本书系湖北省高等学校2018年教学成果奖二等奖项目资助研究最终成果
项目名称：创建涉外交流培育体系，服务和引领海军学员国际化素质培
养的探索与实践（项目编号：2018357）

高校教学工作双语手册

A Practical Chinese-English Book for Universities with International Programs

邓波　徐茜　程飞霞　龚梅　编著

卢甜　金倩　吴振亚　参编

WUHAN UNIVERSITY PRESS

武汉大学出版社

图书在版编目(CIP)数据

高校教学工作双语手册＝A Practical Chinese-English Book for Universities with International Programs:汉、英/邓波等编著.—武汉:武汉大学出版社,2022.7

ISBN 978-7-307-22944-0

Ⅰ.高… Ⅱ.邓… Ⅲ.高等学校—教学工作—手册—汉、英 Ⅳ.G642.0-62

中国版本图书馆 CIP 数据核字(2022)第 033742 号

责任编辑:李晶晶 责任校对:汪欣怡 版式设计:马 佳

出版发行:**武汉大学出版社** (430072 武昌 珞珈山)
(电子邮箱:cbs22@whu.edu.cn 网址:www.wdp.com.cn)
印刷:湖北金海印务有限公司
开本:720×1000 1/16 印张:28.75 字数:292 千字 插页:1
版次:2022 年 7 月第 1 版 2022 年 7 月第 1 次印刷
ISBN 978-7-307-22944-0 定价:74.00 元

前　　言

　　随着世界多极化、经济全球化、文化多样化、社会信息化的深入发展，我们身处的地球村已成为你中有我、我中有你的命运共同体。因其具有基础性、先导性、全局性、支撑性等特点，国际教育交流合作受到世界各国的积极关注。近年来，中国大力推进教育对外开放，已成为全球有影响力的国际教育中心之一，不但拥有世界最大规模的外语学习人口，而且建成世界上影响最大的语言推广机构；不但持续保持世界最大的国际学生生源国地位，而且稳居亚洲最大留学目的国位置；不但成为引进世界优质教育资源开展合作办学最多的国家，而且成为积极探索境外办学、重点为"一带一路"沿线国家提供教育服务公共产品的最大发展中国家。这带来了对教育领域双语人才和教学工作语言文字双语规范化表达的大量而急迫需求。

　　为服务构建人类命运共同体和响应"一带一路"倡议，助力提升高校国际教育交流合作的水平质效，方便广大教育工作者、学生了解和查找高校常用文书、对话地道纯正的英语表达，编者梳理多年高校教学、管理及涉外交流的第一手经验和鲜活案例，编著了《高校教学工作双语手册》。全书以高校交流和留学生培养需求为重点，用中英双语对照的方式，聚焦教学管理、教学活动、学生管理、文娱体育、综合保障、国际交往 6 个板块，内容简洁精练、系统实用，既从规章制度和教学组训方面彰显办学育人的治学态度，又从综合保障和文化交流方面体现细致入微的人文关怀。考虑到书稿内容的通用性，书中所涉及的部分国名、地名、组织机构名和人名为代称。

1

新时代国际教育交流合作是一个快速发展、不断完善的"巨系统"，对双语要求宏大广博。本书只是抛砖引玉，由于水平和时间有限，难免有疏漏和不足，敬请专家同行和读者朋友提出宝贵意见。

编　者

2021 年 7 月

目　　录
Contents

第一章 教学管理篇
Chapter 1 Management of Education

1.1 管理规定 Regulations of Management

1.1.1 留学生教学管理规定 Education Management Regulations for International Students

甲大学留学生教学管理规定
University A's Education Management Regulations for International Students

第一章 总 则

第一条 根据甲大学教学管理有关规章制度，制订本规定。

第二条 本规定的制订旨在规范留学生教学工作，确保留学生学习正规、有序。

Chapter One General Provisions

Article 1 These regulations are formulated in compliance with University A's education management regulations.

Article 2 These regulations are intended to ensure that the international students' education is in good order and sequence.

第二章 入学与注册

第三条 留学生根据中外有关协议来甲大学学习。留学生本人的入学条件、个人情况、学习专业、时段必须与有关备案一致。

第四条 留学生须按规定的日期和方式来校报到，甲大学按招生条件组织入学资格复查和体检，并根据相关专业要求进行文化水平和专业素质等测试。复审合格者，予以注册登记，取得学籍并列编学号；复审不合格者按有关程序退回。

第五条 留学生在校学习时间自入境之日算起到离境之日为止。

Chapter Two   Enrollment

Article 3 International students may apply for University A's courses according to the bilateral agreement. International students' admission qualifications, personal information, course application and course duration should be identical to the record of our party.

Article 4 International students should register at the university according to the university's schedule and in the manner specified by the university. The university may organize a qualification review and a medical check-up for students, and appropriate authorities from different courses may conduct exams on their educational level and knowledge of the course. The eligible may enroll and be admitted as a student of the university, as well as be assigned a number on the roll, while those who are not eligible will be returned with the appropriate procedures.

Article 5 Students' course duration is calculated from the date of their arrival in China to the date of their departure from China.

第三章　学业考核与成绩记载

第六条 留学生必须按照教学计划参加学习、训练和考核，考核成绩记入留学生学籍档案。

第七条 一般不接受学制 1 年以下的留学生对某门课程的免修申请。

第八条 考核分为考试和考查两种。各课程的考核种类由教学计划规定。

第九条 课程最终成绩由卷面成绩（含论文、实作考核，占总成绩 50%）、课堂表现（占总成绩 20%）、到课情况（占总成绩 15%）、课程作业完成情况（含实验报告，占总成绩 15%）四部分综合评定组成。

第十条 考核不及格者可在考试结束一个月内补考一次。留学生因病或其他特殊情况不能参加考核，须在考前申请，经教务处批准缺考的留学生，可在恢复正常上课后一周内进行补考。

第十一条 留学生无故不参加某门课程（含实验、实作）学习，到课率低于 70% 的，或完成作业低于规定总量的 75% 的，不得参加该门课程考核，课程以零分计。

第十二条 任何考试未经许可不得携带电子产品，开卷考试只能携带纸质资料，擅自缺考或考核作弊者，该课程成绩以零分计，不予补考，并由大学视情给予必要的处罚。

Chapter Three　System for Academic Evaluation and Score Reporting

Article 6 International students should participate in the study, training, and evaluations specified in the course syllabus, with the score report card included as part of their file.

Article 7 In general, no application for subject exemption will be accepted if the applicant's course duration is less than one year.

Article 8 The evaluation method may be either an examination or grading, as defined in the syllabus.

Article 9 Each exam's final score is made up of four parts: the exam paper (including course papers and practical sessions) (50%), the class performance (20%), the class attendance (15%), and the assignment (including the experiment report, 15%).

Article 10 Those who fail the exam have one chance of taking a make-up exam within a month. Those who are unable to take the exam owing to illness, among other reasons, are required to submit an application prior to the exam. Those who receive approval from the study administration office for missing a test will take a make-up exam within a week of restarting their studies.

Article 11 Those who are absent from class (including experiment and practical classes) without requesting for leave and have a class attendance rate of less than 70% or an assignment submission rate of less than 75% of the assigned work are not allowed to take the relevant exam, and the final score is zero.

Article 12 Except with previous authorization, no electronic device is permitted in the exam. In an open-book exam, students may only bring paper materials. Those who are absent from the exam without requesting for leave or who are detected cheating during the exam will be penalized by the university, and their final score will be zero. Additionally, no opportunity for a make-up exam is provided.

第四章　退学与转学

第十三条　留学生有下列情形之一者，应予退学。

1. 经补考后，累计仍有两门考试课程不及格者。

2. 累计旷课 30 学时者。

3. 经指定医疗单位诊断，患有精神病、传染病或其他严重疾病者；生病治疗期限超过一个月；因故伤残或手术后不能坚持正常学习者。

4. 因其他原因不宜继续学习者。

第十四条　留学生若需转学，按上级主管部门的有关规定办理。

Chapter Four　Discontinuity of Courses and Transfer to a Different Institution

Article 13　In any one of the following circumstances, the course study should be terminated.

1. Those who do not pass the make-up exams for two subjects.

2. Those who miss 30 class hours without requesting leave of absence.

3. Those who have been diagnosed by a medical institute with a mental illness, an infectious disease, or a serious disease; those whose medical treatment lasts more than one month; and those who are unable to study on a regular basis due to disability or surgery.

4. Those who are unable to complete their studies due to special circumstances.

Article 14　In the case of a transfer to another institution, the students should follow relevant regulations of responsible authorities.

第五章　毕业及鉴定

第十五条　留学生符合毕业条件的，颁发毕业证书，未达到毕业条件的发结业证书。符合学位授予条件的留学生，颁发相应学位证书。

第十六条　一门考试课程经补考后仍不及格者，发结业证书；两门（含）以上补考不及格退学者，发肄业证书。

第十七条　教务处将对留学生学业情况做出鉴定，分为学期鉴定和毕业鉴定两类，并将此作为毕业综合鉴定的主要依据。

Chapter Five　Graduation and Appraisal

Article 15　Students who meet the graduation requirements will receive a diploma; those who do not meet the requirements will receive a course completion certificate. Those who meet the Degree Program criteria will be awarded a degree certificate.

Article 16　Students who fail a make-up test in one subject will receive a certificate of course completion. Furthermore, students who fail two or more make-up tests and are forced to withdraw from the study will receive a certificate of attendance.

Article 17　The Office of Studies will evaluate each overseas student on the basis of their academic record. Semester and graduational evaluations will serve as the critical foundation for a full graduation appraisal.

第六章　教室及课堂管理

第十八条　教室（含实验室）是进行教学活动的主要场所，必须保持严肃而正规的教学秩序和良好的学风。授课教师是教室秩序和管理的第一责任人，履行管理职责。

第十九条 留学生应保持教室的清洁卫生，桌椅要摆放整齐，不得在教学场所吐痰、吸烟、吃零食、乱丢脏物和会客，不得在桌椅、墙壁及黑板等设施上乱刻乱画。

第二十条 留学生应爱护多媒体投影器材、电脑等教学设施和公用物品。上课完毕，由留学生值班员或专业班次班长负责安排留学生擦拭黑板，关闭灯、电扇、空调、门窗等。

第二十一条 未经许可，不得擅自拍照或录像、录音，不得使用教室电脑和自带移动存储设备。

第二十二条 留学生应于上课前五分钟进入教室，保持肃静，准备好学习用品。不得迟到、早退或旷课。上、下课时，由留学生值班员(如仅有一个专业班次，则为该专业班次班长)向教师报告到课情况。如遇领导查课时，由教师履行报告职责。

第二十三条 教室内应保持安静，不准喧哗、打闹和做与学习无关的事情。课堂上，留学生应保持着装整洁得体、坐姿端正，严守课堂纪律，不随意走动。要讲究礼节礼貌，提问前应先举手。

第二十四条 实验课时，应严格遵守操作规程和安全规则，确保人身和设备安全。实验器材准备完毕，须经教师检查无误后，方可通电或启动。实验中发生异常现象，应立即报告教师并采取措施。未经教师允许，不得动用与本次实验无关的器材、设备。离开实验室时，应将所用工具、器材、设备按要求放置妥当，如数交还。实验后应按要求完成实验报告。

第二十五条 爱护教学设施，如损坏教学设备、实验仪器、工具器材等，应及时如实报告教师。因人为原因所造成的损坏，由个人负责赔偿。

第二十六条 未经允许，不得进入无关教学场所。留学生课余时间可以申请使用留学生教室用于自习。

Chapter Six　Classroom Rules and Class Management

Article 18　Classrooms and laboratories are the primary locations for instructional activities. As a result, it is critical to provide a serious yet pleasant educational environment. The instructor is the first person in charge of classroom management.

Article 19　International students should keep the classroom clean and tidy, with desks and chairs arranged neatly; they should not spit, smoke, eat, litter, or meet with visitors in classrooms; and they should not scribble on any facilities such as tables, chairs, walls, or blackboards.

Article 20　International students are expected to take good care of multimedia projection equipment, computers, among other public facilities and resources. When class is finished, the duty student or course leader may assign one student to clear the blackboard, turn off the lights, fans, and air conditioning, and shut the windows and doors.

Article 21　International students should not take photos, films, or audio recordings in class unless they have permission. They are not allowed to utilize the classroom computer or connect it to their own personal mobile storage devices.

Article 22　International students should enter the classroom five minutes prior to the start of class. Maintain silence and be prepared for class. Avoid being late, leaving early, or skipping lessons. At the beginning and end of class, the duty student (or course leader if only students from the same course are present) should report attendance to the lecturer. Instead, when leaders inspect the class, the instructor should report to them.

Article 23　The classroom requires quietness where activities such as shouting, chasing, and horseplay are not permitted. Students are expected to pay attention in class, dress well, and sit up straight. Adhere to the class rules and refrain from walking about during class. Respect lecturers. Raise your hand before approaching lecturers with questions.

Article 24　Students must observe the operating procedures and safety guidelines in the lab to ensure their own safety and the safety of the equipment. After the supplies for the experiment are ready, students should not turn on or start up the equipment until the instructor confirms. Failures in the experiment should be reported to the instructor as soon as possible so that emergency action can be taken. Do not handle or operate any instruments or equipment that are not relevant to your experiment. Before students leave the lab, all tools, equipment, and instruments should be set up and handed back to the instructor. As required, students should produce experiment reports.

Article 25　Take good care of the facilities. In the event that any equipment, tools, or gadgets are damaged, please notify the teacher as soon as possible. If the harm is caused by the student, he or she must bear the cost of reparation.

Article 26　Visits to other instructional locations are not allowed without prior permission. Students may apply for designated independent study classrooms.

第七章　附　　则

第二十七条　本规定解释权在甲大学。

第二十八条　在本规定执行过程中，遇有未列入条款的事项，由教务处负责进行补充修改。

第二十九条　本规定自发布之日起实施。

Chapter Seven　Supplementary Provisions

Article 27　The final authority to interpret the regulations remains with University A.

Article 28　The Office of Studies is in charge of making additional changes to situations that are not covered by the regulations.

Article 29　These regulations take effect on the day of their publication.

1.1.2　留学生行政管理规定 Administrative Regulations for International Students

甲大学留学生行政管理规定
Administrative Regulations for International Students

第一章　总　　则

第一条　为规范留学生在甲大学的日常行为，建立良好的教学和管理秩序，根据《学校招收和培养国际学生管理办法》和甲大学有关管理规章制度，制订本规定。

第二条　本规定所称留学生是指由甲大学招收培养的外国人员。

Chapter One　General Provisions

Article 1　These regulations are written in compliance with *University*

A's Administrative Measures for International Students as well as University A's policies and rules in order to govern international students' everyday performance and promote a positive educational and management environment.

Article 2　In the regulations, the term "international students" refers to foreign personnel recruited by University A.

第二章　权利与义务

第三条　当留学生入学正式取得学籍后，培训期间，即成为甲大学在籍学生，享有以下权利：

1. 留学生参加指定专业、课程学习（含组织的集体参观见学）。

2. 大学按标准为留学生提供饮食保障和住宿保障。

3. 入学阶段，大学为留学生安排一次体检。学制一年以上，每年增加一次常规体检。留学生患病后，由大学医院提供门诊治疗，必要时，转入指定医院诊治。就诊时间一般安排在工作日下午。

4. 留学生可以享受中国的法定节假日，学制超过半年的，可以享受寒暑假。经大学批准，留学生每学期可以享受 1 个本国的节假日（每次 1 天），并可自行组织有关庆典活动。

5. 如无特别申明，留学生可以免费使用学校内的各类对外开放的文体场馆和训练设施。如使用场馆内的收费项目或设施，费用自理。

6. 留学生入学和毕业，参加校方组织的参观见学、集体活动等需要交通保障时，由大学负责。留学生自行外出活动，大学一般不提供车辆保障；如果遇到特殊情况，可以视情为留学生提供方便，并适当收取交通费。

7. 留学生在遵章守纪的前提下，其荣誉、人格尊严、宗教信仰自由、人身自由、风俗习惯受甲大学尊重和保护。

第四条　留学生在中国学习期间，即是甲大学学生，应履行与身份相符的义务：

1. 留学生要注重维护派出国和自身的形象，发扬本国优良传统和作风，遵守中国的法律、法规及大学的规章制度和纪律，不得发表针对中国政府和甲大学的不恰当言论。

2. 留学生要服从甲大学的管理，积极参加各项教学训练和集体活动，不得从事与学习无关的其他职业和营利性活动。

3. 留学生要尊重中国的社会公德和风俗习惯，遵守公共秩序，不得与校内外人员进行不正当的交往，不得进行不健康的娱乐消费活动，不得酗酒、赌博。

4. 留学生在中国境内进行宗教活动，必须遵守《中华人民共和国境内外国人宗教活动管理规定》。留学生参加宗教活动，应当在节假日和课余时间进行，不得影响教学秩序。

5. 留学生之间要团结友爱、相互尊重、和谐相处。

Chapter Two　　Rights and Obligations

Article 3　After obtaining a student ID, international students are accepted as students at University A. Throughout their course, they are entitled to the following rights.

1. International students enroll in designated courses (including the organized visit and study tour).

2. The university provides food and lodging in accordance with relevant norms.

3. During the registration period, the university arranges for a medical check-up. In addition, for individuals whose course duration is one year or more, the medical check-up will be scheduled once a year. If necessary, the sick are to be transferred to the designated hospital from the university hospital which provides outpatient care. A doctor's appoint-

ment is usually scheduled in the afternoon of a working day.

4. Chinese statutory holidays are available to international students. For individuals whose course duration exceeds six months, winter and summer holidays are available. International students are entitled to one day of leave per semester, with prior consent from the institution, to celebrate their home country's Day or Festival.

5. If no particular declaration is made, the public recreational and athletic venues, as well as various training facilities, are available for free. If the fee for using the amenities inside the venues is necessary, students are expected to pay.

6. The university provides vehicles for welcoming newcomers, transporting graduates to airports/railway stations, visit and study tour, and group activities. However, vehicles are not provided to students who go out on their own. In exceptional instances, vehicles are provided, and students are responsible for transportation costs.

7. As long as international students follow the norms and laws, the university will respect and preserve their reputation, dignity, religion, freedom, and cultures and habits.

Article 4 International students are considered students at University A during their time studying in China, and hence must adhere to the following identity-bound obligations:

1. International students should value their country's image as well as their own, carry forward their country's excellent practices, observe Chinese laws and norms, as well as the university's regulations and discipline. Any behavior or words that go against the Chinese government or the university are prohibited.

2. International students must follow administrative instructions and participate in a variety of instructional and group activities. Any other ca-

reer or business that is unrelated to the course is prohibited.

3. International students must adhere to Chinese ethics, values, and customs, as well as maintain public order. It is prohibited to engage in illicit relationships, unhealthy recreations, excessive drinking, or gambling.

4. International students should follow the *Rules for the Administration of Foreigners' Religious Activities in China* and participate in religious activities during holidays and free time. Any behavior that has the potential to impede instructional activities is prohibited.

5. International students should value the spirit of solidarity and friendship, respect each other, and live in peace and harmony.

第三章 会议及事项报告制度

第五条 甲大学主要通过开学典礼、结业典礼、重大节假日庆典、学期教学讲评、季度行管讲评、周交班会等会议通报重要信息和安排、讲评教学和行政管理情况，回复学生重要关切。会议参加人员、地点、时间及着装要求，由国际交流学院根据会议内容确定，并会提前通知。

第六条 留学生应通过书面形式向国际交流学院反映情况或提出申请。程序是：从国际交流学院值班室领取相应表格并填写，经由留学生领队签名后交回国际交流学院值班室；国际交流学院的中国值班教师每天17:00前集中查看，并通过电子公告、信函或口头等形式回复。

第七条 如遇突发疾病、停电、停水、火灾等紧急情况，可以采用口头方式直接向留学生管理教师或中国值班教师报告。

Chapter Three　System for Meetings and Reporting

Article 5　The university's opening ceremony, graduation ceremony, celebrations of major events, briefings on academic comments each semester, quarterly administration meetings, and weekly duty hand-over briefings, among others, are significant occasions for communicating critical messages, arrangements, comments, and administrative information, as well as responding to students' primary concerns. The College of International Exchange will notify the attendees, the location, and time, and the dress code in advance, based on the meeting's topic.

Article 6 If necessary, international students should report to or make an application in writing to the College of International Exchange. The method is as follows: fill out appropriate paperwork accessible at the college's duty room; return completed forms with the signature of the country group leader to the duty room. Every day before 17:00, the Chinese duty staff will review the report or application and reply via electronic notification, e-mail, or verbally.

Article 7 In the event of an emergency, such as an acute ailment, a blackout, a water supply breakdown, or a fire, it is recommended to communicate orally with the administrator responsible for international students or the Chinese duty staff.

第四章 证件管理

第八条 留学生来校报到时，应提交入学通知书和有效健康证明、艾滋病检查证明。甲大学按照《中华人民共和国外国人入境出境管理条例》等规定，自入境之日起 30 日内，协助体检合格的留学生办理在华居留证件。

第九条 留学生应持甲大学发放的外出证出入校门。证件应妥善保管，严禁转借、复制、伪造、涂改，防止遗失和损坏。

第十条 留学生在培训期间临时出入境的，相关手续自行办理。除特殊情况外，留学生应当在毕业后 3 天内离境。需要继续在中国境内停留的，相关手续自行办理。停留期间安全责任自负，甲大学不负责提供食宿和交通保障。

Chapter Four　　Documents Management

Article 8　International students are expected to present their admission notification, a valid health certificate and an AIDS-free certificate when they report to the university. According to the *People's Republic of China's Regulations on Administration of Foreigners's Entry and Exit*, among other regulations, the university will assist international students who are eligible for a medical check-up within 30 days of their entry in filing for a residency visa.

Article 9　When going out, international students should carry the university's going-out pass. Students should keep the pass to themselves and not lend, duplicate, counterfeit, or mark it, nor should it be destroyed or lost.

Article 10　If an international student has to enter or quit China during the course, he or she must complete the necessary formalities on his or her own. Except for special circumstances, they should leave China within three days of graduation. If students want to stay in China after graduation, they must go through the formalities on their own. Furthermore, students must be responsible for their own safety, as the university will not offer housing or transportation during their stay.

第五章　　奖惩及鉴定

第十一条　甲大学实行优秀留学生评选制度，对成绩优异、遵章守纪、表现突出的留学生给予表彰和奖励。学制半年以内的专业（班次）不评选优秀毕业留学生。

第十二条　对有下列突出表现者，将给予表彰奖励：

1. 参加各项文体活动比赛，荣获前 3 名。

2. 每学期遵章守纪或管理能力突出，管理效果明显，所管理留学生无违纪现象。

3. 学制一年（含以上）的留学生，第二学期平均成绩与第一学期相比在本专业排名提升 5 名以上的，无无故旷课或迟到现象，无其他违纪现象，可参评"学习进步奖"。

第十三条　对违反中国法律法令和甲大学规章制度者，将视情节轻重给予批评教育或处罚，并通报其驻华代表机构。有下列情形之一者，给予勒令退学或开除学籍处分：

1. 违反中国法律法令，扰乱社会秩序，有反华行为者。

2. 言行违背两国间协议宗旨，并有明显的破坏行为者。

3. 试图窃取国家机密，危害国家利益者。

4. 违反甲大学各项规章制度，拒不服从管理，组织煽动闹事，破坏教学、生活秩序，情节严重者。

第十四条　学习期满，甲大学将对留学生在华期间的学习成绩、日常表现及发展潜力做出总体评价和鉴定。

Chapter Five　Appraisal, Awards and Punishment

Article 11　University A has implemented a program selecting Excellent International Students to recognize and reward students who have excelled academically, followed the rules and regulations, and excelled in extracurricular activities. Students whose courses last fewer than six months will not be considered.

Article 12　International students will be recognized for their outstanding achievement in the following circumstances.

1. Those who are placed first, second and third in recreational activities and sporting games.

2. Those who follow the rules and regulations or who have exceptional organizational and managerial capabilities as long as no international student breaches the regulations while under their direction.

3. The Academic Progress Award will be given to students whose course duration is longer than one year, if the international student's average score in the second semester is higher than that in the first semester, and the international student's progress in the ranking table is at least 5 places higher in the second semester; in the meantime, there is no absence from class without asking for leave, and no violations of regulations and rules are documented.

Article 13　Anyone who violates Chinese laws or the university's policies and rules faces education or punishment. The university will notify international students' Embassy in China of the violations and the appropriate penalties. Students will be dismissed from the university or academic status if any of the following conditions is met.

1. Anyone who breaches Chinese laws and decrees, disrupts social order, or acts against China.

2. Anyone whose words and actions undermine the bilateral agreement, resulting in sabotage.

3. Anyone who seeks to steal confidential documents from China and harms China's interests.

4. Anyone who violates the university's regulations and rules, challenges the administration system, incites others, and disrupts education and social order, incurring severe repercussions.

Article 14　The university will conduct a complete evaluation of international students' academic performance, everyday performance, and development potential at the conclusion of the course.

第六章　附　　则

第十五条　本规定解释权在甲大学。在规定执行过程中，如遇本规定未列入条款的事项，由甲大学国际交流学院和留学生领队根据具体情况共同协商解决。

第十六条　在认真阅读并完全理解上述规定后，须在《甲大学留学生行政管理规定认知书》上签名。

第十七条　为明确安全责任，国际交流学院将与留学生签署《甲大学留学生安全责任协议书》。

第十八条　本规定自发布之日起实施。

Chapter Six　Supplementary Provisions

Article 15　The final authority to interpret the regulations remains with University A. The College of International Exchange and country group leaders of the students are in charge of making additional changes to situations that are not covered by the regulations.

Article 16　To fully comprehend these regulations, read them carefully. Then, sign the *Confirmation of the Administrative Regulations for International Students*.

Article 17　To define their individual responsibilities, international students and the College of International Exchange should sign the *Agreement on Safety Obligations*.

Article18　These regulations take effect on the day of their publication.

1.1.3 优秀留学生评选细则 Selection Criteria for Excellent International Students

一、参选条件

1. 学习刻苦，成绩优秀(各科平均成绩在 80 分以上，单科成绩不低于 75 分)。

2. 积极参加各项文体活动比赛，成绩突出(校外比赛获奖，校内比赛前 3 名)。

3. 组织管理能力突出，参加国际交流学院指定的管理工作认真负责，管理效果明显。

4. 无无故旷课或迟到现象，无其他违纪现象。

二、量化评分细则

(一)学习成绩

满分 100 分，取所有课程的平均分。

(二)综合表现

满分 100 分，由以下四部分组成：

1. 留学生集体测评分(占总分 20%)：由全体留学生对每名留学生的日常表现进行无记名打分(分值为 0~20)，取平均分。

2. 留学生骨干测评分(占总分 10%)：由留学生委员会主席、副主席、文体委员和后勤委员对所有留学生的日常表现进行打分，由年级长、班长对本年级或本班级留学生的日常表现进行打分(分值为 0~10)，取平均分。

3. 国际交流学院测评分(占总分 40%)：由国际交流学院教师对每名留学生的日常表现进行打分(分值为 0~40)，取平均分。

4. 加减分(占总分 30%)：考查日常管理、遵章守纪、比赛成绩等情况。各项加减分可累加，总分不能高于 30 分，但可低于 0 分。

(1)加分项目：①积极参加大学和国际交流学院组织的各项活动比赛，加起评分 10 分。②获大学、国际交流学院各类比赛前三名，分别加 3 分、2 分、1 分；获校外比赛金银铜奖或荣誉奖，分别加 4 分、3 分、2 分、1

分。③获评月优秀寝室，加 1 分(可累计)；获评季度优秀寝室，加 2 分(只计 1 次)。④担任留学生委员会主席、副主席、年级长、班长、文体委员、后勤委员各加 5 分(如连任同一职务，只计 1 次)；担任留学生国别领队、周值班员加 2 分。⑤每学期平均成绩在本专业排名前三名，分别加 3 分、2 分、1 分(可累计)；第二学期平均成绩在本专业排名与第一学期相比提升 5 个名次及以上加 2 分。⑥考取研究生并认真参加学习，加 5 分。

(2)减分项目：①旷课一次减 1 分。②上课迟到或早退一次减 0.5 分。③请假外出，未在当日 22:00 前归队，1 小时之内的减 0.5 分；2 小时之内的减 1 分。④严重违反《留学生行政管理规定》所列条款，一次减 3 分。

学习成绩和综合表现评分相加后，按从高到低排序，排名前 20% 的即为优秀留学生。

I. Candidate Prerequisites

1. Strive for academic excellence (the average score is above 80 and the mark of any subject is not lower than 75).

2. Compete vigorously in recreational and athletic events and attain outstanding outcomes (e.g. win any award outside the university and the top three award inside the university).

3. Be extremely competent at organizing and managing. Be responsible for the job allocated by the College of International Exchange and capable of doing it successfully.

4. There are no reported absences from class without asking for leave, and no documented infractions of regulations and norms.

II. Quantitative Selection Criteria

A. Academic performance: Based on a hundred-point scale, it is determined by the average of all subjects' scores.

B. Comprehensive performance: Using a hundred-point system, the evaluation is divided into four sections:

1. Evaluation by all international students (20%): All international

students are expected to anonymously evaluate each other, assigning a point value between 0 and 20 based on daily performance. The final result is determined by the total average score.

2. Evaluation by students in authority (10%): The chairman and vice chairman of the International Students Union, the recreation and sports secretary, and the logistics secretary are responsible for evaluating all international students, while the senior prefect and class prefect are responsible for evaluating international students in the same grade or class, assigning a score between 0 and 10 points. The average score determines the final outcome.

3. Evaluation by the College of International Exchange (40%): The College of International Exchange staff are responsible for evaluating each international student and assigning a point value between 0 and 40 based on their daily performance. The final outcome is determined by the average score.

4. Bonus and deduction points (30%): Points are awarded based on daily performance, compliance with laws and regulations, and competition standings, among other things. The total of the points for bonus and deductions should not be more than 30 points, however it is possible to be less than 0 points.

(1) Bonus: ①10 points are planned to be awarded to active participants in various activities organized by the university or the College of International Exchange. ②According to their positions, the top three victors in competitions or games at the university or the College of International Exchange are supposed to receive 3 points, 2 points and 1 point, respectively. In tournaments outside of the university, the gold medalist, silver medalist, bronze medalist, and honorable winner are meant to receive 4 points, 3 points, 2 points, and 1 point, respectively. ③Winners of the

monthly Sanitation and Safety Inspection of the Dormitory are expected to receive 1 point (accumulative total is possible); winners of the quarterly Sanitation and Safety Inspection of the Dormitory are expected to receive 2 points (only once, accumulative total is not possible). ④The chairman and vice chairman of the International Students Union, senior prefects, class prefects, recreation and sports secretary, and logistics secretary are all meant to receive 5 points (each person can only receive 5 points once if they are on the same appointment in a row). The nation group leader and the duty student are both eligible for 2 points. ⑤The best three average scores in their respective courses are meant to receive 3 points, 2 points, and 1 point, respectively (accumulative total is possible). Those whose second semester average score is greater than their first semester average score and whose position in the ranking table has risen by at least 5 places in the second semester are supposed to receive 2 points. ⑥Those who are accepted as postgraduate students and study hard should receive 5 points.

(2) Deductions: ①Deduct 1 point for each absence from class without authorization. ②Deduct 0. 5 point for being late for class or departing early without requesting for leave. ③Deduct 0. 5 point for each late return after 22:00 within 1 hour and 1 point for each late return after 22:00 within 2 hours if you go out with permission. ④Deduct 3 points for any serious infringement of the *Administrative Regulations for International Students*.

The top 20% of international students will be selected as Excellent International Students based on the total points of their academic performance and overall performance.

1.2 教学依据 Course Planning

1.2.1 专业规范 Course Standards

轮机工程专业规范(示例)

培养目标：轮机工程师

培养目的：掌握工程热力学、流体力学等专业基础理论和内燃机、柴油机动力装置等专业基础知识，具备船舶动力相关工作能力、轮机工程师专业素养。

培养单位(地点)：甲大学

学制：4 年

学位类别：工学学士学位(按照国家学位办规定，符合相关资质要求的留学生经批准可授予该学位)

开学时间：每年 1 期，9 月 1 日

招生数量：××名

入学条件：高中以上文化程度，身体健康，熟练掌握英语、法语任何一种语言。高中毕业生年龄原则上不超过 19 周岁，在职学生年龄不超过 22 周岁。有学习汉语的意愿，具有较强的语言学习能力

授课语言：汉语

课程设置：

1. 公共基础课：(1)汉语基础。(2)科学文化。(3)体育基础。

2. 专业课：(1)机械基础。(2)流体力学。(3)工程热力学与传热学。(4)内燃机。(5)船舶动力装置原理。(6)船舶电气设备。(7)船舶生命力与损害管制。(8)柴油机结构实验与操纵管理。

3. 选修课：(1)汉语口语训练。(2)汉语基础训练。(3)法律常识。

（4）计算机及网络运用。

4. 实践环节：（1）岗位任职课程均包含实践性教学内容。（2）船舶实习。（3）参观见学。

5. 论文工作：围绕所学内容，结合本国实际，撰写毕业论文。

其他：

1. 留学生应在开课前 3 天抵达，无故逾期不报到视为放弃入学资格。

2. 第一年通过汉语水平考试(HSK)四级后，方能转入后续三年本科基础教育和专业课程学习。

3. 必须通过汉语水平考试(HSK)五级，并符合有关规定和要求，准予毕业，发给毕业证书；留学生取得毕业资格，达到甲大学有关授予学士学位的标准，并符合有关规定和要求，经甲大学学位委员会审查通过，授予工学学士学位，发给学位证书。

Marine Engineering Program（Example）

Course Objectives：Marine Engineers

Expertise：International students are expected to grasp engineering thermodynamics and fluid mechanics theories, as well as to develop their skillsets in internal combustion engines and diesel engine power plants. They thus possess the capability of power engineering and the expertise of a marine engineer.

Institution & Place：University A

Duration：4 years

Degree Type：Bachelor of Engineering（Accredited international students may obtain the degree of BE with approval from the National Academic Degree Committee）.

School Opening Date：September 1st. Enrollment is limited to once per year.

Enrollment Quota：××.

Admission Requirements：Applicants must be in excellent health and possess a senior high school diploma or above. Applicants should be fluent in English or French. For high school graduates, the maximum age is recommended to be 19, while those having a job should not be older than 22. Furthermore, individuals who intend to learn Chinese and have strong language learning abilities are preferred.

Intermediate Language: Chinese

Curriculum:

1. Preparatory & Basic Subjects: (1)Basic Chinese. (2)Science and Culture. (3)Physical Training.

2. Specialized Subjects: (1)Mechanical Engineering Basis. (2)Fluid Mechanics. (3)Engineering Thermodynamics and Heat Transfer Theory. (4)Internal Combustion Engine. (5)Ship Power Plant Principle. (6)Marine Electrical Equipment. (7)Ship Survivability and Damage Control. (8)Diesel Engine Construction Practice and Operation Managemen.

3. Elective Subjects: (1)Oral Chinese Practice. (2)Basic Chinese. (3)Legal Knowledge. (4)Application of Computer & Network.

4. Practical Sessions: (1)The practical hours are incorporated in the specialized topics. (2)Practice: onboard ship. (3)Study tour.

5. Graduation Thesis: The thesis is the product of the student's course work against the backdrop of his/her country's maritime industry.

Tips:

1. Participants must arrive three days prior to the institution's scheduled opening. Those who fail to register on time for unjustifiable reasons will be considered waivers.

2. Those who pass HSK 4 (Chinese Proficiency Examination) in the first year will continue the undergraduate education and professional training in next three years.

3. Students who pass HSK 5 and meet all other prerequisites are eligible to graduate and receive a diploma. After being approved by University A's Academic Degree Committee, graduates who meet the

requirements for bachelor degree will be granted the dagree of BE and the BE certificate after being reviewed by University A's Degree Committee.

1.2.2　人才培养方案 Curriculum and Schedules

轮机工程专业人才培养方案(示例)

一、招生对象及学制

(一)招生对象

招收对象为高中以上文化程度,身体健康,熟练掌握英语、法语任何一种语言。高中毕业生年龄原则上不超过 19 周岁,有学习汉语的意愿,具有较强的语言学习能力。

(二)学制

4 年。

二、时间分配

(一)时间分配表

表 1.1　各学年时间分配　　　　　　　单位:周

学年	在校总时间	入学训练	教学训练				法定节日	寒暑假	机动
			小计	教学活动	复习考试	毕业论文			
1	××	×	××	××	×		×	×	×
2	××		××	××	×		×	×	×
3	××		××	××	×		×	×	×
4	××		××	××	×	×	×	×	×
小计	×××	×	×××	×××	×	×	×	××	×

(二)课程体系及时间分配

留学生四年全期课程总学时为××××学时,划分为汉语文化课、基础技能课、科学文化课、岗位任职课和主要实践环节五个模块。

27

表 1.2　汉语文化课

课程编号	课程名称	学时	备注
001	汉语基础	××	考试/必修
002	初级汉语综合	×××	考试/必修
003	中高级汉语综合	×××	考试/必修
	小计	×××	

表 1.3　基础技能课

课程编号	课程名称	学时	备注
004	海洋气象	×××	考试/必修
005	船舶概论	××	考试/必修
006	航海基础	××	考试/必修
007	航行操纵	××	考试/必修 （结合航海实习）
008	船舶条令与船艺	××	考试/必修 （结合航海实习）
	小计	×××	

表 1.4　科学文化课

课程编号	课程名称	学时	备注
009	高等数学	×××	考试/必修
010	工程数学	××	考试/必修
011	大学物理	××	考试/必修
012	大学物理实验	××	考试/必修
013	大学化学	××	考试/必修
014	工程力学	××	考试/必修
015	工程材料	××	考试/必修
016	流体力学	××	考试/必修
017	中国国情及传统文化	××	考试/必修
018	海洋法	××	考查/必修
019	当代世界经济与政治	××	考查/必修
020	计算机及网络应用	××	考查/必修
021	程序设计基础（C 语言）	××	考试/必修
022	电子技术基础	×××	考试/必修

续表

课程编号	课程名称	学时	备注
023	机械基础	××	考试/必修
024	工程热力学与传热学	××	考试/必修
025	船舶电路原理	×××	考试/必修
026	工程制图	××	考试/必修
	小计	××××	

表 1.5　岗位任职课

课程编号	课程名称	学时	备注
027	船舶机械计算机控制技术	××	考试/必修
028	船舶动力维修工程	××	考试/必修
029	船舶设备检测与诊断	××	考试/必修
030	轻潜水	××	考试/必修
031	船舶辅助机械	××	考试/必修
032	船舶电机结构	××	考试/必修
033	船舶电气设备	××	考试/必修
034	船舶结构与强度基础	××	考试/必修
035	船体识图与制图	××	考试/必修
036	内燃机	××	考试/必修
037	船舶动力装置原理	×××	考试/必修
038	船舶生命力与损管组织	××	考试/必修
039	柴油机结构实验与操纵管理	××	考试/必修
040	船舶机电专业训练与组织	××	考试/必修
	小计	×××	

表 1.6　主要实践环节

课程编号	课程名称	学时	备注
041	厂所实践与参观见学	×××	考查/选修
042	船舶实习	×××	考试/必修
043	毕业实习	××	考试/必修
	小计	×××	

三、课程设置

表 1.7 课程设置

课程模块	课程名称	学时	理论	实践	学分	学期学时分配								考核方式
						1	2	3	4	5	6	7	8	
汉语文化	汉语基础	XX	XX	XX	X	XX								考试
	初级汉语综合	XXX	XXX	XXX	XX	XXXXXX	XXXXXX							考试
	初级汉语复练	XXX	XX	XXX	XX	XXXXXX	XXXXXX							考试
	中高级汉语综合	XXX	XX	XXX	XX			XX	XX	XX	XX			考试
	中高级汉语复练	XXX	XX	XX	X			XX	XX	XX	XX	XX		考试
	汉语水平考试训练	XXX	XX	XXX	X							XX		考试
基础技能	体育基础	XX	XX	XXX	X	XX	XX	XX	XX					考试
	船舶概论	XX	XX	X	X	XX								考试
	航海基础	XX	X	XX	X		XX	XX						考试
	航行操纵	XX	X	XX	X				XX					考试
	船舶条令与船艺	XX	X	XX	X			XX						考试
科学文化	高等数学	XXX	XXX	XX	X	XXX		XXX						考试
	工程数学	XX	XX	XX	X			XX	XX					考试
	大学物理	XX	XX	XX	X			XX	XX					考试
	大学物理实验	XX	X	XX	X			XX	XX					考试

续表

课程模块	课程名称	学时	理论	实践	学分	学期学时分配								考核方式
						1	2	3	4	5	6	7	8	
科学文化	大学化学	XX	XX	XX	X			XX						考试
	工程力学	XX	XX	XX	X			XX						考试
	工程材料	XX	XX	XX	X					XX				考试
	流体力学	XX	XX	XX	X				XX					考试
	中国国情及传统文化	XX	XX	XX	X	XX								考查
	海洋法	XX	XX	X	X	XX								考查
	当代世界经济与政治	XX	XX	XX	X			XX						考查
	计算机及网络应用	XX	XX	XX	X		XX							考查
	程序设计基础（C语言）	XX	X	XX	X				XX					考试
	电子技术基础	XXX	XX	XX	X				XX	XX				考试
	机械基础	XX	XX	XX	X				XX					考试
	工程热力学与传热学	XX	XX	XX	X			XX		XX				考查
	船舶电路原理	XXX	XX	XX	X			XX		XX				考试
	工程制图	XX	XX	XX	X				XX					考试

课程模块	课程名称	学时	理论	实践	学分	学期学时分配								考核方式
						1	2	3	4	5	6	7	8	
岗位任职	船舶机械计算机控制技术	XX	XX	XX	X				XX					考试
	船舶动力维修工程	XX	XX	XX	X						XX			考试
	船舶设备检测与诊断	XX	XX	XX	X						XX			考试
	轻潜水	XX	X	XX	X				XX					考试
	船舶辅助机械	XX	XX	XX	X					XX				考试
	船舶电机结构	XX	XX	XX	X				XX					考试
	船舶电气设备	XX	XX	XX	X					XX				考试
	船舶结构与强度基础	XX	XX	XXX	X				XX					考试
	船体识图与制图	XX	XX	XX	X				XX					考试
	内燃机	XXX	XX	XX	X					XX				考试
	船舶动力装置原理	XX	XX	XX	X					XX	XX			考试
	船舶生命力与损管组织	XX	XX	XX	X							XX		考试
	柴油机结构实验与操纵管理	XX	XX	XXX	X								XX	考试
	船舶机电专业训练与组织	X	X	XXX	X								XX	考查
实践	厂所实践与参观见学	XXX	X	XXX	XX	XX	XX	XX	XX	XX	XX			考查
	船舶实习	XXX	X	XXX	XX						XX			考试
	毕业实习	XX	X	XX	XX								XX	考试

四、教育训练计划

表 1.8　汉语能力训练计划

活动名称	计划安排	时间
汉语复练	通过课堂游戏、语言实践、科技互动等方式，加强任课教师与学生之间、学生与学生之间的互动，最大程度地激发留学生学习汉语、运用汉语的兴趣，变"被动输入"为"主动输出"，提升留学生在不同场景中的语言应用能力。	详见课程设置
汉语水平考试训练	结合汉语水平考试大纲，通过讲解真题、分析考点、模拟练习，以考代练，以考促学，以考评学，及时发现学习中存在的问题，查漏补缺，让复习备考更有针对性、目的性和实效性。	详见课程设置
备注：汉语能力训练计划学时总数×××学时，其中，汉语复练×××课时，汉语水平考试训练×××课时。		

表 1.9　中国传统文化体验计划

活动名称	计划安排	学时	开课时间
MOOC	初级汉语语法	××	第一学期
	运动与健康	××	第三学期
	中国传统艺术——篆刻、书法、水墨画体验与欣赏	××	第四学期
	走近中华优秀传统文化	××	第五学期
MOOC	合计	×××	

表 1.10 体育训练计划

活动名称	计划安排	学时
五公里	自主学训时间组织集中训练	××
游泳	自主学训时间组织集中训练	××
障碍	自主学训时间组织集中训练	××
防护与急救	暑期训练	××
备注：学生毕业前必须通过前三项体育考试，在大三下学期组织第一次考试，若考试未通过，大四下学期组织补考。		

表 1.11 领导能力培养计划

类别	科　　目	学时	学期安排
1	年级、班级负责人	××	各学期
2	文体委员、后勤委员	××	各学期
3	文体活动负责人	××	各学期
4	与中国学生同班合训	××	第五学期

Marine Engineering Program（Example）

Ⅰ. Admission Conditions and Course Duration

1. Admission Conditions

Applicants must be in good health and possess a senior high school diploma or above. Applicants are expected to be fluent in either English or French. In principle, high school graduates should not be older than 19. Furthermore, individuals who intend to learn Chinese and have strong language learning abilities are preferred.

2. Course Duration

Four years.

Ⅱ. Annual Schedules

1. Holistic Training Timetable

2. Course System and Schedules

A total of ×××× class hours are allotted to five modules throughout the course of four years of study: Chinese Language, Basic Skill Development, Science and Culture, Specialized Subjects, and Practical Sessions.

Table 1.1　A Timetable of Each Academic Year

Time Unit: Week

Academic Year	Cumulative Time at the University	Training for Freshers	Events for Education and Training				Statutory Holidays	Winter and Summer Vacations	Other Events
			Subtotal	Education Events	Exams	Graduation Thesis			
1	××	×	××	××	×		×	×	×
2	××		××	××	×		×	×	×
3	××		××	××	×		×	×	×
4	××		××	××	×	×	×	×	×
Subtotal	×××	×	×××	×××	×	×	×	××	×

Table 1.2　Chinese Language

Serial Number	Name of the Subject	Class Hours	Remarks
001	Basic Chinese	××	Exam/Compulsory Subject
002	Elementary Chinese Listening, Speaking, Reading, and Writing	×××	Exam/Compulsory Subject
003	Intermediate and Advanced Chinese Listening, Speaking, Reading, and Writing	×××	Exam/Compulsory Subject
Subtotal		×××	

Table 1.3   Basic Skill Development

Serial Number	Name of the Subject	Class Hours	Remarks
004	Marine Meteorology	××	Exam/Compulsory Subject
005	An Introduction to Ships	××	Exam/Compulsory Subject
006	The Foundation of Navigation	××	Exam/Compulsory Subject
007	Ship Handling	××	Exam/Compulsory Subject (The performance in Navigation Training is included in the exam)
008	Ship Ordinances and Seamanship	××	Exam/Compulsory Subject (The performance in Navigation Training is included in the exam)
	Subtotal	×××	

Table 1.4   Science and Culture

Serial Number	Name of the Subject	Class Hours	Remarks
009	Advanced Mathematics	×××	Exam/Compulsory Subject
010	Engineering Mathematics	××	Exam/Compulsory Subject
011	Physics (College Version)	××	Exam/Compulsory Subject
012	Physical Experiments	××	Exam/Compulsory Subject
013	Chemistry (College Version)	××	Exam/Compulsory Subject
014	Engineering Mechanics	××	Exam/Compulsory Subject
015	Engineering Materials	××	Exam/Compulsory Subject
016	Fluid Mechanics	××	Exam/Compulsory Subject
017	An Introduction to China and Chinese Culture	××	Exam/Compulsory Subject
018	The Law of the Sea	××	Rating/Compulsory Subject

Continued

Serial Number	Name of the Subject	Class Hours	Remarks
019	The Global Economy and Politics of Today	××	Rating/Compulsory Subject
020	Application of Computer & Network	××	Rating/Compulsory Subject
021	The Foundation of Program Design (C Language Program)	××	Exam/Compulsory Subject
022	The Fundamentals of Ship Electronic Technology	×××	Exam/Compulsory Subject
023	Mechanical Basics	××	Exam/Compulsory Subject
024	Engineering Thermodynamics and Heat Transfer Theory	××	Exam/Compulsory Subject
025	The Fundamentals of Ship Electronic Circuit	×××	Exam/Compulsory Subject
026	Engineering Drawing	××	Exam/Compulsory Subject
Subtotal		××××	

Table 1.5　Specialized Subjects

Serial Number	Name of the Subject	Class Hours	Remarks
027	Computer Control Technology of Ship Machinery	××	Exam/Compulsory Subject
028	Ship Power Maintenance Engineering	××	Exam/Compulsory Subject
029	Ship Equipment Detection and Diagnosis	××	Exam/Compulsory Subject

Continued

Serial Number	Name of the Subject	Class Hours	Remarks
030	Light Weight Diving	××	Exam/Compulsory Subject
031	Marine Auxiliary Machinery	××	Exam/Compulsory Subject
032	The Construction of Ship Electric Machine	××	Exam/Compulsory Subject
033	Marine Electrical Equipment	××	Exam/Compulsory Subject
034	Fundamentals of Ship Architecture and Strength	××	Exam/Compulsory Subject
035	Ship Cartography	××	Exam/Compulsory Subject
036	Internal Combustion Engine	××	Exam/Compulsory Subject
037	Ship Power Plant Principle	×××	Exam/Compulsory Subject
038	Ship Survivability and Damage Control Organization	××	Exam/Compulsory Subject
039	Experiment with the Structure and Operation of Diesel Engine	××	Exam/Compulsory Subject
040	Ship Electromechanical Department Training and Organization	××	Exam/Compulsory Subject
	Subtotal	×××	

Table 1. 6　Practical Sessions

Serial Number	Name of the Subject	Class Hours	Remarks
041	Practice at Workshops, Visits and Study Tours	×××	Rating/Elective Subject
042	Ship Internship	×××	Exam/Compulsory Subject
043	Graduation Field Work	××	Exam/Compulsory Subject
	Subtotal	×××	

III. Curriculum Setup

Table 1.7　Curriculum Setup

Modules	Name of the Subject	Class Hours	Lectures	Practice	Credits	1	2	3	4	5	6	7	8	Evaluation
Chinese Language	Basic Chinese	××	××	××	×	××								Exam
	Elementary Chinese Listening, Speaking, Reading, and Writing	×××	×××	×××	××	×××	×××							Exam
	Revision & Exercises for Elementary Chinese	×××	××	×××	××	×××	×××							Exam
	Intermediate and Advanced Chinese Listening, Speaking, Reading, and Writing	×××	××	×××	××			××	××	××	××	××		Exam
	Revision & Exercises for Intermediate and Advanced Chinese	×××	××	××	×			××	××	××	××	××		Exam
	HSK Training	×××	××	×××	×	××	××					××		Exam
Basic Skill Development	Physical Training	×××	××	×××	××	××	××	××	××	××				Exam
	An Introduction to Ships	××	××	×	×	××								Exam
	The Foundation of Navigation	××	×	××	×		××	××						Exam
	Ship Handling	××	×	×××	×			××	××					Exam
	Ship Ordinances and Seamanship	××	×	××	×			××						Exam

Continued

Modules	Name of the Subject	Class Hours	Lectures	Practice	Credits	1	2	3	4	5	6	7	8	Evaluation
	Advanced Mathematics	XXX	XXX	XX	X		XX	XXX						Exam
	Engineering Mathematics	XX	XX	XX	X			XX	XX					Exam
	Physics (College Version)	XX	XX	XX	X			XX	XX					Exam
	Physical Experiments	XX	X	XX	X			XX	XX					Exam
	Chemistry (College Version)	XX	XX	XX	X			XX						Exam
	Engineering Mechanics	XX	XX	XX	X			XX						Exam
	Engineering Materials	XX	XX	XX	X					XX				Exam
	Fluid Mechanics	XX	XX	XX	X				XX					Exam
Science and Culture	An Introduction to China and Chinese Culture	XX	XX	XX	X	XX								Exam
	The Law of the Sea	XX	XX	X	X	XX								Rating
	The Global Economy and Politics of Today	XX	XX	XX	X			XX						Rating
	Application of Computer & Network	XX	XX	XX	X		XX							Rating
	The Foundation of Program Design (C Language Program)	XX	X	XX	X				XX					Exam

The column group header spanning semesters 1–8: "Class Hours for Respective Semesters"

Continued

Modules	Name of the Subject	Class Hours	Lectures	Practice	Credits	1	2	3	4	5	6	7	8	Evaluation
Science and Culture	The Fundamentals of Ship Electronic Technology	XXX	XX	XX	X				XX	XX				Exam
	Mechanical Basics	XX	XX	XX	X				XX					Exam
	Engineering Thermodynamics and Heat Transfer Theory	XX	XX	XX	X				XX	XX				Exam
	The Fundamentals of Ship Electronic Circuit	XXX	XX	XX	X			XX	XX					Exam
	Engineering Drawing	XX	XX	XX	X				XX					Exam
Specialized Subjects	Computer Control Technology of Ship Machinery	XX	XX	XX	X				XX					Exam
	Ship Power Maintenance Engineering	XX	XX	XX	X						XX			Exam
	Ship Equipment Detection and Diagnosis	XX	XX	XX	X						XX			Exam
	Light Weight Diving	XX	X	XX	X				XX					Exam
	Marine Auxiliary Machinery	XX	XX	XX	X					XX				Exam
	The Construction of Ship Electric Machine	XX	XX	XX	X				XX					Exam
	Marine Electrical Equipment	XX	XX	XX	X					XX				Exam

Continued

Modules	Name of the Subject	Class Hours	Lectures	Practice	Credits	1	2	3	4	5	6	7	8	Evaluation
Specialized Subjects	Fundamentals of Ship Architecture and Strength	XX	XX	XX	X				XX					Exam
	Ship Cartography	XX	XX	XX	X				XX					Exam
	Internal Combustion Engine	XX	XX	XX	X					XX				Exam
	Ship Power Plant Principle	XXX	XX	XX	X					XX	XX			Exam
	Survivability and Damage Control Organization	XX	XX	XX	X							XX		Exam
	Experiment with the Structure and Operation of Diesel Engine	XX	XX	XX	X								XX	Exam
	Ship Electromechanical Department Training and Organization	XX	X	XX	X								XX	Exam
Practical Sessions	Practice at Workshops, Visits and Study Tours	XXX	X	XXX	XX	XX	XX	XX	XX	XX	XX	XX	XX	Rating
	Ship Internship	XXX	X	XXX					XX		XX			Exam
	Graduation Field Work	XX	X	XX									XX	Exam

IV. Education and Training Programs

Table 1. 8　Chinese Language Development Program

Events	Description	Timetable
Revision and Exercises	We hope to strengthen instructor-student communication and boost student-student interaction in class through games, practical platforms, and the use of modern technology, thereby fully motivating students' interest in learning and using Chinese. In diverse language circumstances, students should hopefully shift from being "passive receivers" to "active contributors."	Refer to Curriculum Setup for details
HSK Training	We deliver lectures on previous years' test papers, offer solutions to problems in tests, and organize simulated tests based on the HSK syllabus. Focusing on exams, on the other hand, is thought to be an effective strategy to encourage students to learn from testing and plays a constructive role in the evaluation system. Focusing on exams also prepares students for stronger HSK skills and helps students build confidence through concentrated practice and timely correction of errors.	Refer to Curriculum Setup for details

Notes: Chinese Language Training is structured on a ×××-hour schedule, with ××× hours dedicated to revision and exercises and ××× hours to HSK training.

Table 1. 9　Chinese Traditional Culture Experience Program

Events	Description	Class Hours	Timetable
Massive Open Online Courses	Elementary Chinese Grammar	××	Semester 1
	Sports and Health	××	Semester 3
	Traditional Chinese Arts: Seal Carving, Calligraphy and Wash Painting	××	Semester 4
	A Closer Look at the Chinese Nation's Fine Traditional Culture	××	Semester 5
	Total	×××	

Table 1.10　Physical Training Program

Events	Description	Class Hours
5km Running Race	Arranged at the period of independent study and training	××
Swimming	Arranged at the period of independent study and training	××
Obstacles	Arranged at the period of independent study and training	××
Protective Measures and First-aid Practice	Summer Vacation Training Program	××

Notes: Before graduation, students must pass the test for the top three events indicated on the table. The first test is scheduled for the second semester of the third year. Those who fail the first test are allowed to retake it during the second semester of their fourth year.

Table 1.11　Leadership Development Program

Category	Events	Class Hours	Timetable
1	Designated as student-in-charge for specific classes or years	××	All Semesters
2	Appointed as secretary of the sport and entertainment committee, or as secretary of the logistic committee	××	All Semesters
3	In charge of sports and entertainment events	××	All Semesters
4	Attend the training program alongside Chinese colleagues	××	Semester 5

1.2.3　课程表 Classes Schedule

班级　XX-XXX

专业：船舶总体技术

表 1.12　20××—20×× 课程表（第二学期）

周序	日期	一 12	一 34	一 56	二 12	二 34	二 56	三 12	三 34	三 56	四 12	四 34	四 56	五 12	五 34	五 56	六 12	六 34
1	20××.02.25—20××.03.03	图	图		纵	纵		□	计		图	图		纵	纵		体	体
2	20××.03.04—20××.03.10	图	图		纵	纵		□	计		图	图		纵	纵		体	
3	20××.03.11—20××.03.17	图	图		纵	纵		□	计		图	图		纵	纵		体	体
4	20××.03.18—20××.03.24	图	图		海	海		参	参		图	图		图	图		体	
5	20××.03.25—20××.03.31	图	图		海	海		□	计		图	图		图	图		体	体
6	20××.04.01—20××.04.07	图	图		海	海		□	计		海	海		清明节			体	
7	20××.04.08—20××.04.14	静	静		海	海		□	计		海	海		静	静		体	体
8	20××.04.15—20××.04.21	静	静	参	海	海		□	计		海	海		静	静		体	
9	20××.04.22—20××.04.28	静	静		海	海		劳动节			海	海		静	静		体	体
10	20××.04.29—20××.05.05	静	静		海	海		□	计		海	海		静	静		体	体
11	20××.05.06—20××.05.12	静	静		海	海		参	参		海	海		静	静		体	
12	20××.05.13—20××.05.19	参	参		参	参	参	参	参		参	参	参	参	参	参	参	参
13	20××.05.20—20××.05.26	构	构		构	构		□	计		构	构		构	构		体	体
14	20××.05.27—20××.06.02	构	构		构	构		□	计		构	构		构	构		体	
15	20××.06.03—20××.06.09	综	综		综	综		参	参		综	综		端午节			体	
16	20××.06.10—20××.06.16	综	综		综	综		□	计		综	综	综	综	综		体	体
17	20××.06.17—20××.06.23	综	综		综	综	综	□	计		综	综		综	综		体	体

续表

日期	周序	一 12	一 34	一 56	二 12	二 34	二 56	三 12	三 34	三 56	四 12	四 34	四 56	五 12	五 34	五 56	六 12	六 34
20XX.06.24—20XX.06.30	18	综	综	综	综	综	综	管	管		管	管		管	管		管	管
20XX.07.01—20XX.07.07	19	管	管		管			管			管	管		管	管		管	
20XX.07.08—20XX.07.14	20	管			管													

毕业工作

课程名称	性质	上课场所	简称	时数
船体识图与制图	必修	101教室或实验室	图	XX
船舶海洋环境	必修	102教室或实验室	海	XX
船舶静力学	必修	103教室或实验室	静	XX
船舶结构与强度基础	必修	104教室或实验室	构	XX
船舶总体综合实践	必修	105教室或实验室	综	XX
航海基础与船舶操纵	必修	106教室或实验室	纵	XX
计算机及网络应用	必修	107教室	计	XX
汉语口语	必修	108教室	口	XX
体育基础训练	必修	田径场	体	XX
参观见学	必修	武汉市区	参	XX
船舶损害管制	必修	实验室	管	XX

备注：1. 节假日时间：清明节4月5日，与周末连休；劳动节5月1日；端午节6月7日，与周末连休。
2. 课程考试时间、地点，试卷安排，请提前3天与教务处联系（电话：XXXXXXXXX）。

Class No: XX-XXX

Table 1.12　Classes Schedule of 20XX—20XX （Second Semester）

Major: Ship Overall Technology

Week No.	Date	Mon. 12	Mon. 34	Mon. 56	Tue. 12	Tue. 34	Tue. 56	Wed. 12	Wed. 34	Wed. 56	Thu. 12	Thu. 34	Thu. 56	Fri. 12	Fri. 34	Fri. 56	Sat. 12	Sat. 34
1	20XX.02.25—20XX.03.03	SC	SC		BH	BH		OC	CN		SC	SC		BH	BH		ST	
2	20XX.03.04—20XX.03.10	SC	SC		BH	BH		OC	CN		SC	SC		BH	BH		ST	
3	20XX.03.11—20XX.03.17	SC	SC		BH	BH		OC	CN		SC	SC		BH	BH		ST	
4	20XX.03.18—20XX.03.24	SC	SC		ME	ME		VT	VT		SC	SC		SC	SC		ST	
5	20XX.03.25—20XX.03.31	SC	SC		ME	ME		OC	CN		SC	SC		SC	SC		ST	
6	20XX.04.01—20XX.04.07	SC	SC		ME	ME		OC	CN		ME	ME		Holiday 1				
7	20XX.04.08—20XX.04.14	SS	SS		ME	ME		OC	CN		ME	ME		SS	SS		ST	
8	20XX.04.15—20XX.04.21	SS	SS		ME	ME		VT	VT		ME	ME		SS	SS		ST	
9	20XX.04.22—20XX.04.28	SS	SS		ME	ME		OC	CN		ME	ME		SS	SS		ST	
10	20XX.04.29—20XX.05.05	SS	SS		ME	ME		Holiday 2			ME	ME		SS	SS		ST	
11	20XX.05.06—20XX.05.12	SS	SS		ME	ME		OC	CN		ME	ME		SS	SS		ST	
12	20XX.05.13—20XX.05.19	VT	VT	VT	VT	VT	VT	VT	VT		VT	VT	VT	VT	VT	VT	VT	VT
13	20XX.05.20—20XX.05.26	AS	AS		AS	AS		OC	CN		AS	AS		AS	AS		ST	
14	20XX.05.27—20XX.06.02	AS	AS		AS	AS		OC	CN		AS	AS		AS	AS		ST	
15	20XX.06.03—20XX.06.09	AS	AS		AS	AS		OC	CN		AS	AS		Holiday 3				
16	20XX.06.10—20XX.06.16	IP	IP		IP	IP		VT	VT		IP	IP		IP	IP		ST	
17	20XX.06.17—20XX.06.23	IP	IP		IP	IP	IP	OC	CN				IP	IP	IP		ST	

Continued

Week No.	Date	Mon.			Tue.			Wed.			Thu.			Fri.			Sat.	
		12	34	56	12	34	56	12	34	56	12	34	56	12	34	56	12	34
18	20XX.06.24—20XX.06.30	IP	IP	IP		IP	IP	DC	DC		DC	DC		DC	DC		DC	DC
19	20XX.07.01—20XX.07.07	DC			DC			DC			DC			DC	DC		DC	DC
20	20XX.07.08—20XX.07.14	DC			DC			DC			DC							

Subjects	Classrooms	Codes	Hours
Ship Cartography	C101 or Lab	SC	XX
Ship Marine Environment	C102 or Lab	ME	XX
Ship Statics	C103 or Lab	SS	XX
Fundamentals of Ship Architecture and Strength	C104 or Lab	AS	XX
Integrated Practice of Ship Equipment	C105 or Lab	IP	XX
Navigation Basics and Ship Handling	C106 or Lab	BH	XX
Application of Computer & Network	C107	CN	XX
Oral Chinese	C108	OC	XX
Sports Skills Training	Playground	ST	XX
Visits and Study Tours	Wuhan	VT	XX
Ship Damage Control	Lab	DC	XX

Remarks: 1. Holiday 1: Tomb-Sweeping Day is on April 5, including weekends; Holiday 2: International Labor Day is on May 1; Holiday 3: Dragon Boat Festival is on June 7, including weekends.

2. Please contact the Academic Affairs Office 3 days in advance for the examination time, place and paper arrangement.

1.2.4　**专业通报** An Introduction to Courses

尊敬的史密斯先生、中外同行们、朋友们：

上午好！

我是中国甲大学国际交流学院的院长王建东，很高兴参加此次中外会谈，并向各位介绍甲大学概况及我们设置的船员培训方案。首先请各位观看宣传片。

甲大学坐落于湖北省武汉市，创建于 1949 年。我校以建设世界一流院校，培育一流人才为目标，以培养合格的建设者和未来领导者为己任，在近 70 年的教学实践中，形成了"严谨、求实、拼搏、创新"的校风。我校拥有雄厚的师资、先进的设备、优美的环境、良好的校风、开放的办学理念、丰富的育人经验，先后为国家培养了数十万名人才。我们的对外合作交流活动丰富多样，我们与多个国家的院校建立了常态化、机制化的交流。我校留学生教育工作起步于 20 世纪 50 年代，至今共培养数十个国家近万名外国人才，国别辐射亚洲、非洲、南美洲、北美洲、大洋洲五大洲。留学生在这里学有所获，生活充实，回国后能很快成为为本国发展建设做贡献的有用人才。

我介绍的第一部分是甲大学留学生教育专业设置情况。

依托我校学科和资源优势，结合国外需求和船舶设备建设特点，我们开设了 5 个留学生专业。包括：（1）四年制本科轮机工程专业，使用汉语授课。（2）一年制船舶技术与管理专业，下辖多个方向。（3）半年制船舶设备保障管理专业、船舶损管消防技术专业与船岸智能信息交互系统专业。后面 3 个专业均使用英语和法语授课。

近年来，我们还开展外国留学生研究生培养工作。我校广阔的办学平台和完整的办学体系使得我们有实力根据友好国家的需要，开设专门课程，针对特定层次、特定目标及不同规模的留学生群体进行定制性培训。

我介绍的第二部分是甲大学留学生教育条件。

1. 我校拥有完备的专业人才培养体系。我校学科专业齐全，以船舶相关专业为例，拥有与船舶各专业岗位人才培养密切相关的本科与任职培训体系，同时我校也是船舶岗位专业训练等资格认证的重要基地，培养了大批高素质应用型人才。

2. 我校拥有雄厚的师资力量和全面的教学配套建设。我校在同类型高校中拥有无可比拟的师资优势和教学配套建设，以船舶相关专业为例，专业教师中，硕士以上学历超过 95%，博士学历接近 60%，高级专业技术职务约 70%，骨干教师全部能用英语直接授课。有配套完备的教材、实装、实验室和模拟器。

3. 我校拥有完备的留学生教育后勤保障条件。大家现在所在的这栋楼是我校综合对外培训楼，总建筑面积近 2 万平方米，集教学、住宿、餐饮、娱乐、健身服务等多功能于一体。共有宿舍 100 多间，能容纳 300 多个床位；多功能会议厅、多功能智慧教室、国际礼仪实践俱乐部、体育中心、灯光球场等场所一应俱全，教学、生活区域 WiFi 全覆盖，另外还有 10 套外国留学生陪读家属公寓。

我介绍的第三部分是甲大学贵国留学生培训情况。

贵国先后选派多批次近百名留学生来我校学习，覆盖船舶维修、机电、通信等培训专业。总的来说，贵国留学生表现突出，给我们留下了深刻印象。他们有以下几个特点：一是学习能力强，综合素质好。贵国留学生学习刻苦认真，成绩在各国留学生中位居上流，先后有多人获评为优秀留学生。二是热情开朗，积极参加各类文体活动。不少贵国留学生是我们文体活动的骨干，积极参加迎新春晚会、深蓝文化节等活动，他们还积极组织了大学首次板球比赛，反响很好。三是遵章守纪，荣誉感强。贵国留学生气质和仪表较好，自我要求严格，能够带头遵守中国法律法规和学校的规章制度，服从和配合中方管理。四是重情重义，与中外人员相处融洽。历届贵国留学生都对中国和我校充满感情，与中方人员及各国留学生关系亲密，很多人毕业多年后还和我们保持着微信、邮件联系，向我们报告结婚生子等喜讯。

我介绍的第四部分是甲大学贵国船员培训方案。

第一是课程目标，通过理论学习和模拟器/实装训练，接船人员能够掌握船舶基本理论知识和基本技能，为实操培训做准备。

第二是学制，共计×个月，约××周，共×××学时。

第三是专业介绍。甲大学目前开设船舶机电管理专业 1 个。如需另外开设机械、电气、仓段操作员等专业，与船舶机电管理专业相同的共同科目培训课程将安排合训，专业培训将分开进行。

第四是培训对象要求。参训的船舶机电管理人员，应具有船舶相关工作背景，大学以上文化程度，数理基础较好，身体健康，熟练掌握英语。如需另外开设机械、电气、仓段操作员等专业，参训人员应具有船舶技术岗位相关工作背景，高中以上文化程度，身体健康，能掌握英语。

第五是培训形式。本次培训采取理论授课、模拟器操纵、实船教学等形式组织实施，共分 2 个阶段进行：第一阶段为船员共同科目培训阶段，时间约为×个月，主要内容为船舶构造、损管等基础知识学习和基本技能训练；第二阶段为专业培训阶段，时间约为×个月，主要内容为船舶各专业设备原理、操作使用、维护保养等的学习。

第六是课程安排。大家请看屏幕。正如我们前面提到的那样，整个培训分为理论学习，模拟器操作和实船教学。理论学习包括共同科目和专业科目。共同科目有：船舶概论、船舶装置与系统、船舶损害管制、船舶电力系统概述、船舶设备系统概述、船舶用语及口令、中国国情文化概述；专业科目有：船舶操纵及模拟器实操、船舶生命力、船舶柴油机及装修实作、船舶电气设备及维修实作、船舶动力系统监测与控制、船舶辅助机械。

第七是考核方式。重点考核对本培训课程理论知识和实作技能的掌握与熟练程度，方式包括形成性考核和终结性考核（各占 50%）。其中，形成性考核包括到课情况、平时作业和课堂表现等；终结性考核为理论或实作考试、技能竞赛、岗位资格考核或撰写总结报告。

第八是计分标准。最终成绩采用百分制。形成性考核（50%）包括到课情况（15%）、平时作业（15%）和课堂表现（20%）；终结性考核（50%）指课程结束时的考试、竞赛或考核成绩。成绩认定采用两级制。终结性考核不及格，该课程考核不通过。终结性考核及格，课程成绩为形成性考核与终结性考核加权后的最终成绩，60分及以上为通过。部分课程考核合格后颁发资格证书。

我的介绍就到这里。顺便说一句，我本人曾于20××年赴贵国B大学学习和生活，对贵国人民感情深厚，回国后我经常向同事、朋友和家人分享那段难忘的经历。欢迎各位有机会访问我们甲大学，预祝本次中外会谈取得圆满成功！衷心希望各位外国朋友能积极宣传甲大学，欢迎贵国更多优秀人员来我校交流、学习，以增进我们之间的了解与交流。最后，祝各位朋友身体健康，愿我们的友谊像滚滚长江奔流不息！谢谢！

Mr. Smith, dear friends and colleagues,

Good morning!

My name is Wang Jiandong, and I'm the dean of the College of International Exchange of University A. I feel greatly honored to be invited to the forum. I would like to avail myself of this opportunity to make a presentation on our university and the training program for ship crew members. To begin, please join me in watching a video of the College of International Exchange.

University A was established in 1949 and is located in the city of Wuhan, Hubei province. Since then, our university has chartered the course of building a world-class academy, fostering great personnel and developing talented students and future leaders for our country. Over the 70 years' development, the university has created a motto as "being rigorous, practical, hard-working and innovative." Our university boasts competent professors, advanced equipment, beautiful environment, sound atmosphere, open education philosophy, and rich experience in education. So far our university has incubated around 100 thousand talents for our country. On the other hand, our university is very active and resourceful in international cooperation. We have established the exchange mechanism with other colleges around the world. Furthermore, since the 1950s, our university has welcomed over 10,000 international students from over 50 nations across five continents, including Asia, Africa, South America, North America, and Oceania. After gaining valuable education and living an exciting life here, the students became the backbone of their respective countries soon after their return.

In the first part of my presentation, I will discuss the courses available to overseas students at our university.

We have so far offered 5 courses for international students, supported by the university's disciplines and resources, in response to other countries' demand and ship equipment development. The courses are as follows: (1)A four-year marine engineering course with a bachelor's degree accessible and Chinese is the intermediate language in class. (2)A one-year ship technology and management course that covers a variety of specialized sectors. (3)A six-month course in ship equipment support management, a six-month course in ship damage control and firefighting technology, and a six-month course in ship-shore intelligent information interaction system. The last three courses use English and French in class.

We have recently developed a postgraduate program for international students. Because our university has a large platform and a complete school management system, we are able to tailor courses to overseas students' professional levels and scales, all based on the need and objectives of our friendly countries.

In the second part of my presentation, I will talk about the excellent educational environment available to overseas students.

1. We have an educational system that offers a diverse range of cour-

ses. Our university offers a diverse range of disciplines. Ship-related courses, for example, include both undergraduate and on-the-job training programs for all on-board positions. Furthermore, our university is a major center for crew member qualification accreditation. It has fostered a great number of talented individuals for our country.

2. We have highly skilled instructor resources and comprehensive educational support services. In comparison to other universities of the same type, we have unrivaled professors and educational support facilities. In ship-related courses, for example, more than 95 percent of lecturers have a master's degree, almost 60 percent have a PhD, and 70 percent hold senior academic titles. All of the major instructors are capable of giving lectures in English. The university has a comprehensive set of supporting literature, real-world equipment, labs, and simulators.

3. We have effective logistical support for overseas students. This is a multi-purpose building for overseas students. It incorporates classrooms, dormitories, a dining hall, an entertainment facility, a gym, among other services across a total construction area of 20,000 square meters. Everything is already in place, including over 100 rooms with more than 300 beds, a multi-function conference hall, smart classrooms, an international etiquette workshop, a sport center, a floodlit court, and our WiFi covers throughout the teaching and living building. What's more, there are ten apartments for family-accompanied international students.

Let me discuss about students from your country at our university in the third part of my presentation.

So far, your country has sent nearly 100 students to our university to study ship-repair, electromechanical engineering, and communication engineering. In general, they have significantly impressed us with their outstanding performance. I'll summarize their characteristics as follows:

To begin, they are quite capable of learning and have a high level of quality. They are hardworking in their studies, ranking first among all overseas students. Many of them have received the Excellent International Student Award. Second, they actively participate in cultural and sporting events. Many of them are in charge of sport and culture activities, and spare no efforts to organize events such as the New Year Gala and the Cultural Festival. It is worth noting that the activists organized the first cricket games at our campus, which received positive feedback from all sides. Third, they follow the laws and regulations and have a great sense of honor. They have a good personal bearing and take the lead in adhering to Chinese laws as well as the university regulations. They are very cooperative with the Chinese management authority. Last but not least, they value friendship and have good relationships with both Chinese staff and international students. None of your students who have come to study with us throughout the years have forgotten China or our university, and they have maintained close ties with Chinese personnel and their classmates. Many of them have stayed in touch with us via Wechat and e-mail for years after graduation. We are more than happy to share their excitement at their marriage and the arrival of their children.

Let's go to the training program for your crew members.

The course objectives come first. This course is expected to lay a solid foundation for crew members in their theoretical knowledge and skillset required by the ship, through lectures and simulator/equipment training, preparing for on-board training in the future.

Second is the course duration. there are ×××　class hours in total throughout the course of × months (about ×× weeks).

Third is the course introduction. For the time being, we only offer one course to your students: ship electromechanical management. Depending on your needs, we can also provide various courses such as mechanical engineering, electrical engineering, cabin management, etc. All students will take classes together for general subjects, while students from different courses will take specialized lessons individually.

The fourth are the program's requirements for crew members. To enroll in the ship electromechanical management course, candidates must have previous ship-related experience and a strong grasp of the English language and sciences. They should be physically healthy and have finished university-level or higher education courses. Candidates should have hands-on experience in technical missions and a high school certificate or higher to enroll in courses such as mechanical engineering, electrical engineering, cabin management, and ship maneuvering. They should also be physically fit and able to communicate in English.

The fifth is a description of training process. The training will consist of lectures, simulator manipulation and on-board teaching and will be conducted in two stages: in the first stage, crew members will attend lectures and practice the skillset for general subjects, including ship structure, damage control and basic skills development, which may last up to × months; in the second stage, crew members will focus on the specialized knowledge, such as the principle, operation and maintenance of various ship equipment, which may last up to × months.

The sixth is an overview of the subjects. The table is shown on the screen. The complete training process, as we described in earlier parts, comprises of lectures on theoretical knowledge, simulator manipulation, and on-board teaching. Lectures cover both general and specialized topics. The following are examples of general subjects: An Overview of Ships, Ship Devices and Systems, Ship Damage Control, An Overview of the Ship's Electrical Power System, An Introduction to the Ship's Equipment System, Terminologies and Ship Commands, An Overview of Chinese Culture and the National Situation, and so on. Ship Manipulation and Simulator Practice, Ship Survivability, Installation and Maintenance of Ship Diesel Engine, Ship Electrical Equipment and Maintenance Operation, Ship Power System Monitoring and Control, and Ship Auxiliary Machinery are some of the specialized subjects.

The Seventh is the evaluation method. The evaluation will focus on theoretical knowledge and skillset. The evaluation is divided into two parts: formative assessment (50%), which includes class attendance, assignments, and class performance, and summative assessment (50%), which includes theoretical and practical examinations, skill contests, and qualification examinations or summary reports.

The eighth is the grading criteria. In the final evaluation, a hundred-point scoring system is used for the grading criteria. Formative assessment, which accounts for half of the total, includes class attendance (15%), assignments (15%), and class performance (20%). Summative assessment, which accounts for half of the grade, refers to the results of examinations/contests or evaluations after subjects have been completed. A two-level grading system is used for the Grading System. If they do not pass the summative assessment, students will fail the exam. If students pass the summative assessment, their final score will be the weighed sum of the formative and summative assessments. The minimum passing score for the exam is set at 60 points. For some subjects, if students pass the tests, we will offer the certificates.

This concludes my presentation. It is pertinent to note that in 20××, I was assigned to study at the University B in your country, which strengthened my understanding and friendship with your country and its people. Since returning home, I have always shared the memorable experiences in your country with my colleagues, friends and families. Hereby, I'd like to extend an invitation to all of you to visit our university whenever it is convenient for you. I wish the forum a great success from the bottom of my heart. Sincerely, I look forward to your proactive promotion of our university, as well as welcoming more excellent colleagues from your side to our university for course study and exchange programs, in order to raise mutual understanding and cooperation to new heights. Finally, I'd like to wish all of my friends good health. May our friendship last as long as the tenacious Yangtze River. Thank you very much.

1.3 质量管理 Quality Control

1.3.1 授课满意度问卷调查表 Questionnaire of International Students' Satisfaction with Instructors and Lectures

表 1.13 留学生教师授课满意度问卷调查表

专业		评价等级		
课程名称		优秀	良好	一般
1	汉语口语训练			
2	计算机及网络应用			
3	参观见学			
4	体育训练			
5	电机结构与维修			
6	船舶辅助机械			
7	船舶电气设备			

续表

课程名称		评价等级		
		优秀	良好	一般
8	机电专业训练与组织			
9	柴油机装修实作			
10	机电设备检测维修实践			
11	天线与无线传播			
12	卫星通信技术			
13	无线电测向			
14	短波与超短波通信设备			
15	测速测深仪			
16	导航接收机			
17	自控元件			
18	电气原理与维修			
19	航海基础与船舶操纵			
20	船舶损害管制			
1. 每人只对本专业课程进行评价，注意填写专业名称，不用填写本人姓名。 2. 对课程及教师的意见建议。				

Table 1. 13　Questionnaire of International Students' Satisfaction with

Instructors and Lectures

Course				
	Subjects	Ratings		
		Excellent	Good	Average
1	Oral Chinese			
2	Application of Computer & Network			
3	Visits and Study Tours			
4	Sports Training			

Continued

	Subjects	Ratings		
		Excellent	Good	Average
5	Construction and Maintenance of Ship Electric Machinery			
6	Marine Auxiliary Machinery			
7	Marine Electrical Equipment			
8	Electromechanical Engineering Training and Organization			
9	Repair and Maintenance of Diesel Engine			
10	Detection and Maintenance of Electromechanical Equipment			
11	Antenna and Radio Wave Transmission			
12	Satellite Communication System			
13	Radio Direction Finding			
14	HF and V/UHF Communication Equipment			
15	Speed Log & Deep Sounder			
16	Navigation Receivers			
17	Automatic Control Components			
18	Electrical System Fundamentals and Maintenance			
19	Navigation Basics and Ship Handling			
20	Ship Damage Control Basics and Operation			

1. Please only provide feedback on your course's teachers and lectures. Fill in your course name but do not include your own name.
2. Share your thoughts and ideas about instructors and lectures.

1.3.2　教学会议 Sharing Ideas on International Education

留学生教学工作座谈交流会议程

时间：5月9日15:00

地点：留学生楼二楼会议室

参加人员：国际交流学院领导，留学生教师，留学生代表

主持人：国际交流学院副院长赵长江

议程：

1. 介绍留学生教学大纲有关要求。

2. 留学生代表发言，介绍学习过程中的意见及建议。

3. 留学生教师代表发言，介绍教学过程中的意见及建议。

4. 国际交流学院院长王建东讲话。

Agenda of the Meeting on Teaching Feedback

Time: 15:00 on May 9th

Location: Conference room, second floor of the international students' building

Attendees: Leaders of the College of International Exchange, teachers and student representatives

Host: Professor Zhao Changjiang, deputy dean of the College of International Exchange

Agenda:

1. The host briefs on the syllabus.

2. Student representatives present challenges during their studies,

and offer solutions.

3. Teacher representatives express their thoughts and provide ideas.

4. A speech is given by Professor Wang Jiandong, dean of the College of International Exchange.

留学生教学工作座谈交流会主持词

各位留学生教师、同志们：

大家下午好！非常高兴能有机会与大家沟通交流关于留学生教学的有关问题。今天会议的主要目的就是针对目前留学生教学过程中存在的问题共同商讨对策，到会的既有一线教师，还有留学生代表，希望能听到大家关于留学生教学的困难、意见及建议，以便改进教学工作，共同提高人才培养质量，提升我们留学生教育的竞争力。

今天的座谈会有以下几个议程：

一是由我介绍留学生四年本科教学工作整体情况，主要是教学大纲的一些要求。

二是请留学生代表谈论学习中遇到的一些问题和建议。

三是请留学生教师谈论教学中的意见及建议。

最后请国际交流学院院长王建东讲话。

Host's Remarks of the Meeting on Teaching Feedback

Dear professors and comrades,

Good afternoon! It is my pleasure to join you in this meeting to address some concerns that affect teachers and students over the course of the study. Today's discussion is intended to provide solutions to the problems that have troubled us all. We hope that both professors and students will be able to share their issues and suggestions on various courses during the meeting. We believe that your comments will help to improve our educational quality, foster our talent cultivation mode, and increase our competitiveness in international education.

The meeting today is divided into three halves. To begin, I will provide an overview of the four-year undergraduate program, with a special emphasis on the syllabus. Second, we will invite student representatives to voice their concerns and ideas. Third, we will ask representative teachers to present their solutions. Last but not least, we will welcome Professor Wang Jiandong, the College's dean, to deliver a speech.

国际交流学院院长在留学生教学工作座谈交流会上的讲话

各位老师、同志们：

下午好！今天我们开会就是为了交流前期教学工作的方法和经验，收集教学双方的意见及建议，研究下一步工作举措。

我校于去年9月开始承担留学生本科教学任务，这是一次全新的探索，具有很强的综合效益，既展示了我校的办学实力和国际影响力，也进一步扩大了办学规模，丰富了办学层次和类型，提升了参训院系和教师的对外教学能力和国际交流水平。我们坚持质量标准，迅速建立了一整套规章制度，开设了一系列优质课程，选拔了一支专业的教师队伍，在校内外和国际上产生了良好影响。前期各项工作的顺利推进得益于我校内训教学的扎实基础，得益于各位教师的高度政治觉悟与质量意识。我们各位教师是开拓者，在我校留学生教育历史上留下了重要印迹。

针对留学生汉语学习零基础、学习难度大的实际，我们采取周测试、月讲评等方式随时检验，编印数学、物理等基础课程汉语学习手册，组织专业汉语学习走进实验室，建立早晚自习辅导制度。为了更好地服务于留学生HSK考试，我们申请了HSK考点，改造了"多功能对外汉语语音教室"。我们组织对外汉语教学授课评比，进一步加强对外汉语师资力量建设以提高对外汉语教学水平。

对于后续工作，一是进一步探索并健全不同于中国学生及短学制留学生的教学管理制度。各位教师要把握本科留学生的教育特点和规律，摸索推广针对性强、行之有效的教学方法。我们也会加强与承担留学生教育工作的兄弟院校的合作与交流。特别是在对外汉语和基础课程教学、教材编写、国际文化交流、中国传统文化教育和学术资源等方面，择优采购其他兄弟院校目前使用的留学生教材，聘请高水平的专家教授担任部分课程教师，选派我校对外汉语教师到有关院校接受专业培训等。二是调动教、学、管三方的积极性，增强教师的自豪感和本科留学生的荣誉感，采取倾斜政策和措施支持和推进教学帮带、课后辅导、奖学金等制度的实施。

下一步，我们将在国家和院校级评比中，为各位教师积极争取荣誉，在出国名额上采取倾斜政策，支持和资助专著、教材的出版及论文的发表，为直接使用英语授课的教师提供课时费奖励。在场地建设方面，我们将积极筹措、建设留学生智慧教室、计算机教室，为远程指导和视频答辩提供条件。我们还将常态化、机制化地安排留学生教学工作会议，组织教学经验交流和理论研讨会议，以解剖麻雀的方式来改进有关工作。希望大家对自己有信心，对教师有信心，对学校有信心。

Speech by Dean of the College of International Exchange

Dear professors and comrades,

Good afternoon! The purpose of today's meeting is to exchange prior experience and solutions on course instruction, as well as to collect views and suggestions from both professors and students in order to improve our future work.

In September of last year, our university began offering undergraduate education to international students. It is regarded as a new historical exploration that will benefit all parties involved. The new initiative has highlighted the university's educational strength and international influence, broadened the educational spectrum, and enhanced educational levels and types. Meanwhile, it has improved the teaching skills and the international exchange level of colleges and instructors. We always adhere to quality standards and we have swiftly implemented a set of rules and regulations, provided a series of high-quality classes, and assembled an outstanding teaching team. At this moment, the undergraduate program has received positive response both in and out of the university, as well as abroad. The past work has progressed smoothly due to the solid foundation of the university's education for Chinese students, as well as the professors' quest of high quality education and their high political awareness. Our teachers have left their footprint on the university's history of international education as pioneers of the international undergraduate program.

In response to the fact that international students' zero Chinese language basis has created challenges in their study, we introduced weekly tests and monthly reviews on their Chinese learning, compiled and printed the Mathematics and Physics Handbook in Chinese, offered classes of learning Chinese in labs, and established a tutoring system during morning and evening self-study periods. Following a successful application, we established HSK exam center at our university and modified the multipurpose classroom for teaching Chinese to speakers of other languages. We held competitions on teaching Chinese as a foreign language in order to strengthen the teaching team and improve the teaching abilities of the instructors.

For future work, we propose conducting additional research on an education management system that differs from the current one for Chinese students and the one for international students visiting for a short length of time. We hope teachers are able to identify the educational features and nature of international undergraduates, and in response to their feedback develop effective teaching techniques. We will strengthen our partnerships with other institutions that offer courses to overseas students. In particular, in terms of teaching Chinese to international students, basic subject education, textbook materials, cross-cultural communication, education on Chinese tradition, and academic resources, among other things, we can select and purchase high-quality textbooks currently used by other institutions for international students, recruit renowned professors for lectures in specific classes, and send instructors who teach Chinese to international students to other schools for professional development. Furthermore, we will mobilize three parties: the teaching team, the students, and the management authority, in order to increase teachers' sense of pride and students' sense of honor through preferential policies. We will implement policies to promote win-win cooperation between teachers and students, as well as to improve after-class tutoring and scholarship system.

Next, we will endeavor to provide opportunities for each instructor in national and intra-university competitions, as well as preferential policies for visiting and studying abroad. We intend to sponsor the publication of academic books, textbooks, and academic papers, as well as to compensate those who use English in their lectures.

In terms of infrastructure development, we will finance the building of smart classrooms, computer classrooms and establish circumstances for online tutoring and viva. We will hold international education-related meetings on a regular basis, share teaching experiences and discuss teaching theory. We are determined to improve our work through case studies. We hope that each of us is confident in our international education and has faith in the future of our university.

1.3.3　留学生成绩表 International Student's School Report

表 1.14　留学生成绩表

姓名	萨帕斯		国籍		C 国	
专业	损管消防技术		注册日期		20××.09.01	
			结业日期		20××.02.28	
班级	××-×××		证书编号		58413	
序号	课程				成绩	评语
1	船舶生命力				90	
2	船舶损管组织与管理				98	
3	船舶损管技能与协同管理训练				83	
4	船舶损管综合演练				85	
5	中国国情及传统文化				86	
6	汉语入门				87	
7	参观见学				95	
甲大学国际交流学院意见： 国际交流学院院长： 日期：20××年 2 月 28 日			甲大学国际交流学院 （盖章） 日期：20××年 2 月 28 日			

Table 1.14　International Student's School Report

Name	Sampath		Nationality	Country C
Course	Damage Control and Fire Fighting Technology		Admission Date	1st Sep. , 20××
			Completion Date	28th Feb. , 20××
Class	××-×××		Certificate No.	58413

Continued

No.	Subjects	Score	Remarks
1	Ship Survivability	90	
2	Ship Damage Control Organization and Management	98	
3	Ship Damage Control Technology and Integrated Management	83	
4	Ship Damage Control Integrated Training	85	
5	An Introduction to China and Chinese Culture	86	
6	Basic Chinese	87	
7	Visits and Study Tours	95	

College of International Exchange, University A:	College of International Exchange, University A
Dean:	(Seal)
Date: 28th Feb., 20××	Date: 28th Feb., 20××

1.4 研究生教育 Postgraduate Education

1.4.1 研究生招生简章 Admission Brochure for International Students (Master's Degree Program)

报考须知

(一)报考条件

1. 遵守中国法律法规，品行良好。

2. 身体健康。

3. 具有高等教育学历或学士(含)以上学位。

(二)报考办法

20××年 9 月 19 日至 23 日，考生填写并上交留学生硕士研究生入学考试报名表。

20××年 9 月 24 日至 30 日，教务处对考生进行资格审查。

20××年 10 月 31 日，领取准考证。

20××年 11 月 2 日至 3 日(每天上午 8:30—11:30，下午 14:00—17:00)，组织考试。考试科目为：英语、数学、专业基础、专业综合 4 门。

20××年 11 月中旬，复试，科目为英语和专业面试。公布录取名单。

(三)有关说明

1. 通过入学考试的考生，须提交学位证书复印件或扫描件。

2. 留学生硕士研究生采取课程学习与科学研究相结合的培养方式，实行导师负责制。

3. 学习年限为 2 年(20××年 9 月至 20××年 7 月)。其中，1 年在校学习(20××年 9 月至 20××年 7 月)，1 年回国撰写研究生论文(20××年 7 月至 20××年 5 月)。论文撰写完毕，返校或网上远程进行论文答辩。

4. 留学生须报考与目前所学留学生专业相近的研究生专业。其所学留学生专业的所有课程同时作为硕士研究生专业的必修课程，另外视情增开与报考专业相关的课程。

5. 留学生硕士研究生完成培养计划规定的全部学习内容，修满规定的学分，论文答辩成绩合格，准予毕业，颁发中华人民共和国教育部承认的硕士研究生学历和学位证书。

Application Information

A. Prerequisites

1. Applicants must follow the laws and regulations of the People's Republic of China while exemplifying high moral values and ethics.

2. Applicants must be in good physical and mental health.

3. Applicants must have completed university education or hold a bachelor's degree or higher.

B. Application Procedures

From 19 to 23 September, 20✕✕, applicants must submit a correctly completed Postgraduate Entrance Exam Application Form for International Students.

From 24 to 30 September, 20✕✕, the Office of Studies at University A will evaluate and verify applicants' credentials.

On 31 October, 20✕✕, applicants will receive the Postgraduate Entrance Exam Pass.

Exams will be held from 8:30 to 11:30 and 14:00 to 17:00 on the 2nd and 3rd of November 20✕✕, respectively. English, mathematics, specialist basics, and general professional assessment are all part of the exams.

In the middle of November 20✕✕, the second round of exam is required wherein the knowledge of English and specialization is tested through an interview. The accepted roll will then be made public.

C. Description of the Postgraduate Program

1. Applicants must submit the photocopy or scanned copy of their graduation certificate or degree and the approval letter of their respective countries after successfully passing the entrance exam.

2. The overseas postgraduate program's education technique combines course study and scientific research. Furthermore, the "tutor responsibility" process is emphasized.

3. The duration of the postgraduate program is 2 years (from September 20✕✕ to July 20✕✕) wherein the study for the first year is conducted at University A (from September 20✕✕ to July 20✕✕). There-

on, for the second year study, students must prepare and submit master's program dissertations from their own countries (from July 20××to May 20××). Upon the completion/submission of dissertations, students should participate in the viva at the university or online.

4. Applicants should apply for the postgraduate program that is most closely related to their present program (course). The subjects students cover in their present courses are used as the required subjects for the postgraduate program. In addition, subjects directly related to the particular postgraduate program will be provided.

5. The Ministry of Education of the People's Republic of China will then award the graduation certificate and master's degree, providing that students complete the course study, receive the specified credits, and pass the viva prior to the following issuing of permission for graduation.

1.4.2　研究生招生考试考生注意事项 Points for Attention：Postgraduate Entrance Exam for International Students

研究生招生考试考生注意事项

为确保留学生硕士研究生招生考试的安全、平稳、顺利进行，请考生入场时注意以下事项：

1. 考生凭准考证、护照按规定时间进入考场，自觉接受身份验证核查、安全检查和随身物品检查等，并对号入座，入座后将上述证件放在桌面左上角，以便检查。

2. 考生须着装整洁。

3. 考前 10 分钟，考生可进入考场。

4. 考试时间以北京时间为准，每科开考 15 分钟后不得入场，交卷出场时间不得早于各科考试结束前 30 分钟。

5. 考生要严格遵守考场规则。

6. 考生不允许携带任何计时工具、通信工具和带储存功能的计算器进入考场。

7. 考生应在指定位置填写姓名、考生编号等，并在答题纸规定的区域答题，写在草稿纸或者规定区域以外的答案一律无效。

8. 四门课程满分 500 分，专业综合 100 分、英语 100 分、数学 150 分、专业基础 150 分。

真诚希望各位考生诚信应考。祝愿各位考生考出理想成绩！

Points for Attention: Postgraduate Entrance Exam for International Students

Please read the following information before entering the exam room to ensure a safe, stable and smooth Entrance Exam.

1. You must enter the exam room with your Exam Pass and Passport at the specified time. Your ID must be validated, and your belongings must be inspected. Take the seat with your Pass Number pasted on it. Place your Pass and Passport on the upper left corner of your desk.

2. You must dress appropriately.

3. It is permitted to enter the exam room 10 minutes before the start of the exam.

4. The exam schedule is based on Beijing Time. It is not permitted to enter the exam room beyond 15 minutes of the exam's start time. The exam paper cannot be submitted 30 minutes before the end of the exam.

5. You are expected to follow the exam guidelines.

6. No laptops or communication devices are permitted.

7. In the designated sections on the page, write your name and Pass

Number. Fill in the blanks on the answer page with your response. If the response is on rough/draft paper or outside of the prescribed regions, it is deemed invalid.

8. The tests have a total mark of 500 points, with 100 points for Comprehensive Professional Assessment, 100 points for English, 150 points for Mathematics, and 150 points for specialized subjects.

The exam places a strong importance on honesty. Good luck and success to you.

表 1.15　甲大学留学生研究生招生考试报名申请表

姓名		国籍		照片
出生年月		宗教信仰		
婚姻状况		护照号码		
手机号码		语种		
最高学历及专业				
就读院校及时间				
最高学位及专业				
就读院校及时间				
本校就读专业		申请专业		
教育背景	时间	院系	专业	
工作经历	时间	工作单位	职务	

Table 1.15 Postgraduate Entrance Exam Application Form for
International Students

Name		Nationality		Photo
Date of Birth		Religion		
Marital Status		Passport No.		
Telephone No.		Languages		
Highest Level of Education and Major				
University and Time of Study				
Highest Degree Obtained and Major				
University and Time of Study				
Undergraduate Major at University A		Major Choice		
Educational Background	Time	Department/College		Major
Working Experience	Time	Employer		Title

表 1.16 甲大学留学生研究生复试审定表

姓名		性别		国籍		照片	
出生日期		婚否		语种			
宗教信仰		护照号码		准考证号			
本科专业							
现工作单位							
联系方式	手机：			家庭电话：			
	通信地址：			电子邮箱：			
毕业学校		毕业时间		最后学历			
毕业专业				最后学位			
学历证书编号			学位证书编号				
报考学科专业			研究方向及代码				
拟录学科专业			导师姓名		研究方向代码		
总成绩计算公式	初试成绩（C）		复试成绩（F）		总成绩（Z）		本专业排名
Z＝C÷5×70% ＋F×30%							

Table 1. 16 Postgraduate Interview Application Form

Name		Gender		Nationality			Photo
Date of Birth		Marital Status		Languages			
Religion		Passport No.		Entrance Exam Pass No.			
Undergraduate Major							
Current Employer							
Contacts		Phone No.:			Home Phone No.:		
		Address:			E-mail:		
Education			Graduation Time		Highest Level of Education		
Major					Highest Degree Obtained		
Diploma No.			Degree Certificate No.				
Applied Major			Research Interest and Code				
Accepted Major				Supervisor		Research Interest and Code	
Formula Used to Calculate the Final Score	Score of the Entrance Exam (C)		Score of the Second Round of Exam (F)		Final Score (Z)		Position at the Major Table
$Z=C\div5\times70\%$ $+F\times30\%$							

研究生录取通知书

柯欧：

你已被录取为我校××级××专业研究生，谨向你表示热烈祝贺。

甲大学

（盖章）

××年×月×日

Postgraduate Admission Notice

Dear Keo,

You have been admitted by course ×× as a postgraduate student of class ×× at University A in the People's Republic of China. We would like to express our heartfelt congratulations to you.

University A, PRC

（Seal）

DD/MM/YYYY

1.4.3　在研究生答辩会上的讲话 Speech at the Graduation Viva of Postgraduates

尊敬的主席，各位教授，女士们、先生们：

下午好！首先对各位抽出宝贵的时间参加留学生研究生的毕业答辩表示热烈欢迎和感谢。为适应对外友好交流的快速发展，提升大学国际竞争力和影响力，助力世界一流院校建设，自20××年，我校开办留学生研究生教育工作起，迄今已招收多批共××名留学生研究生。招生比例占每年同期留学生总数的20%，毕业比例约占入学比例的60%。这充分说明，我校留学生研究生教育一直坚持严格的质量标准。按照我校留学生研究生培养及学位管理的有关规定，经过院系，指导教师的严格审核，有10人具备答辩条件，参加本次毕业论文答辩。我谨代表国际交流学院全体人员预祝他们答辩顺利，也祝各位专家和教授工作愉快，身体健康！谢谢！

Respected Chairman, dear professors, ladies and gentlemen,

Good afternoon! To begin, I would like to express my gratitude for your attendance at the graduation viva of international postgraduates. To keep pace with the rapid growth of friendly exchanges, to enhance our university's competitiveness and influence, and to contribute to the development of a world-class university, the university has recruited ×× overseas postgraduates for × consecutive years since 20××, when the overseas postgraduate program was launched. Postgraduate admissions account for 20% of all international students admitted year on year. Around 60% of postgraduates have been offered a master's degree. As seen by the data above, the university has implemented a strict quality control system for its postgraduate programs for international students. According to the application procedures of master's degree, ten students are qualified to attend the dissertation interview with the approval of relevant colleges and professors. I would like to convey my best wishes to them at the interview on behalf of all staff. And I wish all academics the best of luck in your careers and good health. Many thanks.

1.4.4 毕业综合答辩流程 Procedures for Graduation Viva

毕业综合答辩流程

1. 宣布答辩开始。
2. 介绍答辩委员会主席及其他成员。
3. 介绍答辩学生名单及答辩顺序。
4. 答辩学生依次进行答辩。（第一名个人陈述完毕后，答辩委员会提问；第一名离场准备解答，第二名陈述，完毕后答辩委员会提问；第二名离场准备解答，第一名入场回答，第三名陈述……)

5. 答辩活动结束，告知答辩成绩的公布日期。

Procedures for Graduation Viva

1. Declare that the graduation viva has begun.

2. Introduce the viva committee chair and other members.

3. Announce the names of the students and their viva order.

4. Students follow the viva procedure: after the first student's presentation, the viva committee members will ask him questions. While the first leaves with unanswered questions, the second begins his presentation. The first returns to answer the questions, while the second departs with questions from the committee. Following the third one's presentation, the second one returns with the answers...

5. At the conclusion of the viva, the host announces the date for the publication of viva results.

1.4.5 留学生毕业综合答辩稿撰写要求 International Students' Graduation Report Writing Requirements

1. 本综合答辩稿是指留学生在学习结束期满前向甲大学和国际交流学院陈述本人学习、生活等方面情况的书面报告。

2. 综合答辩稿内容应反映留学生在校期间的成绩收获、综合表现等情况，主要指：学习态度、到课情况，学习成绩及收获，配合中方管理情况及自我管理情况，个人素质及外在形象，人际关系，建言献策情况，参加甲大学和国际交流学院组织的文体、参观活动情况，自身学习、管理方面存在的问题和不足等。

3. 综合答辩稿要完整准确、实事求是。

4. 字数在 1000~3000 字，A4 纸打印。口头答辩时间控制在 5 分钟之内。答辩稿及口头答辩可用汉、英、俄、法中的任一语种，但需要事先向国际交流学院声明。

1. This is a written report provided by international students to University A and the College of International Exchange prior to the end of the study. The report includes students' performance in academic and performance in daily life, and so on.

2. The main focus of this report is on students' academic achievements and general performance at this university. The following information is required: the attitude toward studying, class attendance, academic performance and achievements, cooperation with Chinese management authority and self-management, personal image, awareness of solidarity, relationship with others, contribution to suggestions, participation in cultural, sporting and visiting activities organized by University A and the College of International Exchange, difficulties and shortcomings in learning and management, etc.

3. The report should be thorough and truthful.

4. The word count should be between 1,000 and 3,000 words. Use A4 paper to print the report. The report should be completed in 5 minutes. The report can be written in Chinese, English, Russian, or French, and you must notify the College of International Exchange of your language preference in advance.

1.5　典礼活动 Ceremonies

1.5.1　开学典礼 Opening Ceremony

留学生开学典礼议程

时间：10 月 11 日 11：00

地点：国际学术交流会议中心

参加人员：大学领导，机关处(办)领导，承担留学生教学工作的院系领导及教师代表，国际交流学院全体工作人员，全体留学生及陪读家属

主持人：国际交流学院院长王建东

议程：

1. 宣布典礼开始，奏中华人民共和国国歌。

2. 主席台领导为留学生颁发校徽。

3. 留学生代表发言。

4. 教师代表发言。

5. 大学校长讲话。

6. 奏甲大学校歌，宣布典礼结束。

Agenda for International Students' Opening Ceremony

Time：11：00 on October 11

Location：Conference Center for International Academic Exchange

Participants：University leaders, university executive offices' leaders, leaders and teacher representatives from relevant colleges and departments responsible for overseas student education, leaders and staff from the College of International Exchange, and all international students and their families

Host：Professor Wang Jiandong, dean of the College of International Exchange

Agenda：

1. The ceremony is officially opened, followed by the playing of the national anthem.

2. Leaders distribute university badges to students.

3. International student representative makes a speech.

4. Instructor representative makes a speech.

5. President of the university addresses the ceremony.

6. The ceremony concludes with the playing of the university song.

留学生开学典礼主持词

留学生开学典礼现在开始。首先，我向大家介绍在主席台就座的大学领导：大学校长刘鹏海先生，党委书记何中华，副校长白晓林。参加典礼的还有校办公室等机关处(办)领导和承担留学生教学工作的院系领导。让我们对各位领导的到来表示热烈的欢迎！

请全体起立！奏中华人民共和国国歌！

请坐下。

请主席台领导为留学生颁发校徽。

请留学生代表迪亚斯发言。

请教师代表刘永辉发言。

请大学校长刘鹏海先生致辞，大家欢迎！

请全体起立，奏甲大学校歌！典礼到此结束！请主席台领导离席。

Host Remarks at the Opening Ceremony for International Students

I declare that the international students' opening ceremony has begun. First and foremost, please allow me to introduce the following leaders: professor Liu Penghai, president of the university, professor He Zhonghua, university party secretary, and professor Bai Xiaolin, vice president of the university. The ceremony also includes representatives from the administration office, colleges, and departments responsible for international student education. Let's greet them with a round of applause.

All rise! Play the national anthem of PRC.

Please sit down.

Let's invite the leaders to hand out the university badges to all students.

Let's invite the student representative Dias to make a speech.

Let's invite the instructor representative Liu Yonghui to make a speech.

Let's welcome professor Liu, president of the university to address the ceremony.

All rise please! Play the university song. I declare the ceremony concluded! Leaders may be the first to leave the conference room.

校领导在留学生开学典礼上的讲话

女士们、先生们、朋友们：

上午好！经过前一阶段的入学考核和训练，来自五大洲 40 个国家的外国留学生，今天正式加入了甲大学这个大家庭。我校首批本科留学生也顺利完成第一年的汉语和体能素质强化，转入基础和专业课程学习阶段。在此，我谨代表学校领导和全校师生向新入学的外国留学生表示热烈的欢迎和祝贺！

留学生朋友们，你们留学的年份对中国来说，注定是不平凡而又让人难忘的一年。因为今年中华人民共和国迎来了 70 周年华诞，我相信，前几天通过收看在北京天安门广场举行的盛大阅兵仪式和参加校内外的庆祝活动，你们已经充分感受到了全中国喜迎国庆的浓厚氛围。70 年来，中国人民同心同德、艰苦奋斗，取得了令世界刮目相看的伟大成就，一个社会主义中国巍然屹立在世界东方。70 年来，中国坚持和平发展的道路，奉行互利共赢的开放战略，同世界人民一道推动人类命运共同体的建设。近些年来，我校的对外合作交往活动十分丰富多彩，我们与多个国家的高等院校建立了常态化、机制化的交流，迄今为止共为数十个国家培养了近万名人才，招收和培养了多批留学生硕士研究生。每当我听到毕业留学生为各国建设做出突出贡献、得到提拔和重用的喜讯时，每当我听到从异国他乡、大洋彼岸传来的一声声感谢、思念与祝福时，作为校长，我感到由衷的自豪与欣慰！

留学生朋友们，我希望你们珍惜在这里的学习机会，勤奋刻苦，严守纪律，团结互助，争当优秀留学生，认真学习专业知识和技能，积极感受丰富多彩的中国文化，高质量的完成培训任务。同时，我更希望你们能像往届留学生那样，身体力行，情系中国，传承友谊，心中永远埋下中国情结，积极向身边的亲友、同事宣传中国，在促进中外交流、共同合作发展等方面做出贡献。我相信，通过我们的共同努力，大家一定会学有所成、满载而归，并留下一段美好而难忘的中国记忆！

最后，祝在座的各位身体健康！祝留学生朋友在中国生活愉快，学业有成！谢谢！

Speech by the University Leader at the International Students' Opening Ceremony

Ladies, gentlemen and friends,

Good morning! Following the exams and training in the induction stage, students from 40 countries across five continents officially become family members of University A today. The first class of international undergraduates have completed Chinese language and physical training in the first year, and proceed to fundamental and specialized subjects studies. Hereby, on behalf of the university authority, teachers and students, I'd like to extend my welcome and congratulations to new friends from various nations.

Dear friends, the year you settle down in China will be remarkable and unforgettable for this year is China's 70th anniversary. By watching the grand military parade at Tian'anmen Square on TV and participating in numerous celebrations on and off campus, you have witnessed widespread joy throughout China. Over the past seven decades, through concerted efforts and arduous struggle, the Chinese people have accomplished extraordinary feats that have surprised the world. A socialist China now is standing rock-firm in the east of the world. Over the past seven decades, China has steadfastly pursued peaceful development, followed a win-win strategy of opening up, and collaborated with people from all countries to build a community with a shared future for mankind. In recent years, our university has seen an increase in international exchange and partnership opportunities. We have established a regular exchange mechanism with colleges and universities around the world. So far, we've developed nearly 10,000 talents for dozens of countries and admitted international postgraduates for several years in a row. When I learn of their advancement and contributions to their countries, or when we receive compliments and gratitude from across the ocean, I am filled with pride and joy.

Dear friends, I hope you cherish the opportunity to study here, work hard, follow the rules and regulations, work together and help one another, strive for the Excellent International Student award, gain knowledge and skills in your professional fields, embrace diversified Chinese culture, and successfully complete the courses. Meanwhile, I hope you can follow your heart and carry forward the friendship with China, like our past international students did and do introduce the university and China to your family, friends and colleagues, thereby contributing to international exchanges and cooperation between China and your nations. I believe that by working together, all of you will be successful in your studies and return home with your accomplishments. Your time at our university and in China will be etched on your memories for the rest of your life. Finally, I want to wish everyone good health. I wish all international students a pleasant and rewarding stay in China. Thanks.

教师代表在留学生开学典礼上的发言

尊敬的各位领导、同事、留学生朋友们：

大家上午好！

非常荣幸作为教师代表，在今天这样一个热烈、庄重的开学典礼上，代表全体留学生教师向各位留学生的到来表示诚挚的欢迎。

2014年春天，我走上了留学生讲台，回首几年来的教学经历，我深感留学生教学是一种享受。在我的眼里，留学生彬彬有礼、亲和友善，勤于思考、学而不厌。课堂上，我们对专业问题的分析鞭辟入里，在知识的海洋里畅游；课堂外，我们谈笑风生，各抒己见，分享不同的文化及异国趣事。比如说，让我印象比较深的是去年毕业的来自D国的留学生萨科伊，他热爱中国，连续两年来到甲大学求学；他热爱生活、能歌善舞，还让我知道了在他们国家WiFi是装在热气球上的。

留学生朋友们，甲大学为大家准备了丰富多彩的课程，既有介绍中国文化的社科类课程，又有量身定制的专业类课程。我们全体留学生教师期待，在未来的求学中，大家能珍惜当下，做好每天的事情，学有所获；更期待，大家能在今后的工作中，学以致用，崇实去浮。我们也很乐意与大家探讨各类问题，为大家追求真理、了解和平发展的中国指点迷津。最后，祝愿各位留学生朋友，经过系统的学习和愉快的留学生活，成为各自领域的行家，成为增进世界与中国交流的友谊使者！谢谢！

Speech by the Teacher Representative at the Opening Ceremony

Respected leaders, colleagues and friends,

Good morning! It is a great privilege for me, as a teacher representative, to be here at today's friendly and beautiful opening ceremony. On behalf of my colleagues, I would like to extend a warm welcome to all international students.

In the spring of 2014, I began working as a lecturer for international students. Looking back on my teaching experiences, I can honestly say that I appreciate international education from the bottom of my heart. Overseas students, in my opinion, are polished and courteous, pleasant and supportive, attentive in their thinking, and eager and relentless in their pursuit of knowledge. In class, we conduct extensive investigation on the subject as professionals, eager to gain insight into the huge ocean of knowledge. We are cheerful after class, discussing everything in our lives, offering our thoughts on various cultures and hilarious stories from around the world. For example, a student named Saquoi from nation D has tremendously impressed me. He adores China and attended our university for two years in a row. He had a good time with his song and dancing. I learned about the WiFi system that is placed on hot-air balloons in his nation from him.

My wonderful friends, University A is resourceful in its courses. Social sciences can teach you about Chinese culture, and customized courses can teach you about specific topics. We all hope that you will value the opportunity to study at university, that you will benefit from everyday life and your courses, and that you will apply what you have learned to your career and develop practical skills. We are willing to discuss whatever you are interested in regarding China, as well as offer guidance on the path you should take to seek the truth and gain insight into China's peaceful growth. Finally, I wish you all the best in your future careers, as well as a happy time at our university, and may you become ambassadors of friendship to boost country-to-country exchange. Thank you all.

留学生代表在留学生开学典礼上的发言

尊敬的各位领导，各位老师，即将开始学习征程的各国同学们：

大家早上好！我是船舶技术与管理专业的迪亚斯。非常荣幸地站在这里，作为全体留学生代表感谢中国政府不仅为我们提供了一个非常宝贵的学习机会，更为我们提供了一个了解和体验中国文化的机会。尤其要感谢甲大学为我们提供了良好的学习氛围以及优质的生活环境。

尽管这已经是我第二次来中国学习，尽管我曾在中国乙大学、丙学院留学 4 年，但来到这所与新中国同龄的名校——甲大学，我的心情却比之前更为激动、更为期待。夏末秋初的九月就像一场梦，我和在座其他留学生一样，经过激烈的竞争，通过了祖国的层层选拔后，才如愿成行。

身处在一个全新的环境，面对着许多陌生的脸庞，我该如何规划自己的人生？如何充实地度过我的培训生活？经过了一个月的学习、生活，我了解到甲大学是一所以工为主，工管结合，文理兼容，具有鲜明特色的全国重点大学。能够在这样一所学校学习、生活，我感到无比骄傲与自豪。在未来的学习生活中，我会将我们的校训"严谨、求实、拼搏、创新"深深地烙入我的心底，努力学习新知识，并严格遵章守纪，积极交流。学成归国后，我将不忘初心、砥砺前行。我相信多年之后，甲大学将成为我们求学路上无悔的选择。谢谢大家！

Speech by the International Student Representative at the Opening Ceremony

Respected university authority, professors, and friends about to embark on a new journey,

Good morning. I am Dias from ship technology and management.

It is a great honor for me to stand here on behalf of all international students and express our appreciation to Chinese government for this opportunity to study in China. It is also an opportunity to know and experience Chinese culture. Many thanks to the university in particular for providing sound academic and living environment.

This is the second time that I have been in China for study. I have studied at University C and Academy D for 4 consecutive years. However, I am even more excited to be in China this time as I am coming to university A, which is of the same age as the People's Republic of China.

September is the transition of summer and autumn. It's like a dream. All international students including me excelled at the strict selection in our home country and won the place of studying in this university.

Being in a brand new environment full of new faces, how should I make the plan for a fulfilling life here? After one month of study and life, I learned that this university is a higher institution of China. It is very strong in engineering discipline and combines engineering, management, command, technology, science and liberal arts.

I am so proud to study and live in such a first-class university. I will always bear in mind our motto of being "rigorous, practical, hardworking and innovative" in future study. I will be hardworking, self-disciplined, and active in exchanges and presentations. We will always keep true to our original aspiration and strive ahead even going back after the courses in China.

I believe when we recall the days many years later, this university would be the choice without regret. Thank you all.

1.5.2 毕业典礼 Graduation Ceremony

留学生毕业典礼议程

时间：7月20日17：00

地点：国际学术交流会议中心

参加人员：大学领导，办公室、教务处、研究生院、国际交流学院领导，留学生教师代表，全体留学生及陪读家属

主持人：国际交流学院院长王建东

议程：

1. 观看本学年留学生教学训练视频。

2. 奏中华人民共和国国歌。

3. 校领导为留学生颁发毕业证书和纪念牌、为优秀毕业留学生颁发荣誉证书、为毕业研究生颁发学位证书和纪念牌。

4. 留学生代表发言。

5. 校长致辞。

Agenda for International Students' Graduation Ceremony

Time：17：00 of July 20

Location：Conference Center for International Academic Exchange

Attendees：University authority, leaders from the university executive offices, the Office of Studies, the Graduate School, and the College of International Exchange, teacher representatives and all international students and their families

Host：Professor Wang Jiandong, dean of the College of International Exchange

Agenda：

1. Watch this academic year's video on international students' education and training.

2. Rise for the national anthem of the People's Republic of China.

3. University leaders present students with graduation certificates and commemorative badges; award certificates to excellent international students; issue master's degree certificates and commemorative badges to postgraduates.

4. International student representative makes a speech.

5. President of the university addresses the ceremony.

留学生毕业典礼主持词

尊敬的各位领导、留学生朋友们：

大家下午好！

欢迎来到甲大学留学生毕业典礼的现场，刚才我们观看了留学生教学训练剪影，回顾了一年来的学习生活，相信大家感受颇多。

下面，我首先向大家介绍出席今天典礼的领导和嘉宾：大学校长刘鹏海，大学办公室主任曹容，教务处处长蔡亚波，研究生院领导刘鹏，及部分留学生教师代表，让我们对各位领导和嘉宾的到来表示热烈的欢迎和衷心的感谢！

请全体起立！奏中华人民共和国国歌！请坐下。

请大学校长刘鹏海为留学生颁发毕业证书、校徽牌。

请大学校长刘鹏海为优秀留学生颁发荣誉证书。

请大学校长刘鹏海为留学生研究生颁发学位证书及纪念牌。

谢谢刘鹏海校长，请入座。

请留学生代表阿米拉发言，大家欢迎！

下面让我们以热烈的掌声请大学校长刘鹏海致辞！

谢谢刘鹏海校长，请入座。

毕业典礼到此礼成！再次向毕业留学生表示祝贺！请前排领导离席。

Speech by the Host at the Graduation Ceremony

Honorable leaders, dear friends,

Good afternoon. Welcome to the graduation ceremony for international students. We just watched the video about students' education and training, which was a snapshot of their lives and studies over the past year. It has greatly impressed us.

To begin, please allow me to introduce the leaders and guests presented today: professor Liu Penghai, president of the university; Cao Rong, head of the admin office; professor Cai Yabo, head of the Office of Studies, and professor Liu Peng, dean of the Graduate School. Teacher representatives also join us at the gathering. Let's greet them with a round of applause.

All rise, please. Play the national anthem of the People's Republic of China.

Let's invite professor Liu, the university president to present students with graduation certificates and commemorative badges.

Let's invite professor Liu, the university president to award certificates to excellent international students.

Let's invite professor Liu, the university president to issue master's degree certificates and commemorative badges to postgraduates.

Thank you, professor Liu.

Now let's welcome student representative Amira to make a speech.

Now let's welcome professor Liu, president of the university to address the ceremony.

Thank you so much, professor Liu.

The ceremony is concluded. We would like to express our heartfelt congratulations to all international graduates once more.

校领导在留学生毕业典礼上的讲话

留学生朋友们，女士们、先生们：

下午好！一年同经风雨，临别共享荣光。今天是留学生毕业的喜庆日子，我首先代表大学全体教职员工向顺利完成学业的各国留学生及研究生表示热烈祝贺，同时也向为留学生工作付出辛勤劳动的全体同志表示慰问！

留学生朋友们，一年前，你们肩负各自国家的期望，心怀求学的壮志，相聚到甲大学。一年来，大学的教室、实验室和训练场，留下了你们求知若渴、挥汗如雨的身影。军运会火炬接力、志愿者服务、庆祝中华人民共和国成立 70 周年、庆祝建校 70 周年、构建海洋命运共同体国际研讨会、毕业综合演练、中外迎新春晚会、基层足球联赛等活动都留下了你们的身影。深圳罗湖村、湛江海港、广船国际船台、博鳌亚洲论坛会址……你们一路走访、一路学习，一路感悟、一路收获。一年时间很短，但你们收获了扎实的专业和技能知识，体验了中国的文化，真切地感受到了中国和甲大学的发展，有了中国的朋友圈和微信群，成为了大学一道亮丽的风景线。

留学生朋友们，2020 年注定是不平凡的一年，新冠肺炎疫情肆虐全球，中国人民在习近平总书记的领导下，众志成城、共克时艰，国内疫情防控取得重大战略成果，再一次刷新了中国速度、中国力度与中国温度，展示了中国能力、实力与魅力。中国还为许多国家提供了医疗援助，与许多国家进行病毒防治研究国际合作和经验共享等，用实际行动诠释了人类命运共同体的理念。病毒没有国界，疫情不分种族，处在疫情中心的你们与我们一道参与疫情防控的战斗，你们服从命令、听从安排，克服了身体和心理上的不适应，主动配合防疫管控措施和医疗检测，积极参加线上教学和室内外体育锻炼，让每一天都过得无比充实。留学生朋友们，你们不仅是这段人类历史的见证者，更是亲历者。可以预见，新冠肺炎疫情常态化防控将伴随我们的生活，你们回国后要宣传中国防控经验，帮助你们的同胞及家人远离病毒，健康生活。

留学生朋友们，希望你们把学到的知识运用到你们国家的发展建设中；希望你们把中国的情谊带回去，把甲大学的问候带回去，做我们之间的友好使者和桥梁，积极向你们的同事、亲友宣传中国！更欢迎你们常回家看看，母校的大门永远为你们敞开！甲大学永远是你们的家。

最后，祝留学生朋友们返程顺利，身体健康，家庭幸福，前程似锦！谢谢大家！

Speech by the University Leader at the Graduation Ceremony

Dear friends, ladies and gentlemen,

Good afternoon. In the past year, we've been through all ups and downs together and now it's time to share the glory before parting. On this auspicious graduation day, on behalf of all faculty, I would like to congratulate students from various nations on your successful completion of the courses, and to thank everyone who contributes to the international education.

Dear friends, one year ago, you came to our university with high hopes of your respective countries and the desire to explore the academic world. Short as the past year is, the classrooms, labs and training fields have witnessed your perseverance and thirst for knowledge. Your expertise has played prominent role in diverse events like the torch relay and volunteer services for the Military World Games, celebrations for China's

70th anniversary and our university's 70th anniversary, the symposium of "building a maritime community with a shared future", integrated exercise for graduation, football game and New Year gala. You learn and gain along the tours to Luohu village in Shenzhen, Zhanjiang port, Guangzhou shipyard and Bo'ao Forum venue in Hainan. Short as the past year is, you have acquired solid professional knowledge and skills, experienced the profound Chinese culture, and witnessed the development of China and the university. At the end of the year, you have your own circle of Chinese friends and wechat groups, and you are always the center of attention on our campus.

Dear friends, the year of 2020 is extraordinary. Despite the global COVID-19 outbreak, under the strong leadership of general secretary Xi Jinping, Chinese people united as one to tackle challenges. The pandemic prevention and control efforts in China yield major strategic results. The national response to the pandemic renews the Chinese speed, resilience and compassion, and also demonstrates Chinese capacity, strength and charisma. Amid the global pandemic, China provides medical assistance, collaborates with many countries in COVID-19 prevention and control research and shares relevant experience globally. What China has done interprets the vision of community with a shared future for mankind. Dear friends, viruses respect no borders or races. In the pandemic epicenter, you fight with us in this unforgettable battle, follow the command, disregard all discomfort and inconvenience, and cooperate in the medical check and lockdown management. Besides, you show great interests in online classes and enrich every single day by study and workouts. You are absolutely the witness of the history and great warriors. It is predictable that we're entering a post-epidemic era when regular prevention and control response will be in place all the time around us. It is hoped that when you return home, you will help your people and family keep viruses away by providing the Chinese solution.

Dear friends, we sincerely hope that you can apply what you have learned here to the development of your country, become friendly messengers and solid bridges between our nations, and promote China and our university to more and more people in your country. We look forward to seeing you again in your Alma Mater! The university will be your home forever.

Finally, I wish everyone a safe journey home, good health, a happy family and a bright future! Thank you.

留学生代表在毕业典礼上的发言

尊敬的刘鹏海校长，各位领导、各位老师，留学生朋友们，女士们、先生们：

下午好！很荣幸能站在这里作为本届留学生代表发言。当我开始考虑我该说些什么的时候，我发现我和甲大学的故事可以连续讲几个小时，这里的经历让我们准备好了迎接未来。

三年前，我就曾到过甲大学学习，从某些方面来说，那时的我是个问题学生，小毛病不断。中国史书《左传》说："人谁无过，过而能改，善莫大焉。"很幸运，去年我再次成功申请来到了来甲大学学习的机会。这一次我倍加珍惜、勤勉自律。天道酬勤，我通过了大学留学生硕士研究生入学考试，成为本学年少数几名留学生研究生之一，学年课程平均成绩超过90分，最后还被光荣地评为优秀毕业留学生。

过去的一年里，我们各国留学生像一家人一样互帮互助，在大学的精心培育下，努力学习，掌握了专业知识和技能，了解了中国文化和语言，进一步加深了对中国的感情。过去的一年，我们经历了很多喜庆的大活动，也遭遇了席卷全球的新冠肺炎疫情，但我们十分幸运，在大学领导和教师、管理人员的照顾下，我们全体留学生安然无恙，顺利完成学业。在这场防疫战争中，我们也看到，中国人民迅速集结，奔赴抗疫一线，并且向几十个国家和地区开展医疗援助，体现了与中国人民、世界人民同呼吸、共命运、心连心的胸怀大爱。

离别将近，思乡渐浓，但我却不舍离开。获知有些留学生朋友因为疫情暂时没有航班回国，我竟然有些羡慕他们。在我们共庆毕业之时，让我代表全体留学生朋友再道一声感谢，因为我坚信，在甲大学所经历的一切将会使我们受益无穷！

谢谢中国！谢谢甲大学！

Speech by the International Student Representative at the Graduation Ceremony

Honorable leaders, friends, ladies and gentlemen,

Good afternoon. It's an honor for me to speak here on my colleagues' behalf. As I began thinking about what I should say to you, I discovered that I could go on for hours talking about the difficulties and successes we faced together here in this university, for the experience we have got here surely prepared us to do more in future.

Three years ago I had an opportunity to come to China, specifically, in this university. In one way or another I can say I was a trouble maker. *The Commentary of Zuo* omce said: "Our greatest glory is not in never falling; but in rising every time we fall." The saying that "God helps those who help themselves" is known by everyone of us. I was selected once again to join this university but luckily being among a few of international students that pursuing postgraduate. My average score was higher than 90 points and I was awarded the excellent student honor. In my life I will never forget this.

In the past year, we learned professional knowledge and skills, Chinese culture and language, and forged stronger ties with China.

Last year was an eventful year since the coronavirus disease broke out around the world. However, we're lucky to be healthy all the time and complete all the courses due to the leadership of the university authorities. We've been taken care of through out the time. In the response to COVID-19, we see Chinese servicemen assemble in the first time heading to the front line of the battle. China also provides medical assistance to dozens of countries and regions, which shows Chinese people's great compassion for their counterparts.

It's about the time to say goodbye now, but I feel reluctant to leave. When I heard that some students cannot leave because of the suspension of flights, I was a bit jealous. On this joyful occasion, please allow me to express my sincere gratitude on behalf of my colleagues. I always believe that what we have experienced here will be helpful when we in our future life after we go back in our countries.

Thank you China! Thank you University A!

第二章 教学活动篇
Chapter 2 Pedagogical Activities

2.1 理论教学用语 Discourse for Theoretical Sessions

一、上课(Beginning a Class)

1. 上课！Class begins!

2. 起立。Stand up, please.

3. 坐下。Sit down, Please.

4. 请坐下。Please be seated.

5. 我们现在开始。Let's start now.

6. 我们现在开始上课了。Let's begin our class/lesson.

7. 上课时间到了。It's time for class.

二、打招呼(Greetings)

1. 大家早上好！Good morning, class/everyone.

2. 今天怎么样？How are you today?

3. 今早怎么样啊？How is it going this morning?

4. 好久不见，欢迎回来。Haven't seen you for a long time, welcome back to the class.

5. 新学期有新开始。As the new term begins you will have a new start.

6. 你们应该收心学习。You should get your minds back to school.

三、介绍（Introduction）

1. 现在，我来自我介绍。Now, let me introduce myself.

2. 我来介绍一下我自己。I'll just tell you a bit about myself.

3. 我的名字是李华，LI HUA 这样拼写。My name is Li Hua, spelt L-I-Li, H-U-A-Hua.

4. 我已经教书 10 年了。I've been teaching for 10 years.

5. 我是武汉人。I am from Wuhan.

6. 直到去年我都在报社工作。I worked for a newspaper until last year.

7. 那么你们呢？And what about you?

8. 你可以自我介绍一下吗？Would you please introduce yourself?

四、考勤（Checking Attendance）

1. 好！我现在要开始点名了。Right! Let's have a roll call.

2. 注意！我要开始点名了。Now! I'll take mark the register.

3. 注意！仔细听你们的名字！OK! Listen while I call out your names.

4. 请安静，我点名的时候注意听。Quiet, please. Pay attention as I shout out your names.

5. 注意！我们看看谁缺勤。Now! Let's see who's absent.

6. 所有人都在吗？Is everyone（everybody）here?

7. 有人没有来吗？Is anyone（anybody）absent?（Who's absent?）

8. 好了！我们来看看谁不在。Right! Let's see if anyone's away.

9. 今天谁是值日生？Who is the duty student today?

10. 今天谁值日？Who is on duty today?

11. 你们班上有多少学生？How many students are there in your class?

12. 有多少学生在场？How many students are present?

13. 请回到座位上。Go back to your seat, please.

14. 今天星期几？What day is it today?

15. 今天几号？What is the date today?

16. 下次不要迟到。Don't be late next time.

17. 你知道他为什么没有来吗？Do you know why he is absent today?

五、回顾与小结（Review and Summary）

1. 今天我们讲新课。We'll start（begin）a new lesson today.

2. 我们学一些新东西。We'll learn something new.

3. 好了，我们来学第八课。Well, let's learn Lesson 8.

4. 我想带你们进入一个新的课程。I'd like to introduce to you a new program now.

5. 我们来复习一下。Let's do some revision.

6. 首先我们开始复习。First, let's review.

7. 昨天/上节课我们学了些什么呢？What did we learn yesterday / last time?

8. 现在，谁记得上节课我们讲了什么？Now, who remember what we were mainly talking about in our last class?

9. 好了，有谁能告诉我上节课我们练习了些什么？Well, can any of you tell me what exercises have we done last time?

10. 我想请一名学生告诉我上节课我们学习/阅读/用到了什么？OK, I'd like a student to tell us what we have learned/read about/used in the last lesson?

11. 准备好了么？Ready? /Are you ready?

12. 明白了么？Got it? / Clear? /Did you get it?

13. 明白我说的吗？Do you get me?

14. 今天我们主要讲三点。Today we have three steps to go.

15. 首先我想讲一下有关……接下来……First I'm going to talk about... And then...

16. 首先；其次/然后/在这之后；最后。First/first of all; and then/ later（on）/after that; finally/in the end.

17. 在课程进行到一半的时候。In half way through the class.

18. 在这节课的最后，你们可以讨论一下各自的观点。By the end of

the lesson, you'll be able to share ideas with the class.

19. 这节课快结束的时候，如果我们有足够的时间，我们可以……
When we've finished… （near the end of the lesson/at the end of the lesson） if we have enough time （if time permits/if there's time）, we may spend a few minutes on…

六、鼓励（Encouraging）

1. 你愿意试试么？Will you try it?

2. 请给他/她一些掌声。Please give him （her） a big hand.

3. 尽力试试。Try your best.

4. 尽量做。Do your best.

5. 来吧！你能做到的。Come on! You can do it.

6. 有人有不同意见吗？Who has a different idea/ opinion?

7. 我相信你，而且信任你。I believe you, and I believe in you.

8. 别害怕(害羞/紧张)。Don't be afraid （shy/ nervous）.

9. 别担心。放松点。Don't worry. Take it easy!

10. 想一想，再试一次。Think it over and try again.

11. 努力就会有结果。Great efforts will be rewarded by great progress.

12. 如果你愿意，我会尽力帮你的。I'll try/ do my best to help you if you like.

13. 我相信你在一个月内会有很大进步。I'm sure you'll make a great progress within a month.

14. 我为拥有你们这样的学生而感到骄傲。I am proud of having students like you.

15. 你们应该互相学习互相帮助。You're encouraged to help and learn from each other.

16. 你应该下决心赶上别人。You shall decide/ make up your mind to catch up with others.

七、指令（Issuing a Command）

1. 请举手。Hands up, please.

2. 如果有问题请举手。Put up your hands if you have any questions.

3. 不要说，请举手。Just hands. No voices.

4. 请放下手。Hands down, please.

5. 请停下来。Stop now. / Stop here, please.

6. 请继续。Go on, please.

7. 请做笔记。Take notes, please.

8. 拿出你们的书。Please take out your books.

9. 翻到第……页。Turn to page...

10. 打开书的第……页。Please open your books at page...

11. 请回答我的问题。Please answer my question(s).

12. 请大声朗读。Please read it aloud. / Loudly, please.

13. 关上书。Close (Shut) your books, please. /Books closed.

14. 仔细听/看。Listen /Look carefully, please.

15. 请看黑板/屏幕。Look at the blackboard/screen, please.

16. 现在我们开始学习文章。Now we will read the passage.

17. 请坐好。Sit straight, please.

18. 请脱帽。Take off your cap/hat, please.

19. 自己做，这是为考试准备的练习。By yourself. This is practice for the exam.

20. 回到你的小组，每个人都有机会。Back into groups, each person say it in turn.

21. 看看我是怎么写的。Watch how I write it.

22. 看看这个怎么做。Watch how to do it.

23. 看我来给你演示。Watch me and I'll show you.

24. 现在，转过身，不要看黑板。Now, turn round, face the back without looking at the board.

25. 到前面来。Please come to the front.

26. 回到你的座位。Please go back to your seat(s).

27. 你们准备好听了吗? Are you ready to listen?

28. 你们在听吗? 那么现在开始。Are you all listening? OK, then.

29. 现在讲解一些新的! 我们改变一下话题。Now something new! Let's change the topic.

30. 非常好, 我们再来一次。That was quite good, let's do it once more.

八、维持纪律 (Keeping the Class in Drder)

1. 请安静。Silence. /Be quiet, please.

2. 不要说话。Stop talking. /Don't talk.

3. 请别再打扰别人了! Please stop interrupting the others!

4. 请别小声说话! Would you mind not whispering?

5. 安静。你最好别在课堂说话! Keep silent. You'd better not talk in class.

6. 别打扰别人! Don't disturb the others.

7. 好了! 现在所有人请安静。不要说话了! OK! Then everybody be quiet now please. No more talking.

8. 如果你继续打扰别人, 你会有麻烦的。There will be trouble if you go on disturbing the others.

9. 如果你继续这样, 我会向××报告。You will be reported, if you go on!

10. 不准说话! No talking!

11. 不准聊天! No chatting!

12. 别发出噪音! Stop making a noise!

13. 别大呼小叫了! No more shouting!

14. 别聊天了。还有你! Stop chatting now. And you!

15. 你不应该这样做! You shouldn't behave (be behaving) like that!

16. 醒一醒，别做梦了！No dreaming! Wake up!

17. 不准乱跑！Stop turning round!

18. 安静！Be quiet!

九、评价与反馈（Comments and Feedback）

1. 好！/很好！/非常好！/太好了！/好极了！Good! /Great! /Fabulous! /Fantastic! /Wonderful!

2. 做得好！Well done! /Good job! /You did well!

3. 你表现得特别礼貌(聪明，好)！You've been really polite (smart, good...).

4. 你很有进步。You've improved a lot.

5. 你进步很大！You've got a big progress.

6. 挺好的。That was good.

7. 不错啊。Not bad.

8. 比之前好了一点，但是……That was a little better, but...

9. 好很多了，但是你做的时候忘记了一些步骤。That's much better, but you forgot something when you do it.

10. 你不觉得你有进步了吗？Don't you think you have made a little progress?

11. 接近正确答案了，但是你最好……Nearly right, but you'd better...

12. 不太对，你没有……That was not quite right, you didn't...

13. 听起来不太对。That doesn't sound very good.

14. 不对。Not really! /Not quite!

十、下课（Ending a Lesson）

1. 今天就到这里。That is all for today.

2. 下课铃响了。The bell is ringing. / There goes the bell.

3. 时间到了，就到这儿吧。Time is up. Let's stop here.

4. 有问题来找我。Come to / ask me if you have any questions.

5. 下节课见。Goodbye. / Bye, see you next time.

6. 等一两分钟，你们做完了就可以走了。One or two more minutes, just complete the task you're doing and then we'll stop.

7. 时间到了，我们就到这里，你们已经做了足够多了。Now time is up. We'll stop now. You've done enough of that (enough practice at that).

8. 你们做的比上次好多了。Most of you have done it better than last time.

9. 我要收作业了。I'll collect your papers/worksheets now, please.

10. 请上交你的作业本。Please hand in your workbooks.

11. 我来收上次的作业。I'd like to take in your last homework.

12. 请从最后一排传上来。Please will you pass it from the end of the row?

13. 你们离开的时候，把作业放在桌上。Put your work on my desk as you leave.

14. 谢谢大家，这节课非常好。Thank you, everyone. Well done.

15. 你们走前，能不能检查一下书本都放好了吗？Before you all leave, would you check that all the books are put away?

16. 李明，你今天的工作就是把黑板擦干净。Li Ming, it's your job today to clean the board.

17. 下课前我有些事情要交代，请认真听。I have some announcements to make before you go. Could you listen carefully, please?

十一、作业布置（Homework）

1. 完成课后的练习。Finish the exercises on your workbook.

2. 完成上课没有做完的练习。Finish the exercise undone in class.

3. 复习第八章。Review Chapter 8.

4. 学习第八页课程总结。Learn the summary on Page 8.

5. 把问题答案写在一张纸上。Write down the answers on a piece of paper.

6. 写关于……的论文，至少一千字。Write an essay about... for at least 1,000 words.

7. 今天晚上在家，做第九页的练习。Do the exercise on page 9 at home tonight.

8. 今天你们回去后在作业本上写一个关于今天所学知识的文章，明天交上来。You are going to compose a piece of writing about today's topic in your workbooks and turn it in tomorrow morning.

9. 我想让你们把这个当作家庭作业做完。For homework, I want you to finish this piece of work.

10. 下节课前，你们必须复习 12 单元所学内容。Before next lesson you must go over what we've just learnt from unit 12.

11. 下节课之前必须完成这个。It must be done by the next lesson.

12. 下星期上课前你们必须把这个作业写完。The piece of writing must be completed by this time next week.

十二、教学专用词汇（Specialized Vocabulary）

1. 小测验 test/quiz

2. 期中考试 mid-term exam

3. 期末考试 final exam/term exam

4. 口试 oral exam/spoken test

5. 笔试 written exam

6. 补考 makeup exam/ supplementary exam

7. 教学目标 teaching objectives

8. 教学计划 teaching programs

9. 教学原则 teaching principles

10. 教学大纲 syllabus

11. 课堂教学 classroom teaching

12. 现场教学 on-site teaching

13. 公开课教学 open class

14. 观摩课教学 demonstration class

15. 教学小结 teaching summary

16. 补课 make up the lessons

17. 教案 teaching plans

18. 教学要求 teaching requirements

19. 教学重点 key teaching points/ focal points

20. 难点 difficult points

21. 总复习 overall review

22. 标准答案 answer key

23. 互相听课 to sit in on each other's class/to visit each other's class

24. 备课 to plan a lesson/lesson planning

25. 集体备课 lesson co-planning

2.2　实践教学用语 Discourse for Practical Sessions

一、课堂活动(Classroom Activities)

1. 我们轮流来。Let's do it one after another/in turn/by turns.

2. 现在到你了。Now you, please.

3. 该你了(学生名字)。It's your turn,(student's name).

4. 下一个。Next, please.

5. 不要说出来。Don't speak it out.

6. 一起来。All together.

7. 现在请两名学生上台在黑板上写下来。I ask two students to write on the blackboard.

8. 有人自愿么? Any volunteers?

9. 谁愿意到黑板上来做? Who wants to do it on the blackboard?

10. 有谁想来试一试? Who want a try/go? Who want to try/ give it a go?

11. 有人想试一试么？Who would like to have a try?

12. 找出重难点以及你不理解的地方。Find out the difficulties and what you don't understand.

13. 我给你们一个问题来讨论。I give you a question for discussion.

二、进行分组活动（Dividing up the Class）

1. 我希望你们一起回答这个问题。I want all of you to answer the questions together.

2. 我想让一个人来回答问题。I'd like just one person to answer.

3. 我希望这边的同学来回答。I want students in this part to answer the question.

4. 我们两两一组来做这件事。Now let's do it out in pairs.

5. 我想要把你们从中间分成两组来做这件事情。For this, I'm going to divide you down the middle.

6. 现在我要把你们分成两组。Now I'll divide you in half.

7. 现在轮到谁了？不是你/轮到你了。Whose go is it? Not yours/You be quick!

8. 首先是第六组，到你们了。快点，就是这样。It's group 6 first. Now you. Quickly! That's it.

9. 你们第二批上。You'll go as the second.

10. 我现在在黑板上计分，看看哪组赢了。We'll score on the board and see which team wins.

11. 我想让你们分组来完成。I'd like you to work in groups.

12. 四人一组。In fours. /In groups of four.

13. 转身面向你身边的人。Turn round and face your neighbor.

14. 你没有人组队是吗？You haven't anyone to work with, have you?

15. 加入他们组怎么样？What about joining in with them?

16. 请分组练习/请分组。Practice in groups, please. /In groups, please.

17. 请问你们能不能组成三人小组？Could you possibly arrange your-selves to make a group of 3?

18. 请组成五人小组。Arrange yourselves to form a group of 5.

三、处理交际中的语言障碍（Addressing Communication Issues）

1. 你说什么？Pardon/ Pardon me?

2. 请再说一遍。Please say that again.

3. 请慢点说。Please say that slowly.

4. 你所指的……是什么意思？What do you mean by...?

5. 不好意思，我没有明白你说什么。I'm sorry I can't follow you.

6. 不好意思，我英文不太好。I'm sorry I only know a little English.

7. 我听不清，请大点声音。I can't hear you clearly. Louder, please.

四、组织课堂（Getting Organized）

1. 你能不能把你的凳子往前挪？Would you move your chairs forward?

2. 你们三个能不能把桌子往前挪？Could the three of you move your desks forward, please?

3. 你们俩能不能把桌子移到这边？Will you both move your table this way please?

4. 你可以把椅子摆齐么？Would you mind straightening the chairs please?

5. 你能不能往后一点？Do you mind moving back a bit?

6. 你能不能留出大一点的空间？Will you make a bigger space here?

7. 能不能把椅子搬到第三排？Would you arrange your chairs in row 3?

8. 请找到我们上节课发的材料。Would you find the handouts we were using last time please?

9. 请拿出上节课的复印件。Could you get out the photocopies you had last time please?

10. 请拿出昨天开始做的练习。Will you take out the worksheets you began yesterday please?

11. 找到我们上次学到的段落。Let's find the passage we were reading last lesson.

12. 请收起其他的书。Put your other books away, please.

13. 不需要了。这就够了。No others! That's all.

14. 我们不需要这些图片了。你能把它放一边吗？We don't need these pictures. Will you put them away?

15. 不是那本书，是这本。对的，红色这本。Not that book, the other one. Yes, the red one.

16. 准备好了我们就开始。Now we shall start if you are ready.

17. 你没有带你的吗？那你和同桌共用一下吧！Haven't you brought yours? Well, you'll have to share with your neighbor.

18. 你的丢了吗？你可以和李雷一起用。Have you lost yours? Well, you may share with Li Lei.

19. 你没有带吗？忘记了？好吧，你用我的吧，但是下次别忘了。Haven't you got yours? Forgotten? Well, you may use mine, but don't forget it next time.

20. 我现在发试卷。I have papers to give out now.

21. 今天又有一些新书发给你们。I have more new books to give out today.

22. 现在我发一些练习题。Here are some worksheets to hand round.

23. 你能帮我发这些练习题吗？谢谢。Will you please give these sheets out? Thanks.

24. 请把这些卷子交上来(发下去/传下去)。Please pass these papers back (round, along), please.

25. 拿出一张然后发下去。Take one and (then) pass the others on.

26. 你们保管这些。They're for you to keep.

27. 你可以拿着。You may have them.

28. 请归还教具。I want the materials back please.

29. 我会在课程结束时收回。I want them back at the end of the course.

30. 你们之后还要交上来，请不要在上面写字好吗？You'll give them in later, so please don't write on them. OK?

31. 你能帮忙擦一下黑板吗？Can you clean the blackboard (the whiteboard/the board)?

32. 让我们来对答案。Let's check the answers.

五、启发思路（Inspiring）

1. 假设一个朋友想要你关于这门课的建议。Suppose a friend needs your advice on this course.

2. 你可以同意他人观点，然后提出你的观点。You could agree with the other person and say something else.

3. 你可以问问原因。You may ask the reason.

4. 我来演示一下好吗？Shall I demonstrate? OK?

5. 你怎么想的？What do you think?

6. 我给你一点提示。I'll give you a cue.

7. 我来帮帮你。Let me give you some help.

六、考试用语（Exam Languages）

1. 阅卷 Marking/Scoring.

2. 不要忘了书写整洁。Don't forget to write neatly.

3. 文字之间注意空格。Make sure your spaces between words are clear.

4. 你们必须在 10 分钟之内完成。You must finish it in ten minutes.

5. 别交头接耳。Stop whispering. /Don't whisper to each other.

6. 不准抄袭。No cheating, please.

7. 作弊记零分。You will be marked zero if you cheat.

8. 你们为什么传纸条？Why are you passing notes?

9. 不准抄袭！自己做！You can't copy! Do it on your own!

10. 在我说之前请不要打开试卷。Do not open the exam booklet before I announced.

11. 你们现在可以开始了。Now you can start.

12. 现在你们有 60 分钟来完成这张试卷。Now, you have 60 minutes to finish this paper.

13. 你有 10 分钟把答案填写到答题卡上。Now you have 10 minutes to transfer your answers to the answer sheet.

14. 好了，时间到了，请上交试卷。OK/Well, time is up. Hand in your papers, please.

2.3　线上教学 Online Classes

2.3.1　线上学习须知 Online Learning Guidance

留学生线上学习须知

疫情防控期间，大学将组织留学生参加线上教学，具体方案和要求如下：

学习时间：×月××日至×月××日

学习内容：各专业方向留学生一同学习船舶损害管制、电路原理、计算机及网络应用、汉语口语训练、深蓝汉语夜校、中国文化鉴赏等专业基础和通用课程，并进行基础技能训练。

学习方式：(1)各门课程通过微信群进行授课，留学生使用个人手机或笔记本电脑，单人独立在宿舍或住所参加在线学习；(2)教师在微信群布置学习任务、推送课件资料、进行辅导答疑和批改作业；(3)留学生按照课程表和教师要求开展自学和提交作业，并参加线上教学互动；(4)国际交流学院指定教学管理人员担任课程微信群联络员，进行教学保障，收集意见建议；(5)基础技能课程由体育教研室教师和留学生管理教师按周制订训练计划并进行指导督促，留学生按时自行组训。

有关要求：(1)每名在校留学生应熟悉课程安排，严格课堂考勤，按时登录上课微信群打卡，班长清点统计到课人数并向教师和联络员报告；（2）上课期间，留学生须在宿舍认真进行自学、训练或参加线上学习，不得睡觉或进行休闲娱乐活动，学院值班员和留学生管理教师将不定期进行检查；（3）已回国留学生，可以根据所在国家时差和网络条件，灵活安排时间登录课程微信群进行自学；（4）保持良好的学习状态，按时按量完成学习任务，认真预习和复习，做好课堂笔记，积极参加教学在线互动，准时上传、提交作业，坚持开展体能训练；（5）线上教学以理论授课为主，实操实验课将在疫情结束恢复正常时补上；（6）结合疫情期间线上学习实际表现，课程最终成绩按规定由终结性考核卷面成绩（占50%，疫情结束后择时安排）、课堂表现（占20%）、到课情况（占15%）、课程作业完成情况（占15%）等四部分综合评定组成。

Online Learning Guidance

During the epidemic prevention and control period, the university will offer online classes to international students. The details and requirements are as follows:

Time: From DD/MM to DD/MM

Contents: Students from all majors participate in online lessons of professional basic subjects and general subjects including Ship Damage Control, Fundamentals of Ship Electronic Circuit, Computer and Internet, Oral Chinese, "Blue Water" Night Mandarin Session, and Chinese Culture Appreciation. Students also have to do basic fitness traning.

Methods: (1)Online lessons are held in Wechat groups (please scan the code below for each subject). International students participate in online classes using their cellphones or laptops in their own dormitories. (2)Teachers give assignments, share learning materials, provide tutoring and feedbacks in their Wechat groups. (3)Students learn independently, complete exercises and interact online according to the class schedule and the assignments. (4) The College of International Exchange assigns an administrative staff member to each group, who is responsible for necessary support and collecting suggestions. (5) Weekly basic fitness training is designed and monitored by the PE teacher and the student advisor. Students shall train themselves according to the schedule.

Requirements: (1) Each international student at the university should know the class schedule, and attend online classes on time. Class prefects are supposed to check attendance before reporting to the teacher and admin staff. (2) During class hours, students should study individually, learn online or train in dormitories. Sleeping or leisure activities are forbidden during the class hours. Duty staff of the College of International Exchange and student advisor will inspect randomly. (3) Given differences in time and Internet accessibility, students in their own countries may log in to Wechat online classrooms and study at their convenience. (4) Maintain a positive learning attitude. Always finish all assignments on time, preview and review the lessons, take notes, upload your work on time and interact with group members. Continue your fitness training. (5) The online classes are primarily lecture-based, with practice and experiments resumed following the epidemic. (6) Each subject's score is constituted of 50% of the final test paper (Exam will take place after the epidemic control), 20% of the class performance, 15% of the attendance, and 15% of the assignments.

2.3.2 线上教学用语 Language Used in Online Classes

一、常用词汇(Words and Phrases)

1. 上课/会议平台: class/meeting platform

2. 下载: download

3. 安装：install

4. 注册：sign up/register

5. 创建账户：create an account

6. 音频/视频会议：audio/video meeting

7. 开启课程/会议：start/host a class/meeting

8. 加入课程/会议：join a class/meeting

9. 离开课程/会议：leave the class/meeting

10. 结束课程/会议：end/quit the class/meeting

11. 安排课程/会议：schedule a class/meeting

12. 参与人：participants

13. 屏幕共享：screen sharing

14. 课件：PPT/slide

二、常用句子（Sentences）

1. 请打开你的摄像头和麦克风。Please turn on your camera and microphone.

2. 能将麦克风调成静音吗？/打开麦克风吗？ Can you please mute/unmute your microphone？

3. 大家能听到我说话吗？ Can everyone hear me？ / Can you guys hear me？

4. 可以调高/低音量吗？ Could you please turn up/down the volume of your mic？

5. 咱们看一下课件。Let's get into the slides.

6. 咱们继续 11 页的讨论。Let's get onto the discussion on page 11.

7. 同学，你的网络好卡。There's something wrong with your network.

8. 我将发放答题卡。I am going to give you the answer sheet.

9. 请把你的答案输入对话框。Please type the answer in the text box.

10. 你的声音卡住了，你能重新讲一下嘛？ Sorry, your voice just

froze, could you please back up a little bit?

11. 选一个同学来回答一下这个问题。I'm going to nominate one student to answer this question.

12. 我的笔记本没有反应，我得重启一下。My laptop is not responding. I'm trying to restart it.

13. 我什么都不能做，屏幕动不了了。I can't do anything. The screen is frozen.

14. 对不起，我没听懂，你能再讲一遍吗？I'm sorry I didn't catch that, could you run that by me again?

15. 我的互联网连接崩溃了。My internet connection crashed.

16. 发送答案。Post your answer.

17. 设置倒计时。Set a time limit.

18. 我的屏幕上看不到东西。I cannot see anything on my screen.

19. 网络不太稳定。The line is choppy here.

20. 我的手机运行速度很慢，我需要清理一些内存。My phone is running slow. I have to clear up some memory.

21. 这个网太卡了。The internet is really laggy.

22. 抱歉，我断开连接了。Sorry, disconnected.

23. 连线会中断。The connection is on and off.

24. 对不起，我的摄像头有一些技术问题，我会找人修理。Sorry, I have some technical issues with my camera, I will find someone to fix it.

25. 稍等一会儿，我调整一些设定。Please hold on, let me adjust some settings.

26. 你的声音有一点杂音。There are（static）noises in your voice。

27. 对不起，我的钉钉刚才有问题。Sorry, my Dingding just crashed.

28. 不好意思，我耳机故障。Sorry, my headset is broken.

29. 不好意思，我检查一下我的耳机。Excuse me, let me check my headset.

30. 不好意思，我重拨给你。Excuse me, let me call you right back.

2.4　学科竞赛用语 Language Used in Skill Competition

2.4.1　柴油机装修实作学科竞赛 Diesel Engine Maintenance and Repair Skill Competition

柴油机装修实作竞赛安排

为丰富教学形式，增强教学效果，拟结合"船舶柴油机装修实作"课程教学内容及其在船舶设备方面的实际应用背景，面向机电专业留学生开展学科竞赛活动。本竞赛由赛前准备、现场操作及考核总结三个环节组成。具体时间安排如下：

×月×日：公布竞赛题目及评分细则。

×月×日：听取留学生的反馈意见，完善评分细则等内容。

×月××日：柴油机实作竞赛。上午 10:30 开始，11:10 统计成绩，11:30 公布成绩、颁发证书。地点为实验室。

竞赛完成后，现场公布成绩并颁发相应证书。竞赛设一等奖一名；二等奖一名；三等奖一名。按照留学生教学管理规定，此次竞赛成绩视为课程考核部分，按 50% 的比例计入该课程的最终成绩。

Diesel Engine Maintenance and Repair Skill Competition Plan

We intend to link the Ship Diesel Engine Maintenance and Repair class with the ship equipment application through a competition for electromechanical students in order to enrich teaching forms and achieve the desired effect. This competition comprises of pre-competition preparations, on-site operation, and post-competition review. The following information is provided：

On DD/MM：The topics and scoring guidelines are to be released.

On DD/MM：Update scoring guidelines based on students' comments.

On DD/MM：The competition will kick off at 10：30. At 11：10, we will compute the scores. At 11：30, the results will be released and certificates will be issued. The site is at the lab.

The organizer will announce the results and award the winners following the competition. There will be one first-prize winner, one second-prize winner and one third-prize winner. According to the education management regulations, the competition results are included in the subject's final exam, accounting for 50% of the total points.

柴油机装修实作竞赛评分细则

柴油机喷油器的拆卸、装配与调试：

一、得分表

表2.1　得　分　表

得分项	得　分　规　则	得分
检查工具	检查工具，确定没有工具缺少或损坏。	
操作得分（60分）	1. 按照正确的顺序拆卸喷油器得 10 分。	
	2. 完成清洗部件得 10 分。	
	3. 喷油器启喷压力正确得 15 分。	
	4. 雾化效果好得 5 分。	
	5. 没有喷孔堵塞得 5 分。	

续表

得分项	得 分 规 则	得分
操作得分 （60分）	6. 没有渗漏得 5 分。	
	7. 正确使用测试台得 5 分。	
	8. 拧紧护帽得 5 分。	
安全得分 （20分）	9. 喷油器的零部件或工具无损坏得 10 分。	
	10. 操作人员没有受伤得 10 分。	
时间得分 （20分）	时间（按照计时器）： 　　时间得分公式 = $\left(20-\dfrac{T_C-T_{fastest}}{T_{slowest}-T_{fastest}}*10\right)*$（质量分/质量配分）	

二、操作规程

1. 所有参赛者必须服从裁判员的指令。

2. 当参赛者准备好后需要向裁判报告"准备完毕"。

3. 一局比赛时间为 20 分钟。在裁判下命令"开始"后，参赛者启动计时器。然后，开始操作。

4. 当参赛者完成操作后，自己结束计时器并报告"操作完成"。

三、工具清单

表 2.2　工 具 清 单

序号	名　　称	数量
1	活动扳手	1
2	加力杆	1
3	扁口螺丝刀	1
4	梅花扳手	1
5	开口扳手	2
6	力矩扳手	1
7	探针	2

序号	名 称	数量
8	零件盘	1
9	承油桶	1
10	平口钳	1
11	油嘴偶件	1
12	铜垫圈	2
13	抹布	1
14	检验平台	1

Scoring Guidelines for Diesel Engine Maintenance and Repair Skill Competition

Diesel Engine Injector Disassembly, Reassembly, and Testing

Ⅰ. Scoring Criteria

Table 2.1 Scoring Criteria

Items	Scoring Guidelines	Scores
Tools Checking	Check the tools and make sure no items missing or broken.	
Operation (60 points)	1. You will receive 10 points when the injector is disassembled in the correct order.	
	2. You will receive 10 points when you finish washing the parts.	
	3. You will receive 15 points when the injecting pressure is correct.	
	4. You will receive 5 points when the atomization spray is perfect.	
	5. You will receive 5 points when no nozzle hole is blocked.	

Continued

Items	Scoring Guidelines	Scores
Operation（60 points）	6. You will receive 5 points when no leakage happens.	
	7. You will receive 5 points when you use the file bench correctly.	
	8. You will receive 5 points when you tighten the covering nut.	
Safety （20 points）	9. You will receive 10 points when no part of the injector or tool is damaged.	
	10. You will receive 10 points when the operating person is not injured.	
Timekeeping （20 points）	Timekeeping(according to the timer)： timekeeping formula = $\left(20-\dfrac{T_C-T_{fastest}}{T_{slowest}-T_{fastest}}*10\right)$ *（Quality points/Quality distribution points）	

Ⅱ. Operating Procedures

1. All competitors must follow the referee's instructions.

2. The competitor must report to the referee when he/she is ready, announce "Ready!"

3. A single round lasts 20 minutes. The competitors start the timer after the referee says " Begin!"Then competitors start to operate.

4. Competitors stop the timer after they finish the operation and report "Finish!" to the referee.

Ⅲ. Tools List

Table 2. 2　Tools List

Item	Name	Quantity
1	Adjusting wrench	1
2	Extension bar	1
3	Screwdriver	1
4	Ring spanner	1
5	Open end ring spanner	2
6	Torque wrench	1
7	Probe	2
8	Disk	1
9	Fuel bucket	1
10	Flat pliers	1
11	Needle valve couple	1
12	Copper washer	2
13	Cloth rag	1
14	Testing bench	1

2. 4. 2　模拟联合国大会 Model United Nations Conference

模拟联合国大会开幕式议程

时间：××月××日 10：00—10：30

地点：国际学术交流会议中心

参加人员：大学领导，校办公室、教务处、国际交流学院领导，大会外请嘉宾，深蓝国际俱乐部成员，校内参会学生，校外线上学生

着装要求：全体人员着正装

主持人：陈广宇(模拟联合国大会副秘书长)

活动流程：活动前，观看甲大学宣传视频

1. 奏唱中华人民共和国国歌。

2. 中国联合国协会副会长王思旭寄语。（视频连线）

3. 模拟联合国大会主席团代表发言。（视频连线）

4. 模拟联合国大会秘书长发言。

5. 甲大学副校长致辞，给模拟联合国大会主席代表授锤。

Agenda for the Opening Ceremony of the Model United Nations Conference

Time: 10:00—10:30, DD/MM

Place: Conference Center of International Academic Exchange

Participants: University leaders, heads of the admin and study offices, leaders of the College of International Exchange, guests of the ceremony, members of the Blue Water International Workshop, students on campus and students online from other universities.

Dress code: Formal wear

Host: Mr. Chen Guangyu (deputy secretary general of MUN)

Agenda: Prior to the ceremony, watch the propaganda video of University A

1. Sing the national anthem of the People's Republic of China.

2. Mr. Wang Sixu, co-chairman of China UN Association makes an online speech.

3. Representative of the conference chairman committee makes an online speech.

4. Secretary general of MUN conference makes a speech.

5. Vice president of University A makes a speech and hands over the gavel to the MUN conference representative.

模拟联合国大会开幕式主持词

尊敬的各位领导，老师们，女士们、先生们，同学们：

大家上午好！受有关因素影响，甲大学模拟联合国大会采取线上线下相结合的方式召开，欢迎各位参加今天的开幕式，衷心感谢各位校外嘉宾、代表与我们积极连线，热烈欢迎各位校领导、代表的莅临。

首先，我想隆重介绍参加今天开幕式的各位领导：甲大学副校长白晓林，校办公室主任曹荣，教务处处长蔡亚波，国际交流学院院长王建东，国际交流学院副院长赵长江。另外校外嘉宾还有中国联合国协会副会长王思旭先生，北京乙大学教授张波。此次模拟联合国大会还有 30 个国家 80 多所高校的 200 多名中外青年精英应邀参加。让我们以热烈的掌声欢迎他们！

下面进行第一项活动，请全体起立，奏唱中华人民共和国国歌。

请坐。今天，我们很荣幸地邀请到了中国联合国协会副会长、联合国科教文组织亚太非物质文化中心顾问委员会主席王思旭先生作为大会的特邀嘉宾，考虑到常态化防控要求，王思旭先生没能来到现场，但他给我们发来了寄语，下面我们一起观看视频！

此次模拟联合国大会不仅得到大学各级部门的全力支持和亲切指导，也得到了众多大学模拟联合国大会同仁的积极参与。下面，让我们欢迎本届模拟联合国大会主席团代表——丙大学学生李晓峰发言致辞。

谢谢李晓峰。甲大学模拟联合国大会组委会主体成员为大学深蓝国际俱乐部骨干。深蓝国际俱乐部成立于20××年，是大学生实践优秀俱乐部之一，也是全体大学生提升国际化素养的实践平台，在学生中极具影响力。下面，让我们有请甲大学深蓝国际俱乐部主任兼本届模拟联合国大会秘书长张冠宇发言。

谢谢张冠宇。近年来，在大学领导的亲切关心和指导下，我校学生积极参加各大高等院校模拟联合国大会，秉持世界眼光，始终瞄准一流大学，全方位、多层次、宽领域地参与到大学国际交流活动当中，综合能力和国际视野得到拓展，一批外事知识丰富、外语口语流利、外事礼仪娴熟、涉外交流能力优秀的外事人才脱颖而出。下面让我们以最热烈的掌声欢迎大学副校长白晓林致辞。

谢谢白晓林副校长。下面，请白晓林副校长为主席代表授锤。

至此，开幕式即将结束，希望每一位参会代表享受此次大会时光，展现出新一代青年学子的外交风范。再次感谢在座的各位嘉宾，感谢各位的参与。祝本次活动圆满成功！我们赛场见！

Host Remarks at the MUN Conference Opening Ceremony

Respected leaders, teachers, ladies and gentlemen, friends,

Good morning! We organize the MUN Conference both online and offline due to some circumstances. We are very happy to have you at the opening ceremony. And we would love to extend our heartfelt gratitude to distinguished guests and delegates for your generous support. We also welcome the university leaders and delegates who are present here.

To begin, I am honored to introduce the leaders at the ceremony: professor Bai Xiaolin, vice president of University A; Cao Rong, head of the Administration Office; professor Cai Yabo, head of the Office of Studies; professor Wang Jiandong, dean of the College of the International Exchange; professor Zhao Changjiang, deputy dean of the College of the International Exchange. The distinguished guests online are Mr. Wang Sixu, co-chairman of China UN Association and professor Zhang Bo from University B in Beijng. Additionally, we invited over 200 delegates from 80 universities in 30 contries for this event. Let's welcome all of them with a round of applause.

Now comes the first event for the ceremony. Please rise for the People's Republic of China's national anthem.

Sit down, please. Today, to our great honor, online we have a special guest, Mr. Wang Sixu, the China UN Association co-chairman, and the Consultative Committee Chairman of UNASCO Asia-Pacific Intangible Culture Center. Mr. Wang was unable to join us on the scene due to the routine prevention and control response. However, he sent us his best wishes via video. Let's watch this video now.

The conference is not only fully supported and guided by the university authorities, but also backed by colleagues from other universities. Mr. Li Xiaofeng from University C, the MUN presidium representative will now take the floor.

Mr. Li, thank you for your wonderful speech. The core members of MUN Conference Organization Committee of University A are students from the Blue Water International Workshop. The workshop was established in 20××. It is a practical platform for students' international competence development, bearing exceptional leverage among students and has been recognized as a wonderful workshop. Mr. Zhang Guanyu, the workshop coordinator and secretary of the MUN conference, will now take the floor.

Mr. Zhang, thank you for your wonderful speech. Our students have actively participated in MUN conferences conducted by numerous universities throughout the years, thanks to the guidance of university authorities. And they have engaged themselves in international exchanges in all aspects keeping the global map in mind and aiming for the best. The students' comprehensive talents and international perspective have developed as a result of their unwavering efforts. On top of that, they have stood out as talents who have a good knowledge of foreign affairs and are proficient in foreign languages, familiar with diplomatic protocal and confident in communication through international exchange. With a round of applause, let's welcome professor Bai Xiaolin, vice president, to give a speech.

Professor Bai, thank you very much. Professor Bai will now hand over the gavel to the representative.

At this point, we will conclude the opening ceremony. We hope that each delegate has a good time and that you can demonstrate your diplomatic professionalism as university students. We'd want to thank everyone again for coming to the event. We wish the conference the best of luck. I'll see you later.

模拟联合国大会秘书长在模拟联合国大会开幕式上的发言

尊敬的各位来宾，女士们、先生们：

上午好！非常荣幸有机会与80所高校的中外才俊在网上相聚，共同见证和参与甲大学模拟联合国大会。首先，我谨代表甲大学模拟联合国协会对各位参赛代表表示热烈的欢迎，对各位领导、嘉宾的莅临表示衷心的感谢！

甲大学模拟联合国大会至今已成功举办多次，来自各大高校的参赛代表在会场上施展才华，用青春的热情灌溉着这片充满希望的热土，并取得了较好的反响。特殊年份总会给予人们汲取智慧、继续前行的力量。今年是不平凡的一年，也是充满希望与感动的一年，我们在成长中历练，参与了全面抗疫、线上课程学习、复课演练等非同寻常的事情。这次我们的模拟联合国大会，也相应采取了线上线下相结合的方式，其主题是"共享浩瀚深蓝——构建海洋命运共同体"，这是我们甲大学学子积极响应和践行中国国家主席习近平在人民海军成立70周年会见各国海军代表团团长时提出的重要理念的举措。在此，我也倡议各位参会代表，积极参与与海洋密切相关的国际问题的讨论，展现当代青年学子的知识见地和志向抱负，为建设人类社会的持久和平，为促进世界的和谐与繁荣发展，发出属于自己的时代最强音。

"江山代有才人出，各领风骚数百年。"朋友们，历史的接力棒传递到我们手中，我们是实现世界和平与发展的希望，也是实现中华民族伟大复兴的主力军。衷心祝愿大家充分利用模联这一特殊平台，拓展国际化视野和眼界，锤炼综合能力。用我们的热情感染身边的每一个人，世界需要倾听青年的声音，世界需要青年的行动，未来正在我们脚下。

谢谢大家！

Speech by Secretary General of MUN Conference at the MUN Conference Opening Ceremony

Respected guests, ladies and gentlemen,

Good morning! It is my great honor to have the opportunity to join talents from 80 universities online both at home and abroad to witness and participate in the Model United Nations Conference at University A. To begin, on behalf of University A's Model United Nations Association, I would like to extend my warm welcome to all delegates and my heartfelt thanks to all the leaders and guests at the event!

For years, University A has successfully organized the Model United Nations Conference, which has received excellent feedback from delegates from many universities. Young delegates with strong goals have dedicated their abilities to MUN conferences. Extraordinary years inject impetus for people to gain wisdom and progress. In this special year, it has also been full of optimism and meaningful moments. We have experienced and participated in exceptional events such as fighting the pandemic on all fronts, attending online classes and class resuming rehearsals, and so on. This Model United Nations Conference incorporates both online and offline sessions. The theme of this conference is "Sharly the Boundless Ocean: the Journey to Build the Maritime Community with a Shared Future". This topic is motivated by an important proposal suggested by Chinese President Xi Jinping during a meeting with chiefs of naval delegations from other countries on the occasion of the PLA Navy's 70th anniversary. As a result, I would like to propose that all delegates participate actively in the discussion of international issues closely related to the ocean, demonstrating the knowledge, insight, and aspirations of today's young students, and contributing your ideas to the lasting peace of human society and the harmony and prosperity of the world.

"On this noble land, each age brings forth new genius, with their talents lasting for ages to come." My friends, the torch of history has been passed to us. We are the hope for world peace and development, as well as the driving force behind China's great rejuvenation. I sincerely hope that each of us takes full advantage of this unique opportunity to broaden our international horizons and forge our comprehensive abilities and competence. I hope those around us can feel our enthusiasm. The world needs our voices and actions because we are the future.

Thank you very much.

校领导在模拟联合国大会开幕式上的讲话

尊敬的王思旭副会长、张波教授，各位参赛代表：

大家上午好！由于目前国内常态化疫情防控要求，我们以这种特殊的方式举行开幕式。在此，我代表大学全校师生对各大高校代表团的出席表示热烈的欢迎。众所周知，模拟联合国大会是一项国际性的学术活动，对当代大学生了解各国国情，探讨国际形势，丰富知识体系，提高思辨能力具有重要意义。自20××年甲大学模拟联合国协会成立以来，我们学校的学生在模拟联合国大会的舞台上耳闻窗外事，心系天下情，努力拓展自己的国际视野并培养战略思维和文化底蕴。同时他们也怀着谦虚进取的态度，积极向外校模拟联合国大会同仁取经，吸取各方先进理念和创新做法来提高自己。可以说，模拟联合国大会是我校教学改革的试金石，是培养国际化人才的重要平台，是优秀大学生的必修课。本届大会，将不仅是各大高校青年代表华山论剑、指点江山的比武场，也是大学模拟联合国协会的练兵场和一次阶段性的成果展。

中国国家主席习近平在出席中国人民解放军海军成立 70 周年活动时，提出构建海洋命运共同体的理念。这是对人类命运共同体思想的丰富和发展，是共护海洋和平、共筑海洋秩序、共促海洋繁荣的中国方案，顺应时代潮流，契合各国利益。

当今世界，我们面临百年未有之大变局，中国智慧、中国声音、中国方案在国际大环境中绽放光彩，希望大家通过这个平台去建立基本的国际思维、视野，参与国际热点问题的研究，共同探讨、创新解决思路，为世界的和平发展提供青年智慧和力量。

习近平总书记 2017 年 5 月 3 日在中国政法大学考察时曾说："中国的未来属于青年，中华民族的未来也属于青年。"历史的接力棒终要传递到大家手中，希望你们树立远大志向，锤炼各项能力，增长才干，与国同成长，为建设社会主义强国的伟大工程、伟大事业注入自己的青春才智和无限力量！祝本届大会取得圆满成功，愿各位代表能在本次模拟联合国大会中度过一段精彩难忘的时光，收获真挚美好的友谊！

谢谢大家！

Speech by the University Leader at the MUN Conference Opening Ceremony

Respected Mr. Wang Sixu, professor Zhang Bo, dear delegates,

Good morning. Today we attend the opening ceremony online as per our country's guidelines for routine epidemic prevention and control. Hereby, on behalf of faculty and students of our university, I would love to extend a warm welcome to delegations from different universities. It is well-known that as an international academic event, the MUN conference is of great significance for modern university students in learning about the national situation of various countries, discussing the international situation, enriching their knowledge system and improving their critical thinking skills. Since the establishment of the MUN Association in 20×× , students at our university have spared no efforts to forge the skillset to expand their international vision, develop their strategic thinking and enhance their cultural foundation through the MUN stage which has a strong bond with the international community. Meanwhile, with humble attitude and strong aspiration they have drawn successful experience from colleagues outside, improving themselves through innovative implementation of MUN philosophy. It is fair to say that the MUN practice is the litmus test for the ongoing reform at our university and the important platform for global talents incubation, and it's essential to the development of exceptional students. At this conference, all delegates are supposed to share their ideas and debate over hotspot issues. On top of that, the MUN Association of our university will take advantage of this opportunity to put their skills to test and exhibit their growth.

The Chinese President, Xi Jinping, proposed the concept of building a maritime community with a shared future at the commemorative event for the 70th anniversary of PLA Navy. This proposal has greatly enriched and developed the philosophy of building a community of a shared future for mankind. This proposal has been recognized as Chinese solution for safeguarding maritime peace and order, and fostering maritime prosperity. And this proposal comforms to the trend of the times and aligns with the interests of different countries. Today, despite the greatest uncertainty, the world stage shines brightly with Chinese wisdom, voice, and solution. At this point, I hope that the MUN platform will allow you, as a young generation, to join in the study of international hotspots and improve your solutions through brainstorming, thereby donating your wisdom and strength to the world.

When he visited China University of Political Science and Law on May 3, 2017, President Xi said, "The future of China belongs to the youth, and the future of the Chinese likewise belongs to the youth." You will be expected to take over the torch from your predecessors. I hope you will set your goals high, hone your skills in all areas in response to the call of our country. I hope you will contribute your wisdom and strength to the construction of our country, and to the building of a great socialist nation at large. I wish this MUN conference a great success and wish each of you a memorable experience at the conference. Finally, I wish all of you would become good friends at this event.

Thank you all!

模拟联合国大会闭幕式议程

时间：××月××日 10:00—11:00

地点：国际学术交流中心

出席人员：国际交流学院领导、全体留学生、校内外模拟联合国大会代表

着装要求：全体人员着西装

主持人：陈广宇（模拟联合国大会副秘书长）

活动流程：

1. 播放模拟联合国大会总结视频。

2. 模拟联合国大会秘书长宣布获奖人员名单。

3. 国际交流学院党委书记为获奖代表颁奖。

4. 校外获奖代表发言。

5. 国际交流学院院长致闭幕辞。

Agenda for Closing Ceremony of MUN Conference

Time: 10:00—11:00, DD/MM

Location: International Academic Exchange Center

Participants: Leaders of the College of International Exchange, all international students, all delegates

Dress code: Business suit

Host: Mr. Chen Guangyu(deputy secretary general of MUN conference)

Agenda:

1. Watch the conclusion video of the conference.

2. Secretary general of MUN conference announces prize winners.

3. Party secretary awards prizes to winners.

4. Prize-winner representative makes a speech.

5. Dean of the College of International Exchange delivers the closing speech.

模拟联合国大会闭幕式主持词

尊敬的各位领导、嘉宾、老师们、同学们，女士们、先生们：

大家下午好。欢迎各位参加甲大学模拟联合国大会闭幕式。首先请允许我介绍出席今天闭幕式的领导和专家，他们是国际交流学院院长王建东和国际交流学院党委书记张嘉琪。欢迎各位领导的莅临。

刚刚过去的一天半，各位参会同学扮演来自不同国家的外交代表，围绕各自委员会设置的热点问题进行辩论、磋商、游说，会场气氛热烈，议事程序规范，你们也更好地学习到了联合国等多边议事机构的运作方式和外交知识。首先，让我们观看闭幕式视频，回忆会场精彩时刻。

接下来，有请模拟联合国大会秘书长张冠宇宣布模拟联合国大会获奖名单。

恭喜以上获奖同学。

让我们用热烈的掌声邀请国际交流学院党委书记张嘉琪为获奖代表颁发证书。校外代表的获奖证书后期将邮寄给大家。

再次祝贺所有代表。谢谢你们在会场上的精彩表现。

下面有请校外获奖代表北京丙大学程海娟发言。

谢谢程海娟。下面请国际交流学院院长王建东致辞。

谢谢王建东院长。在过去一天半的会议期间，全体参会人员精心准备，认真撰写立场文件，形成决议，为我们呈现了一场高水平的模拟联合国会议。全体志愿者努力工作，为此次模拟联合国会议的顺利召开提供了周到、一流的服务。让我们用热烈的掌声对全体同志的辛勤付出表示衷心的感谢。

尊敬的各位嘉宾、亲爱的同学们，现在我宣布甲大学模拟联合国大会到此结束，期待明年再次与你们相见。

Host Remarks at the Closing Ceremony

Respected leaders, distinguished guests, colleagues, ladies and gentlemen,

Good afternoon! Welcome to the closing ceremony. To begin, I am honored to introduce the leaders and professors present: professor Wang Jiandong, dean of the College of International Exchange; professor Zhang Jiaqi, party secretary of the College of International Exchange. Let's welcome them with a round of applause.

During the one-and-a-half-day conference, acting as diplomats from different countries, you debated, consulted and lobbied on hot issues provided by relevant MUN committees, in a heated atmosphere in accordance with established protocols. As a result, you have gained a better understanding of the functioning method of international organizations such as the UN, as well as the diplomatic knowledge. Now let's watch the closing ceremony video and review our fantastic moments.

Now Mr. Zhang Guanyu, secretary general of MUN conference will announce the prize winners.

Congratulations to all of the winners!

Now let's welcome professor Zhang, party secretary to award certificates to winners. Winners of the online session will receive their certificates by mail.

Congratulations to the award winners and thanks for your wonderful performance at the conference. Now Miss Cheng Haijuan from University C in Beijing will take the floor.

Thank you Miss Cheng. Now professor Wang Jiandong, dean of the College of International Exchange will deliver a speech.

Professor Wang, thank you so much. Throughout the sessions, delegates have worked tirelessly to write position papers and launch motions, demonstrating a high-quality MUN conference. Besides, all volunteers tried their best to support the conference. Let's give them our applause to express our heartfelt appreciation for their efforts.

Distinguished guests, dear friends, now I have to declare the conclusion of the MUN conference. I am looking forward to having you at the next conference.

校外获奖代表在模拟联合国大会闭幕式上的发言

尊敬的各位领导、各位代表、各位来宾：

上午好！非常荣幸能作为校外代表在甲大学模拟联合国大会闭幕式上发言。非常感谢甲大学举办模拟联合国大会，这次活动我和其他各校模拟联合国大会代表收获颇丰。

在为期一天半的会议中，参会的各校代表以联合国外交官的身份，以"共享浩瀚深蓝——构建海洋命运共同体"为主题，投入"海洋能源开发与安全""共建海上丝绸之路"和"维护海洋安全，打击海上恐怖主义"三个议题的探讨中，依照联合国的程序阐述观点、展开磋商与辩论。大家畅所欲言，突破物理距离，通过在线讨论、谈判和磋商，最终完成了各项决议案。

在本次模拟联合国大会中，我们各个代表带着使命感关注世界、发现自我，锻炼了自己的演讲能力、批判性思维能力及团队协作能力。同时大家通过视频云端连线的方式相互交流和学习，提升了人文素养，拓展了国际视野，强化了责任担当，积极参与构建海洋命运共同体、人类命运共同体。

不仅如此，我还收获了沉甸甸的国际友谊，但是我们的友谊始于模拟联合国大会，却不会终于模拟联合国大会。希望我们在此次模拟联合国大会上收获的经历和友谊，将成为我们生命中一笔宝贵的财富。期待在未来的外交场上我们还能再相见，谢谢大家！

Speech by Prize-winner at the MUN Conference Closing Ceremony

Respected leaders, dear delegates and guests,

Good morning! It's my great honor to make a speech as a delegate of the conference at the closing ceremony. I would like to extend my heart-felt gratitude to University A for a wonderful event in which I along with others have gained so much.

During the past one-and-a-half day conference session, under the theme "Sharing the Boundless Ocean: The Journey to Build a Maritime Community with a Shared Future", as the United Nations diplomats, the delegates from various universities actively participated in the discussion and debate on three topics: "Marine Energy Exploitation and Security", "Jointly Build Maritime Silk Road", and "Safeguard Maritime Security & Fight against Maritime Terrorism", in accordance with the procedure of United Nations Conference. Despite the geographical distance, we discussed our opinions, and made negotiations during the online sessions. We ultimately finalized resolutions among divergent viewpoints and various ideas.

We focused on global concerns during this MUN conference, identified our potential, and honed our public speaking skill, and improved our critical thinking ability and cultivate our teamwork spirit. Meanwhile, we learned from one another via internet connections, increasing our humanistic literacy, broadening our global perspective, and bearing in mind our responsibility to actively contribute to the development of a maritime community with a shared future and a human community with a shared future.

Additionally, I made friends with international students. Our friendship was established at the MUN conference, but it will not be limited to the MUN conference. I hope that the experiences and friendships we have at the conference will prove to be a priceless asset in our life. I'm looking forward to seeing you again in the diplomatic world. Thanks very much.

国际交流学院院长在模拟联合国大会闭幕式上的讲话

女士们、先生们，中外朋友们，各位参会代表们：

上午好！经过一天半紧张而充实的会期，甲大学模拟联合国大会完成所有议程，即将圆满落幕。

中外青年朋友就"海洋能源开发与安全""共建海上丝绸之路""维护海洋安全，打击海上恐怖主义"等话题积极阐述先锋观点，加强沟通合作，相互学习和交流。在一场场的唇枪舌战中，在聆听中国模拟联合国大会副会长、北京乙大学专家的精彩讲座中，我们开阔了眼界，培养了能力，收获了友谊，展现了风采。受大学领导委托，我谨对各位代表的优秀表现及10个获奖单位、40名获奖个人表示热烈祝贺！向大会工作人员及志愿者表示亲切慰问！

模拟联合国大会旨在为大家创造一个共同探讨国际热点问题的平台。随着社会多极化、经济全球化、社会信息化、文化多样化深入发展，国与国之间的联系日益加深，具备战略思维和国际眼光成为中外青年的共同追求。

从各位积极参与的热情和全身心的投入可以看出这项活动的意义。希望大家发扬模拟联合国大会精神，加强合作交流，共同努力，把包括甲大学在内的各高校模拟联合国大会办成全国知名的学术研究机构和实践平台。

本届大会的主题是"共享浩瀚海洋——构建海洋命运共同体"。中国国家主席习近平指出，海洋对人类社会的生存和发展具有重要意义，海洋孕育了生命、联通了世界、促进了发展。海洋是高质量发展战略要地。当今世界和平合作的潮流奔涌，开放融通的势头强劲。我们都在同心协力，构建人类命运共同体、海洋命运共同体，为共创和平安全、繁荣开放的世界而奋斗。

青年是社会力量中最积极、最有生气的组成部分，是国家和民族真正的希望，衷心祝愿同学们把握时代大势，响应时代号召，立大志、强素质、勤奋斗、做先锋，在中华民族伟大复兴的中国梦的奋斗中体现个人价值，不负青春韶华，不忘使命重托。

最后，再次感谢各位模拟联合国大会同仁的热情参与和大力支持，愿我们高校"模联人"的友谊地久天长！祝中外青年朋友及家人身体健康，新年快乐！

谢谢大家！

Speech by Dean of the College of International Exchange at the MUN Conference Closing Ceremony

Ladies and gentlemen, friends and delegates,

Good morning! We are about to conclude the conference which lasted one and a half days in a tight-scheduled and productive fashion.

At this conference, friends from both home and abroad expounded on respective points, strengthened collaboration and learned from each other in the vanguard of international hotspots such as "Marine Energy Exploitation and Security", "Jointly Build Maritime Silk Road", and "Safeguard Maritime Security & Fight against Maritime Terrorism". Undoubtedly, you widened your horizons and enhanced your capabilities, gained friendship, and displayed your professionalism by exchanging fire in the war of words and attending lectures provided by the co-chairman of China MUN conference and professors from University B in Beijing. Authorized by the university's leaders, I'd like to send my heartfelt congratulations to 10 units and 40 people on their remarkable achievements, as well as my best wishes to the staff and volunteers who made the conference a big success.

The MUN conference aims to provide a platform for us to study the international hot issues. As is known to all, the connectivity and mutual dependence between countries have deepened amid the ever-increasing multi-polarization, economic globalization, social informatization and cultural diversity. In order to keep abreast of the time, it is common goal for young generation around the world to develop strategic minds and global vision.

The significance of the MUN conference can be found in your enthusiasm and full engagement in related events. I hope you can carry forward the spirit of the MUN conference, and enhance cooperation and exchange to make the MUN conference a nationally recognized intellectual and practical platform.

The theme of this conference is "Sharing the Boundless Ocean: The Journey to Build a Maritime Community with a Shared Future". According to President Xi Jinping, the ocean is of vital importance for the survival and development of human society since it is where the life begins, the world is connected, and the social progress is achieved. Meanwhile, the ocean is being prioritized as a strategic resource for high-quality development. The world today is riding the waves of peaceful cooperation, building momentum for global openness and circulation. We are all working together to develop a human community with a shared future and a maritime community with a shared future, in order to create a world of peace, safety, openness and prosperity.

The young generation is the most active and vigorous force in our society, as well as the hope of a country. I wish from the bottom of my heart that all of you would set lofty goals, push your capabilities to new heights, strive for the best and play the role as pioneers in response to the call of the era. I hope you will make due contribution to the Chinese Dream of the great rejuvenation of China, live up to the prime of youth and bear in mind the mission entrusted to you by our country.

Finally, again I wish to extend my gratitude to colleagues from all universities for your passionate participation and tremendous support. Long live our friendship. I wish all of you and your family good health. Happy New Year to you all.

Thank you.

2.5 参观见学 Visit and Study Tour

2.5.1 参观见学行前安全教育 Education Prior to the Visit and Study Tour

参观见学动员教育提纲

留学生朋友们,

大家好! 今天我们开会的主题是通报下周赴外地参观见学的具体行程及要求。

根据留学生教学计划总体安排, 为进一步加深大家对中国国情和文化的认识, 经学校批准, ××月××日至××日, 我们将组织大家前往中国千年古都陕西省省会西安、中国革命圣地延安等城市参观见学。我现在给大家通报具体安排:

一、总体情况

我们这次共有××个国家的留学生××人。我们为大家制订了详细活动计划, 对乘车、住宿、就餐等进行了分组, 购买了旅游意外保险, 还安排了医生随行提供保障。我们委托旅行社协助安排各项参观、食宿、交通和英语向导事宜。

按时间顺序，我们将先后参观西安明城墙，轩辕黄帝陵园，延安革命纪念馆，毛泽东、朱德等老一辈革命家在延安时期的办公地和居所——枣园、杨家岭，以及世界八大奇迹之一的秦始皇陵兵马俑等。我们还将体验中国速度最快的火车——高铁。

二、参观要求及规定

这次活动是一项正规的教学安排，中外人员加起来有××人。为确保出行安全顺利，在这里我们明确几条要求：

1. 自觉遵守社会公共秩序和社会公德，尊重当地风俗习惯。大家来自不同的国家，一言一行都代表你们国家的形象。参观过程中，大家要注意言谈举止，不要随地吐痰，不要乱闯非开放场所，不要在公共场合大声喧哗。要爱护旅游资源，保护生态环境，不要乱刻乱画，做一个文明的传播者和国家形象的展示者。

2. 一切行动听安排，无条件服从国际交流学院教师的管理。这次参观，我们将到访×个城市××处场所，换乘两次高铁和多次汽车，环节多，转换复杂。大家一定要遵守以下规定：

(1)严格按照计划表参加各项活动，提前 5 分钟到达指定地点集合等候，建议大家参访时戴手表。

(2)按照要求统一着装(即红色马甲、运动裤和黑色帽子)，这也是为了方便大家找到团队。

(3)参观时注意人身财物安全。因参观时间仅为×天，大家不要携带太多行李，特别是笔记本电脑等贵重物品。所有行李请放到我们统一发放的双肩包中。进出火车站、上下汽车时注意检查和清点自己的行李、物品。乘车时头手不得伸出窗外。参观时普通物品可以放在旅行车上，贵重物品必须随身携带。一旦丢失任何物品，由留学生自行负责。在酒店住宿时，未经国际交流学院教师同意，不得擅自离开酒店。离开房间在酒店内活动，要向同房间人员告知自己的去向。晚上9点(第一天为晚上9:30)会进行查房。注意保持手机通信畅通。如果留学生们的手机号码有变动，请在出发前及时告知。

(4)参观过程中，大家要团结互助，及时帮助有困难的同伴。要紧跟中方向导，在国际交流学院教师的带领下开展活动。各组负责人和安全员要与本组人员在一起，对本组人员的安全负责，及时清点人数。

(5)外出参观期间要注意根据天气情况及时增减衣物，防止生病。我们安排了医生同行，带了感冒药、晕车药和急救箱，旅途中大家身体如有不适，及时向我们报告。要按时集中就餐，不得单独用餐或购买路边不干净的小吃、饮料，防止吃坏肚子。

(6)另外建议大家不要在景点购买纪念品或礼品，价格较贵，也不方便携带。如确实需要购买，注意选择正规商店，购买前，仔细询问和查验物品价格和品质，避免不必要的麻烦。

(7)请大家参观时注意认真听讲解，认真做好记录，参观结束一周后，每人上交不少于1000字的参观报告和3张照片，参观报告主要包括参观整体情况及自己的所见所闻所感等。会后，大家就可以着手准备各项外出物品，也可以上网查询参观景点的介绍。

(8)回校后，我们将评选参观见学优秀报告并举办优秀摄影作品展。根据参观见学报告、摄影作品质量来进行奖励。希望大家积极准备，认真参与。

最后，祝大家旅行愉快！

Education Outlines for the Visit and Study Tour

Dear friends,

Good afternoon! At this meeting, I will brief on the itinerary for the visit and study tour in other cities, which is scheduled for next week. We acquired approval from the university authority for the visit and study tour from DD/MM to DD/MM in accordance with international students' educational programs, to expand your understanding of our national situations and cultures. Among the cities on the itinerary are Xi'an, the millennium capital city and current provincial capital, and Yan'an, a Chinese revolutionary base. Let me now go over the specifics.

Part Ⅰ　The General Picture

It is worth noting that there are ×× international students from ×× nations participating in this tour. To ensure a safe journey, we have made detailed plan and divided international students into groups for transportation, lodging, and meals. We also bought travel insurance for everyone. A doctor from the university hospital will join us to provide necessary support. And we entrusted the travel agency with the task of arranging the itinerary, accommodation and transportation. During the journey, tourist guides will speak English.

We will visit the following places in chronological order: the Ming Dynasty City Wall of Xi'an, Mausoleum of Yellow Emperor(Huang Di), Yan'an Revolutionary Memorial Hall, Zaoyuan and Yangjialing, where Mao Zedong and Zhu De, the old generation of revolutionists' offices and residence were located; and the Qin Dynasty's terra cotta warriors and horses, one of the eight wonders in the world, among other places. Besides, we will go by high-speed train, known as the fastest train in China.

Part Ⅱ　Tour Requirements, Rules and Regulations

Because the visit and study tour is part of the educational program and will be attended by more than ×× people, the following points should be highlighted to ensure a safe and seamless journey.

1. Respect public ethics and order, as well as local custom. Because you are from different countries, your behavior represents the image of your own country. Do not spit in public, do not enter restricted areas, and do not make loud noises. Take good care of tourism resources and protect the environment from pollution. Graffiti is not permitted, as everyone is aware. Please be kind and act as a messenger of civilization and an envoy of your country during your visit.

2. Stick to the schedule for all activities. You must unconditionally follow the administration and arrangements of the College of International Exchange staff. We will visit ✕✕ scenic locations in ✕✕ cities and take the high-speed train twice and take bus several times during our trip, which implyies that both the visit and the transportation are quite complicated. As a result, you are required to:

(1)Participate in the activities as outlined in the itinerary and arrive at the designated location 5 minutes early. If feasible, use a watch.

(2)Follow the dress code (e.g. the red vest, pants, and black cap), which will allow you to easily spot the team in crowded scenic areas.

(3)Take care of yourself and keep your stuff to yourself. Please do not bring too many items, especially valuables such as your laptop, with you during your ✕-day visit. Please place your items in the pack bag that we have given to you. Check your bags as you board and disembark from the bus or train. Please do not extend your hands and head out of the windows of a bus or train. It is kindly recommended that you carry your valuables with you and leave other items on the bus during your visit. In the event of a loss, you must bear responsibility. You are not permitted to leave the hotel without the consent of the college staff. Before you leave the hotel room, your roommate is supposed to be informed. We will conduct a room inspection round at 21:00 (or 21:30 on the first night). Check your phone's balance and battery to ensure that you can stay connected at all times and from anywhere. If your cell phone number has changed, please notify us of the change before the visit.

(4)Please help one another, especially those in need. Stay close to the tourist guides and follow the instructions of the College of International Exchange staff. Students in charge of group and group safety are expected to stay with their respective groups and count the members on a regular basis.

(5)Please change your clothes to avoid contracting a cold. The doctor will have cold medicine, car sickness medicine, and first-aid supplies on hand. Please notify us if there is a physical problem. Please make sure that the meals are served on schedule. To avoid potential health risks, please do not buy food or beverages from unlicensed vendors.

(6)It is strongly advised not to buy gifts or souvenirs at scenic locations because they are expensive and inconvenient to carry. If you do want to buy some, please go to a licensed store. To avoid unnecessary problems, inquire about the price and carefully check the quality of the goods before you pay.

(7)Please pay close attention to the introduction of the scenic spots and take notes carefully. The report (minimum 1,000 words) and photos (minimum 3) are need to be handed in within one week after the visit and study tour. Your report should include the general description and your own experiences. Following the meeting, you can begin your preparation for the tour by researching online the tourist destinations we will visit.

The selected reports and photographs will be exhibited in the College of International Exchange. The award will be given based on the quality of the reports and photos submitted. We hope that everyone will take the assignment seriously.

Finally, I wish you a pleasant journey.

2.5.2 参观见学活动手册 Visit and Study Tour Guidance

一、参观流程

表 2.3 参 观 流 程

日 期	时 间	活动安排	地点
××月××日 (第一天)	06:30	早餐	留学生餐厅
	07:10	集合、检查物品	国际交流学院 综合训练场
	07:20	乘车前往武汉站	武汉火车站东广场
	09:22—14:37	武汉站乘坐高铁赴西安北(中餐为高铁餐)	西安
	15:00	乘车前往明城墙	
	16:40	参观大雁塔广场、外观大雁塔	
	18:30	乘车前往餐厅吃晚餐	
	20:00	餐厅门前集合，乘车前往酒店	
	22:00	查房	

续表

日期	时间	活动安排	地点
××月××日 （第二天）	06:30	自助早餐，退房（酒店06:00叫醒，全体留学生早餐时将行李拿至大厅，早餐后不再回到房间，直接退房）	西安
	07:30	集合登车前往黄帝陵景区参观	
	12:00	前往餐厅吃午餐	
	13:00	乘车赴壶口瀑布参观	
	17:00	赴延安吃晚餐	
	20:00	入住酒店	
	22:00	查房	
××月××日 （第三天）	07:00	自助早餐，退房（酒店06:30叫醒，全体留学生早餐时将行李拿至大厅，早餐后不再回到房间，直接退房）	延安
	08:00	乘车前往延安革命纪念馆参观	
	10:00	前往枣园参观杨家岭	
	11:50	前往餐厅吃午餐	
	13:00	乘车前往延安大桥参观	
	13:30	乘车赴临潼吃晚餐	
	19:30	乘车前往酒店	
	22:00	查房	
××月××日 （第四天）	07:00	酒店早餐，退房（酒店06:30叫醒，全体留学生早餐时将行李拿至大厅，早餐后不再回到房间，直接退房）	临潼
	08:30	乘车前往秦始皇陵兵马俑博物馆	
	13:00	前往火车站乘坐高铁返回武汉（晚餐为高铁餐，出武汉站集合清点人数）	

Part I Itinerary

Table 2. 3   Itinerary

Date	Time	Events	Location
DD/MM Day 1	06:30	Breakfast	Students' Dinning Hall
	07:10	Muster and check luggage	Multi-purpose training ground
	07:20	Take the bus to Wuhan Railway Station	East square of Wuhan Railway Station
	09:22—14:37	Take high-speed train to Xi'an Bei Railway Station(Lunch served on the train)	Wuhan Railway Station
	15:00	Depart for a tour to Ming Dynasty City Wall	Xi'an
	16:40	Visit the square of the Great Wild Goose Pagoda	
	18:30	Leave for dinner at a restaurant	
	20:00	Muster in front of the restaurant and proceed to the hotel	
	22:00	Room inspection	
DD/MM Day 2	06:30	Buffet breakfast, check out (Morning call service is at 06:00. Bring your luggage to the lobby prior to breakfast. Leave from the hotel following breakfast)	Xi'an
	07:30	Muster and depart for a tour to the Yellow Emperor's Mausoleum (Huang Di)	
	12:00	Depart for lunch at the restaurant	
	13:00	Depart for a tour to the Hukou Waterfalls	
	17:00	Depart for Yan'an, where you will have dinner	
	20:00	Check-in at the hotel	
	22:00	Regular room inspection	

Continued

Date	Time	Events	Location
DD/MM Day 3	07:00	Buffet breakfast, check out (Morning call service is at 06:30. Bring your luggage to the lobby prior to breakfast. Leave from the hotel following breakfast)	Yan'an
	08:00	Depart for a tour to Yan'an Revolutionary Memorial Hall	
	10:00	Depart for a tour to Zao Yuan	
	11:50	Depart for lunch at the restaurant	
	13:00	Depart for a tour to Yan'an Bridge	
	13:30	Depart for Lintong county, where you will have dinner	
	19:30	Take the bus for the hotel	
	22:00	Regular room inspection	
DD/MM Day 4	07:00	Breakfast, check out (Morning call service is at 06:30. Bring your luggage to the lobby prior to breakfast. Leave from the hotel after breakfast)	Lintong
	08:30	Depart for a tour to Museum of Terracotta Warriors and Horses of Qinshihuang Mausoleum	
	13:00	Take the bus for railway station. Return Wuhan by high-speed rail (Dinner is served on the train. Muster and count people at the square of Wuhan Railway Station)	

二、乘车安排

从学校往返武汉火车站以及陕西当地参观时，我们将协调 2 辆大巴进行保障，根据各专业划分乘车人员。

Part Ⅱ   Transportation

We will arrange for two buses to transport students from our university to and from Wuhan Railway Station as well as during the visit and study tour. The bus schedule is determined by your separate courses.

三、就餐安排

除每日的早餐是自助餐外，中餐和晚餐均为圆桌就餐，每桌可容纳 10 ~12 人。根据专业划分餐桌，就餐全程不提供酒精性饮料。

Part Ⅲ   Meals

Except for breakfast, 10 to 12 people will dine at the same table for lunch and dinner. The tables are set up according to your courses. There are no alcoholic beverages offered.

四、住宿安排

我们在陕西的住宿按照两人一间进行安排，具体安排参见住宿安排表。

Part Ⅳ   Accommodation

Two people share one double room in Shaanxi province. See the table for details.

表 2.4 住 宿 安 排

姓名	房号	姓名	房号	姓名	房号

Table 2.4 Room Arrangement

Name	Room No.	Name	Room No.	Name	Room No.

五、物品携带

根据天气预报，届时陕西省将会有雨，并且温度较武汉低很多，建议每名留学生带好自己的雨伞和衣服；另外，酒店会为我们提供洗漱用品，因此不必自己携带。

Part V Necessary Personal Stuff

According to the weather forecast, it is most likely to rain in Shaanxi province during the tour and the temperature will be substantially lower than that in Wuhan. It is recommended that you bring your umbrella and clothes. Furthermore, the toiletries are provided by the hotel, so you do not need to bring your own.

第三章 学生管理篇
Chapter Three Administration

3.1 入学迎新 Enrollment Procedure

3.1.1 入学阶段活动安排 Events at the Enrollment

入学阶段活动安排

第一阶段：入学注册(个人信息登记、入学考试)

第二阶段：规章制度通报(管理规定和法律法规学习、课程介绍)

第三阶段：体育训练

第四阶段：参观校园

第五阶段：开课

第六阶段：体检

第七阶段：办理在华居留许可

第八阶段：开学典礼

Events at the Enrollment

Stage 1：Enrollment(personal information registration and academic foundation examinations)

Stage 2：Lectures on Regulations(study laws and regulations, and introduce courses)

Stage 3：Physical Exercises

Stage 4：Campus Tour

Stage 5：Class Begins

Stage 6：Medical Check-up

Stage 7：Residence Permit Application

Stage 8：School Opening Ceremony

3.1.2　高校对外介绍稿范例 Introduction Scripts for Universities

丁大学对外介绍稿

丁大学是教育部直属的全国重点综合性大学，是国家"211 工程"和"985 工程"重点建设和发展的高校。

丁大学的前身是丁学院，成立于19××年，其在发展演变的过程中，几经更名，最终于19××年更名为丁大学，是我国近代成立最早的综合性大学之一。到19××年年底，这所大学已经建立了××个学院，包括文科、法律、科学、工程、农业和医药等。

一个世纪以来，丁大学建成了一座古朴典雅、富丽堂皇的建筑群，将东西方建筑风格完美地融合在一起，被评为"中国最美大学"。丁大学具有百年人文积淀，其校训"自强不息，求实创新"简洁明了。

目前，丁大学正努力把自己建设成为国内外一流的综合性研究型大学。

An Introduction on University D

The University D is a comprehensive and key national university directly under the administration of the Ministry of Education. It is also one of the

"211 Project" and "985 Project" universities with full support in the construction and development from the central and local government of China.

The history of University D can be traced back to the College D, which was founded in 19××. In the process of development and evolution, the college changed its name several times before it was finally named University D. It is one of the earliest comprehensive national universities in modern China. By the end of 19××, the university had established ×× colleges comprising liberal arts, law, sciences, engineering, agriculture and medicine.

Throughout the last century, University D has built an elegant palatial architectural complex of primitive simplicity which blends perfectly the eastern architectural style with that of the west. It has been honored as "the Most Beautiful University in China." Furthermore, University D's centennial humanistic accumulation boils down to its succinct motto, that is, "self-improvement, perseverance, truth-seeking and innovation."

Now University D is endeavoring to shape itself into a world-class comprehensive research university domestically and internationally.

甲大学对外介绍稿

甲大学地处中国湖北省武汉市，是全国重点大学，是集教学与科研于一体并共同发展的高等教育院校。甲大学是中国人才培养和科学研究的重要基地。

一、发展历程

学校前身为××学校，创办于 1949 年××月××日，1999 年与××学院合并并组建成甲大学。学校经过多年的建设和发展，形成了"严谨、求实、拼搏、创新"的校风，为中国培养了 10 多万名高素质专业人才，并为几十个国家培养了近万名优秀人才。

二、职责任务

学校以本科、研究生教育为主体，学历教育与任职教育相结合，专业包括众多领域，形成了以工学为主，工学、管理学、文学、理学、经济学等五大学科门类协调发展的综合化学科环境，拥有学士、硕士、博士学位授权点和博士后科研流动站。现有教员千余人，其中中国工程院院士××人，教授、副教授××人。

三、机构设置

学校机关编设办公室、教务处、教保处等部门；下设基础部、船舶学院等××个教学院(部、系)以及研究生院、船舶综合试验训练中心等，管理各类学生数万名。

四、教学训练

学校以"厚基础、强实践、求创新"为培养理念，构建思想政治、科学文化、专业技术、管理能力与身体心理协调发展，岗位任职能力与职业发展潜力均衡发展的教育培养体系，按照政治理论、科学文化基础、工程技术基础和专业基础四个模块设置各类课程，培养信念坚定、基础扎实、视野开阔、勇于创新的现代高素质人才。

五、科学研究

学校为适应国家发展需要，坚持科研为国家培养人才的方向，突出基础研究、创新研究，在船舶动力、机械、材料、综合电力等领域取得突破，具备较强的自主创新能力。近年来，有上千项成果获国家科技进步奖。

六、交流合作

学校始终秉承开放办学的理念，与多国院校建立了机制化合作关系；接待了数十个代表团、××余国数千余名外国人员来校访问；与多个国家院校互派学生、开办专家论坛，增进了相互间的信任与友谊；构建了以专业教师为主体的国际学术活动机制，先后派出几百批次、近千人次专家教授出国参加各类技术交流，邀请了美、英、韩、新加坡等国专家教授来校开展学术活动。

"有朋自远方来，不亦乐乎!"新时代有新展望，甲大学将以更加开放包容的姿态，欢迎来自世界各地朋友！我们也愿和更多国家和地区的同行互相学习、共享人才培养经验！愿我们的友谊天长地久、共同进步！

A Brief Overview of University A

University A is a key national university in Wuhan, Hubei Province, China. It is a higher educational institution that integrates education and scientific research in order to achieve coordinated progress in both areas. It has grown into a significant center for education and scientific research.

I. History

The predecessor of University A is the ×× Academy which was established on DD/MM in 1949. The ×× Academy and the ×× College amalgamated to form University A in 1999. Years of development have created the school motto: "Improve oneself, seek truth, encourage perseverance and make innovations." So far, the university has cultivated more than 100,000 high-caliber talents for China, as well as approximately 10,000 international students from dozens of countries or so.

II. Missions

University A is committed to undergraduate and graduate education, and its educational missions include on-the-job training. The courses have covered a variety of professional fields, with engineering as the primary focus, in order to foster an academic environment that coordinates the development in five disciplines: engineering, management, liberal arts, sciences, and economics. University A is authorized to confer bachelor's, master's, and doctoral degrees. Additionally, it offers Post-Doctoral Research Centers. There are over 1,000 skilled lecturers, including over ×× professors and associate professors. It's worth noting that ×× professors are Chinese Academy of Engineering academicians. The annual maximum number of students could be 10,000.

Ⅲ. Administration

The university administration authority is set up by the Admin Office, the Office of Studies, and the Office of Education Support, among others. There are ×× schools, colleges and departments under the administration sector, such as School of Basic Education, College of Ship Architecture, Graduate School, and Ship Testing and Training Base and so on. The administration authority is responsible for the management of tens of thousands of students enrolled in various courses.

Ⅳ. Education & Training

Following the philosophy "build a firm foundation, intensify practical efforts, and pursue innovations", University A has developed an educational system that promotes coordinated growth in ideology, science and culture, professional expertise, leadership, and physique and psychology, while balancing job and future career development. The courses are divided into four modules: political theories, science and culture, engineering technology, and specialist foundations, with the goal of developing high-caliber professionals who have a strong faith in their beliefs, a solid foundation in their professional expertise, an open-minded vision, and the ability to innovate.

Ⅴ. Scientific Research

To align with national development, University A holds that scientific research should serve the cultivation of professionals for our country. It has long placed a premium on basic science research and innovation research. Its ability to innovate has been demonstrated by technological breakthroughs in ship power engineering, machinery, materials, and integrated electrical power systems, among other areas. Up to 1,000 scientific research products have been recognized with the National S & T Progress Award.

Ⅵ. International Collaboration

University A has created bilateral collaboration mechanisms with higher educational institutions worldwide in accordance with the principle of educational openness. Over the past years, it has welcomed thousands of overseas visitors, organized student and lecturer exchange programs with universities from other countries, and hosted specialty forums attended by presidents and experts from international institutions. As a result, mutual trust and friendship have grown significantly between University A and its overseas counterparts. Academic exchange programs for lecturers have been established at University A, with about 1,000 instructors being sent overseas in hundreds of batches for international interactions. Additionally, it has invited professors and professionals from the United States, the United Kingdom, South Korea, and Singapore to participate in academic activities.

Confucius, the Chinese sage, says, "Isn't it a delight to have friends come from afar?" With fresh aspirations for new era, a more open and inclusive University A looks forward to meeting friends from all over the world. We are open to exchanging ideas and educational experience with colleagues from every corner of the world. Long live our friendship and let's go forward together.

3.1.3 入学阶段行政管理宣讲 Lecturing on Administrative Regulations

留学生入学整体安排介绍

留学生朋友们：

下午好！

首先非常欢迎各位来到中国武汉市，来到甲大学。这里是国际交流学院，也是你们将要生活一年的新家。我是国际交流学院留学生办公室老师吴君鹏，这位老师是蔡成凯。我们主要负责行政管理和活动安排。之后你们会陆续认识国际交流学院的其他工作人员。下一步，国际交流学院领导将专门会见大家。留学生朋友们，你们是我校历史上第五批 Y 国留学生，也是今年到校的第一批留学生，还有其他很多国家的留学生正分批来校报到。为了迎接大家的到来，国际交流学院做了认真充分的准备。

我们先看一段大学介绍片，建立一个对大学的初步印象……接下来，我介绍一下入学阶段的整体安排，包括法规宣讲、入学考试、信息登记、课程介绍、校园参观、体检、在华居留手续办理、开学典礼等环节。今天，也就是第一天，先安排填表、照相、换汇、购物等事宜。第二天上午进行英语摸底考试、发放教材及课程表、宣讲行政管理规定。第三天上午进行数学摸底考试、宣讲教学管理规定。第四天上午进行物理摸底考试、宣讲生活指南。第五天上午介绍培训计划及课程设置、进行专业摸底考试。第五天下午和第六天休息。从第七天上午开始按照课程表上课。以后每个星期一和星期三下午的体育锻炼时间将统一安排跑步、球类或其他类型体育锻炼。校园参观、体检、在华居留手续办理、开学典礼这 4 个环节，等其他国家的留学生到校后集中安排。除按照课程表上课以外，其他国际交流学院组织的活动，我们都会在一楼保安室对面的大屏幕上公布具体时间、地点及着装要求。你们要注意阅读，按照要求做好相关准备并提前 5 分钟就位。

大家先找时间好好看看《留学生行政管理规定》《留学生教学管理规定》和《武汉留学生生活指南》，上面有很多关于留学生学习生活方面的规定和要求，也有很多实用的留学信息和提示。明天开始我们会逐一宣讲。先强调两点，一是早饭和中饭要统一去餐厅。二是不能随便进出大学校门，外出时必须写外出申请，并领取专门外出证。

我的介绍完毕，考虑到大家刚来，国际交流学院为每人提前准备了一套洗漱用品。为方便大家与家人联系，宿舍有互联网接口，105 教室还有可以上网的电脑。如果需要，我们还可提供收费手机电话卡，每张已预存100 元。衷心希望我们在今后的一年时间里能够相处融洽，也希望大家在中国学有所成、生活愉快。现在给大家 15 分钟时间填表，然后集合去照相、换汇、购物。晚上 5:30 开餐，明早 7:10 开餐。

Guidance for Enrollment Procedure

Dear friends,

Good afternoon!

To begin, I would like to welcome all of you to University A and Wuhan, China. You are at the College of International Exchange, your new home for the academic year ahead. My name is Wu Junpeng, a teacher from the College's administration office, and my colleague on the same team is professor Cai Chengkai. We are both in charge of student administration and other events. Later, you will meet with other College staff. The College authorities will meet with you on another occasion. Dear friends, you are the fifth batch from country Y to attend our university, and the first group of overseas students to arrive this year. Students from many other countries are en route to our university. We have done all necessary arrangements in advance of your arrival.

Let's watch the film on our university to learn about its development. Now I would like to give you a broad summary of the enrollment procedure, including lectures on the laws and regulations, examinations on your academic foundations, information registration, course overview, campus tour, medical check-up, residency permit application, school opening ceremony and so on. Today, you will fill out information forms, take ID photos, exchange currencies and go shopping. On the morning of day two, you will take the English foundation examination, collect course books and class schedule, and attend the lecture on administration regulations. On the morning of day three, you will sit for the Mathematics foundation examination, and attend the lecture on education management regulations. On the morning of day four, you will take the physics foundation examination, and attend the lecture on living in China. On the morning of day five, we will introduce course syllabus, and subjects and conduct the professional foundation examination. There are no additional events planned for you on day six or the afternoon of day five. As from the morning of day seven, you will attend classes according to the class schedules. Every Monday and Wednesday afternoon, we will organize physical training including running, ball games, among others. The campus tour, medical check-up, residency permit application and school opening ceremony will take place when other students arrive at the university. Apart from class schedules, we will post activities hosted by the College of International Exchange on the first floor's TV facing the security room, including the time, location and dress code required by the activities. Please read the information and reach the specified location five minutes early.

At your free time, please read the *Administrative Regulations for International Students*, *Education Management Regulations for International Students* and *Guidance for International Students in Wuhan*. You can learn about the legislation governing your education and living, as well as a wealth of other important information during your stay in Wuhan. As from tomorrow, we shall begin lecturing on the above three materials one by one. I want to stress two points: you must attend to the dining hall together for breakfast and lunch, and you must submit a written application to go out. It is not permitted to exit and re-enter the university without a going-out pass.

My briefing is over. Given that you are newcomers, we prepared a set of toiletries for each of you. Your dormitory offers internet connection, allowing you to stay in touch with your family whenever you want. In addition, PCs in Classroom 105 are connected to the internet. If necessary, we can provide you with a SIM card with an RMB 100 deposit in the balance. I sincerely hope that we will become friends in the coming year and that each of you will be successful in your respective fields, and I wish you all a pleasant stay in China. You now have 15 minutes to complete information forms, then muster before departing for ID photos, money exchange and shopping. Dinner is scheduled at 5:30 pm, and breakfast at 7:10 am.

3.1.4 行政管理规定认知书 Confirmation of Administrative Regulations

留学生行政管理规定认知书

我是来自 M 国的留学生，我已认真学习并完全理解《甲大学留学生行政管理规定》。我决心在甲大学学习期间，认真遵守并执行以上各项规定，圆满完成学业。

留学生：

（签名）

年　月　日

Confirmation of the Administrative Regulations for International Students

I am an international student from Country M. I have read carefully and understood the *Administrative Regulations for International Students*. I promise to observe the regulations strictly and complete my studies successfully at University A.

International Student(Signature):

DD/MM/YYYY

3.1.5 安全责任协议书 The Agreement on Safety Obligations

留学生安全责任协议书

1. 为提高留学生的安全意识，明确留学生在校培训期间的相关安全责任，根据中华人民共和国有关法律及甲大学相关规章制度，甲大学国际交流学院(以下简称"甲方")与_____国留学生（以下简称"乙方"）经过友好协商，签订本协议。

2. 乙方在我校学习期间，受中华人民共和国法律保护和约束。乙方应当遵守中国的法律、法令、风俗习惯和甲方的规章制度，增强自我保护意识，注意自身安全。

3. 下列情况下，甲方承担乙方的安全责任：

(1)乙方参加甲方组织的教学和训练，并按教师的要求实施时；

(2)乙方(包括家属)在甲方校区内按甲方的规章制度生活、居住时；

(3)乙方参加甲方组织的参观见学、实习和游览，按照甲方要求活动时；

4. 下列情况下，甲方不承担乙方的安全责任：

(1)乙方因违反中国的法律、法规(包括交通规则)以及甲方的规章制度而受到人身和财产伤害时；

(2)乙方参加甲方组织的教学和训练，未按任课教师的要求实施时；

(3)乙方参加甲方组织的参观见学、实习和游览，未按甲方的要求行动，自行安排活动时；

(4)乙方自行到甲方校区以外的地区活动，因意外事故(例如交通事故、受到不法分子袭击等)而导致伤亡时；

(5)乙方自行乘坐民用交通工具(包括公共汽车、出租汽车、火车、飞机、轮船等)时；

(6)乙方与家属在甲方校区外住宿时；

(7)乙方自行赴本市以外的中国境内其他城市游览、旅行或回国探亲时；

（8）乙方自然死亡、猝死或因其他不可抗力导致伤亡时；

（9）乙方在本国驻华使、领馆活动时。

5. 乙方违反中国的法律、法令（如进行反华政治活动、赌博、嫖娼、违反交通规则等）以及甲方的规章制度，伤害或危及他人人身和财产安全时，应当承担法律、安全和赔偿责任。

6. 乙方来校陪读家属的安全责任由乙方本人承担，甲方建议乙方自费为陪读家属购买人身意外伤亡保险和财产保险。

7. 乙方及陪读家属因不可抗力遭受意外伤害时，甲方按照中国有关法律、法令和甲方的有关规定，协助乙方所属国驻华机构处理善后事宜。

8. 本安全协议于_____年_____月_____日在甲大学签署。

9. 本协议一式两份，每份均用中文和英文写成，甲乙双方各执一份，两种文本具有同等效力。

甲方代表：　　　　　　　乙方（留学生）：

（签名）　　　　　　　　（签名）

年　月　日

The Agreement on Safety Obligations for Intremational Students

1. The Agreement on Safety Obligations is made by and between the College of International Exchange of University A (hereinafter referred to as Party A) and the International Student _____ from _____ (hereinafter referred to as Party B) through amicable negotiations in accordance with relevant laws of the People's Republic of China and relevant regulations of University A, with the goal of increasing the International Student's safety awareness and clarifying the safety obligations.

2. Party B is protected and bound by the laws of China during the

course. Party B should follow Chinese laws and specifications as well as Party A's regulations and norms, respect Chinese customs and habits, and raise awareness of self-protection and personal safety.

3. Party A is held accountable for Party B's safety in the following circumstances:

(1) Party B follows instructors at education and training organized by Party A.

(2) Party B (including Party B's family) lives in the area administered by Party A and in compliance with Party A's laws and regulations.

(3) Party B adheres to Party A's instruction throughout visits and study tours, practical sessions and sightseeing events planned by Party A.

4. Party A is excluded from liability for Party B's safety in the following circumstances:

(1) Party B suffers damage or property loss as a result of a violation of both Chinese laws and rules (including traffic law) and Party A's regulations.

(2) Party B does not follow instructors during education and training organized by Party A.

(3) Party B does not follow Party A's instructions throughout visits and study tours, practical sessions and sightseeing events scheduled by Party A, and arranges otherwise.

(4) Party B stays in locations other than those under the administration of Party A, and his/her injury or death is caused by an accident, such as a traffic accident or a criminal attack.

(5) Party B travels by civil transportation by himself/herself (including bus, taxi, train, plane or ship, etc.)

(6) Party B and his/her family live beyond the administration region

of Party A.

(7) Party B travels to other cities in China other than Wuhan or returns home to visit his/her family alone.

(8) Party B's death results from natural or sudden death, or Party B's injury and death results from another force majeure.

(9) Party B remains in China at the Consulate or Embassy of his or her country.

5. Party B should assume corresponding responsibilities and be punished accordingly if he/she violates Chinese laws and statutes (for example, if Party B organizes and participates in anti-Chinese activities, gambling, whoring, and violating traffic laws), Party A's regulations, and harms or threatens the personal and property safety of others.

6. Party B should be held accountable for his/her family's safety in China. As a result, Party A recommends that Party B get Life Accident Insurance and Property Insurance for his/her family.

7. If the force majeure causes injury or death to Party B and his/her family, Party A will help the Embassy of Party B's nation in China in managing the aftermath in accordance with Chinese laws and norms as well as Party A's applicable regulations.

8. The agreement on Safety Obligations is signed at University A in Wuhan on DD/MM/YYYY.

9. This agreement is written in both Chinese and English and delivered in duplicate, one held by Party A and the other by Party B. Both texts/versions are legitimate in their own right.

Party A: Party B:

(Signature)   (Signature)

DD/MM/YYYY   DD/MM/YYYY

3.1.6 个人情况表和联络表 Information Form and Contacts

表 3.1 留学生个人情况表

姓名		国籍		照片
出生时间		工作时间		
宗教信仰		教育程度		
身高（厘米）		体重（千克）鞋码（厘米）		
职务级别		现任职务		
特长		毕业拟任职务		
婚否		语种		
家庭主要成员信息				
教育背景				
留学经历				
工作简历				

Table 3.1   Personal Information Form for International Students

Full Name		Nationality		Photo
Date of Birth		Years of Employment		
Religion		Diploma/Certificate		
Height (cm)		Weight (kg) Shoes Size(cm)		
Seniority		Current Appointment		
Special Talent(s)		Appointment after the Course		
Marital Status		Languages		
Family Members				
Education Background				
Overseas Study				
Positions Held				

表 3.2 留学生联络表

姓名		国籍	
家庭住址			
家庭电话		邮政编码	
邮箱		手机	
工作单位			
单位地址			
办公室电话		邮政编码	
配偶			
父母			
主要社会关系			

Table 3. 2   Contact Details of International Students

Full Name		Nationality	
Home Address			
Home Tel. No.		Postcode	
E-mail		Mobile Phone No.	
Work Unit			
Work Unit Address			
Office Tel. No.		Postcode	
Spouse			
Parents			
Major Relatives			

3.2　讲评信函 Remarks at Meetings and Letters to Students and Faculty

3.2.1　点名讲评 Comments at a Weekly Meeting

留学生朋友们：

下午好！

刚才大家介绍了本周的学习和工作情况，这一周课程任务较重、活动较多，大家表现积极，我感到很欣慰，但仍有个别留学生存在课前集合迟到的情况，希望大家今后能够注意，尽量避免此类情况再发生。另外，近期天气转冷，教学楼和宿舍内有空调，但室外气温比较低，希望大家外出时注意保暖，避免冷热交替导致感冒。下周主要有以下几项事情……希望大家保持上周的积极态度，在抓好学习的同时积极参加各项活动。

Dear friends,

Good afternoon!

Just now you made a briefing on your study and living of last week. Despite the hectic class schedule and activities, you showed excellent passion in all of your work, which impressed me greatly. However, some of you were late for the pre-class muster. I hope you won't be late for mustering in the future. Furthermore, it is becoming cold. There are air conditioners in classrooms and dormitories, but due to the cold outside, I recommend that you keep warn when you are outside. When we alternate between staying in cold and warm places, we should be cautious about developing a cold. We shall do... the following week. I hope that every-one of you will maintain your positive attitude and actively participate in various activities while completing your course work.

3.2.2　骨干座谈会 Meeting for Students in Charge

1. 留学生骨干座谈会主持词

留学生朋友们：

下午好！

今天召集大家开会的主要目的是让上学期的骨干和新任的骨干坐在一起进行经验交流。上学期我们一共任命了×名骨干，他们在管理服务以及各项活动的组织中发挥了重要作用，×名骨干中×名已顺利结业离校回国，×名继续留任或改任到其他岗位，×名未继续担任。这×名留学生希望你们离岗不离心，继续支持和参与到我们的留学生管理工作和活动组织中，并将自己的宝贵经验传授给新任骨干。

下面请各位留学生骨干代表依次发言……

由于时间有限，今天只安排部分新老骨干发言，其他未发言的可以在会后进一步交流。还是那句话，关于管理服务保障工作，我们反映的渠道是畅通的，有任何建议随时欢迎你们向留学生管理办公室和教师反映。

下面掌声有请国际交流学院副院长赵长江讲话。

谢谢赵副院长。会议到此结束。谢谢大家。

1. Host Speech at the Meeting with Students in Charge

Dear friends,

Good afternoon!

Today's meeting is for experience-sharing on administration management between former students in charge and the newly elected team. Last semester, altogether × international students undertook their responsibilities as students in charge, and played a significant role in various work as organizers and coordinators of student management and activities. Among them, × students have finished their courses and returned home, × students have continued their posts or shifted to other posts, while another × students haven't taken their post any longer. Here I hope that those of you who are leaving your positions will continue supporting and participating in activities related to student administration and organization, and share your experience with the newly appointed team.

Now please take turns expressing yourself.

Due to time constraints, we only have × students in charge today to present their experience and work plan. Others, if you wish, are welcome to speak with us after the meeting. I want to stress that we are always available at the administration office and encourage you to meet with us to share your thoughts on administration and logistics.

Professor Zhao Changjiang, Deputy Dean of the College of International Exchange will now take the floor.

Professor Zhao, thank you very much. The meeting is concluded. Thank you all.

2. 国际交流学院副院长在留学生骨干座谈会上的讲话

刚才，×名上学期优秀留学生骨干交流了在实际工作中的宝贵经验，×名本学期新任留学生骨干表明了态度、阐明了工作思路。听了你们的发言，我很感动，感动于你们对甲大学的深厚感情，感动于你们对我们工作的理解和支持，你们都把自己看成是这个国际大家庭的成员，都为了把这个家建设得更加团结、和谐、融洽而贡献着自己的力量和智慧。过去的一个学期，全体骨干较好地发挥了模范带头作用，严格落实教学管理规章制度，加强留学生的教育引导和各项活动的组织，并取得了丰硕的成绩。在此，我对上一届骨干的辛勤劳动表示由衷的感谢，同时我也代表国际交流学院领导对新学期通过民主选举产生的骨干表示祝贺。

骨干的身份代表了全体留学生对你们的信任，你们要比其他学生付出更多，这是一种考验和锻炼，相信担任骨干的经历，日后一定会成为你们的人生财富。借此机会，我也想给大家提几点要求：一是发挥模范带头作用。中国有句古话是"打铁还需自身硬"，希望你们带头并引导全体留学生共同遵守大学的各项规章制度，树立良好的形象，为你们的管理工作打下良好的基础。这些规章制度和做法都是在多年来留学生工作实践中积累的经验，得到了各级领导和中外朋友的认可。你们要做好榜样，用无声的行动感染人，影响人，当其他留学生出现违纪行为时，要提醒他们，你们要做规章制度的捍卫者。二是发挥管理的桥梁和纽带作用。本学期大事、喜事、要事多，如中国建国 70 周年、深蓝国际文化节、市内外参观见学、大学基层运动会和篮球赛，还有各个国家节日庆典等，这些都需要大家的积极参与和密切配合，希望你们能以饱满的热情和高度的责任意识，发动全体留学生，加强组织引导，把新学期的各项活动完成好。三是处理好工作和学习之间的矛盾。留学生骨干的管理工作会占用你们部分个人时间和精力，你们需要比其他留学生付出更多，希望你们能处理好这个矛盾，在做好骨干工作的同时，学习成绩也能走在前列。根据以往情况，很多被评为优秀毕业留学生的人都来自留学生骨干，我相信你们也能和往届骨干一样，工作和学习两不误，成为优秀留学生的有力竞争人选。

谢谢大家！

2. Speech by Deputy Dean of the College of International Exchange at the Meeting with Students in Charge

Just now, × outstanding international students in charge for last semester shared their personal experiences in administration, and × newly elected students in charge clarified their attitude and explained their work plan for future administration. I am greatly impressed by your genuine affection for the university and the College of International Exchange, as well as your understanding and support to our work. You have regarded yourselves as members of a big international family, and contributed your ideas and wisdom to building a more united and harmonious international student family. In the past semester, all of the students in charge have done well in their administrative duties, exerting positive influence to other international students. They made significant contributions by enforcing administrative and educational management standards and procedures, advising overseas students, and arranging a range of events. I'd want to express my heartfelt gratitude to you for your hard work. At the same time, I'd like to congratulate the newly elected team on behalf of the College of International Exchange's authority.

The identity as students in charge represents your colleagues' trust. It is also a challenge for you have to spare more efforts than others. But I believe, your experience as international students in charge here will be a precious asset in your future career. Today, I want to take this opportunity to put forward some requirements to all of you. Firstly, be a role model in all aspects. In China, an old saying goes like that " to strike iron, one must stay strong". I hope you will set a good example for other international students by following laws and regulations in order to define your image and lay a solid foundation for your future work. The regulations and practices are summarized from many years' work and recognized by higher authorities. As a role model, you will guide and influence others. You also must defend procedures and regulations and remind your colleagues when they violate or are about to break the rules. Secondly, be bridge and messenger between the College of International Exchange and international students. This semester will mark a series of tremendous, major and delighted events, including the 70th anniversary of the founding of the People's Republic of China, the Blue Water International Culture Festival, tours in and outside Wuhan, the university's sports meeting and basketball match, as well as celebrations and national festivities of international students. It requires your active participation and cooperation. I hope you will be enthusiastic and responsible in the abovementioned events, and I hope you will encourage other students to participate in by offering your organizational talents to ensure the success of all events. Thirdly, maintain good balance between your work and study. The work as students in charge will definitely distract you from your studies. So you have to put up more efforts in your studies than others. I hope you are able to balance your work and studies, becoming an excellent student in charge while excelling in your course. As in previous years, the majority of Excellent Graduates come from the student leadership. I also believe you are as capable as your predecessors, that you will balance your work and studies and that you will become candidates of Excellent Graduate Award.

Thank you!

3.2.3 教学讲评表彰会 Commendation for Brilliant Academic Achievements

教学讲评表彰会主持词

留学生朋友们：

下午好!

今天我们在这里进行教学讲评表彰会。首先，请国际交流学院副院长赵长江宣布上学期学习成绩优秀的留学生名单。

下面，请国际交流学院党委书记张嘉琪为学习成绩优秀的留学生颁发获奖证书及奖牌。

下面，请国际交流学院院长王建东进行教学讲评。

今天的会议到此结束。

Host Address at the Academic Award Ceremony

Dear friends,

Good afternoon!

Today, we are gathered at the Academic Award Ceremony to witness the recognition of brilliant students. To begin, professor Zhao

Changjiang, Deputy Dean of the College of International Exchange will read the names of those who excelled in their course work.

Now let's invite professor Zhang Jiaqi, the College party secretary to award certificates and medals to the students.

Now let's welcome professor Wang Jiandong, Dean of the College to make a speech.

The ceremony has been concluded.

国际交流学院院长在教学讲评表彰会上的讲话

留学生朋友们、学院全体工作人员：

下午好！

今天召开这个久违的教学讲评表彰会，主要是为了总结和分析上学期留学生教学工作，以表彰先进，鞭策后进；也是为了更好地迎接从明天开始的线下复课及 8 月份的毕业工作，以厘清重点，讲清要求。

首先，我代表学院领导及全体工作人员，对在前一阶段学习中取得优异成绩的同学表示祝贺，对为教学任务圆满顺利完成付出辛勤劳动的教学、管理及保障人员表示慰问和感谢！

按照教学计划安排，上学期我们共开设了××个专业、××门课程。全体留学生遵章守纪、刻苦钻研、互相帮助，已顺利通过了全部课程的考核。××个专业顺利结业，××名留学生通过 HSK 一级考试，×××名留学生通过 HSK 二级考试，×名外国研究生被录取。我们还组织了深蓝汉语桥大赛、基层足球赛、中华人民共和国成立 70 周年联欢会、中外学生迎新春嘉年华、赴广州海南参观见学等大型活动，并选派××名留学生参加武汉军运会火炬传递，组织全体留学生观看军运会比赛等。

经过统计，上学期轮机工程专业留学生总平均分 83 分，平均成绩最高 87 分。船舶总体专业留学生总平均分 85 分，平均成绩最高 92 分；动力专业总平均分 81 分，平均成绩最高 88 分；电气专业总平均分 80 分，平均成绩最高 86 分。全体留学生中，平均成绩 90 分以上的，即学习优秀的占总留学生数的 20%；平均成绩 80 分以上的，即学习良好的占总留学生数的 60%。

本学期，按照学校"停课不停教、停课不停学"的倡议，我们从×月下旬开始线上授课，线上教学时间长达×个月，共开设了×个专业、××门课程。期间，你们积极配合学校和国际交流学院疫情防控要求，做好个人防护。你们主动参与线上教学，用学习和锻炼充实每一天。为此，我想代表国际交流学院领导和工作人员，向你们表示感谢！

按照学校的有关要求，我们拟制了接下来两个月的课程表，将于明天恢复线下授课。根据教学计划安排，一年制船舶技术与管理专业的留学生将在×周内完成××门课程的学习，于 8 月底前完成学业并离校。这一阶段我们主要安排了专业课程学习，包括实践课程，还专门为大家保留了线上参观见学等公共课程。四年制本科轮机工程专业留学生将利用双休日、暑假等节假日进行补课，计划在×月参加 HSK 三级考试、×月参加 HSK 四级考试。为了让全体留学生安心生活、放心锻炼、专心学习，我们已经组织专业公司对所有留学生教室、餐厅、电梯、楼道等公共区域及宿舍进行了一次彻底的卫生清扫和全面消杀，并完成了对所有教室多媒体设备的检查及故障维修，保证教室恢复到常规使用状态。复课后，我们还将安排保洁人员每日对留学生教学场所进行卫生清扫和消毒，也希望大家在复课后坚持做好日常个人防护。

今天大家进行了复课预演，目的是为了让大家熟悉复课后如何落实常态化防控的一些要求，这里我也想再强调两点：第一，要继续落实常态化防控要求，做好个人防护。大家都知道，截至今天，新冠肺炎疫情已波及全球×××多个国家和超过××××万人，N 国已经超过×××万人确诊，疫情防控不能松懈。2020 年 5 月 24 日，中国国家主席习近平参加第十三届全国人大三次会议湖北代表团审议时强调，"针尖大的窟窿能漏过斗大的风"，意思是关于疫情防控任何疏忽和大意都可能产生极其严重的后果。中国的疫情防控效果与其他许多国家形成鲜明对比，这是因为我们有毅力和决心遵守严格的防疫措施，阻断病毒传染的途径，这是科学理论指导实践的体现。为此，课上课下、生活当中请大家配合体温测量、戴口罩、勤洗手、不要聚集等。大家现在可以在校园部分教学区域活动，但目前依然不得前往家属区、超市，不得出校门，这也是学校根据当前校内外形势作出的要求。后续学校如果调整管控措施，我们也会及时作出相应调整。任何时候如有身体不适，请及时向任课教师或学院的工作人员报告。第二，毕业前我们将组织"优秀留学生"评选。这个评选从20××年开始，已经连续评选了×届共××名综合表现优秀的留学生，其中不少优秀留学生回国后得到了提拔和重用，大学优秀留学生品牌效应明显。优秀留学生也是大学颁给留学生的最高褒奖与荣誉，要考查学习成绩和日常综合表现等多个方面。我希望大家以历届优秀留学生为榜样，努力学习，严守纪律，积极表现，争当优秀留学生。

对于我们的学院工作人员，我也提两点要求，一是要在复课后严格落实各项教学规章制度，加强听查课工作，紧抓正规教学工作，确保本学年的教学工作圆满完成。二是要继续做好疫情防控的服务保障工作，确保复课安全稳定，为留学生营造规范有序、健康温馨的学习和生活环境。

最后祝大家圆满完成学业、顺利毕业，也祝大家及家人健康幸福。谢谢大家！

Speech by Dean of the College of International Exchange at the Academic Award Ceremony

Dear friends, staff of the College of International Exchange,

Good afternoon!

This long-cherished meeting will summarize the teaching work of the previous semester, acclaim the excellent, motivate the others to move forward, and better prepare you for the start of regular classes tomorrow and the graduation process in August. During the meeting, I will underscore key aspects and clarify the requirements.

First, on behalf of the College of International Exchange's leadership and staff, I'd like to extend my congratulations to top scoring international students, as well as my appreciation to the teaching, management and logistic staff who have worked tirelessly to ensure the successful completion of teaching task.

According to the syllabus, we had ×× courses and ×× subjects accessible last semester. All international students observed the rules, worked hard, supported each other and passed all of their exams. Students from ×× courses graduated, ×× students passed HSK 1, ××× students passed HSK 2, × students were admitted as postgraduates. We held many activities, such as Blue Water Chinese Bridge Contest, football games, celebrations of the 70th anniversary of the PRC, Chinese New Year Gala, visit and study tour to Guangzhou and Hainan. We selected ×× international students for the torch relay at the 7th Military World Games and all of the international students watched the Military World Games.

According to statistics, students of Marine Engineering have an average score of 83, with the best score being 87; students of Ship Overall Technology score an average of 85, with a maximum score of 92; students of Power Engineering score an average of 81, with a maximum score of 88; and students of Electrical Engineering score an average of 80, with a maximum score of 86. Twenty percent of all overseas students excelled in their courses, with an average score of more than 90. Those with an average score of 80 or higher demonstrated strong academic performance, accounting for 60% of all.

In response to the initiative of "no suspension of teaching and learning when school is closed", the College of International Exchange has offered online classes since late February. So far, we have set up ×× online subjects in × courses over the period of × months. Thanks to your cooperation, we were able to carry out successfully the pandemic prevention and control response launched by both the university and our college, and so far all of you have maintained personal protective measures. Additionally, you have actively participated in online sessions, focusing on your course work and physical activities to make the most of your time day after day. Therefore, I would like to thank you all on behalf of all leaders and staff of the College of International Exchange.

We have made the class schedule for the next two months of regular classes which will begin tomorrow, in accordance with the university's guidelines. According to the schedule, international students enrolled in the one-year Ship Technology and Management program will complete the course and leave our university by the end of August after attending ✕✕ subjects in ✕ weeks. During this time, you will attend classes on specialized topics including practical sessions, as well as classes on more general topics, such as an online tour of China. International students enrolled in the four-year Marine Engineering program will have make-up lessons on weekends and during summer vacation, as well as HSK 3 in MM and HSK 4 in MM. To give you confidence in your exercises, studies, and daily life, all dormitory rooms and public places such as classrooms, canteens, elevators, and stairs have been carefully cleaned and disinfected. All classroom multimedia equipment has been inspected and troubleshooted. We will ensure that all classrooms are returned to normal. Every day following the resumption of classes, the classrooms will be cleaned and disinfected. And I call on everyone to continue practicing personal protective response as usual.

From the class resuming rehearsal we had today, you will gain an understanding of the requirements for regular prevention and control. Here I want to stress two points. The first is to strictly implement the requirements for regular prevention and control, which includes taking personal protective measures. As we all know, so far COVID-19 has hit over ×× × countries and affected more than ××× of thousands of people worldwide. In country N, over ××× of thousands of people have been confirmed infected. Thus, prevention and control measures can't be relaxed. In 24 May, 2020, Chinese President Xi Jinping attended the deliberation by Hubei delegation at the third Session of the 13th National People's Congress and said, "A powerful wind can blow through a tiny hole as small as a pinpoint". It tells us that even minor ignorance or negligence will result in severe consequences regarding the pandemic response. The Chinese people's perseverance and commitment on strict measures which block the transmission of virus is the reason why China has a far better situation of pandemic control than many other countries. It shows how scientific theory guides practices. I urge everyone to cooperate with the COVID response by checking your temperature, wearing masks, cleaning your hands, and not gathering whenever and wherever you are. Now you are free to roam in the designated areas on campus but still not allowed to visit family quarters, supermarkets or leave the university. Based on the current pandemic scenario both inside and outside the university, the university has mandated this obligation. If additional measures become available in the future, we will make the necessary adjustments. If you are physically uncomfortable, please notify our college's lecturers or office personnel as soon as possible. The second concern is the selection of Excellent Graduates. The honor began in 20××. We have selected ×× excellent international students in × years, and many of them were promoted to prominent positions when they returned to their home country. It shows that the honor really weighs a lot. The Excellent Graduates Award is the highest distinction granted to international students by the university. It is determined by academic and daily performance. I hope you will be inspired by the accomplishments of prior honorees. Strive for honor by studying hard, and adhering to the rules.

As for the staff of the College of International Exchange, I also have two requirements. The first is to strictly enforce education management regulations, conduct inspection rounds in classes, and focus on standard education procedures, in order to successfully complete the teaching task this academic year. The second is to carry on the logistical support for pandemic response so as to create a sound environment for study as well as a healthy, organized and comfortable way of living.

Finally, I wish you all best of the luck in your academic endeavors. I wish you and your family good health and happiness! Thank you all.

3.2.4　致留学生新生的一封信 A Letter to Newcomers

亲爱的留学生朋友：

欢迎来到甲大学学习深造！

甲大学是一所与新中国同龄的国家重点大学，是工程与管理、技术与管理相结合，覆盖多学科门类、包含多层次培养的综合大学，也是中国重要的教学科研基地。主校区位于湖北省武汉市中心城区，是读书治学的理想园地，你们将在这里品味丰富多彩的中国文化，全方位感受中国高校氛围，留下一段美好而特别的人生回忆！

甲大学和国际交流学院已经为你的学习生活做了精心准备，请尽快阅读《留学生行政管理规定》《留学生教学管理规定》，了解有关信息及要求。在入学阶段，我们将安排法规宣讲、入学摸底考试、课程介绍、教材发放、信息登记、体检及在华居留手续办理等事项。请注意观看一楼电视屏幕的通知，了解各事项开始的时间、地点等有关要求，事先做好准备并提前5分钟就位。

需要提醒的有两点：（1）每天三餐就餐时间分别为7:10、12:10、17:30。（2）到校外购物、参观或处理其他事宜，须提前填写外出申请表，并经国际交流学院批准后，方可领取外出卡，从大学北门、南门或西门（正在维修）进出，返回后请将外出卡放回原位。

从 20××年×月新留学生楼运行以来，各类条件得到了较大的改善，但为了给留学生朋友提供更优质的学习生活环境，我们利用暑假时间维修改造了留学生楼部分设施，目前整体工程基本完工，有部分工程正处于收尾阶段，部分设施设备正在组织采购，请留学生朋友注意安全，不要穿越安全警示护栏、不要靠近施工现场和操作施工设备，以防发生意外！感谢你们的理解和配合！

祝大家学有所成、生活愉快！如需要任何帮助，请到留学生楼 2 楼西侧留学生管理办公室与中方教师取得联系。

甲大学国际交流学院

年　月　日

Dear friends,

Welcome to University A.

University A is one of the prestigious national universities, which is the same age as the People's Republic of China. It is a comprehensive university with multiple-discipline and multi-dimensional education where engineering is incorporated into management science and technology is integrated into management science. It is also a significant educational, scientific, and research center in China. The main campus is in the city of Wuhan, Hubei province. Here at the university, an ideal place to study, you will develop an understanding of the diverse Chinese cultures and gain an all-around experience of living in a Chinese institution. As a result, you will remember the pleasant and special days at University A for the rest of your life!

Your arrival has been meticulously planned by the university and the College of International Exchange. Please read the *Administrative Regulations* and the *Education Management Regulations* to learn more about the information and requirements for life here. Lectures on laws and regulations, academic foundation exams, course briefings, course book handover, personal information registration, medical check-up, and residency permit application are all part of the enrolling procedure. The announcements, which include the event's time, location, and other details, will be broadcast on the first floor's television. Please engage in the activities as directed and come five minutes early at the appropriate location.

Two points are highlighted here: (1) The three meals are scheduled at 7:10, 12:10 and 17:30 respectively. (2) Before leaving the campus, you should always fill out the application form. With your going-out pass, you can exit and re-enter through the North Gate, the South Gate, and the West Gate (under maintenance) after receiving approval from the College of International Exchange. Please return the going-out pass in its original place when you come back.

Conditions have substantially improved after the new international student building opened in MM, 20×X. However, in order to provide you with a high-quality environment, we initiated a renovation project, with the bulk of facilities refurbished during the summer holiday. The renovation is almost finished, and the remaining project is nearing completion. To avoid an accident, please take care, do not cross the fenced-in area, approach the construction site, or operate the equipment. Thank you for your understanding and cooperation.

Finally, we wish you all best of the luck in your academic endeavor and in your life. If you need support, please visit Chinese staff at the administration office on the west side of the second floor.

With best regards!

Yours Sincerely,

College of International Exchange of University A

Date: DD/MM/YYYY

3.2.5　致往届留学生校友的一封信 A Letter to Alumni of University A

亲爱的×××：

展信好！时光如梭，光阴荏苒，虽然你早已完成学业，回国建功立业，但你在校培训的情景依然留藏在我们心中。

甲大学自开展留学生教育以来，已经为亚、非、南美、北美、大洋五大洲××个国家培养了数千名留学生。近年来，国际交流学院在原来的基础上进行了合并组建，并且搬迁至学校西区新留学生楼，学习和生活环境得到极大的改善。与此同时，大学留学生教育类型增多、招生规模加大、承训能力变强，除原一年制船舶技术与管理专业8个方向之外，新增四年学制轮机工程、半年学制船舶设备保障与管理、船舶损管消防技术与船岸智能信息交互3个专业，同时也开办了研究生学历教育。我们欢迎各位留学生朋友回校深造，也欢迎大家推荐更多同胞来校学习。

留学生朋友们，2020年是不平凡的一年，新冠肺炎疫情在全球蔓延，给我们的国际教育交流合作和留学生学习生活造成了极大的影响。我们虽然位于中国疫情中心地区，但在中外人员的共同努力下，我们实现了全体留学生零感染的目标。在联手抗疫期间，我们收到许多往届留学生通过电话、微信、邮件等方式发来的关心和问候，我们深受感动。在此，我们想向所有关心、挂念、祝福我们的毕业留学生校友道一声感谢。同时，我也期待更多地了解你们的近况，希望与你们一起分享晋升、结婚、生子的喜悦，因为我们永远都是一家人。目前，我们正在建设留学生校友录，收集整理所有来校学习的留学生的近况，加强学校与各位留学生之间的联系。如条件允许，我们也将邀请大家再回母校看看，希望你们收到信函后及时与我们联系，也请向其他你们熟悉的同学转告此信。我们的对外联络电话是：××××××××，邮箱是：××××××@163.com。

最后，祝工作顺利，身体健康，家庭幸福！

Dear ×××,

We sincerely hope everything has been going well since you returned home. And we are amazed at how time flies and slips away while looking back on the wonderful moments that you impressed us. We know your fantastic contribution to your country has gained accolades in the professional world since you completed the course at our university.

Dear friend, since we developed international programs, we have fostered thousands of talents for ×× countries in Asia, Africa, South America, North America and Oceania. Over the past years, the previous College of International Exchange has reshuffled into a new one. We are now using a new building for international students in the west side of our campus, with much improved learning and living conditions. We are presently offering more education types in international programs than ever before, and student enrollment is increasing, claiming unprecedented international education capacity in history. Apart from the traditional one-year program—Ship Technology and Management, which offers eight courses, more programs are opened to international students, including a four-year Marine Engineering course, three six-month courses in Ship Equipment Support and Management, Ship Damage Control and Fire Fighting Technology, and Ship-to-shore Intelligent Information Interaction. Besides, postgraduate programs for international students are accessible. You are welcome to further advance your expertise at our university. And we believe you will be able to recommend the above-mentioned programs to more of your friends at home.

Dear friend, the year of 2020 was fraught with ups and downs. As is known to all, the COVID-19 virus has spread worldwide, wreaking havoc on the cooperation and exchange in international education and the study and living conditions of international students. Despite the fact that our university was located at the epicenter of the pandemic in China, through joint efforts of the Chinese staff and international students, we made our goal: there were zero infection cases from international students. During the period when we were fighting the pandemic together, we embraced a lot of greetings, words of consolation and encouragement from international students via phone calls, Wechat and email, which made us deeply moved. Hereby, we want to say thanks to all for your care, love and support. At the same time, we are looking forward to hearing from you, sharing the great moment when you are promoted in position, married and blessed with a baby. Please bear it in mind that we are family forever. Currently, to create an alumni book, we are updating the information of international students who once followed courses at our university, so as to strengthen the ties between our university and each of the international students, as well as boost the friendship between international students from different countries. If permitted, we would like to invite you to come back and visit the university. We hope you would contact us as soon as you receive this letter and pass the word to other graduates that you know. Please contact us at the number: ××××××××. Our e-mail is: ×××××@163. com.

Finally, wish you a success in work. May you enjoy happy family, stay safe and sound.

3.2.6 突发疫情形势下致在校学生的一封信 A Letter to International Students at the Pandemic Outbreak

各位留学生朋友们:

大家好!

2020 年春节,新冠肺炎疫情突如其来,谁也没有想到,我们会以这样的方式迎来新年。我们给大家安排的所有新年娱乐和文化体验活动都被迫取消了，武汉这么大一座城市万人空巷，我们彼此见面也都戴上了口罩……但城市封闭不会隔断彼此的关心，隔离病毒不会隔离爱，无论是坚守在国际交流学院和我们并肩作战的你们，还是已经结业返国的往届留学生们，大家都通过各种渠道向我们表达了关心、支持与鼓励。我们感谢大家对国际交流学院的关心与牵挂，也高度赞赏你们在疫情防控战斗中表现出来的良好个人素养。

我们当前最首要的任务就是内防发生、外防输入，所以学校和国际交流学院采取了封闭式管理，国际交流学院及时发布了通告信息，印发了防控手册，发放了防护用品，也给大家强调了很多注意事项，比如尽量不要离开国际交流学院，如有特殊情况应及时报告；出门戴口罩；勤用流动水洗手，洗手液在手上停留时间至少二十秒；保持房间干净和通风，用配发的消毒液给房间消毒；在餐厅就餐时分开就座，不要跟他人闲聊；自觉做到不串门、不聚集。国际交流学院每天会在电梯、餐厅等公共区域做好消毒工作，大家不要过于担心。同时为确保安全，即日起每日由值班留学生收集购物需求，每天下午四点由中方老师带领一名留学生代表去超市采购。需要强调的是，每日的体温检测要认真执行，如果有任何不舒服或者发现异常情况，请立刻向国际交流学院值班员或中方管理教师反映，我们会及时处理。以上这些要求大家一定要遵照执行，大家也要及时关注一楼大屏幕发布的有关通知。

我们了解到，随着疫情的发展，大家或多或少地会有一丝紧张或者担忧，在这场全面战"疫"面前，大家除了要做好身体上的防护外，还要重视打好心理战，不能让过度的焦虑影响身心的健康。现在网上各种信息层出不穷，也有很多不切实际的谣言，大家要学会甄别，多从央视、人民日报、长江日报等主流媒体获取消息，不要以讹传讹。中华民族是一个伟大的民族，武汉是一座英雄的城市，不论是"九八年抗洪"，还是"抗击冰雪灾害"，我们都不畏艰险，迎难而上，取得了最终胜利！现在，全国人民的目光都投向武汉，人力物力都集结武汉，习近平主席亲自部署疫情防控工作，李克强总理亲临武汉检查指导，中国人民解放军医疗队除夕夜紧急驰援，上演了"最美逆行"，这些带给我们的是勇气、信心和力量。大家也从新闻看到了，一周左右时间我们新建了两所医院——火神山医院和雷神山医院，并已经开始转运病人，这也算是一个奇迹了。我们相信，在大家的共同努力下，我们很快就能战胜这场疫情。学校目前各项防控工作也在有序展开，校内形势比较稳定，大家在这里是安全的。我们的假期将延长，具体开学时间要等待通知，大家要安排好自己的生活，鼓励大家进行单人室内锻炼，增强体质和抵抗力，鼓励大家多看书学习。

中国有句古话：上下同欲者胜。疫情防控是攻坚战、科普战，更是心理战、意志战，只要我们始终坚定信心、戮力同心、团结一心，只要我们每个人都有一颗向上、向善、向前的心，我们就一定能够击穿疫情的阴云，迎来胜利的曙光！

最后，祝您和家人身体健康、阖家幸福！

Dear friends,

None of us expected to see the arrival of the Chinese New Year 2020 with the sudden onslaught of COVID-19. All the recreational and cultural events we had planned for you had to be canceled. The bustling Chinese metropolis of Wuhan fell silent during those days. We had to wear masks when we met with each other... However, the city's shutdown may not cut off the care for each other and the block of virus may not prevent us from loving each other. You, along with us, fought the virus dauntlessly, and the graduates who had returned to their home countries, supported in our struggle with their care and encouragement via various channels. We really appreciate your concern for the College of International Exchange, as well as your professionalism demonstrated in the pandemic response.

At the moment, our paramount mission is to avoid pandemic out-break inside the university as well as imported infections from outside sources. Therefore, in response, the university and the College of International Exchange imposed the close-door management. Besides, we timely issued information and handed out booklet for pandemic prevention and control, distributed personal protective equipment and put emphasis on the following: leave the college building only when necessary; report immediately in special circumstances; wear masks when leaving your room; wash hands with running waters from time to time with sanitizer retaining on hands at least 20 seconds; keep your room clean and ventilate frequently; disinfect your room with the provided disinfectant; sit separately and do not converse with others when dining in the canteen; and the visit to others' rooms and gatherings are not permitted. We will disinfect public facilities such as the lift and the canteen on a daily basis, so please don't worry about the hygiene in those places. Meanwhile, to avoid health problems, as from today, the duty student will collect your grocery list on a daily basis. At 16:00 every day, the Chinese staff will accompany one of you to the grocery for shopping. One thing that should be mentioned is that all of you should monitor your body temperature seriously every day. If you feel physically uncomfortable or notice something wrong, please notify the Chinese duty staff or teachers right now. We will respond as quickly as possible to your information. Everyone must follow the guidelines outlined above. Furthermore, you should read the announcements broadcast on the first floor's television.

We have noticed that as the outbreak has progressed, you've become increasingly apprehensive or concerned. However, when faced with a virus war, you must not only protect yourself against infection, but also engage in psychological warfare to combat excessive anxiety, which has a negative impact on both your physical and mental health. A large amount of information about the virus, which is spreading at an alarming rate, as well as baseless words and rumors, appear on the Internet. You should learn to distinguish between the good and the evil. To avoid distributing misleading information, it is advised to rely on the mainstream media sources such as China Central Television, People's Daily and Yangtze River Daily. The Chinese nation is a great nation and Wuhan is a city of heroes. We have faced a variety of crises, including the catastrophic flood in 1998 and the unprecedented snow disaster in 2008. We fought fearlessly in the face of every disaster, winning battle after battle. Now, people throughout China are offering to help Wuhan. We have received professionals on all fronts and material resources for the viral war. The Chinese President Xi Jinping personally deployed the pandemic preventive and control strategy, while Premier Li Keqiang gave instructions during his inspection in Wuhan. The medical teams from PLA rushed to Wuhan on the eve of Chinese Spring Festival, being hailed as heroes in harms way. All of this has given us courage, confidence, and strength. You must have heard that two hospitals, Huoshenshan and Leishenshan, which have being built in just one week. They are now being utilized to receive patients with COVID-19. It can be considered a miracle to some extent. We believe, with the joint effort, we will eventually be able to defeat the virus. At the moment, the university has carried out the prevention and control response in a systematic manner. You are safe on campus because the situation is mostly stable. The winter vacation will be extended, and the exact start date of the second semester has not yet been determined. Please create good plans for your own life. It is recommended that you exercise alone in your room to improve your physique and immunity, and that you spend more time on self-study.

One old saying in China goes that success belongs to those who share. The battle against the pandemic is full of challenges, which requires the scientific approach as well as spiritual support that requires our willpower. We will undoubtedly rise from the doldrums and welcome the sunshine of victory as long as we have confidence, work together, unite as one, and are resolute to forge ahead in adversity.

Finally, I wish you and your family good health and happiness.

With best regards!

Yours Sincerely

3.2.7 "停课不停教，停课不停学""No Suspension of Teaching and Learning When School is Closed"

留学生朋友们：

你们好！疫情防控工作已进入攻坚期，学校和国际交流学院实行了严格的封闭式管理，最大限度地减少了病毒外来输入的风险。大家都积极调整生活习惯以适应这种特殊时期的生活，每天出门戴口罩、测体温，平时勤洗手、多通风，单人单间住宿，不串门、不聚集，就餐分时分批、一人一桌，生活必需品集中采购。目前，留学生身体状态良好，情绪稳定，学习生活秩序井然。

这里要感谢所有留学生及你们的国家、家人给予的理解、关心、支持和鼓励。最近，我们陆续收到多个国家往届留学生向学校和国际交流学院发来的问候，有的打电话询问情况，有的发来鼓励的话语和暖人的视频。同时，在校留学生也自发地集体撰写了《给大学领导的一封信》，感人肺腑、催人奋进。有的留学生还发挥特长，创作并演唱了歌曲《中外同心抗疫情》，这些都极大地鼓舞了我们，也坚定了我们国际交流学院全体师生与中国武汉、与学校一起战胜疫情的信念和决心。

最近，按照学校"停课不停教、停课不停学"的要求，为确保疫情防控期间教学进度和质量，促进留学生身心健康，我们利用网络平台和资源针对线上教学做了大量的准备工作，并对课程设置进行了相应调整。部分课程已经试行一段时间了，自×月开始全体留学生要同时进行多门课程学习。希望你们尽快阅读有关通知，熟悉课程安排，把手机、微信等设备和软件调试好，找到相应课程微信群或线上资源，保持良好的学习状态，做好预习、复习和授课笔记，按时提交作业，积极参与线上讨论、师生互动；同时，还要认真遵守上课期间的纪律和要求，不做与教学训练无关的事，更不能在房间睡觉或娱乐，国际交流学院将加强检查和抽查。请大家特别注意，按照《留学生教学管理规定》，每门课程最终成绩由终结性考核成绩（占 50%，疫情结束后择时安排）、课堂表现（占 20%）、到课情况（占 15%）、作业完成情况（占 15%）四部分组成。

最后，让我们中外同心、团结一致，共同战胜疫情！不久的将来，我们的生活将会恢复到往常的阳光快乐、健康舒适状态。

Dear friends,

The pandemic prevention and control response has reached a critical and decisive stage. Our university and the College of International Exchange have imposed stringent close-door management to reduce the likelihood of infection from outside sources. You have all adjusted to the new norms during this special period: wear masks when leaving your room; take your body temperature every day; wash your hands from time to time, keep your room clean and ventilate it frequently; live alone in the dorm; sit in separate tables and attend the canteen in different batches; hand over daily purchase to designated people; and don't visit other's rooms and attend gatherings. At the moment, all students are in good physical and mental state and lead an orderly life.

Here I want to thank all the international students, your countries, and family members for their understanding, care, support and encouragement. Recently, we have received greetings from previous students in various countries in a row. Some made a phone call to tell their concerns about the situation in Wuhan, while others supported us with their kind words and videos. Meanwhile, international students remaining on campus wrote *A Letter to the Authority of University A*, which touched us deeply in the heart and encouraged us to strive forward amid the pandemic. Some international students made good use of their talents, writing a song *Battle against the Epidemic with Joint Efforts by China and the International Community*. All this greatly boosted our spirit in the fight and strengthened the faith and commitment of college staff and international students to defeat the pandemic, together with Wuhan city and University A.

Recently, in accordance with the university's initiative of "no suspension of teaching and learning when school is closed", we have done tremendous work for online classes through the Internet platforms and resources while adjusting part of the subjects, to avoid compromise in class schedule and education quality during pandemic response, and to ensure students' physical and mental health. Students have attended online classes for several subjects. From MM, students will begin taking more online classes. I hope you will follow the instructions and learn about the online class schedule, install Wechat APP, join relevant Wechat group for online classes or online resources. I hope you will remain enthusiastic about learning, preview and review the lessons, take notes, finish all assignments and post them on time, and interact with group members in class. You must follow the class rules and requirements: do not do anything that is unrelated to teaching and training. Sleeping and leisure activities are forbidden during online learning. The college will conduct random inspections. According to *Education Management Regulations*, the subject grade is constituted of 50% of the final test paper (exam will take place after the pandemic control), 20% of class performance, 15% of attendance, and 15% of assignments.

Finally, let's fight together as one for the decisive victory. I believe that our lives will soon return to the good old days of happiness, health, and comfort.

3.2.8　致全校教职员工的一封信 A Letter to the University Faculty

近期，湖北武汉出现新冠肺炎疫情，全校上下都在积极开展疫情防控工作。学校按照统一部署要求，采取切实有效的措施开展疫情防控，目前各项防控工作正有序展开。

防控疫情，人人有责。为保障教职员工和广大学生的身体健康、生命安全，以自身安全稳定为武汉疫情防控做贡献，特向全校人员发出如下倡议：

一、把疫情防控作为当前最重要的任务，坚决贯彻习近平总书记重要指示精神，严格落实当地防控指挥部和学校防控工作部署要求，高度重视，坚定信心，严密防控。

二、对新冠肺炎病毒的致病力、传播力保持高度警惕，外出时必须佩戴口罩，勤通风，勤洗手，不串门，不聚餐，避免到公共场所和人多的地方去，从我做起，从每个卫生习惯做起，把每项防控措施落到实处。

三、严密落实省市人员交通管控和学校校园管理规定，严格门岗管理，严控人员进出，教育引导家属子女配合做好相关工作，共同维护校园安全环境。

四、校内人员如感身体不适或有发烧等症状，请按照人员分类管理和属地管理原则，第一时间向所属单位报告，及时就医就诊。离汉休假人员要自觉落实当地防控措施，及时报告情况。

五、科学理性对待疫情防控，做到不造谣、不信谣、不传谣，凝聚正能量，振奋精气神，保持正规有序的值班执勤和工作秩序。

我们坚信，有党中央的坚强领导，有当地政府和医护人员的立体防治，有全校同志的严密防范，我们必能万众一心、众志成城，打赢这场疫情防控战。

最后，祝大家新春快乐，身体健康，阖家幸福！

甲大学

年　月　日

Recently, our university has taken a proactive approach to fight the COVID-19 pandemic. Effective efforts have been put in place to prevent the spread of the virus in accordance with the guidelines. We are currently carrying out the epidemic prevention and control response in a systematic manner.

Everyone bears his share of the responsibility in the pandemic response. The city will be safe if everyone is safe and healthy. To protect each of us against viral attack, we would like to propose the following initiatives:

1. The pandemic response is taken as the paramount mission at present. We will steadfastly follow General Secretary Xi Jinping's instructions and put in place local government and university prevention and control measures. We will prioritize pandemic response instructions and proceed with confidence in an intense response.

2. Be vigilant against the virus's virulence and transmissibility. Wear a mask while leaving your house; ventilate your house regularly; wash your hands frequently; do not drop by other people's houses; do not gather for meals and avoid crowds and public places. Each of us should follow the guidelines and develop a hygiene habit for the pandemic response, in order to implement all of the preventative and control measures.

3. Strictly adhere to the Wuhan government's traffic control regulations as well as the university's administration requirements. We shall have control over the exit and entry points at the university gates. Please encourage your family members to assist us in our efforts to create a safe campus environment.

4. At our university, we classify people based on their category and place of residence. If you have health problems or a fever at the universi-

ty, please report to your work units and see a doctor as soon as possible. Those on leave outside of Wuhan should follow the local pandemic response and, if necessary, notify their situation.

5. In the pandemic response, we should take a scientific approach. We should also avoid starting, following, or spreading rumors. We must collaborate in upbeat spirit and raise our morale in order to maintain a standard and orderly working environment.

We are confident that, with the strong leadership of the CPC central committee, the multi-dimensional protection of the local government and medics, and our university's pandemic response, we will be able to unite as one in the fight against the pandemic and win the war.

Finally, I wish you all happiness and good health. Happy New Year!

University A

DD/MM/YY

3.3　行为规范 Conduct Code

3.3.1　一日生活制度 Daily Regime

1. 起床。正常工作日(一般为周一至周六)上午 06:30 起床, 遇周日或中国法定节假日可推迟至 07:00。

2. 就餐。正常工作日就餐时间分别是早上 07:10、中午 12:10、晚上 17:30。

3. 上课。留学生应提前 10 分钟到达指定教室准备上课。仅遇到以下情况, 可不参加上课:

(1)遇所在国重大节假日, 经书面申请, 并报请批准。

(2)患病, 凭学校门诊部病假条, 并经书面申请。

4. 自习。正课时间如没有安排课程, 留学生应在指定教室或宿舍内进行自习。

5. 午休。午休时间留学生应在宿舍内原地休息，保持肃静，不得影响他人。

6. 体育锻炼。自行前往健身房或田径场进行锻炼。

7. 会客。留学生在上课时间不得会客。课余时间可会见来访人员，来访人员不得在校内留宿。

8. 就寝。熄灯前半小时，留学生应回到自己宿舍准备就寝。熄灯铃响后，留学生应抓紧时间就寝，不准从事娱乐活动或影响他人休息。

表3.3　作息时间表

内　容	时　间
早上	
起床	06:30
打扫卫生	06:40—06:55
早餐	07:10—07:30
第一节课	08:10—08:55
第二节课	09:05—09:50
课间休息	09:50—10:15
第三节课	10:15—11:00
第四节课	11:10—11:55
午餐	12:10—12:50
中午	
午休	12:50—14:10
第五节课	14:30—15:15
第六节课	15:25—16:10
体育锻炼	16:30—17:25
晚餐	17:30—18:10

内　　容	时　　间
晚上	
自由活动	18:20—19:00
晚自习	19:00—19:45
晚自习	19:55—20:40
洗漱	21:50—22:20
就寝	22:20—22:30
熄灯	23:00

1. Getting up. From Monday to Saturday, international students should rise at 06:30; on Sundays and Chinese holidays, time to get up might be delayed until 07:00.

2. Food. Meals are planned at 07:10 for breakfast, 12:10 for lunch, and 17:30 for dinner on working days.

3. Classes. Students should arrive 10 minutes early in class. Students are only permitted to miss lessons in the following circumstances:

(1) During the important holidays in the home country of the international students. Students should submit an application to the College of International Exchange to acquire prior approval.

(2) On sick leave. To gain approval, students must submit an application along with a sick leave note from the university hospital.

4. Study session on your own. If no classes are scheduled during the class periods, students should study in designated classrooms or dormitories.

5. Break for lunch. Students should stay in their dormitories and re-

frain from doing anything that would disturb others.

6. Physical activities. International students are welcome to work out in gyms or on the training grounds.

7. Guests. During class, international students are not permitted to meet with guests. In their spare time, they may meet with visitors. Visitors should not, however, spend the night on campus.

8. Bedtime. Students should return to their rooms 30 minutes before the lights go off. Students are not permitted to disrupt others by engaging in recreational activities after the bell for lights-out has rung.

Table 3.3 Daily Schedule

Events	Time
Morning	
Getting up	06:30
Washing & Cleaning	06:40—06:55
Breakfast	07:10—07:30
The First Class	08:10—08:55
The Second Class	09:05—09:50
Break	09:50—10:15
The Third Class	10:15—11:00
The Fourth Class	11:10—11:55
Lunch	12:10—12:50
Afternoon	
Lunch Break	12:50—14:10
The Fifth Class	14:30—15:15
The Sixth Class	15:25—16:10
The Sports Time	16:30—17:25
Supper	17:30—18:10

Continued

Events	Time
Evening	
Liberty	18:20—19:00
Self-Study Session A	19:00—19:45
Self-Study Session B	19:55—20:40
Washing	21:50—22:20
Bedtime	22:20—22:30
Light-Out	23:00

3.3.2 着装及举止 Dress Code and Etiquette

1. 留学生进入教室、图书馆等教学场所，着装须规范得体。男士不得着背心、短裤、拖鞋等；女士不得穿吊带裙、超短裙、拖鞋等。参加中方组织的重大活动时，按通知要求着装。如遇本国重大节日，经报备国际交流学院，可着本国礼服。

2. 留学生在公共场所应当举止端正，保持良好的个人形象和仪容，着装整齐干净。不准背手和将手插入衣袋；不准边走边吸烟、吃东西；不得随地吐痰、乱扔垃圾；不准赤背、赤脚或穿拖鞋。

3. 留学生离开校园时，应当遵守公共秩序和交通规则，不准聚集街头、追逐打闹、高声喧哗，不准携带违禁物品。乘坐车、船和飞机时，要按秩序上下，不准争抢座位，提倡主动给老人、幼儿、孕妇和伤、病、残人员让座。

4. 留学生称呼中方领导和教师时，通常称××教授或副教授，或者××老师。

1. When entering educational facilities such as classrooms and libraries, international students should dress appropriately. Male students may

not wear vests, shorts, or slippers; female students may not wear braces, miniskirts, or slippers. When attending important events organized by the Chinese side, international students should dress appropriately. Additionally, students may wear national ceremonial clothing with permission from the College of International Exchange during their home country's important festivals.

2. International students should keep a professional demeanor and a positive personal image, while dressing properly. In public places, hands behind the back or in pockets are not recommended. Smoking or eating while walking is not recommended, as is spitting or litering in public. Being barebacked, barefooted, or wearing slippers is not permitted in public areas.

3. While off campus, intermational students should observe public order and traffic rules, and refrain from participating in street gatherings, horseplay, or making loud noises. Get on and off cars, boats, and airplanes in an orderly manner and do not compete for seats. Seats should be reserved for the elderly, minors, pregnant women, the injured, the sick, and the crippled.

4. When addressing Chinese leaders and lecturers, please refer to them by their academic titles or by their surnames.

3.3.3　场所管理制度 Facility Management Regulations

留学生教室管理规定

一、授课教师是教室秩序和管理的第一责任人，应根据学校有关规定进行全面管理。

二、教室内应保持安静，不准喧哗、打闹，严禁做与学习无关的事情。

三、教室内不得随地吐痰、吸烟、乱丢杂物，不得以任何形式破坏墙壁和其他设施，不得随意在桌椅、黑板等一切公用设施上乱涂乱画。

四、教室内的课桌椅和电教设备不得随意挪动或搬出。严禁随意损坏多媒体设备、教具、黑板等教学设施和窗帘、衣帽钩、玻璃等公用物品。

五、值班留学生要及时打扫教室卫生，保证室内地面无杂物，桌椅排列整齐，黑板擦拭干净。

六、严禁带充电宝等易燃易爆电子产品到教室充电、使用。

七、离开教室时，要及时将灯、电扇、空调、门窗等关闭。

八、未经许可，不得拍照或录像、录音。

九、留学生应于上课前 5 分钟进入教室，保持肃静，准备好学习用品。按时上下课，不得迟到、早退或旷课。上、下课时，值班留学生向任课教师报告到课人数、缺课人数及原因。

十、留学生应严格遵守课堂纪律，专心听讲。如须向任课教师提问，应先举手示意。

Classroom Management Regulations

Ⅰ. The first person in charge of classroom management is the instructor. He/She should oversee classroom management in all aspects.

Ⅱ. The classroom is a tranquil environment where actions like shouting, chasing, and horseplay are prohibited. Activities unrelated to coursework are not permitted.

Ⅲ. Students are not permitted to spit, smoke, eat, or litter in classrooms, nor are they permitted to damage walls or facilities, nor are they permitted to doodle on any facilities such as desks, chairs, or blackboards.

Ⅳ. It is not permitted to move or relocate desks, seats, or equipment. Damage to facilities such as multi-media equipment, tools, blackboards, and public resources such as curtains, coat hooks, and windows is prohibited.

V. Duty students should tidy classrooms to maintain the floor clean, align desks and chairs, and clear the chalkboard.

VI. It is forbidden to charge and use power banks in classrooms, as well as to bring other flammable and dangerous e-devices inside classrooms.

VII. Before leaving classrooms, turn off the lights, fans, and air conditioning, and shut the windows and doors.

VIII. Students should not take photos, films, or audio recordings in class unless they have permission.

IX. Students should arrive 5 minutes early for class. Keep quiet and be prepared for class. Do not arrive late, leave early, or skip classes. When class begins and ends, the duty student should inform the lecturer of the number of students present and absent, as well as the reasons for absence.

X. Students must strictly adhere to classroom discipline and pay close attention in class. When approaching the instructor with questions, please raise your hand.

留学生电子教室管理规定

一、使用电子教室必须遵守《中华人民共和国计算机信息网络国际互联网管理暂行规定》《中华人民共和国计算机信息网络国际互联网安全保护管理办法》有关规定。严禁利用国际互联网从事危害中国国家安全、扰乱社会治安等犯罪活动，严禁利用国际互联网查阅、复制和传播淫秽、色情信息；严禁利用国际互联网从事恶意攻击、病毒传播、信息窃取、人身攻击等非法网络活动。对于违反以上规定者，电子教室管理人员有权取消其上机资格，并按中国政府有关规定和大学管理制度严处。

二、未经许可，不得在电子教室使用自带移动存储设备(U 盘、移动硬盘、MP3 等)。个人需存储下载文件，请将文件设置为共享，由管理教师将下载文件刻录至光盘。

三、爱护电子教室内的各种设备和电子资料，不得私自挪动电脑及其附属设施，不得私自安装和删除各种程序和文件。出现故障，应及时向管理教师报告。如发生人为损坏情况，照价赔偿。

四、电子教室内的各种设备和各种电子资料仅供留学生在本教室内阅览，概不外借。

五、电子教室内应保持安静，不准喧哗、打闹，使用耳机时请控制音量，以免影响他人。

六、要按指定位置就坐，使用相应的计算机，并进行使用登记。

Regulations for E-classrooms

Ⅰ. Comply with *China's Provisional Regulations for the Management of the Internet of the Computer Information Network* and *China's Security Regulations for the Management of the Internet of the Computer Information Network* when you are in the electronic classroom. The illegal activities such as compromising the national security of China and jeopardizing the public order are strictly prohibited. Searching, reviewing, copying and distributing pornography and obscene information are not allowed. Intentional attack, virus spread, information theft, personal calumniation and other illegal network activities are prohibited. Those who violate the above regulations will be driven away from the classroom and severely punished by the Chinese government as well as the university.

Ⅱ. Personal storage devices, such as USB drive, removable hard disk and MP3, are not allowed to use in the electronic classroom without permission. If you want to save the downloaded files, please set the files as "shared" and ask the administrator to save your files to a CD.

III. Take good care of all the equipment and electronic resources. Do not move the computers and the accessories, nor install or remove any programs or files without permission. If you discover any issues, please notify the administrator. Any damage to classroom equipment should be compensated

IV. All the equipment and electronic resources in the electronic classroom are intended for use exclusively in the classroom and should not be borrowed for use outside of the classroom.

V. Keep quiet in the classroom. Do not yell, scream or make any other kind of noise. Use earphones and control your volume to avoid disturbing others.

VI. Take your designated seat to utilize the assigned computer. Keep a log for your usage.

留学生实验室管理规定

一、实验室是重要的教学场所，参加实验的人员必须自觉遵守实验室的各项规定。

二、要爱护实验室的一切设施，不准随意动用与本实验无关的其他仪器设备，遇到事故要采取紧急措施，并及时报告实验室管理教师。

三、要严格按照操作规程使用仪器设备，在设备运行时，操作人员必须坚守岗位，不准擅自离开。

四、要服从实验室管理教师的管理，对违反操作规程或实验室规则不听劝告者，实验室管理教师有权进行干预直至令其停止实验。对违章操作造成事故者要追究责任。

五、实验室的设备、器材要严格进行登记。

六、教学器材和设备如发生损坏、丢失，应及时报告，查明原因，并按相应规定认真处理。

七、实验室内应保持安静，不准喧哗、打闹和做与实验无关的事情。

八、保持实验室清洁卫生，不准在实验室内吐痰、吸烟、吃零食、乱丢脏物，不得以任何形式破坏墙壁。

九、实验结束应进行安全检查，要断开电源、气源、水源，关好门窗。

Regulations for Laboratories

Ⅰ. Laboratories are important educational facilities. Any people in laboratories must follow all the rules and regulations herein.

Ⅱ. Take good care of all the equipment in laboratories. Do not touch or operate instruments and equipment unrelated to your experiment. Take emergency actions for any accidents and report to the laboratory administrator immediately.

Ⅲ. Strictly follow the operation procedures to use instruments and equipment. The operator should not be absent when the machine is functioning.

Ⅳ. Strictly follow the laboratory administrator's instructions. The laboratory administrator has the authority to interfere or halt the experiment of anyone who violates operation procedures or laboratory regulations in defiance of the administrator's warning. The person who violates regulations should indemnify the laboratory for any damage caused by him/her.

Ⅴ. All the equipment and materials in the laboratory should be documented.

Ⅵ. Any damage or loss of instructional equipment or laboratory supplies should be reported immediately for investigation of the causes.

Ⅶ. Keep quiet in the laboratory. Do not shout, scream, make noise or do anything unrelated to experiments.

Ⅷ. Keep the laboratory clean and tidy. Do not spit, smoke, eat or litter in the laboratory. Do not cut, scratch or write on walls.

Ⅸ. Safety inspection should be performed at the end of the experiment. Be sure to turn off the power supply, gas and water and close doors and windows.

3.3.4　值班制度 Duty System

一、国际交流学院设总值班、副总值班、留学生学生会主席、副主席、年级长、班长、文体委员、后勤委员、留学生领队等留学生日常事务管理与值班岗位。

二、总值班由中方值班教师担任，代表学校和国际交流学院负责留学生各项事务的管理。

三、副总值班即留学生值班员，隶属中方值班教师管理，由留学生骨干轮流担任，交接班每周组织一次。留学生值班员职责为：

1. 值班期间，协助中方教师管理全体留学生，检查和维护留学生一周的学习、训练、作息和安全秩序，填写周值班登记本。

2. 负责全体留学生就餐、上课、体育锻炼、会议时的人员召集、人数清点。

3. 受理留学生领队申请和情况报告，并及时汇总向中方值班教师报告，传达中国值班教师信息。

4. 组织周交班点名，讲评值班期间的各项情况。

5. 协助中方安排好留学生的伙食、参观和节假日生活。

6. 完成中方人员交付的其他工作。

四、每个年级设 1 或 2 名年级长。入学之初，国际交流学院指定正、副年级长各 1 名。入学一个月进行民主竞选。每半年进行一次换届竞选。其职责为：

1. 协助国际交流学院管理本年级留学生，维护日常的学习和生活秩序，落实安全措施，预防各类事故的发生。

2. 组织本年级留学生认真学习专业理论知识，积极配合任课教师维护教学秩序，努力完成学业。

3. 组织本年级留学生认真遵守《留学生行政管理规定》和《留学生教学管理规定》，带领本年级留学生养成良好的作风纪律和学习生活习惯。

4. 熟悉本年级人员情况，了解掌握所属留学生的思想和心理状况，关心同学，增强团结。

5. 组织本年级留学生积极开展体育锻炼和文化娱乐活动。

五、文体委员入学之初，由国际交流学院从有文体特长的留学生中指定。入学一个月进行民主竞选。每半年进行一次换届竞选。职责：

1. 协助国际交流学院开展全体留学生的日常文化、体育、娱乐活动。

2. 制订每学期的文化体育活动计划，组织开展形式多样的文化体育活动和比赛，积极鼓励留学生参加体育锻炼。

3. 组织全体留学生积极参加国际交流学院组织的相关文艺演出和比赛。

六、入学之初，由国际交流学院从各班留学生中指定班长 1 名。入学一个月进行民主竞选。每半年进行一次换届竞选。其职责为：

1. 值班期间，认真填写留学生到课记录本，负责向任课教师报告。

2. 协助任课教师维护课堂秩序，督促留学生完成好课后作业。

3. 定期向中方值班教师和任课教师报告留学生学习情况，提出合理建议，协商解决存在的问题。

七、留学生数超过 2 人(含)的国家可推荐 1 名资历最高的留学生，经国际交流学院批准同意后担任留学生领队；对于留学生数少于 2 人的国家，由国际交流学院根据语言、国别地域、宗教习俗相近的原则指定部分资历较高的留学生担任留学生领队。留学生领队隶属中方值班教师、留学生值班员管理。留学生领队对所属留学生管理负主要责任，其职责为：

1. 协助中方值班教师、留学生值班员对所属留学生实施管理，督促其自觉遵守各项规定，教育指导其服从中方值班教师和留学生值班员管理，发现违规现象或问题立即纠正。

2. 检查和维护所属留学生的学习、训练、作息和安全秩序。

3. 掌握所属留学生动态、去向，每天就寝前检查留学生在位情况并向留学生值班员报告。

4. 定期向中方值班教师和留学生值班员报告所属留学生的学习、生活情况，提出合理建议，协商解决存在的问题。如遇突发事件随时报告。

5. 担任留学生值班员时履行其相关职责。

6. 完成中方教师交付的其他工作。

Ⅰ. The College of International Exchange has established a duty system that includes positions such as chief duty staff, deputy duty staff, chairman of the International Students Union, vice chairman of the International Students Union, senior prefect, class prefect, recreation & sports secretary, logistics secretary, and country group leader to manage the affairs of international students.

Ⅱ. Teachers of the College of International Exchange serve as chief duty staff, managing student affairs on behalf of the University and the College.

Ⅲ. The on-duty student serves as the Chinese duty staff's deputy, reporting to the Chinese duty staff. On a weekly basis, students in the authority team serve as duty students. The duty rotation is scheduled once a week. The following are the responsibilities of duty students:

1. Assist Chinese duty staff with student management. Inspect and maintain the order and safety of the students in their education, training, and living. And don't forget to fill up the log book.

2. Manage activities such as meals, classes, and physical training. When there is a meeting, the organizer is the duty student who is in charge of calling in fellow students and checking the number.

3. Submit country group leaders' briefing and applications to the Chinese duty instructor as soon as possible and give feedback to country group leaders.

4. Organize a weekly meeting on the occasion of duty transfer to discuss the week's events.

5. Assist the Chinese staff with food, visits and holiday celebrations.

6. Perform any other tasks delegated by the Chinese staff.

Ⅳ. Each grade/class sets one or two senior prefects. The College of International Exchange appoints one senior prefect and one deputy prefect during the enrollment period. A month following enrollment, a running campaign for the posts stated above begins. Every six months, students in authority are elected. Their responsibilities are as follows:

1. Assist the College of International Exchange in managing students belonging to the same grade/class. Maintain order in study, exercise, and daily life. Take precautions to avoid accidents.

2. Supervise and encourage fellow students to work diligently to acquire professional knowledge and to collaborate with teachers to preserve classroom order.

3. Provide directions to fellow students regarding the rules of *Administration of International Students Regulations* and *Education Management Regulations for International Students*. Take the initiative to follow the discipline and build healthy living habits.

4. Prefects must be familiar with their fellow students on all levels and get an understanding of their opinions and attitudes. Additionally,

take care of them and foster a sense of community.

5. Organize physical training and leisure events.

Ⅴ. During the enrollment period, the College of International Exchange appoints students with athletic and artistic talent as recreation and sports secretaries. The college arranges the election for the aforementioned position one month after enrollment. Every six months, students in authority are elected. Their responsibilities are as follows:

1. Assist the College of International Exchange in organizing cultural, sporting, and recreational events.

2. Create a semester-long strategy for cultural, sports, and recreational events, organize a variety of leisure activities and sports games, and encourage their fellow students to participate in sports.

3. Encourage their fellow students to take part in performances and games put on by the College of International Exchange.

Ⅵ. The College of International Exchange appoints one prefect for each class throughout the enrolling period. The college arranges the election for the aforementioned position one month after enrollment. Students in authority are elected every six months. Their duties are as follows:

1. Complete the attendance log book and report to teachers in class.

2. Work with teachers to maintain classroom order. Supervise and encourage other students to do after-class work.

3. Report international students' situation in coursework on a regular basis to Chinese duty staff and lecturers. Offer constructive suggestions and solve problems through negotiation.

Ⅶ. Countries with two or more students may recommend members with the highest seniority as country group leaders and the recommendation should be approved by the college authority. Additionally, for nations with fewer than two students, the college administration assigns group leaders with the higher seniority according to their linguistic, geographic, and religious characteristics. The group leaders are responsible for their respective nation groups and report to the Chinese duty staff and the duty student. Their responsibilities include the following:

1. Assist the Chinese duty teacher and the duty student in managing students from the same country groups and supervise them to make sure they are following the rules. Give directives to their fellow students on how to follow the management of the Chinese duty teacher and the duty student. Correct infractions and misbehavior as soon as they are discovered.

2. Examine and uphold the rules governing their fellow students' studies, physical training, living arrangements, and safety.

3. Ascertain the whereabouts of fellow students. Verify the number of the international students in dormitories and report to the duty student before bedtime.

4. Inform Chinese duty staff and duty students on a frequent basis about their fellow students' academic and living situations. Offer constructive suggestions and solve problems through negotiation. In the event of an emergency, report immediately.

5. Assume appropriate obligations while serving as a duty student.

6. Assume any other responsibilities allocated by the Chinese staff.

3.3.5 请假制度 Requesting Leave

留学生外出，必须按级请假，按时返回；未经批准不得外出。外出期间的各种费用全部自理，安全自负。

1. 上课时间内，无特殊事由不得请假。如确有特殊情况，须由本人申请，经留学生领队和中方管理教师同意后，方可外出。

2. 请假外出必须在当日 22:00 前返回。确有特殊情况无法按时返回的，应在 21:30 前向中方管理教师续假；返回后，及时向中方管理教师报告。

3. 一般情况下不允许请假离开所在城市或在校外留宿。如确有特殊情况，待学校和国际交流学院批准后方可成行。

4. 利用中国法定节假日或寒暑假外出旅游或回国休假，待大学和国际交流学院批准后方可成行，各种费用自理，安全自负。

Before leaving campus, international students should obtain permission from the college authorities at various levels and return on time. It is not permitted to leave without obtaining permission. When staying outside, students should bear all the expenses themselves and be responsible for their own safety.

1. Except in special circumstances, it is not permissible to request leave during class periods. Before going out in the event of unusual circumstances, students are expected to submit an application and obtain prior approval from the group leader and the Chinese teacher in authority.

2. Students must return by 22:00 on the same day. Those who are unable to return on time due to unforeseen circumstances should report to the Chinese teacher in authority before 21:30 for an extension, and report to the Chinese teacher in authority upon return.

3. Generally, requests to leave the residence for other locations or to spend the night outside will be denied. Students may depart for their destinations or continue as scheduled in exceptional situations, with the approval of the university and the college.

4. With the approval of the university and the college, students may depart for their destinations or return to their home countries on vacation

during Chinese holidays or winter and summer breaks. When students stay outside, they are responsible for their own expenses and safety.

3.3.6　留学生生活指南 Daily Life Guidance

甲大学留学生生活指南

一、武汉概况

(一)城市概貌

武汉,湖北省省会,简称"汉",俗称"江城",位于中国中部、湖北省东部、长江与汉江交汇处,是国家历史文化名城、中国中部地区的中心城市和全国重要的工业基地、科教基地和综合交通枢纽,地理位置为北纬29°58′~31°22′,东经113°41′~115°05′。在平面直角坐标上,武汉市东西最大横距 134 千米,南北最大纵距约 155 千米,形如一只自西向东翩翩起舞的彩蝶。长江、汉江纵横交汇通过市区,形成了武昌、汉口、汉阳三镇鼎立的格局,通称武汉三镇。全市土地面积 8569.15 平方千米,城区面积812.39 平方千米。至 2020 年 11 月 1 日零时,全市常住人口为 12 326 518人。

武汉具有 3500 年建城史,历史文化悠久。武汉号称"九省通衢",不仅是长江黄金水道与京广铁路大动脉的十字交汇处,同时也是全国四大铁路枢纽中心之一、六大航空枢纽之一。随着多条高铁的开通,武汉至北京、上海、广州、香港、成都等地的交通时间缩短至 5 小时左右。武汉高校众多,在校大学生超过 110 万人,是中国乃至世界在校大学生人数最多的城市。

武汉属于亚热带湿润季风气候,春季温暖湿润,秋季天高气爽,四季分明。年平均降雨量为 800~1600 毫米,年平均气温为 18~22℃。每月平均气温情况参见表 3.4。

表 3.4　武汉月平均气温

月份	1 月	2 月	3 月	4 月	5 月	6 月
平均气温	3℃	5℃	10℃	16℃	21℃	26℃
月份	7 月	8 月	9 月	10 月	11 月	12 月
平均气温	29℃	28℃	22℃	16℃	10℃	5℃

(二)旅游景点

武汉旅游资源丰富，景色优美。市区有位列于江南三大名楼之首的黄鹤楼，国家级风景区东湖，以五百罗汉、玉佛及悠久历史著称的归元禅寺和古琴台等名胜古迹。

黄鹤楼毗邻长江，是中国 5A 级风景区，享有"天下绝景"的盛誉，与湖南岳阳楼、江西滕王阁并称为中国的"江南三大名楼"。黄鹤楼传说是为了军事目的而建，至唐朝，其军事性质逐渐褪化，演变为著名的名胜景点，历代文人墨客到此游览，留下不少脍炙人口的诗篇，使黄鹤楼名声大噪。由于战火频繁，黄鹤楼屡建屡废。1981 年 10 月，黄鹤楼重修工程破土开工，1985 年 6 月落成。从楼的纵向看，各层排檐与楼名直接有关，形如黄鹤，展翅欲飞。整座楼在雄浑之中又不失精巧，富于变化的韵味和美感。

东湖位于武汉市之东，是国家重点风景名胜区。整个风景区面积 88 平方千米，规划建设范围 73 平方千米，约占市区面积的四分之一，是武汉市最大的风景游览地。秀丽的山水、丰富的植物、浓郁的楚风情和别致的园中园，是东湖风景区的四大特色。

归元寺坐落在汉阳区翠微路西侧，是武汉市著名景点和最具代表性的寺庙。清顺治十五年(1658 年)，由高僧白光、主峰创建。禅寺取名"归元"，出自佛经《楞严经》："归元无二路，方便有多门。"归元即归真，就是超出生灭之界，还归于真寂本源的意思。

武汉长江大桥于 1957 年 10 月 15 日建成并通车，它是连接长江南北的第一座大桥。武汉长江大桥是公路、铁路两用桥，分两层（上层公路、下层铁路），全长 1670 米。

武汉景点分类如下：

名胜古迹系列：古琴台、长春观。

楚文化系列：湖北省博物馆、武汉市博物馆。

自然风光系列：木兰山风景区、木兰湖生态旅游区。

休闲娱乐系列：武汉森林野生动物园、新世界水族公园、东湖鸟语林、东湖海洋世界、武汉极地海洋世界。

都市文化系列：武汉江滩风光带、楚河汉街、中山公园、长江二桥、龟山电视塔、武汉国际会展中心。

绿色生态系列：武汉植物园、武汉动物园、马鞍山森林公园。

时尚购物系列：江汉路步行街、汉正街、武汉广场、楚河汉街。

Guidance for International Students' Daily Life

Ⅰ. Wuhan's Profile

A. General Picture of Wuhan City

Wuhan, also known as Jiangcheng (River City) and Han, is located in the eastern Hubei province of central China, near the confluence of the Yangtze River and Han River. Wuhan, the capital city of Hubei province, is renowned for its rich history and culture. Furthermore, it is considered a central city in China's central area, as well as an important industrial base, research and education center, and an interconnected transit hub. The coordinates are 113°41 ~ 115°05 East Longitude, 29°58 ~ 31°22 North Latitude. The metropolis looks like a colorful butterfly fluttering from west to east in the grid coordinates, spanning 134 kilometers in horizontal space and 155 kilometers in longitudinal distance. The Yangtze River and Han River converge in downtown Wuhan, splitting the city into three sections: Hankou, Hanyang, and Wuchang, together known as the Three Towns of Wuhan. The city has an area of 8569. 15 square kilometers, with an established area of 812. 39 square kilometers, and a permanent population of 12, 326, 518 as of November 1, 2020.

Wuhan is a city with a 3, 500-year history and culture that has long been known as the "thoroughfare to nine provinces" at the crossing of the Yangtze River's golden passage and the main artery of the Jingguang Railway (Beijng to Guangzhou), while also serving as a transportation hub for four major railways and six major airlines. With the expansion of high-speed trains, travel time from Wuhan to a number of cities including Beijing, Shanghai, Guangzhou, Hong Kong and Chengdu, has been cut to around 5 hours. It is home to universities with over 1. 1 million students enrolled, making it the city with the highest enrollment of university students in both China and the world.

Wuhan has a subtropical humid monsoon climate that is warm and moist in spring and clear and pleasant in autumn. There is a notable difference between the four seasons. The yearly average rainfall is between 800 and 1600 mm, while the annual average temperature is between 18 and 22℃. For your convenience, the monthly average temperature is provided below.

Table 3. 4   Monthly Average Temperature

Month	Jan.	Feb.	Mar.	Apr.	May.	Jun.
Average Temp.	3℃	5℃	10℃	16℃	21℃	26℃
Month	Jul.	Aug.	Sept.	Oct.	Nov.	Dec.
Average Temp.	29℃	28℃	22℃	16℃	10℃	5℃

B. Tourism

Wuhan is rich in tourism resources, and picturesque landscapes. There are famous scenic spots and historic resorts in downtown, including the Yellow Crane Tower, which is the No. 1 of the three famous towers in Jiangman (south of the Yangtze River), East Lake (a national scenic spot), Guiyuan Temple with a time-honored history known for its five hundred skillfully sculptured arhatstatues and the Jade Buddha, and Guqintai, where Chinese old geniuses developed friendship by performing the melody "I meet with my bosom buddies despite the high mountains and rivers".

The Yellow Crane Tower is located adjacent to the Yangtze River and is a National 5A Scenic Spot. It has earned a reputation for having "second to none" scenery and is one of the three famous towers in south of the Yangtze River, the other two being Yueyang Tower in Hunan province and Tengwang Pavilion in Jiangxi province. According to the folklore, the Yellow Crane Tower was constructed to allow the acient army to observe the enemies. With the transition of dynasties, the tower developed into a renowned scenic attraction in the Tang Dynasty, with the military aspect fading away. Numerous literatus visited this location in ancient times and composed hundreds of poems in admiration of the majestic tower, earning the tower a prestigious name. Many conflicts had devastated the tower over the years, and it had been rebuilt again and again. The current tower is a total restoration that began in October 1981 and was completed in June 1985. The tower's eaves are designed like the wings of a crane extending to fly high. The spectacular style incorporates the ever-lasting aesthetic appeal into the tower's delicate construction.

East Lake is a national scenic resort located to the east of Wuhan. With a size of 88 square kilometers and a planned construction area of 73 square kilometers, it has become the largest scenic spot in Wuhan, accounting for one-quarter of the city's total area. It is mainly comprised of four elements: gorgeous mountains and rivers, an abundance of botanical diversity, a rich traditional culture in Hubei, and unique gardens.

Guiyuan Temple, a popular scenic place and the most representative temple in Wuhan, is located in District Hanyang to the west of Cuiwei Road. The temple was built during the reign of Emperor Shunzhi in the early Qing Dynasty (1658) by two master monks named Baiguang and Zhufeng. The word Guiyuan translates as "return to primordial purity". The term is derived from the *Surangama Sutra*, which states that "with purity retained in mind, one has the thoroughfare everywhere".

Wuhan Yangtze River Bridge was completed and opened to traffic on 15 October, 1957. It is the first bridge across the Yangtze River, connecting the north and south banks. It is a double-deck, rail (upper deck) and highway (lower deck) bridge across the Yangtze River with a total length of 1,670 meters.

For your convenience, the category guide is as follows:

Scenic Spots and Historic Resorts: Guqintai, and Changchun Temple.

Chu Culture: Hubei Provincial Museum, and Wuhan City Museum.

Natural Scenery: Mulan Mountain Scenic Area, and Mulan Lake Eco-tourism Area.

Relaxation: Wuhan Wild Animal Zoo, New World Aquarium, East Lake Bird Forest, East Lake Aquatic World, and Wuhan Polar Ocean World.

City Life: Beach of Yangtze River, Chu River Han Street, Zhongshan Park, Second Yangtze River Bridge, Tortoise Hill TV Tower, and Wuhan International Exhibition Center.

Go Green：Wuhan Botanical Garden，Wuhan Zoo，and Ma'anshan Forest Park

Shopping：Jianghanlu Pedestrain Street，Hanzhengjie Market，Wuhan Plaza，and Chu River Han Street

二、日常生活提示

留学生由大学统一安排住宿，不得自行调换房间或在校园外租住。留学生须在入住一个月内交纳 500 元人民币作为宿舍及室内设施物品使用押金；毕业离校前经检查无物品丢失或损坏，将全额予以退还。要注意爱护宿舍的各种设施、设备，如损坏或丢失，须照价赔偿。

1. 室内各类物品要本着整洁、有序、方便生活的原则统一定点摆放。不得随意增加、拆除、移动宿舍内的电气设备及大型家具。

2. 严禁在宿舍使用酒精炉、煤油炉、电炉、电磁炉等用火、用电设备加工食物、取暖。因违反规定引起火灾等事故，将追究其责任，并责成赔偿损失。

3. 自行负责打扫宿舍卫生、清理垃圾，经常开窗通风。保持门窗、桌面、墙面、地面和盥洗室的干净整洁，无灰尘、蛛网、污渍和异味。桌面和窗台上的物品摆放整齐，不要堆放箱包等大件物品。

4. 起床后，须叠被并放置在靠近床头的位置(或将被褥铺平)，枕头置于被子上面。床单铺直、铺平。床面不要堆放杂物。床下鞋子等物品须放置整齐。

5. 不得在墙面打洞、钉钉子、悬挂装饰物；不得在宿舍内存放腥臭、腐烂、有毒及易燃、易爆物品。不得在宿舍内酗酒。不得饲养宠物。不得往地面、窗外、楼下扔东西、吐痰、泼水。

6. 保持宿舍安静，不得妨碍他人休息；离开宿舍时，应当关闭电灯、电风扇、热水器、洗漱设备阀门和窗户等，锁闭房门。未经允许，不得邀请非国际交流学院人员进入宿舍。

7. 中方领导和管理教师将不定期对宿舍安全情况进行检查。

8. 中国使用为 220V、50Hz 交流电。进入宿舍后须将门禁卡(兼房间取电卡)插入取电盒，方可接通电源。宿舍内安装了限流器(当电路负荷超过安全标准时，限流器将会自动切断电源)，为保证用电安全，不得在宿舍内使用 200W 以上的大功率电器。

9. 宿舍内全天供应冷热水，仅供洗浴，不可直接饮用。

10. 宿舍安装有冷热双制式中央空调系统，请通过空调遥控器调至正确模式使用。夏季使用时，请将温度设置在 26℃ 以上；冬季使用时，请将温度设置在 22℃ 以下；离开房间时请关闭空调。

11. 宿舍垃圾注意放入垃圾桶内，每天早上 7:30 前将垃圾桶摆放到宿舍门前，上午国际交流学院保洁人员会前来清理，中午 12:00 后自行收回垃圾桶。请勿将烟头、垃圾等废弃物丢入坐便器内，如因人为原因造成的下水道堵塞，留学生将承担相应的疏通费用。

12. 宿舍电视为液晶屏幕，请勿用尖锐物品或手指触碰屏幕。

13. 宿舍安装木制地板，容易因水或烟头等物受损。如因人为原因造成宿舍地板损坏，留学生将按照受损面积承担维修费用。

14. 请勿在宿舍墙面、家具表面刻画、钉钉子、粘挂钩。发现后我们将进行清除，并视损坏情况由留学生承担维修费用。

15. 请勿在浴室毛巾架晾晒衣物，如因此造成毛巾架脱落，留学生将承担部分维修费用。

16. 请勿在宿舍窗台上堆放物品、晾晒鞋袜、向窗外丢弃废弃物或坐卧于窗台上。

17. 离开学校，须提前请假；进出学校，须出示外出证。学校设有医院、体育馆、超市、邮局、银行、电信营业厅、书店、体育用品店、照相馆、理发店、餐馆、洗衣店等生活服务设施，不出校门即可购买各类日常生活用品。

18. 妥善保管个人财物和重要证件，离开宿舍关好门窗，随身携带钥匙和门禁卡。外出时尽量不要携带大量现金和护照。在校内和武汉市，可凭国际交流学院发放的学生证或外出证证明你的身份。

19. 留学生楼 1 楼大门装有智能门禁系统，进入时须使用门禁卡。该门禁系统每天 06:30~22:30 使用，其余时间无法进出。如将钥匙遗忘在宿舍，可找 1 楼值班室借用钥匙开门。门禁卡或钥匙丢失或损坏，费用自理。

Ⅱ. Daily Life Reminders

The university arranges dormitories for international students. It is not permitted to change dormitories or rent a house outside of campus without approval. Each international student should pay RMB 500 as a deposit for the facilities and objects in the dormitory during the first month of the enrollment, which is expected to be refunded on the eve of graduation if there is no damage or loss confirmed by the College of International Exchange. Take good care of the dormitory's amenities and belongings. In the event of damage or loss, compensation is needed.

1. To achieve convenience, keep the dormitory tidy and the objects in good order. It is not permitted to install new facilities or to disassemble or relocate the dormitory's furniture and appliances.

2. It is forbidden to use an alcohol heater, a kerosene burner, an electric stove, or an induction cooker. In the event of a fire caused by a violation, the students involved must face responsibility and recompense for the loss and damage.

3. International students are responsible for cleaning and waste removal in their dormitories. It is beneficial to one's health to open the windows for ventilation on a regular basis. To keep dust, cobwebs, stains, and odors at bay, clean the door, windows, windowsill, tables, walls, floor, and washroom on a regular basis. Place no luggage or bags on tables or windowsills.

4. After getting out of bed, make your bed. Place the quilt at one end of the bed or unfold it on the bed. Place the pillow on top of the quilt. The bed sheet needs to be straightened. Nothing else should be placed on the bed. The shoes or other items under the bed should be neatly placed.

5. Drilling, nailing, or hanging ornaments on the wall is not permitted. The rotten, stinking, flammable, explosive, and hazardous things are not permitted in the room. Excessive drinking and pet ownership are prohibited. Littering, spitting, or dumping water or debris on the floor or through windows is not permitted.

6. Maintain quiet in the dormitory and do not disturb others. Before leaving the dormitory, turn off the lights, fans, heating appliance, and valves, and lock the door. Without prior authorization, it is not permitted to bring anyone other than the College of International Exchange staff to the dormitory.

7. The Chinese staff will make random inspection rounds in the dormitory area.

8. The alternating current in China is 220V and 50Hz. When you insert your access card into the box on the wall of your dormitory, power is turned on. For the purpose of safety, a power limiter has been installed. When the power load exceeds the safety limits, the power is turned off. To ensure the safe use of electricity, no high-power appliances exceeding 200W are permitted in the dormitory.

9. Cold and hot water are accessible 24 hours a day in your dormitory, but they are exclusively for washing and bathing, not drinking.

10. In the dormitory, an air conditioning system (heating and cooling modes) has been installed. Please use the remote controller to select the appropriate mode. Please set the temperature above 26℃ in summer and below 22℃ in winter. Before you leave your dormitory, turn off the air conditioning.

11. Drop trash in the dustbin. Before 07:30 in the morning, place the dustbin in front of your dormitory. The garbage will be collected in the morning by cleaners. After 12:00, return the dustbin to your dormitory.

Kindly refrain from dropping wasted items such as cigarette ends and trash into the flush toilet. Otherwise, you will be responsible for dredging costs.

12. To avoid damage, please do not touch the LCD TV screen with your fingers or anything sharp.

13. The floor of the dormitory is built of wood, which is susceptible to damage from water and cigarette ends. You are expected to pay for the repair based on the damaged area.

14. It is prohibited to affix pictures and hooks, scrawl or nail on the wall, and so on. Once caught, the substances/scribbling will be removed. You are expected to pay for the repair based on the extent of the damage.

15. Please do not hang clothes or other heavy items on the bathroom towel rack. If the rack is damaged, you are supposed to pay for the repair.

16. You are not allowed to stack items, shoes and socks or sit/lie on the windowsill, or throw trash out of the window.

17. You are required to ask for leave prior to leaving the university. When passing through the university gate, present your going-out pass. For your convenience, the university has living facilities such as hospital, gymnasium, supermarket, post office, bank, China Telecom Service Center, book store, sport goods store, photo shop, barbershop, restaurant, laundry and so on. It is easy to obtain all of your everyday essentials.

18. Keep your valuables and documents to yourself. While leaving your dormitory, take your key and access card with you. It is strongly advisable that you do not bring a big sum of money or your passport with you when you go out. Your student ID and going-out pass serve to validate your identification both at the university and in Wuhan.

19. The dormitory building's gate is equipped with a smart access control system. When you enter the building, you must present an access card. The system is available from 06:30 to 22:30 every day. At other time, the gate is closed and the system is unavailable. If you forget your key at the dormitory, please use the key at the first-floor duty room. If your key or access card is lost or destroyed, you must pay for a new one.

三、可提供的有偿服务

为方便留学生、家属在武汉及校内生活，可以提供部分有偿服务（详见下表）。

表 3.5　可提供的有偿服务表

项目或服务名称	收费标准	预约时间
文字翻译(中英互译)	×××元/千字	提前 3 天
文字翻译(中法互译)	×××元/千字	提前 3 天
个人房间保洁(公寓楼房间)	×××元/次	提前 1 天
个人房间保洁(留学生楼房间)	×××元/次	提前 1 天
传真	发送国际传真×元/页(国内 × 元/页，不含通话费)，接收×元/页	正课时间均可
复印、打印(自带电子版文档)	×元/页	正课时间均可
刻录光盘(自带光盘)	×元/张	正课时间均可
上网	×元/小时	电子教室开放时间均可
家属公寓楼房屋租住	房屋租金详见《租赁合同》	提前 1 个月
留学生楼单人间租住	房屋租金×××元/天，××××元/月	提前 1 个月

Ⅲ. Paid Services

The following paid services are available to facilitate you and your family during your stay at the University and in Wuhan.

Table 3.5　Paid Services Table

Services /Items	Standard of Charging	Time for Ordering
Translation(Chinese & English)	RMB ×××/1,000words	3 days ahead of schedule
Translation(Chinese & French)	RMB ×××/1,000words	3 days ahead of schedule
Cleaning (Family Apartment)	RMB ×××/time	1 day ahead of schedule
Cleaning (Dormitory)	RMB ××/time	1 day ahead of schedule
Fax	International: RMB ×/ page Domestic: RMB ×/ page Receiving: RMB ×/ page (telephone charge not included)	Working hours
Photocopy and Printing	RMB ×/page	Working hours
Burning Disc (Disc not available)	RMB ×/disc	Working hours
Internet	RMB ×/hour	When the E-Classroom opens
Family Apartment Leasing	see "Leasing Contract"	1 month ahead of schedule
Leasing of a Single Room in the Dormitory Building	RMB ×××/day RMB ××××/month	1 month ahead of schedule

四、邮政通信

校园内有邮局和快递公司，可办理多种邮政业务。

在中国境内通信，通常需要用中文书写信封正面。格式是：收信人的邮政编码、地址在上，姓名居中；寄信人的地址、姓名、邮政编码在下。如图 3.1 所示：

邮政编码：$\boxed{1}\boxed{0}\boxed{0}\boxed{0}\boxed{8}\boxed{7}$　　　　　　　　　　　邮票

北京市中关村大街×××号乙大学　留学生院 2 号楼 305 房间

雅克　先生　收

湖北省武汉市民族大道×××号甲大学国际交流学院　阿里

邮政编码：430000

图 3.1　通信格式（中国）

寄往国外的信件，信封正面可以按国际惯用格式书写。如果用中文、英文以外的文字书写，须用中文或英文注明寄达国国名和城市名。

如果希望收到别人寄来的信，一定要把准确的地址告诉他们。地址一般用英文或中文。如图 3.2 所示：

FROM：Arthur

PO BOX 567

ATLANTA GA　30318—9997

USA

　　TO：Mr. John Williams

　　College of International Exchange, No. ××× Minzu

　　Avenue, Wuhan, Hubei, 430000

　　China

Stamp

图 3.2　通信格式（国际）

如对方使用快递给你邮寄物品，可建议其选择中国邮政或中通、申通等快递，这样便于在校内直接领取。取包裹、汇款时，须出示有效证件（学生证或护照）。

在武汉市及大学校园内可购买中国联通、移动、电信 SIM 卡及充值卡拨打国内、国际长途(资费标准参见下表)，方便与家人、朋友联系。

表 3.6　通话资费标准

类　　别		费　　用
市内电话		0.22 元/分钟（前 3 分钟）+ 0.11 元/分钟（3 分钟之后）
中国内地长途		0.3 元/分钟，不加收市话费
中国港、澳、台长途		1.5 元/分钟，须加收市话费
国际长途	美国、加拿大(含阿拉斯加和夏威夷，不含其他代码为"1"的国家和地区)	2.4 元/分钟
	英国、法国、意大利、德国、新加坡、韩国、日本、澳大利亚、新西兰、马来西亚、印度尼西亚、菲律宾、泰国	3.6 元/分钟
	其他国家和地区	4.6 元/分钟

Ⅳ. Postal Services and Communications

The campus post office and express delivery service can provide a variety of postal services.

Please write the envelope in Chinese if you send letters to the addressee who is in China. The format is as follows: the addressee's zip code and address are on the top of the envelope, the addressee's name is in the centre of the envelope, and the addresser's address, name, and zip code are on the bottom of the envelope. The following format is for your reference.

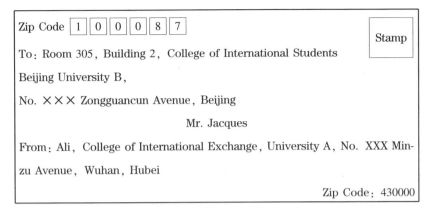

Figure 3.1　The Format to Mail a Letter (China)

Please use the international format when sending a letter abroad. However, if you write an envelope in a language other than Chinese or English, please translate the name of the addressee's city and country on the envelope into Chinese or English.

Please give the sender a correct address if you wish to receive his/ her letter. Either English or Chinese can be employed. The following format is for your reference.

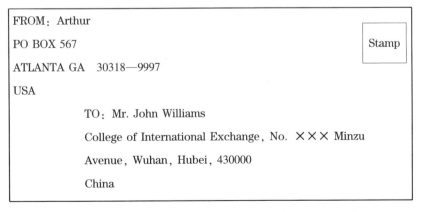

Figure 3.2　The Format to Mail a Letter (International)

233

It is recommended that you choose China Postal, SD and ZT express delivery services for your convenience. Please present your proper identification (student ID or passport) at the parcel claim or post office for remittance.

To make domestic and international calls to family and friends, SIM cards from China Union, China Mobile, or China Telecom, as well as relevant recharge services, are available at the university and other places throughout the city.

Table 3. 6   Call Tariff Standard

Categories	Charge
Local call	RMB 0. 22 (for the first three minutes), plus RMB 0. 11 per minute (after the first 3 minutes)
Long-distance call in mainland	RMB 0. 3 per minute (no additional charge)
Call to Hong Kong, Macao and Taiwan	RMB 1. 5 per minute (charge for local call is required)
Call to the USA and Canada (including Alaska and Hawaii, but excluding other countries and regions with code 1)	RMB 2. 4 per minute
Call to the UK, Italy, France, German, Singapore, South Korea, Japan, Australia, New Zealand, Malaysia, Indonesia, Philippines and Thailand	RMB 3. 6 per minute
Call to other countries and regions	RMB 4. 6 per minute

五、货币银行

(一)中国货币

中国货币为人民币，缩写符号是 RMB。人民币的单位是元，辅币是角。币值有 100 元、50 元、20 元、10 元、5 元、2 元、1 元、5 角、2 角、1 角共 10 种。硬币有 1 元、5 角、1 角。

换算关系为：10 角 = 1 元。

(二)兑换外币

美元、欧元、英镑等货币都可以在中国银行兑换成人民币，兑换时须出示护照。请不要在街头随便换钱，以免遭受经济损失。

如须兑换旅行支票，可以到中国银行湖北省分行进行兑换，兑换时须出示护照。

地址：武汉市建设大道 677 号。

电话：027—82787982。

校园内有中国工商银行、中国银行可以办理人民币的存款、取款和兑换外币业务。开账户时须出示护照。

Ⅴ. Foreign Currency Exchange and Banks

A. Chinese Currencies

The Chinese currency is known as RMB for short, with Yuan as its u-nit, and Jiao as the fractional unit. Paper currencies have values of 100 Yuan, 50 Yuan, 20 Yuan, 10 Yuan, 5 Yuan, 2 Yuan, 1 Yuan, 5 Jiao, 2 Jiao, and 1 Jiao, whereas coins have values of 1 Yuan, 5 Jiao, and 1 Jiao.

One Yuan is equal to 10 Jiao in terms of conversion.

B. Foreign Currency Exchange

When exchanging US dollars, Euros, and pounds for RMB at the Bank of China, you must show your passport. To avoid financial loss, do not exchange money somewhere other than the bank.

When you exchange a travel check for cash at the Bank of China (Hubei Branch), you must show your passport.

Address：No. 677 Jian She Da Dao，Wuhan.

Tel：027-82787982.

You can make RMB deposits and withdrawals, as well as exchange foreign currencies, on campus at China ICBC or Bank of China. Your passport is necessary if you want to open a bank account.

六、武汉公共交通

(一)公共汽车

学校周围有很多公交车线路，出行很方便。但由于武汉市发展十分迅速，所以公交车的线路和站牌也经常发生变化，出行前请认真确认。公交车票价为 1.6 元。

(二)出租车

武汉出租车一般都提供昼夜服务。出租车车顶有"TAXI"的标志灯，车内仪表盘上方的监督卡有司机的照片、姓名、单位和监督电话，未载人的出租车的前挡风玻璃会有"空车"(FOR HIRE)的标志，下车时出租车司机会打印出乘车费发票，最好保留好发票，如果有问题可以凭发票联系到出租车司机或其所在的公司。目前出租车收费标准为：

表 3.7　出租车收费标准

路　　程	费　　用
3 千米以内	10 元
3 千米至 10 千米	10 元加 1.8 元/千米
10 千米以上	23 元加 2.7 元/千米

另外，目前有很多网络租车平台，例如 T3 出行、高德打车、美团打车、斑马智行、51 用车、花小猪打车等。

(三)轨道交通

目前武汉轨道交通大致情况如下：1 号线汉口北至泾河，2 号线天河机场至佛祖岭，3 号线宏图大道至沌阳大道，4 号线武汉火车站至柏林，5 号线中医药大学至武汉站东广场，6 号线新城十一路至东风公司，7 号线园博园北至青龙山小镇，8 号线金潭路至军运村，11 号线武汉东站至葛店南站，16 号线国博中心南至周家河，阳逻线后湖大道至金台。

（四）火车

武汉市主要有武汉火车站、汉口火车站和武昌火车站三个火车站。每天均有开往全国各地的列车。如果想在节假日外出旅游，经批准后，可以提前 5 天到火车站订票，或者通过订票点订票。

（五）飞机

武汉天河国际机场是武汉市唯一民用机场，距离武汉市中心 25 公里，是中国中部首家 4F 级民用国际机场、中国八大区域性枢纽机场之一、国际定期航班机场、对外开放的一类航空口岸。全市民用航空航线 124 条，其中，国际及地区航线 16 条，国内航线 108 条。机场巴士、长途客车、轨道交通（2 号线）和城际铁路连通机场和武汉市区、周边城市。

Ⅵ. Public Transport in Wuhan

A. Bus

There are many bus lines near our university, making travel in Wuhan quite convenient for you. The bus lines and stop signs in Wuhan often change due to the city's rapid expansion. Before you board a bus, double-check the information. Ticket cost is 1. 6 Yuan.

B. Taxi

Taxis are convenient since they are available 24 hours a day, seven days a week. On top of it is a "TAXI" sign lamp. A supervision card above the gauge board shows the driver's portrait, name, taxi firm, and phone number. When a taxi has the word "FOR HIRE" displayed behind its windshield, it is available. When you get off, you should get a receipt so that you can call the taxi company if necessary. The following are the current charging standards:

Table 3.7 Taxi Charging Standards

Kilometers	Charge
Within 3 kilometers	10 Yuan
From 3 kilometers to 10 kilometers	10 Yuan plus 1.8 Yuan/km
For distance greater than 10 kilometers	23 Yuan plus 2.7 Yuan/km

Additionally, online car rental platforms are available such as T3 Chuxing, Amap, Meituan Taxi, Banma Zhixing, 51 Yongche, and Huaxiaozhu Taxi.

C. Metro

The general situation of metro lines in Wuhan is as follows: Metro Line 1 runs from Hankoubei station to Jinghe station, Line 2 from Tianhe International Airport station to Fozuling station, Line 3 from Hongtudadao station to Zhuanyangdadao station, Line 4 from Wuhan Railway station to Bolin station, Line 5 from University of TMC station to Dongguangchang of Wuhan Railway station, Line 6 from Xincheng 11 Road station to Dongfeng company station, Line 7 from Yuanboyuanbei station to Qinglongshanxiaozhen station, Line 8 from Jinyintanlu station to Junyuncun (Military Games Village) station, Line 11 from Wuhandong station to Gediannan station, Line 16 from International Expo Center South station to Zhoujia River station. and Yangluo Line from Houhu dadao station to Jintai station.

D. Train

Wuhan has three main railway stations: Hankou Railway Station, Wuchang Railway Station, and Wuhan Railway Station. Every day, trains run to every part of China. On holidays or festivals, you can reserve tickets at stations or booking offices up to 5 days ahead of departure after obtaining authorization from the College of International Exchange.

　　E. Airport

The only civil airport is Tianhe International Airport. It is 25 kilometers from downtown Wuhan and is rated as a first-class outbound airport, the first 4F civil international airport in central China, and one of China's eight regional airline hubs, hosting regular international flights. There are 124 civil airlines, with 16 connecting locations outside of China and 108 inbound airlines. The airport shuttle buses, the long-distance buses, the metro (Line 2), and the inter-city railroads connect the airport to the city center and neighboring cities.

　　七、武汉宗教场所

　　1. 上海路天主教堂，位于江岸区上海路 16 号。

　　2. 花园山天主教堂，位于武昌区胭脂路花园山 2 号。

　　3. 圣高隆庞堂，位于汉阳区显正路 163 号。

　　4. 博学中学教堂，位于硚口区解放大道 347 号。

　　5. 汉口荣光堂，位于江岸区黄石路 26 号。

　　6. 武昌圣米迦勒堂，位于武昌区复兴路。

　　7. 起义门清真寺，位于武昌区起义街 67 号。

　　8. 江岸区清真寺，位于江岸区发展大道二七横路。

　　9. 宝通寺，位于武昌区武珞路 549 号。

　　10. 古德寺，位于江岸区解放大道黄埔路 75 号。

　　Ⅶ. Religious Activities Venues

　　1. Shanghai Road Catholic Church, Address: No. 16 Shanghai Road, Jiang'an.

　　2. Huayuanshan Catholic Church, Address: No. 2 Huayuanshan, Yanzhi Road, Wuchang.

　　3. St. Columban Church, Address: No. 163 Xianzheng Road, Hanyang.

4. Wilson Memorial Church, Address：No. 347 Jiefang Avenue, Qiaokou.

5. Griffith Church, Address：No. 26 Huangshi Road, Jiang'an.

6. St. Michael's Church, Address：Fuxing Road, Wuchang.

7. Qiyimen Mosque, Address：No. 67 Qiyi Street, Wuchang.

8. Jiang'an District's Mosque, Address：Erqihenglu, Fazhan Avenue, Jiang'an.

9. Bao Tong Temple, Address：No. 549 Wuluo Road, Wuchang.

10. Gu De Temple, Address：No. 75 Huangpu Road, Jiefang Avenue, Jiang'an.

八、生活保障场所使用规定

(一)洗衣房(熨衣房)管理办法

1. 开放时间为每日 07：00—22：00。

2. 爱护室内设备、设施，正确操作，节约水电。严禁搬动洗衣机或乱动各种水电阀门。

3. 使用电熨斗等高温设备时，防止烫伤；为避免起火，设备断电前，人员不得离开洗衣房(熨衣房)。

4. 各种熨衣物品和设备仅限洗衣房(熨衣房)内使用，不得带离。熨烫完毕，将使用物品摆放整齐。

5. 清洗过的衣物统一在晾衣场晾晒，洗衣房内仅限雨雪天气晾晒！任意挂放者，国际交流学院有权没收至一楼值班室，自行领回。

6. 尊重先来后到的公共秩序，提倡互谅互让；保持室内整洁卫生，不准吐痰、吸烟、吃零食、乱丢脏物。

7. 洗衣房(熨衣房)为自助开放式管理，洗衣和晾晒过程中出现衣物损坏或丢失现象，责任自负。

8. 出现故障，应及时向中方人员报告。如发生人为损坏情况，照价赔偿。

9. 离开洗衣房时及时关闭电灯。

（二）俱乐部管理办法

1. 开放时间为每周一至周五 17:00—21:00、周末和节假日 10:00—21:00。

2. 爱护俱乐部内的物品、设备，轻拿轻放，不得随意挪动大型设备。

3. 各项物品和设备仅供留学生在本俱乐部内使用，不得带离。无大人陪同，严禁留学生子女单独使用。使用完毕，将物品放回原位，摆放整齐。

4. 保持俱乐部整洁卫生，不准在房间内吐痰、吸烟、吃零食、乱丢脏物。

5. 出现故障，应及时向中方人员报告。如发生人为损坏情况，照价赔偿。

6. 离开俱乐部时及时关闭门窗及电灯、空调等用电设备。

（三）综合训练场管理办法

国际交流学院综合训练场是留学生开展教学、训练、健身及集会活动的涉外场所，由国际交流学院负责管理。本训练场紧邻国际交流学院办公、教学及留学生宿舍区，为确保良好的办公、教学及生活秩序，入场活动请遵循以下管理办法：

1. 开放时间：工作日为 16:30—21:30，节假日为 08:00—12:00 和 15:00—21:30。其他时间不开放。

2. 开放时间，本训练场供留学生优先使用。非开放时间，留学生须向国际交流学院申请，经批准后方可使用；不受理其他单位或个人非开放时间的使用申请。

3. 未经国际交流学院批准，严禁其他单位或个人使用本训练场组织集会、舞蹈、体育比赛等影响办公及留学生生活秩序的活动。

4. 保持场地卫生，严禁在场内吸烟、吐痰、吐口香糖，乱扔杂物，随意挪动物品设施；严禁携带化学溶剂、易燃易爆物品和宠物进入场地；严禁各种车辆(含自行车)进入场地；无大人陪同，严禁儿童单独使用场地设施。

5. 进入训练场运动，请着运动鞋。不得在场内滑滑板、溜冰、嬉笑打闹、大声喧哗。

6. 凡违反上述管理办法者，国际交流学院工作人员有权劝其离场。对违规使用场地者，视情节轻重，给予一定的罚款；对故意损坏场地及设施者，我们将追究责任，并责成照价赔偿。

Ⅷ. Rules for Living Facilities

A. Rules for Laundry (Ironing Room)

1. Daily hours of operation: 07:00—22:00.

2. Take good care of the laundry facilities/equipment, save water and electricity, and use the facilities/equipment as directed. Moving the washing machine or turning on/off the water/electric valves without permission is absolutely prohibited.

3. Be careful when using high-temperature equipment such as an electric iron to avoid being scalded. To avoid a fire, switch off the power before leaving.

4. The equipment and facilities are solely for use in the laundry and should not be brought outside. After washing/ironing, return the facilities/items to their original location.

5. Dry your clothes in the drying yard or the laundry on rainy and snowy days. If you dry your clothes elsewhere other than the above-mentioned locations, the clothes will be collected and sent to the duty room on the first floor. Then you should file a claim in the duty room for those clothes.

6. Wash and iron in the order of arrival. The spirit of mutual understanding and a harmonious environment are encouraged. Maintain a clean and neat laundry and drying yard. In the laundry, do not spit, smoke, eat, or litter.

7. The laundry and drying yard areas are open and self-help. You are liable for any damage or loss to your garments while they are in the laun-

dry/drying yard.

8. Report equipment/facilities failures to the Chinese duty staff as soon as possible. In the event of a man-made loss or harm, compensation is necessary.

9. Before leaving, turn off all the lights, the washing machine and the electric iron.

B. Rules for Club

1. Hours of operation: 17:00-21:00 from Monday to Friday, 10:00-21:00 on weekends and holidays.

2. Please utilize the club's equipment/facilities with caution and care. Without permission, do not move the huge equipment.

3. All equipment and facilities are only for use within the club and should not be taken outside. Students' children are not permitted to use the equipment/facilities without the presence of their parents. Before leaving, return the facilities/items to their original locations.

4. Maintain a clean and orderly club. In the club, do not spit, smoke, eat, or trash.

5. Report equipment/facilities failures to the Chinese duty staff as soon as possible. In the event of a man-made loss or harm, compensation is necessary.

6. Before leaving, close the door and windows, and switch off all the lights and the air conditioner.

C. Management of Multi-purpose Training Ground

The multi-purpose training ground serves as a location for international students to carry out teaching activities, get training, practice gymnastics, and conduct gatherings. The College of International Exchange is in charge of venue management. Because the training ground is adjacent to offices, classrooms, and dormitories of the College of International Exchange, the management specified below must be followed to ensure a conducive environment for the staff and students.

1. Opening hours: From Monday to Friday, 16:30-21:30. Weekends and holidays, 08:00—12:00, and 15:00—21:30. It is not opened at other time.

2. International students are given priority during opening hours. In other cases, if students want to use the training ground, they must submit an application to the College of International Exchange. Application for use of the venue at other times by groups or individuals other than international students will not be approved.

3. Groups or individuals other than international students are not permitted to use the venue to conduct events such as meetings, dances, and sports games that have a detrimental influence on the college without prior clearance from the College of International Exchange.

4. Maintain the sanitation of the ground. It is forbidden to smoke, spit, spit gums, litter, or move the equipment. It is prohibited to bring chemical solvents, flammable and combustible materials, pets, or vehicles including bicycles to the venue. Minors should not use the facilities on their own.

5. Sneakers are required. Skateboarding, skating, horseplay, and screaming are all prohibited.

6. The College of International Exchange staff have the authority to urge those who violate management to leave the training ground. Those who violate the venue's use will be penalized according to the gravity of the offense. Those who intentionally damage the ground and facilities should be held accountable for their actions, and compensation is needed.

3.4 节日庆典 Festivities

3.4.1 中国国庆节庆典 Celebrations on China's National Day

中外学生庆国庆招待会议程

时间：9 月 30 日

地点：国际交流学院综合训练场

参加人员：大学领导，机关处领导，留学生教师代表，国际交流学院全体工作人员、全体留学生，深蓝国际俱乐部学生

主持人：国际交流学院院长

活动流程：

1. 宣布留学生管理骨干名单。

2. 为留学生管理骨干颁发委任状。

3. 为集体过生日留学生赠送生日礼物。

4. 大学校长致辞。

5. 领导与留学生代表一同切蛋糕，招待会开始。

6. 中外学生文艺表演及游戏互动。

National Day Reception Agenda

Time：September 30

Location：Multi-purpose training ground of the College of International Exchange

Participants：University leaders, heads of administration offices, teacher representatives, faculty of the College of International Exchange, all international students and members of the Blue Water International Workshop

Host: Dean of the College of International Exchange

Agenda:

1. The name list of students in charge is officially announced.

2. The appointment certificates are issued to students in charge.

3. Leaders present students with birthday gifts.

4. President of the university addresses the audience.

5. The reception begins following the ritual in which leaders and student representatives cut the cake together.

6. Students present their performances and play games.

中外学生庆国庆招待会主持词

尊敬的刘鹏海校长，各位领导，各位老师，女士们，先生们，中外同学们：

大家晚上好！

金秋送爽山河美，丹桂飘香庆辉煌。在即将迎来中华人民共和国 70 周年华诞的特别日子里，中外朋友们欢聚一堂，共话友好情谊，共表期盼喜悦。首先，请允许我介绍出席招待会的领导：大学校长刘鹏海，办公室主任曹荣……让我们对各位领导和留学生教师代表的到来表示热烈的欢迎和衷心的感谢。

留学生朋友们，你们是一股注入大学的新鲜血液，大学因为有了你们而多了一抹别样的风景，开学以来，你们很快适应大学生活，融入教学、管理等工作，表现出了较高的个人素质。特别是亚伦、布兰登等几位新生骨干，表现尤为突出，看到你们的汉语每天都在进步，我们感到由衷的高兴。通过前期推荐考察，我们产生了本学年第一届留学生管理骨干。下面请国际交流学院党委书记张嘉琪宣布留学生管理骨干名单并颁发委任状。

谢谢张书记。希望留学生骨干们身先士卒、以身垂范，做好国际交流学院和广大留学生之间的纽带，服务好广大留学生。此次招待会我们也特别要为与新中国同期生日的留学生朋友们庆祝生日，感受我们祖国华诞的同时，也分享你们的快乐。相信你们在中国度过的首个生日会令你们终身难忘。下面请大学办公室主任曹荣为过生日的留学生朋友们赠送礼物。

……

谢谢曹荣主任。最后，让我们以热烈掌声欢迎大学校长刘鹏海致辞。

……

谢谢刘鹏海校长。如此良辰美景，如此欢庆时刻，有请各位领导与我们一起共同切蛋糕，为中华人民共和国 70 周年华诞喝彩!

……

招待会现在开始，请大家尽情享用美食，欣赏中外学生表演的精彩节目。

Host Speech at the National Day Reception

Respected university president Liu Penghai, leaders, professors, ladies and gentlemen and students:

Good evening!

The golden autumn illuminates the picturesque landscape, while the fragrant osmanthus blossoms chant great success across the nation. On the occasion of the People's Republic of China's 70th birthday, friends from home and abroad are gathered together to express our friendship, hopes and happiness. To begin, please allow me to introduce the participants today: professor Liu Penghai, university president, professor Cao Rong, head of administration office... Let's extend a warm welcome and heartfelt gratitude for leaders and teachers with a round of applause.

Dear students, you have infused our university with vitality. Thanks to your participation, our university is bearing a unique picture. Since the start of classes, you have aligned fast with the campus life, collaborating in education and other management-related activities. Your high standard of excellence has been displayed in all aspects, with Aaron and Brandon serving as model students in charge. And we are overjoyed to watch how your Chinese is being improved day by day. The first team of the international students in charge is introduced through recommendation and observation. Let's invite professor Zhang Jiaqi, the College of International Exchange's party secretary to read the names of the students in charge, followed by the issuance of appointment certificates.

Thank you, Professor Zhang. We hope that all students in charge may take the lead, set examples for others, and act as a liaison between the College of International Exchange and the international students, as well as work for your international colleagues. At the reception, we would like to wish students whose birthdays coincide with the PRC a happy birthday. We hope that you can enjoy the pleasure of the celebration of the National Day and share your joy at the meantime. And you will remember your first birthday party in China for the rest of your life. Professor Cao Rong will now present birthday gifts to you.

...

Thank you professor Cao Rong. Let's now welcome professor Liu, our university president to address the reception.

...

Thank you professor Liu.

On this beautiful and joyful moment, let's invite leaders to join us in cutting the cake for the 70th birthday of the People's Republic of China.

...

Now the reception has begun. Please enjoy yourselves and the wonderful performance by students from home and abroad.

校长在中外学生庆国庆招待会上的讲话

女士们、先生们，留学生朋友们：

大家晚上好！很高兴与来自亚洲、非洲、南美洲、北美洲、大洋洲的各国留学生朋友们共庆中华人民共和国 70 周年华诞。在此，我谨代表全校教职员工，向出席招待会的各位来宾、朋友表示热烈的欢迎！也向集体过生日的留学生说声生日快乐！

70 年风雨兼程，70 年沧桑巨变！70 年，中国成为世界第二大经济体、制造业第一大国、货物贸易第一大国和外汇储备第一大国，探索出一条发展中国家走向现代化的光辉道路，彻底改变了"一穷二白"的面貌，实现了由站起来、富起来到强起来的历史性飞跃，创造了让世界刮目相看的发展奇迹。这 70 年，中国不断加强与世界各国的联系，加深与各国人民的友谊，深化和拓展各层面的交流与合作。习近平主席提出的"一带一路"伟大倡议，已经得到了 136 个国家和 30 个国际组织的响应，成为全球最受欢迎的倡议之一。

我校与新中国同龄，70 年来，奋勇向上，发展成为中国重点教学和科研院校，我们不断加强国际合作和多边交流，积极拓展留学生教育层次、专业、类型和规模。截至目前，已为近百个国家培养了万余名人才，很多优秀留学生还走上了本国相关部门、领域的重要领导岗位，我们为他们感到骄傲。

留学生朋友们，你们是各国遴选出的精英，肩负着光荣的使命来到这里。希望你们能够充分利用宝贵的时间，学好专业知识，积极感受中国文化，与中外学生全方位交流，增进了解和友谊。留学生朋友们，我们非常珍视与各位的情谊，希望通过我们的实际行动，深化与各国的务实合作，携手创建和谐海洋，共同推进和平发展、合作共赢。

最后，祝我们的祖国繁荣昌盛、兴旺发达，祝在座的中外朋友节日快乐、身体健康！祝各位留学生在中国生活愉快、学业有成！谢谢！

Speech at National Day Reception by University President

Ladies and gentlemen, dear students,

Good evening! I am very delighted to celebrate the 70th anniversary of the People's Republic of China with international students from countries across Asia, Africa, South America, North America and Oceania. Hereby on behalf of our university faculty, I'd like to extend my warm welcome to all the guests and friends here today. Additionally, I'd like to wish a happy birthday to students who are on their birthdays today.

Over the past seven decades, China has marched forward regardless of hardships. Over the past seven decades, China has seen dramatic development in all facets. Over the past seven decades, China has become the world's second largest economy, the world's largest manufacturer, the World's largest commodity trader and the country with the most foreign currency reserves. It has blazed a trail for developing countries on the way to modernity. It has lifted its impoverished situation, realizing the historic leap of rising up, becoming rich and strong, creating a development miracle that astounded the world. Over the past seven decades, China has continued its efforts to strengthen the ties with the rest of the whole world, boost the friendship with people from all countries, deepen and expand exchanges and cooperation at all levels. The "Belt and Road" initiative proposed by Chinese President Xi Jinping has attracted support from 136 countries and 30 international organizations, making it one of the most popular initiative today.

Our university was established concurrently with the founding of the People's Republic of China. It has steadily risen over the last seven decades to become a major education and research center in China. We have committed to increasing international collaboration and multilateral exchanges, as well as enriching the courses and types and expanding the scale of our international programs. Some outstanding students were promoted to important positions in their professional communities upon their return to their native countries. We are really proud of them.

Dear students, you are elites from diverse countries who have come to study at our university with the hope of your people. So, I hope you can make the most of your time here to obtain professional knowledge, gain insight into Chinese culture, and engage in all-around exchanges with Chinese and international students to develop mutual understanding and friendship. Dear friends, our university values friendship with each of you very much, we hope that through concerted efforts, we will deepen our pragmatic cooperation with other countries, create a harmonious ocean and promote peaceful development and win-win cooperation.

Last but not least, may our beloved country flourish day by day. I wish you all a happy festival and good health. And I want to wish all international students a pleasant stay in China and best of the luck in your academic careers. Thank you all.

3.4.2 中国春节庆典 Chinese New Year Celebrations

新春招待会议程

时间：×月××日 12:00

地点：国际交流学院餐厅

参加人员：大学领导，国际交流学院工作人员及家属，全体留学生及陪读家属

主持人：国际交流学院院长

着装：中方着正装，留学生着本国礼服

活动流程：

1. 观看留学生学习生活视频。

2. 向留学生赠送春联和书籍。

3. 大学领导致春节贺词。

Chinese New Year Reception Agenda

Time：12：00, DD/MM.

Location：The dining hall of the College of International Exchange

Participants：University leaders, staff of the College of International Exchange and their families, international students and their families

Host：Dean of the College of International Exchange

Dress code：Formal attire for the Chinese side; national ceremonial attire for overseas students

Agenda：

1. Watch the film about students' study and life in China.

2. Leaders present students with books and Spring Festival couplets.

3. University leader delivers new year message.

新春招待会主持词

尊敬的白晓林副校长、同志们、留学生朋友们：

大家中午好！

在中国除夕这个喜庆的日子里，我们在此欢聚一堂共同庆祝中国传统佳节——春节。刚才我们一起观看了国际交流学院留学生们的学习生活视频，相信大家都深有感触。首先请允许我介绍出席今天招待会的领导：大学副校长白晓林，办公室主任曹荣。让我们以热烈的掌声对莅临学院新春招待会的领导表示欢迎和感谢。

下面，请大学领导为留学生赠送春联和书籍。

......

今天我们不仅为大家准备了松鼠桂鱼、珍珠丸子、水饺、炸春卷等中国团年饭传统菜品，还特意为大家准备了烤全羊、番茄牛肉羹、奥尔良烤鸡、泰式鲜虾粉丝煲、披萨等深受大家喜爱和想念的家乡美食。下面请大家落座。

......

现在请大学副校长白晓林致新春贺词。

Host Address at the New Year Reception

Respected professor Bai Xiaolin, vice president of the university, dear comrades and friends,

Good afternoon!

On the joyful eve of Chinese New Year, we are gathered to celebrate the Spring Festival, a traditional Chinese festival. Just now we watched the video about your study and life in China, and it is so incredible. To begin, please allow me to introduce leaders present: professor Bai Xiaolin, vice president of the university, and professor Cao Rong, head of the Administration Office. With a round of applause, let's express our heartfelt welcome and thanks to them.

Now, let's invite leaders to present students with books and Spring Festival couplets.

On the menu for today you will find Chinese traditional family reunion dishes such as fried mandarin fish with sweet and sour sauce, meatballs with glutinous rice, dumplings, and fried rolls, etc. And you'll also find food that is your favorite and your home flavor, such as roast whole lamb, tomato and beef soup, Orleans roast chicken, Thai style prawn noodle, and pizza. Please take a seat.

...

Professor Bai Xiaolin will now deliver the New Year message.

校领导在新春招待会上的讲话

女士们、先生们，亲爱的留学生朋友们：

你们好！今天是中国的除夕，这是阖家团圆的日子，此刻我很高兴与各国留学生朋友们相聚在国际交流学院这个大家庭，共庆中国春节，共享节日喜悦。首先，我代表大学全体教职员工，向大家以及你们的家人，致以诚挚的祝福。

过去的一年，不论是对学校还是对你们留学生而言，都是极不平凡的一年。我们携手共进、风雨同舟，一道打赢了疫情狙击战，实现了全体留学生师生的"零感染"，确保了大家的身体健康和生命安全。过去的一年，我们克服空间阻碍，组织线上教学，落实了"停课不停教、停课不停学"的政策，确保了学习和生活正常有序进行。进入20××年我们严格执行国家有关规定，"就地过年"、放弃寒假休假，调整教学计划，为国家疫情防控大局贡献自己的力量，这些都体现了你们良好的个人素质和修养。也许你们在生活中会遇到困扰和问题，但看到你们在磨砺中进步和成长，我感到很欣慰和自豪，为你们点赞！

朋友们，春节是中华民族最隆重的传统佳节，有着大地回春、万象更新、新岁开启的寓意。我们即将迎来的是中国农历牛年，牛在东西方都象征着勤劳和力量，牛年是耕耘的年份，也必将是收获的年份。在此，我祝愿在座的各位及家人牛年身体健康、学习进步、阖家幸福！谢谢大家！

Speech by the University Leader at the New Year Reception

Ladies and gentlemen, dear friends,

Good afternoon! Today is the Chinese New Year's eve, as well as the first day of family reunions. At the moment, I am overjoyed to join students from different nations at the College of International Exchange for a family reunion, enjoying the auspicious occasion of the New Year's celebration. To begin, let me express my warmest greetings to you and your families on behalf of the university faculty.

The past year has been very difficult for both our university and you. However, we came together as a team to battle the virus, resulting in zero confirmed infections among international students and your teachers and ensuring physical health and safety. We planned online classes last year, despite quarantine-related problems, in order to implement the policy of "no suspension of teaching and learning when school is closed". As a result, we ensured an orderly study and life environment. With the approach of 20×× , we adhered to the national policy that encourages residents to stay put during the Spring Festival holiday, canceled the winter vacation, restructured education plan and made contribution to the national pandemic prevention and control work. All this has demonstrated your good quality and culture. I know you may encounter troubles and problems in your life. But I feel so gratified and proud when I learn about your growth and success in adversity. Let me thumb up for your endeavors.

Dear friends, the Spring Festival is the grandest traditional festival in China, since it signifies the return of spring to the earth, the renewal of everything, and the start of the New Year. The year we are about to enter is known as the Year of the Ox. The ox is a symbol of dedication and strength in both east and west civilizations. The Year of the Ox is the year of diligence and accomplishments. Hereby I wish you and your family good health and the best of luck in your academic careers and family life. Thank you.

表 3.8　新春期间活动安排及要求

序号	时间		活动名称	活动地点	活动要求
1	2月11日(除夕)	11:00— 13:00	留学生新春招待会(招待会前留学生体验包饺子)，招待会菜单： 1. 主菜：烤全羊，奥尔良烤鸡，泰式鲜虾粉丝煲，吉布提番茄牛肉羹，羊肉串，松鼠桂鱼，海派红烧肉，珍珠丸子，腰果西芹炒百合，黄金玉米烙； 2. 主食：至尊披萨，水饺，花样南瓜饼，炸春卷； 3. 甜品：纸杯蛋糕，提拉米苏，绿豆糕，现制冰淇淋； 4. 水果：草莓，哈密瓜，香蕉，冰糖桔； 5. 饮品：咖啡，柠檬水，橙汁，牛奶，雪碧，可乐。	餐厅	1. 集合时间：11:00，先包饺子，然后开始招待会 2. 着装要求：正装 3. 包饺子期间全程佩戴红色口罩
		20:00— 22:00	观看春晚	二楼俱乐部	1. 19:50自行前往俱乐部 2. 着装不限
2	2月14日	10:00— 16:00	参观东湖	东湖	1. 集合时间：08:00 2. 集合地点：学院综合训练场 3. 着装要求：运动服 4. 除午餐外全程佩戴口罩
3	2月15日	09:30	"新春杯"拔河比赛	第一田径场	

续表

序号	时间		活动名称	活动地点	活动要求
4	2月15日	11:00—11:50	师生趣味游艺会: 1. 猜灯谜 2. 撕名牌 3. 套圈圈	学院综合训练场	1. 集合时间:09:00 2. 集合地点:学院综合训练场 3. 着装要求:运动服 4. 全程佩戴口罩 5. 拔河后返回学院综合训练场参加游艺会

备注:
1. 休整期为 2 月 11 日至 17 日,全体留学生必须按照要求参加所有活动,无活动时间为在校休整。
2. 休整期除 16 日外,每晚 19:00 在俱乐部播放中外著名影片,留学生自愿观看。
3. 休整期,每日将在微信群推送微课"过年的那些传统习俗",留学生自愿观看。
4. 休整期,每日加做一道留学生推荐的各国特色菜肴。

Table 3.8　Events and Requirements during the Chinese New Year

No.	Time		Events	Locations	Requirements
1	Feb. 11 (New Year's Eve)	11:00—13:00	New Year Reception(Students learn to make dumplings before the reception) Menu: 1. Dishes: roast whole lamb, Orleans roast chicken, Thai style prawn noodle, tomato and beef soup, mutton shashlik, fried mandarin fish with sweet and sour sauce, stewed pork with sauce, meatballs with glutinous rice, cashew nut, celery fried with dried lily bulb and corn pie	Dinning hall	1. Muster Time: 11:00. Learn to make dumplings before the reception 2. Dress code: ceremonial attire 3. Wear red masks while making dumplings

Continued

No.	Time		Events	Locations	Requirements
1	Feb. 11 (New Year's Eve)	11:00— 13:00	2. Staple food: pizza, dumplings, pumpkin pie, fried rolls 3. Dessert: cakes, Tiramisu, green bean cake, and ice-cream 4. Fruit: strawberry, hami-melon, banana and oranges 5. Drinks: café, lemonade, orange juice, milk, Sprite and Coke		
		20:00— 22:00	Watch the New Year gala on TV	Second floor, club	1. At 19:50, please go to the club 2. Any dress is allowed
2	Feb. 14	10:00— 16:00	A tour to the East Lake scenic area	East Lake	1. Muster Time: 08:00 2. Location: the multi-purpose training ground. 3. Dress code: sportswear 4. Wear your masks throughout the tour except during lunch
3	Feb. 15	09:30	The "New Year Cup" tug-of-war game	The first training ground	

Continued

No.	Time		Events	Locations	Requirements
4	Feb. 15	11:00—11:50	Games for Fun: 1. Riddles 2. Rip the nameplate 3. Ring toss	Multi-purpose training ground	1. Muster Time: 09:00 2. Location: the multi-purpose training ground 3. Dress code: sportswear 4. Wear your masks throughout games 5. Join the games for fun following the tug-of-war game

Notes:

1. The relaxation period is set from Feb 11 to 17. All students should participate in scheduled events. All should stay on campus when there are no arrangements for you.

2. Except for 16 Feb., you are welcome to see films in the club at 19:00 every night.

3. You are welcome to attend lectures on "The Traditional Customs of the Spring Festival" via Wechat group on a daily basis.

4. Everyday one foreign cuisine recommended by students is served in the dining hall.

3.4.3 中国端午节庆典 Dragon Boat Festival Celebrations

"迎端午，庆开斋"中外招待会议程

时间：×月××日 12:00

地点：国际交流学院餐厅

参加人员：大学领导，国际交流学院工作人员及家属，全体留学生及陪读家属，深蓝国际俱乐部学生

主持人：国际交流学院院长王建东

着装：中方着正装，留学生着本国礼服

活动流程：

1. 留学生代表发言。

2. 大学领导致辞。

3. 请大学领导、国际交流学院领导、留学生代表切烤全羊。

4. 招待会开始。

Reception Agenda for Dragon Boat Festival and Eid

Time：12：00，DD/MM.

Location：The dining hall of the College of International Exchange

Participants：University leaders, staff of the College of International Exchange and their families, all international students and their families, members of Blue Water International Workshop

Host：Dean of the College of International Exchange

Dress code：Formal attire for the Chinese side；national ceremonial attire for overseas students

Agenda：

1. Student representative makes a speech.

2. University leader makes a speech.

3. The university and college authorities cut the toast lamb with student representatives.

4. The reception begins.

"迎端午，庆开斋"中外招待会主持词

尊敬的校领导、各位来宾，女士们、先生们：

大家中午好！

六月夏半，粽米飘香。在中国的传统节日端午节到来之际，我们在这里举行"迎端午，庆开斋"中外招待会，首先向各位的光临表示热烈欢迎，祝你们节日快乐！今年的端午节又恰逢穆斯林斋月结束，在这里我祝大家端午节安康，祝穆斯林留学生朋友们开斋节快乐！

下面，请留学生代表 P 国默哈迈德发言。

……

请大学领导致辞。

……

请大学领导、国际交流学院领导、留学生代表切烤全羊。

……

下面，我宣布国际交流学院"迎端午，庆开斋"中外招待会现在开始，请大家尽情享用美食。

Host Speech at the Dragon Boat Festival and Eid

Respected leaders, dear guests, ladies and gentlemen,

Good afternoon! In mid-summer, the air smells of delicious Zongzi. On the verge of the traditional Chinese festival, we are gathered at the reception for both Dragon Boat Festival and Eid. First of all, I would like to extend a warm welcome to all of you and wish you all the best of luck. This year's Dragon Boat Festival coincides with the conclusion of Ramadan, therefore I'd like to wish you all a healthy and peaceful Dragon Boat Festival, as well as a happy Eid to my Muslim friends.

Now let's invite student representative Mohamed from country P to make a speech.

…

Let's invite our university leader to deliver a speech.

…

Let's invite our university and college authorities to cut the toast lamb with student representatives.

…

Now the reception has begun. Please enjoy yourselves.

大学领导在"迎端午，庆开斋"中外招待会上的讲话

女士们、先生们、留学生朋友们：

中午好！今天是中国的传统佳节端午节假期的第一天，也是全世界穆斯林的重要节日——开斋节，与各国朋友一起分享节日的快乐，我感到非常高兴！

端午节是中华民族最为古老的传统节日之一，也是中国的法定节假日，其已被列入世界非物质文化遗产名录。人们在端午节祈祷庄稼苗壮成长、国家风调雨顺，后来人们也在端午节纪念伟大诗人屈原。这一天人们会以赛龙舟、吃粽子的形式来庆祝祈福。刚才，他们告诉我，今天国际交流学院专门准备了各种口味的粽子让大家品尝，希望你们能够喜欢。

目前我校有部分穆斯林留学生朋友。在刚刚过去的一个月里，你们按照教义进行白天禁食的斋戒，也克服困难，认真参加了各种教学和文体活动。我对你们的表现表示赞赏，也祝你们及家人开斋节节日吉祥。

全体留学生朋友们，时光荏苒，还有一个月的时间你们就将结束这里的学习和生活，回到自己的祖国。借此机会，我希望你们在剩下的日子里把主要精力放在学习和毕业总结上，为自己在大学的学习和生活画上圆满的句号，争取学成回国后为你们的国家建设做贡献！

最后，我提议，让我们共同举杯，为我们之间的友谊干杯。祝大家身体健康、节日快乐！

Speech by the University Leader at the Reception

Ladies and gentlemen, dear friends,

Good afternoon!

Today is the first day of the Dragon Boat Festival holiday, as well as the important festival Eid for Muslims around the world. I feel really delighted to share the festive happiness with friends from various countries. The Dragon Boat Festival is one of the China's oldest traditional festivals and a national holiday; it is also listed on the UNESCO list of intangible cultural heritage. This festival began as a way for people to pray for good weather for crops, but later evolved into a single memorial day for the renowned poet Quyuan. On this day, people compete in dragon boat races and pray with sticky rice dumplings called zongzi. I was just informed that the College of International Exchange had prepared a large quantity of zongzi in a variety of flavors for you. I hope you will enjoy them. Some Muslim students have fasted for the past month by following religious rituals. Despite this, they continued to attend classes and other recreational and sports activities as usual. I truly appreciate your efforts and would like to wish you and your families an Eid Mubarak.

Dear friends, how time flies. In less than one month, you will complete your courses here and return to your home countries. I hope you can cherish the remaining days and focus on your studies and graduation report to make a happy ending of your study here and contribute more to your countries in the future.

Now please join me to raise your glass, I would love to propose a toast to our friendship and our health. Cheers!

3.4.4 中国中秋节庆典 Mid-Autumn Day Celebrations

中秋迎新招待会

时间：9 月 12 日 12：00

地点：国际交流学院餐厅

参加人员：国际交流学院领导，国际交流学院工作人员，全体留学生，深蓝国际俱乐部学生

主持人：国际交流学院副院长赵长江

着装：正装

活动流程：

1. 学院领导致辞。

2. 招待会开始。

A Mid-Autumn Day Reception for Newcomers

Time：At 12：00, Sept. 12

Location：The dining hall of the College of International Exchange

Participants：College leaders and staff, all international students, members of the Blue Water International Workshop

Host：Deputy dean of the College of International Exchange

Dress code：Formal attire

Agenda

1. The College dean delivers a speech.

2. The reception begins.

中秋迎新招待会主持词

各位留学生朋友，

晚上好！

截至目前，已有××国×××名新留学生抵达学校，加上高年级学历教育留学生和后续抵达的新留学生，他们将组成一个庞大的队伍。中国有句老话，相聚就是缘。今天我们聚集在这里，共同庆祝中秋节，这就是一种特别的缘分。

下面请国际交流学院院长王建东讲话。

……

谢谢王建东院长！下面我宣布中秋迎新招待会开始，祝大家用餐愉快！

Host Speech at the Mid-Autumn Day
Reception for Newcomers

Dear students,

Good evening!

So far the university has welcomed ××× entrants from ×× countries. Together with senior undergraduates and students on their way to our university, newcomers will form a sizable team. As an old Chinese saying goes, "We are predestined to meet each other." It is the special fate that brings us together to celebrate on Mid-Autumn Day.

Let's now welcome professor Wang Jiandong, dean of the College of International Exchange to deliver a speech.

…

Thank you professor Wang. The reception has begun. Please enjoy yourselves.

265

国际交流学院院长在中秋迎新招待会上的讲话

女士们、先生们，留学生朋友们：

大家晚上好！

明月朗照，秋风送爽！非常高兴能够在这样美好的夜晚与中外朋友相聚一堂，共庆传统佳节、共叙友好情谊。在此，我首先代表国际交流学院领导和全体工作人员，向你们的到来表示热烈欢迎，并致以衷心的祝福，祝愿大家中秋快乐、阖家幸福！

按照中国历法，明天就是中秋节，这是中国四大传统节日之一，更是一个充满人情味的节日，它寓意着亲人团圆和幸福美满。这些天各国留学生朋友们陆续报到了，因为友谊，因为缘分，我们相聚在了一起。"每逢佳节倍思亲"，中秋节这一天中国人都会与家人一起赏月、吃月饼，而我们就是你们在中国的家人，让我们一同享受节日的快乐。正如我们在会见时对大家所说的，甲大学是中国重点教学和科研机构，大学科学的教育理念、先进的教学设备、完善的保障体系，将为你们的学习提供强有力的支撑。同时，丰富多彩的文化体育活动，也将帮助你们感受中国的文化和语言，了解中国和中国人。希望你们能尽快适应这里的一日生活制度，投入到学习生活中去。我们看到，二年级的本科留学生经过一年多的努力学习，取得了可喜的成绩，这不仅表现在遵章守纪和体能素质方面，还表现在汉语水平和基础知识方面。你们暑期还进行了文化补习和体能基础训练，比较辛苦，也希望你们能够突破学习瓶颈，调整好心态，继续完成好学业，带好你们的学妹、学弟。国际交流学院是一个国际大家庭，大家都是来自各自国家的优秀代表，希望各国留学生朋友能够相互团结，相互包容，相互帮助，支持骨干留学生的工作，不断巩固各国之间的友谊，让这段学习经历成为一段美好的记忆。

各位留学生朋友们，10月18日至27日第七届世界军人运动会将在武汉举行。我们学校将承办相关赛事，国际交流学院全面负责相关赛事的礼宾接待工作。据我了解，截至目前，已有93个国家报名参赛，我校很多留学生都来自这些国家，相信在座的各位留学生一定希望能够前往赛场为自己的同胞加油助威，你们放心，我们会尽力协调安排。同时，我们还将遴选部分留学生代表作为本次军运会的火炬手，这是一项莫大的荣誉。在这里我预祝各国选手在比赛中取得好成绩，也希望各位留学生积极配合相关工作，与我们一起携手办好这项世界盛会。

最后，祝在座的各位及家人中秋节快乐，身体健康，阖家幸福！谢谢！

Speech at the Mid-Autumn Day Reception for Newcomers by Dean of the College of International Exchange

Ladies and gentlemen, dear friends,

Good evening!

On this beautiful autumn evening, I am very delighted to be with you to celebrate traditional Chinese festival. Hereby on behalf of authorities and staff of the College of International Exchange, I'd like to extend a warm welcome to you and my best wishes for a great Mid-autumn Day.

According to Chinese lunar calendar, tomorrow is the Mid-autumn Day which is one of the four traditional holidays in China. It is a festival of love and compassion, and symbolizes the reunion of a family. These days, friends from various countries have been arriving one after another. We believe that we get together here because of friendship and predestination. As a Chinese poem goes, "On festive occasions more than ever people miss their far-flung family members." On this very day, Chinese people enjoy the full moon and have moon cakes with their family members. We are your family members in China, so let us enjoy this joyful moment together. Just as I told you at our first meeting that our university is a key education and research institute in China. The scientific educational philosophy, cutting-edge teaching facilities, complete logistical system will give solid support for your studies. In the meantime, colorful cultural and sports activities will help you gain insight into Chinese culture and language, as well as China and Chinese people. I hope you can quickly adapt to the daily routine here and focus on learning. We saw that the second year students worked really hard throughout the year, producing excellent results not just in discipline and physical training, but also in Chinese language level and basic knowledge. In the past summer vacation, they have attended tutoring sessions and basic physical training. Your endeavors are highly appreciated. I do hope that you will be able to break through academic bottleneck, adjust your attitude to continue with your course work and set a good example for junior fellow students. The College of International Exchange is an international family, and you are all talents from your country. I do hope all international students can unite as one, and be tolerant, helpful and cooperative with the students in charge, to consolidate the friendship between countries. Let's work together to make our academic experience a memorable one.

Friends, during October 18th and 27th, the 7th Military World Games will be held in Wuhan. Our university will be the host for related sports events. The College of International Exchange will be responsible for the reception of foreign guests. As far as I know, by far 93 countries have signed up for the games, including the home countries of our students. I believe that all of you desire to cheer on your countries at the stadium and I can assure you that we will do our best to coordinate this. In the meantime, we will select torchbearers of the games from among international students. This is a tremendous honor for students who are chosen. And here I wish all athletes from different countries a great success. I hope all international students will help with the necessary tasks. Let's work together to make the world games a successful one.

Finally I wish everyone and their families a nice Mid-autumn Day, good health and a happy family. Thank you!

3.4.5　留学生国庆日庆典 International Students' National Day Celebrations

T 国国庆日庆典仪式安排

时间：7 月 6 日 07:00

地点：国际交流学院综合训练场

参加人员：国际交流学院领导，T 国留学生

主持人：国际交流学院留学生办公室教师吴君鹏

着装：正装

议程：

1. 升 T 国旗、奏 T 国歌。

2. 国际交流学院领导向 T 国留学生赠送鲜花并合影。

3. 国际交流学院领导致贺辞。

4. T 国留学生代表爱德华致答谢词。

Celebrations at Country T's National Day

Time：07:00, July 6

Location：The multi-purpose training ground

Participants：Authorities of the College of International Exchange and students from county T

Host：Mr. Wu Junpeng, from the administration office of the College of International Exchange

Dress code：Formal attire

Agenda：

1. Raise Country T's national flag and play the country's national anthem.

2. College leaders present students of Country T with flowers and

pose for a group photograph with them.

3. College leader delivers a congratulatory message.

4. Student representative, Mr. Edward makes a speech.

国际交流学院领导在 T 国国庆日庆典仪式上的讲话

T 国留学生朋友：

早上好！今天是贵国 70 周年国庆日，在这里我们代表国际交流学院领导和全体工作人员，向你们和你们的家人表达节日的祝福！

T 国和中国自 19××年××月××日建交以来，始终平等相待，相互支持，两国关系发展顺利。截至目前，共有多批近百名留学生来我校培训。虽然相比其他部分国家，来校培训的人数还不算太多，但今年你们来了首批多名本科学历教育留学生，开创了历史，我相信今后会有更多贵国留学生来校学习。今年贵国留学生给我留下了深刻的印象，特别是马拉凯，自担任文体委员以来，他积极参加并协助中方人员组织开展了各项文体活动，受到大家的一致好评。贵国其他留学生的表现也非常不错。

现在距离毕业只剩下两周不到的时间了，所以我想祝愿你们。首先，祝愿你们伟大的 T 国繁荣昌盛；其次，祝愿包括你们的家人在内的 T 国人民幸福安康；最后，祝愿我们两国友谊长存！我也希望你们回国后多多宣传我们学校，介绍更多的贵国留学生来校学习。

Speech by the College Leader at the Celebrations

Dear friends from Country T,

Good morning! Today is the 70th anniversary of your National Day. Here, on behalf of the college's administration and faculty, I wish you and your families the best of luck.

Since the establishment of diplomatic relations between China and your country on DD/MM, 19××, we have consistently adhered to mutual support on an equal basis. Bilateral relations have remained extremely steady. So far, our university has admitted around 100 students from your nation in multiple batches. Although the number of students from your country is relatively small in comparison to other countries, we received more students from your country this year for undergraduate courses, which made history. And, I believe, we will witness an increase in the number of students from your country. This year, students from your country, particularly Maracay, are incredibly amazing. Since assuming the position of secretary of recreation and sports, he has not only participated actively in activities, but also assisted the Chinese staff with the organization work. Everyone lauded his outstanding performance. Other students from your country also did quite well.

There are only two weeks till your graduation from now on. So I want to give you some wishes. first, I wish a prosperous future for your country. Second, I wish people in your country, including your families a healthy and peaceful life; third, long live our friendship. I also hope that you will introduce our university to people in your country and recommend more students to our university.

3.5　毕业送行 Graduation and Departure

3.5.1　毕业通报 A Pre-Graduation Meeting

毕业安排通报议程

时间：×月×日

地点：国际交流学院智慧教室

参加人员：国际交流学院领导、全体留学生

主持人：留学生管理教师

议程：

1. 国际交流学院留学生管理教师通报毕业前主要安排。

2. 国际交流学院院长讲话。

3. 全体留学生测评打分。

4. 年级长、班长测评打分。

Agenda for Graduation Arrangements Meeting

Time：DD/MM

Location：Smart classroom at the College of International Exchange

Participants：College leaders and all students

Host：One staff member from the administration office of the college

Agenda：

1. The staff from the administration office delivers a lecture on the graduation arrangements.

2. Dean of the college addresses the meeting.

3. For evaluation purposes，all students should mark each other.

4. Senior and Class prefects assign grades to fellow students.

毕业前主要安排通报

各位留学生朋友们：

下午会议主要安排三个项目。首先由我向大家通报毕业前的主要安排；然后请国际交流学院院长王建东就毕业安排和优秀毕业留学生评奖事宜讲话；最后由全体留学生骨干对优秀毕业留学生进行测评打分。

经学校批准，我们将于 7 月××日下午举行留学生毕业典礼，7 月××

日开始组织各国留学生分批离境回国。按照时间顺序，我们安排了以下毕业事宜：

1. 7 月××日下午组织授课满意度调查、优秀毕业留学生测评打分。

2. 7 月××日和 7 月××日上午组织课程考试，7 月××日上午进行师生座谈总结。

3. 7 月××日上午 11:00 组织留学生宿舍安全、卫生及物品检查，如合格将退还宿舍押金。

4. 7 月××日下午至××日，留学生自行整理行李及个人物品。

5. 7 月××日上午 8:30，组织毕业典礼彩排；上午 10:30，举行毕业典礼；中午，举行毕业招待会。

6. 7 月××日、××日晚，我们将分两批组织各位留学生朋友乘火车赴北京。我的介绍完毕，下面掌声有请国际交流学院院长王建东讲话。

……

下面我们开始集体测评打分，并填写授课满意度调查表。

Pre-Graduation Arrangements

Dear friends,

The afternoon schedule includes three events. First, I will provide an overview of the pre-graduation arrangements; second, professor Wang Jiandong, dean of our college will speak about the graduation arrangements and discuss the detaile rules for the awards for excellent students; third, the students in charge will assign marks to their fellow students.

The graduation ceremony will take place on the afternoon of DD July according to university authorities. As of DD July, we will arrange student departures in groups. In chronological order, the pre-graduation activities are as follows:

1. On the afternoon of DD July, students will complete the question-

naire on their satisfaction with instructors and lectures, and by scoring, identify excellent students.

2. On the morning of DD July, you will take the exams of some subjects. On the morning of DD July, a seminar for both teachers and students will focus on course idea sharing.

3. At 11:00 on DD July, the college will conduct a safety and sanitation inspection in dormitories, and check the objects in dormitories. You are eligible for a refund if your dormitories meet the inspection and object examination requirements.

4. From the afternoon of DD till DD July, you may pack your luggage.

5. On DD July, at 08:30, you will take part in a graduation ceremony rehearsal. The ceremony will commence at 10:00, and a reception will follow at lunchtime.

6. On the evenings of DD and DD July, we will schedule your train to Beijing in two groups.

My briefing is finished. Professor Wang Jiandong, dean of the college will now take the floor.

...

Now please evaluate your classmates one after another by scoring them, then complete the questionnaire.

国际交流学院院长在毕业安排通报会上的讲话

留学生朋友们:

下午好!

时间过得很快,还有 10 天时间,大家就要毕业了。回想大家的学习生活,我认为是丰富多彩且富有成效的。你们在课堂上学习认真,全部顺利通过了各门课程的考核；你们参加文体活动积极踊跃，取得了包揽"湖北省外国留学生武术大赛前四名"在内的一系列好成绩。我们大家还一道参观了西安、宜昌和武汉等地的风景名胜。武汉媒体多次报道了大家的学习生活，这在以前是不多见的。虽然也有少数留学生在学习生活中犯了些小错误，但我对大家的总体表现还是满意的。上个月，我们分批和各国留学生进行了座谈，我也认真看了每个人的学习总结和"我眼中的中国"征文作品。我能够清晰地感受到大家对学校、对学院的热爱与不舍。

刚才吴君鹏老师已经讲过，你们毕业前，要参加一些考试和正式活动。你们自己也希望外出购物、会友或是到外地旅游。这段时间大家都很忙，但我希望大家随时关注学院的通知，合理安排好自己的时间，按要求参加正式活动；同时注意毕业前不要生病，确保人身和财物安全。

关于优秀留学生评选，我想说的是，按照学校有关规定，我们要对留学生在华期间的遵纪守法情况、学习成绩、个人素质、管理能力、文体活动等日常表现和发展潜质做出总体评价和鉴定，并一式三份，通报中国教育部、你们的驻华使馆及留学生本人。按照公平、公正、公开的原则，我们安排了自我评议、集体评议、学院和学校审批等环节。你们自己撰写的总结将作为附件和学习成绩、校方鉴定、毕业证书等一起通报相关部门。"优秀毕业留学生"是对你们综合表现的最高褒奖和评价，届时，我们将邀请大学校长在毕业典礼上专门为优秀留学生颁发荣誉证书。我们评选优秀毕业留学生是择优选拔，有比例限制，只有少数留学生能够获此殊荣。评价里面有加分项和扣分项，大家看了评选办法，应该就很清楚了。评选工作会持续到毕业前，希望大家重视这项评选，善始善终，通过自己的实际行动和表现来积极争取这项荣誉。等会儿我们将进行无记名测评，我希望也相信你们会本着实事求是和对自己、对各国同学负责的态度来打分。

最后，我想预祝大家在"损害管制"课程的考试中取得好成绩，圆满完成在甲大学的学业！谢谢大家！

Speech at the Pre-Graduation Meeting by Dean of the College of International Exchange

Dear friends,

Good afternoon!

How time flies. In less than ten days you will graduate from this university. I think you have experienced a colorful and fruitful life in China so far. Each of you has worked hard and passed all of your examinations successfully over your academic years. You actively participated in a variety of cultural and sporting activities and achieved outstanding success in competitions, including the top four prizes in the Hubei Martial Arts Competition for Overseas Students. Besides, we enjoyed a fantastic tour of Xi'an, Yichang, and Wuhan. The media in Wuhan covered your life and studies, which was unheard of in the past few years. Generally speaking, I am satisfied with your performance although a few students committed minor mistakes. We had formal discussions with you in various groups last month to solicit recommendations and comments. I read each of your graduation summaries as well as your essays on "China in My Eyes". I can sense your strong affection for our university and college, as well as your unwillingness to say goodbye, through your ideas.

Mr. Wu Junpeng has provided information on pre-graduation arrangements such as exams and official activities. And you want to go shopping, attend parties with your pals and even travel to different places. All of your schedules will keep you busy. I hope you will be able to read our college's notices, budget your time wisely, and attend official activities on time. Additionally, please take good care of yourselves and avoid getting sick. And it is important to ensure the safety of your own and your belongings.

I wish to say a few words on selecting excellent students. In accordance with our university's regulations, the College of International Exchange is obligated to conduct an extensive evaluation and appraisal of international students during their stay in China in the following aspects: discipline, academic work, personal image, management ability, performance in cultural and sporting activities and self-development potential. The appraisal is made in triplicate, two of which are submitted to the Ministry of Education of PRC and your embassy respectively, one of which is kept by yourself. The appraisal procedures, which include self-evaluation, peer review, and approval from our college and university, conform to the values of fairness, impartiality, and transparency. Your graduation summary will be submitted to relevant authorities as an attachment to your academic report, graduation assessment, and diploma.

The title "Excellent International Graduates" is the highest commendation and rating you can receive. At the graduation ceremony we will invite the president of our university to award certificates to excellent international students. We can only award a few students because we only select the best due to limited quota. You will understand the points for bonus and deduction when you finish reading the selection criteria. And the criteria are valid till graduation. I hope all of you attach great importance to the selection and strive for this honor through your actions. Later you will all evaluate your classmates one after another by scoring them in anonymity. I believe each of you will assign grades to your classmates in a responsible and honest manner.

Last but not least, I wish you all the best of luck with your Damage Control exam, as well as your academic work at our university. Thank you.

3.5.2 毕业分国别座谈会 Pre-Graduation Meeting with Students in Country Groups

S国留学生朋友：

你们好！

很高兴在毕业前，与你们进行一次专题座谈，这次座谈是我们毕业工作的一项正式安排，也是我们加强彼此交流、增进师生感情的重要举措。国际交流学院对此次谈话工作高度重视，所有领导和教师几乎都参与进来，为的就是更加全面、系统、准确地收集大家的意见及建议，了解你们的需求，解决存在的困难和问题，更大程度地改进我们的工作。中国有句老话，"知无不言、言无不尽"，希望大家在课程安排、教师能力水平、授课质量、实践性教学设置、行政管理、教学和后勤服务保障、课外文化生活等方面，毫无保留地畅所欲言，向我们提出建设性的意见及建议。

因为你们国家人数比较多，我认为最好以一名代表发言为主，其他留学生可以等代表发言完毕后进行补充。现在，我想听听你们的意见。

……

听了你们的发言，我很感动。首先，我觉得，你们对大学和国际交流学院充满了深厚的感情，你们对我们的工作也非常理解和支持。你们把自己当作大学的一分子，认真学习、认真观察、认真思考，以强烈的主人翁意识，给母校和国际交流学院提出了这么多有建设性的意见及建议。我谨代表学校和国际交流学院对你们表示感谢。

第二，我想说，我们国际交流学院像中国一样，正在快速发展。我们国际交流学院及我们组织的留学生教学工作，既存在好的方面，也可能有一些亟待改善和不尽如人意的地方。你们刚才所提的问题和建议，我们已经认真进行了记录，下一步还会召开专门的会议进行研究，能马上解决的，我们会及时研究解决；对于那些牵涉面比较大的、情况比较复杂的问题，我们也会加强请示、认真研究，逐步采取措施改进，也请你们能够理解。

第三，还有不到一个月你们就要毕业了，还有好几门核心专业课程要进行结课考核，国际交流学院还要组织优秀留学生评选，希望你们在毕业前把主要精力放在课程学习和毕业总结上，认真进行考试准备，参与优秀留学生这个重要荣誉的竞争，为自己在大学的学习生活画一个圆满的句号。

最后，我也衷心祝愿你们顺利完成在中国的学业，充分运用在我校所学到的知识，更好地为你们国家的建设服务，回国后继续关心大学和国际交流学院的发展，并与我们保持良好的沟通和联系！祝愿我们友谊长存，希望你们能作为友好的使者，多宣传中国、宣传我校，为增进中国与你们国家、人民的交流做出新的贡献！最后衷心祝愿你们前程似锦，身体健康，家庭幸福，欢迎你们再回中国、再回母校！

Dear friends of County S,

Good afternoon!

I'm very glad to meet with you before your graduation. This meeting is not only an indispensable part of our graduation work, but also an important way for us to strengthen mutual exchanges and friendship. The College of International Exchange attaches great importance to this meeting, with the involvement of all leaders and staff from the college. The goal is to collect your recommendations and opinions in a more complete, methodical, and accurate manner in order to better understand your needs, current difficulties and problems and to greatly improve our work as well. In China, there's one popular saying, that is, "Say everything you know, and say it without reservation." I hope you can share what you know about the class schedule, instructors' expertise, educational quality, practical class scheduling, administration and teaching management, logistics assistance, and extracurricular activities, and make constructive remarks about them.

Given the large number of members in your country group, I believe it would be preferable if you could designate one representative to inform us of your suggestions. Of course, others can offer suggestions after the representative's statement. Now it is time for you. You may start right now.

...

I'm really moved by your comments. Firstly, I can feel that you have strong affections for the university and the College of International Exchange, as well as a great deal of understanding and support for our work. Besides, you regard yourselves as university members, study hard, observe carefully, and concentrate on thinking, and provide such helpful proposals to the university and our college with a strong sense of ownership. I want to say thanks to you on behalf of the university and our college.

Secondly, I'd like to point out that the College of International Exchange is growing at the same rate as China. We have achieved strides in the education of international students. However, there are several areas that we can improve. Concerning the issues and suggestions you raised, we have made notes and written them down. We shall convene a special conference in the future to debate and research them. If we can do it now, we will be able to improve immediately. However, for those complicated and involved more negotiations, we will report to university authorities, conduct an investigation, and progressively take action. As a result, we hope you can understand.

Thirdly, there is less than a month till graduation. However, you must attend examinations on specialist topics. In addition, we will organize the selection of excellent graduates. So I hope you may devote all of your work to your studies and graduation summary, prepare well for exams and tests, and participate in the selection of Excellent International Graduates to successfully complete your studies at our university.

Finally, I hope all of you can achieve great success in your studies upon graduation and apply what you have learned here to the construction of your country. I also hope that you will continue to support the growth of the university and our college and keep in touch with us after you go home. I hope our relationship lasts forever, and I hope you will be a friendly messenger in promoting China and the university, as well as contributing to communications and exchanges between our two countries. Last but not least, I wish you a bright future, a healthy physique, and a happy family. We look forward to seeing you again in China and at our university.

3.5.3 毕业送站活动安排 Departure Arrangements

毕业留学生行李托运

时间：8 月×日

地点：学院综合训练场

参与人员：全体毕业留学生

具体流程：

1. 8 月×日，收集信息，预估留学生拟托运行李重量，与中铁快运集团了解托运费用。

2. 8 月×日，发布通知，告知留学生托运时间和相关禁运物品，提醒留学生提前打包行李。

3. 8 月×日，与中铁快运集团协调车辆来学院办理托运。

4. 8 月×日，为毕业留学生办理行李托运手续。

Baggage Check-in

Time：DD, August

Location：The multi-purpose training ground

Participants：All graduates

Steps：

1. On DD，August，we will collect the quantity and the approximate weight of your luggage，and communicate the cost of consignment with China Railway Express.

2. On DD，August，we will inform you of the consignment time，prohibited items in luggage check-in，and remind you of the packing in advance.

3. On DD，August，we will negotiate vans from China Railway Express to transport the luggage.

4. On DD，August，check-in luggage wil go through formalities.

毕业留学生核酸检测

时间：8月×日

地点：学院综合训练场

参与人员：毕业留学生

具体流程：

1. 8月×日，发布通知，告知毕业留学生8月×日需前往当地医疗机构进行核酸检测，提醒留学生戴口罩。

2. 8月×日，协调车辆以保障留学生外出做核酸检测。

3. 8月×日，前往当地医疗机构进行核酸检测，前往途中查看留学生健康码并截图保存。

Nucleic Acid Testing

Time：DD，August

Location：Multi-purpose training ground

Participants：Graduates

Steps：

1. On DD, August, we will notify all graduates of the testing at the local medical institute on DD, August and all should wear masks as required.

2. On DD, August, we will negotiate with vehicle team for the transportation.

3. On DD, August, we will arrange the testing at the local medical institute. On the way, we will scan students' health QR code and save the screenshot.

毕业留学生送站安排

时间：8月×日

地点：学院综合训练场/武昌火车站

参与人员：毕业留学生

具体流程：

1. 8月×日，前往武昌火车站协调绿色通道及指定候车厅，减少与外界人员接触

2. 8月×日，协调车辆送毕业留学生前往火车站。

3. 8月×日，发布通知，公布毕业离境安排。

4. 8月×日，组织毕业留学生从火车站出发前往出境城市。抵达出境城市后，带领留学生前往酒店入住。根据留学生离境行程，组织留学生前往机场，协助留学生填写健康信息，办理值机手续。

Departure

Time：DD, August

Location：Multi-purpose training ground/ Wuchang Railway Station

Participants：Graduates

Steps：

1. On DD，August，we will negotiate with Wuchang Railway Station to provide a green passage and a designated waiting room for us，thereby minimizing our contact with other passengers.

2. On DD，August，we will coordinate transportation with the vehicle team.

3. On DD，August，we shall notify graduates of their departure plans.

4. On DD，August，we will organize graduates' departure for the railway station. When we arrive at the departure city，we will arrange hotel for graduates. And we will arrange the transportation to airport according to graduates' itinerary for their home countries. At the airport，we will help students complete health documents and check-in.

表 3.9　留学生离境送站安排表

日　　期	时间点	国别(人数)	事　　项	中方负责人	备　　注
8 月×日	08：00	全体留学生	与中铁快运预约行李托运		
	16：30	全体留学生	宿舍物品清查，退还押金		
8 月×日	15：30	全体留学生	毕业典礼彩排		
8 月×日	07：00	全体留学生	前往当地医疗机构进行核酸检测		
	20：00	全体留学生	前往武昌火车站		乘坐软卧，每个包厢 4 名留学生
8 月×日	08：11	全体留学生	抵达××火车站，出站后就近吃早餐		
	09：00	全体留学生	前往××景区参观		

续表

日　　　期	时间点	国别(人数)	事　　项	中方 负责人	备　　注
8月×日	13:00	全体留学生	前往酒店办理入住		
	17:00	全体留学生	根据留学生行程，组织留学生前往机场，协助留学生填写健康信息，办理值机手续		机场快餐
8月×日	待定	送站人员	送站工作人员返校		

Table 3.9　Departure Plan

Date	Time	Nation (number of students)	Events	Chinese Staff in Charge	Remarks
DD, August	08:00	All students	Schedule a consignment with China Railway Express		
	16:30	All students	Examine dormitory items and return the deposit		
DD, August	15:30	All students	Graduation Ceremony rehearsal		
DD, August	07:00	All students	Proceed to the local medical institute to have a nucleic acid testing		
	20:00	All students	Proceed to Wuchang Railway Station		All Stay at the soft-berth chambers with four students sharing one chamber

Continued

Date	Time	Nation (number of students)	Events	Chinese Staff in Charge	Remarks
DD, August	08:11	All students	Arrive at ×× Railway Station. After exiting the station, we have breakfast nearby		
	09:00	All students	A tour to ×× scenic area		
	13:00	All students	Proceed to the hotel		
	17:00	All students	Based on the students' itinerary, transport them to the airport, and assist them in filling the health documents and finishing the check-in procedures		Fast food restaurant at the airport
DD, August	Undetermined	Chinese stuff	Chinese staff return to the university		

第四章　文娱体育篇

Chapter 4　Cultural, Recreational and Sports Events

4.1　国际文化节 International Cultural Festival

4.1.1　深蓝国际文化节开幕式议程 Opening Ceremony Agenda for Blue Water International Cultural Festival

时间：×月××日 16:00—17:30

地点：体育馆前广场

参加人员：大学领导，国际交流学院全体人员、全体留学生、中方学生代表

主持人：国际交流学院副院长赵长江

活动流程：

1. 国际交流学院院长王建东宣布深蓝国际文化节开始。

2. 主席台领导为征文比赛获奖留学生颁奖。

3. 大学副校长白晓林致辞。

4. 参观中外展台，观看文艺节目表演。

文艺节目顺序：

1. 中外学生"快闪舞"（表演者：中外学生）

2. 中国武术表演（表演者：武术队学生）

3. S 国舞蹈（表演者：S 国留学生）

4. C 国民族舞蹈(表演者：C 国留学生)

5. 中国歌舞表演(表演者：舞蹈社学生)

6. M 国传统舞蹈(表演者：M 国留学生)

7. T 国风情舞蹈(表演者：T 国留学生)

Time：16:00—17:30, DD/MM

Location：The square in front of the gymnasium

Participants：University leaders, staff of the College of International Exchange, all international students and Chinese student representatives

Host：Professor Zhao Changjiang, deputy dean of the College of International Exchange

Agenda：

1. The Cultural Festival is officially opened by Wang Jiandong, the college's dean.

2. The essay competition prize winners are awarded by the leaders.

3. Vice president Bai Xiaolin addresses the ceremony.

4. Visit the booths and watch the performances.

Programs：

1. Quick flashing dance (performers：Chinese and international students)

2. Chinese martial arts show (performers：Chinese students from Kongfu club)

3. Dance of Country S (performers：students from Country S)

4. Traditional dance of Country C (performers：students from Country C)

5. A Chinese song-and-dance performance (performers：Chinese students from dancing club)

6. Traditional dance of Country M (performers：students from Country M)

7. Dance of Country T (performers：students from Country T)

4.1.2 深蓝国际文化节开幕式主持词 Host Speech at the Blue Water International Cultural Festival Opening Ceremony

女士们、先生们、朋友们：

为加强中外学生的交流融合，集中展示中国和目前在校留学生所属国家的地域文化和风土人情，增进各国学生之间的相互了解，今天我们在此举行大学深蓝国际文化节开幕式。首先，我介绍一下出席文化节活动的各位领导：大学副校长白晓林，办公室主任曹荣，国际交流学院院长王建东，我是国际交流学院副院长赵长江。参加此次文化节的还有全体留学生、学校教职员工、中国学生及家属代表，让我们对各位中外朋友们的到来表示热烈的欢迎和衷心的感谢。

现在进行活动第一项，请国际交流学院院长王建东宣布深蓝国际文化节开幕。

……

朋友们，文化铸就校园气质。深蓝国际文化节已成为我校对外交流和展示的品牌！今年的文化节既有继承，也有创新，由一系列活动组成，包括大学微型国际马拉松、国际论坛、模拟联合国大会和中外文化展览交流会等。我们还举办了此次文化节征文比赛，其中获得征文比赛一等奖的是S国萨帕斯；二等奖的是P国万斯、K国罗尚；三等奖的是T国克劳斯、F国萨拉、S国达沙。

请获奖留学生上台领奖。现在，让我们以热烈的掌声欢迎大学副校长白晓林致辞。

……

开幕式到此结束，请各位领导和中外朋友们一起享受接下来的文化盛宴吧！

Ladies and gentlemen, dear friends,

Today we are gathered here for the Blue Water International Cultural Festival opening ceremony, The Cultural Festival is held to strengthen the interactions, understanding, and friendship between international and

Chinese students, as well as to highlight regional cultures and traditions of China and international students' home countries. First of all, let me introduce our honorable leaders: professor Bai Xiaolin, vice president of the university, professor Cao Rong, head of the administration office, professor Wang Jiandong, dean of the college of International Exchange. My name is Zhao Changjiang, deputy dean of the College. All international students, teacher representatives, Chinese students and families are also present at the ceremony. With a round of applause, let us convey our heartfelt greeting and gratitude to all of our friends. To begin, let's invite professor Wang Jiandong, dean of the College of International Exchange to officially kick off the Cultural Festival.

...

Dear friends, it is the culture that shapes the university environment. The Blue Water International Cultural Festival has established a name for itself in the field of foreign exchanges. This year's Cultural Festival continues the history while also introducing new events, including the Campus International Marathon, the International Forum, the Model United Nations Conference as well as the cultural expo. We also have an essay competition. Sampath from Country S is the first prize winner; Vance from Country P and Roshan from Country K are the second prize winners; and Kloss from Country T, Sara from Country F, and Dasha from Country S are the third prize winners.

Let's now greet the winners and present them with their prizes. Let's now welcome professor Bai Xiaolin, vice president of the university to deliver a speech.

...

The opening ceremony has come to an end. Please join us to enjoy the following Cultural Festival.

4.1.3 大学领导在深蓝国际文化节开幕式上的讲话 Speech by the University Leader at the Blue Water International Cultural Festival Opening Ceremony

女士们、先生们、中外学生朋友们：

下午好！今天我们在此举办中外文化展览交流会，共庆中国的生日。其实，从上周开始，大学深蓝国际文化节系列活动就已拉开了帷幕，中外学生朋友们以不同的方式表达了对大学的祝福。其中有大学微型国际马拉松大赛、深蓝国际电影周、模拟联合国大会，还有在我校训练中心举办的招待会。今天的交流会是文化节的最后一项活动。相信中外学生朋友们一定收获满满。在这个喜庆的时刻，我代表大学领导和全校教职员工向刚才获奖的留学生表示热烈祝贺！来我校学习以来，你们的生活多姿多彩，学习取得了成效。你们既积极活跃、奋勇争先，又遵章守纪、行为有度，是一个朝气蓬勃、和谐友爱的优秀团队。因为你们，校园里多了一抹别致的色彩。

中外朋友们，"和平"与"发展"是当今世界的最强音，中国国家主席习近平提出的"一带一路"倡议已经得到了越来越多国家的积极响应。在座的各位大多来自"一带一路"沿线国家。共同打造政治互信、经济融合、文化包容的利益共同体、命运共同体和责任共同体，已成为我们的共识。越来越多不同肤色、不同民族的外国友人在这里相识、相知，斑斓多彩的异国文化在这里交融互通，折射的恰恰是中外深度融合、发展的大愿景、大趋势。

借此机会，我也向中外学生朋友提三点希望。一是希望留学生进一步加强对中国文化的学习与了解，多交中国朋友。二是希望中国学生积极与留学生沟通交流，开阔视野，增长见识，全面提升对外交往能力。三是希望大家高扬深蓝国际文化节的风帆，让代表着和平、合作、友谊的巨轮驶向大洋、挺进深蓝！

最后，预祝深蓝国际文化节取得圆满成功！谢谢！

Ladies and gentlemen, friends,

Good afternoon! The Blue Water International Cultural Festival has opened to commemorate China's birthday. Actually, the Blue Water International Cultural Festival has been inaugurated with a series of events, including the Campus International Marathon, the Blue Water Film Week, the MUN Conference, and the reception at the training facility, since last week. So far, both Chinese and international students have sent their best wishes to China in a variety of ways. The cultural expo today is the festival's final event. I believe that by participating in the expo, you will all be able to accomplish gain a lot. At this joyful time, I would like to extend my heartfelt congratulations to the prize-winners on behalf of the university's administration and faculty. Since your arrival at the university, you've had a diverse and prosperous life. You have been active and striving for excellence while adhering to the discipline and behavior rules. It is fair to say that you are a great team brimming with vitality and love. Our university looks unbelievably beautiful because of you.

Dear friends, peace and development are the strongest voice in the world. The "Belt and Road" initiative proposed by Chinese President Xi Jinping has gained support from a growing number of countries. The majority of international students come from countries along the Belt and Road. The creation of a community of common interest, shared future, and shared responsibility, characterized by mutual trust in politics, economic integration and cultural inclusiveness has been widely accepted. Nowadays, an increasing number of international students from different countries find friendship at our university, and diverse cultures coexist here, reflecting the great vision and primary trend of in-depth integration between China and other countries.

Here I would like to take this opportunity to present three points.

To begin, I hope international students would be able to develop a greater understanding of Chinese culture and make more Chinese friends. Secondly, I hope Chinese students can interact with international peers to broaden your horizon, increase your knowledge and strengthen your capacity in foreign exchanges. Thirdly, I hope all of you are able to raise high the sails of the Blue Water International cultural Festival, steering the ship of peace, cooperation and friendship to blue waters.

Last but not least, I wish the Blue Water International cultural Festival a successful conclusion. Thanks!

4.2　文艺联谊 Gala

4.2.1　中外学生迎新春联欢晚会节目单 Playbill for the New Year Party

1. 开场舞《斗鼓》

表演：非洲鼓队、××学院腰鼓队、锣鼓队

篇章一：异域风情

2. 拉丁舞《激情拉美》

表演：B国、D国留学生，××学院学生

3. 幽默剧《和谐亚洲》

表演：M国留学生、××学院学生

4. 舞蹈《热力非洲》

表演：C国、S国留学生，留学生家属。

5. 中外歌曲联唱《天下一家：甲大学欢迎你》

表演：D国、S国、T国、Y国留学生、××学院学生

篇章二：华夏魅力

6. 武术表演《中国功夫》

表演：C 国、S 国等国留学生；大学飓风武术队

7. 笛子和钢琴联奏《江河情》

表演：××学院教师

8. 舞蹈《沂蒙颂》

表演：郭敏飞等教师

9. 歌曲《前门情思大碗茶》

表演：××学院刘雯

篇章三：多彩大学

10. 光影舞《铸剑》

表演：××学院学生

11. 舞蹈《大学的快乐时光》

表演：D 国、M 国留学生

12. 三句半《我给大学点个赞》

表演：S 国、T 国、Y 国留学生

13. 龙狮歌舞《中国龙》

表演：S 国、Y 国、Z 国留学生，大学龙狮队

主持人：S 国留学生家属（女）、P 国留学生（男）、××学院学生（女）、××学院学生（男）

1. Opening Dance：*Drum Show*

Performers：African students' drum team, Chinese students' gong and drum team

Part Ⅰ　Cultures and Traditions

2. Latin Dance：*The Passion of Latin America*

Performers：students from Country D and B, Chinese students

3. Comedy：*Harmonious Asia*

Performers：students from Country M, Chinese students

4. Dance：*Hot Africa*

Performers: students from Country S and C, and their families

5. Songs: *We are family*; *Welcome to University A*

Performers: students from Country D, S, T, and Y, Chinese students

Part Ⅱ　The Charm of Chinese Nation

6. Martial Arts Show: *Chinese Kungfu*

Performers: students from Country S and C, the university's Martial Arts Team

7. Flute and Piano Show: *Memory on Rivers*

Performers: teachers from ×× College

8. Dance: *Ode to the Yimeng Mountains*

Performers: Mrs. Guo Minfei and her team

9. Song: *Qianmen's Tea Stall*

Singer: Liu Wen from ×× College

Part Ⅲ　A Vibrant University

10. Dance: *The Making of Warriors*

Performers: Chinese students from ×× College

11. Dance: *Fantastic Moments at the University*

Performers: students from Country D and M

12. A Three-and-a-half-line Ballad: *Thumbs up for the University*

Performers: students from Country S, T and Y

13. Singing and Dancing: *Chinese Dragon*

Performers: students from Country S, Y and Z, the university's Dragon & Lion Dancing Team

Host Team: one international student's wife from Country S, a student(male) from Country P, a Chinese student (female) from ×× College, and a Chinese student(male) from ×× College

4.2.2 中外学生迎新春联欢晚会主持词 Host Lines at the New Year Party

张露："尊敬的领导，各位来宾！"

赵帅："Respected leaders, dear friends！"

张露："亲爱的老师们，同学们！"

赵帅："Dear professors, colleagues！"

Fernando："大家晚上好！"（Da jia wan shang hao.）

张露："今夜的明月如此夺目，让我们共同欢歌，用最诚挚的微笑欢送20××。"

赵帅："We enjoy the gala with the splendid moon, smile at our lovely memories, and say goodbye to the year of 20××."

张露："明天的旭日更加辉煌，让我们携手相约，用最真诚的祝福喜迎新的一年。"

赵帅："In the first sunshine tomorrow, let's join our hands to greet the new year with our warmest wishes."

张露："我们相聚于此，共同珍藏这份友谊，使异域文化活跃在和谐校园的方方面面。"

赵帅："We are together in the name of friendship to promote diversified cultures and traditions on campus."

张露："我们携手共进，不懈追求那片和平，让来自不同国家的火热的心紧紧地贴在一起。"

赵帅："Hand in hand, we strive for peace, and bring closer the hearts from various nations."

Fernando："Today, we are witnessing the magical blend of human skills."

张露："我们秉持着同一个传统，严谨求实，拼搏创新；我们流淌着同一种血液，坚持不懈，英勇顽强；我们传承着同一类精神，服务人民，服务国家。因为我们同是甲大学的儿女。下面请欣赏由我们留学生和××学院学生带来的大合唱《美丽的大学》。"

赵帅："We embrace the tradition of being rigorous, practical, diligent and innovative; we are the next generation of our forefathers who have their perseverance and fearless spirit on all fronts; we uphold the principle of serving our people and homeland. We are the children of University A. Let's enjoy the chorus *Our Beautiful University* performed by international students and the Chinese students from ×× college."

张露："《美丽的大学》唱出了我们在校留学生对母校的赞美、眷恋之情。记忆中那童年的点点滴滴也逐渐涌上心头，浮现眼前。下面请欣赏由大学街舞队带来的街舞《童年的记忆》。"

赵帅："A beautiful university shows international students' ode as well as affections for alma mater. The song has brought back childhood memories. Let's now enjoy the dance *When I Was a Kid*, by the university hip-hop team."

张露："下面请欣赏由来自 D 国 5 名留学生带来的《D 国民族歌曲》。"

赵帅："Let's now enjoy the dance *Colorful Days* by students from Country D."

张露："青春，是我们怀揣理想，投身科技的动人旋律；是我们迎接挑战，所向披靡的感人诗章；是我们对践行使命、履行职责掷地有声的应答。这一切只因我们是新时代大学生，把青春交给党是我们无悔的选择。请欣赏舞蹈《青春学子》。"

赵帅："Youth offers the best opportunity for us to practice our ideal in scientific and technological research; Youth offers the best opportunity for us to forge ahead in the face of adversity; Youth responds to the call of our missions. As students in new era, we will never regret to contribute our youth to the CPC. Let's now enjoy the dance *Students on Campus*."

Fernando："We all have dreams as young people. Let's now enjoy the dance *Students on Campus*."

张露："Malaika 在 Swahili 语里代表天使的意思，它是纯真友谊和美好祝愿的象征。下面请欣赏由 T 国和 S 国的留学生带来的歌曲 *Malaika*。"

赵帅："Malaika is Swahili for angels. Angels bestow kindness and well-wishes upon us. Let's now enjoy the song *Malaika* by students from Country T and S. Please enjoy the Swahili song *Malaika*."

张露："今天，我们的老朋友海豚乐队又来到了我们的晚会现场。这次他们又给我们带来了什么节目呢？请欣赏英文歌曲 *My love*。"

赵帅："Our old friend Dolphin Band has come for tonight's show. What song they will play on this stage? Let's enjoy the song *My Love*."

张露："看完我们中方学生的演出，我们的 M 国和 N 国留学生也都按捺不住，跃跃欲试了。下面请欣赏他们自编自导自演的情景歌舞。掌声欢迎!"

赵帅："Students from Country M and N are so enthralled by the performances of Chinese students that they can't wait to give it a shot. They wrote and directed the play on their own. Let's enjoy their singing and dancing."

张露："这是一个神秘的花园，蝴蝶纷飞，虫鸣鸟唱，稻香四溢，雨点纷纷，是谁打破了这片宁静……下面让我们一起走进奇幻的魔术世界，有请赵帅为我们带来的魔术《缤纷魔术秀》。"

赵帅："Who disturbed the peace of a mysterious garden filled with fluttering butterflies, twittering birds, aromatic crops, and misty air? Let's join the magician to enjoy Zhao Shuai's *Magic Charm*."

张露："今天我们的现场来了一位强人，他说他要向舞坛天王迈克尔·杰克逊发出挑战。掌声有请郭飞为我们带来舞蹈 *Dangerous*。"

赵帅："A genius makes his debut tonight. He wants to compete with Michael Jackson, the dance king. Let's welcome Guo Fei with a big applause. His dance is *Dangerous*."

Fernando："A genius wants to challenge Michale Jackson by his dance of *Dangerous*."

张露："是和平友好的共同追求让我们齐聚在这里，是携手进步的美好祝愿让我们欢聚一堂。让我们共同祝愿友谊之花长开，让我们共同祝愿友谊之树常青。请欣赏由中外学生为我们带来的大合唱《友谊地久天长》。"

赵帅："It is our common goal of peace and love that binds us together; it is the best wishes for common progress that brings us together. May our friendship thrive forever. Let's now enjoy the chorus *Auld Lang Syne* by Chinese and international students."

Fernando："Tonight the friendship brings us together and we hope our friendship will last forever, now please enjoy the song *Auld Lang Syne*."

张露："今夜，中华大地上开遍了友谊之花。绿色的橄榄枝也将和平之光洒向了世界每一个角落。"

赵帅："Tonight, the flower of friendship blooms across our nation; the light of peace shines every corner of the world."

张露："我们让快乐永存，永存在灯光辉煌的夜空；我们让友谊永驻，永驻在万家团圆的春天!"

赵帅："May the joy last forever, sustaining the lovely night in our memory; may our friendship last forever, sustaining the spring when everyone enjoys family reunion."

Fernando："Dear College of International Exchange, thank you very much for creating a family for us all."

张露："大学中外学生迎新联欢晚会(合)到此结束! 祝大家(合)晚安!"

张帅："The New Year Gala(together) is concluded. Good Night to all(together)."

Fernando: "All good things must come to an end. Have a Good night."

张露: "请领导和演职人员上台合影。"

赵帅: "Leaders and the cast please join us for a group photo."

4.2.3 中外学生迎新春联欢晚会情况通报 A briefing on the New Year Party

为迎接新年的到来，促进中外学生之间的交流，我们计划于×月×日晚，与中方学生联合举办中外学生迎新春联欢晚会，届时将有舞蹈、歌曲表演和小游戏，并邀请大学领导和你们的任课教师参加。希望大家认真准备相关节目，在晚会中充分展示才艺和风采，尽情地享受节日的欢乐。晚会结束后，我们还将评选最受观众喜爱的节目，并为表演者颁发奖品。近期大家要做的是：

1. 每个国家准备一个表演节目，当然也可以和别的国家合作表演（主要是传统民族舞蹈、哑剧等肢体动作丰富的节目），如果家属、小孩有这方面特长和兴趣的，我们也特别欢迎他们参加。今天会后，请值班员详细询问各国领队，填好节目单，于×月×日交给我们。我们将从中精选出部分节目，在晚会上演出。

2. 学会中文歌曲《相亲相爱的一家人》。我们会利用下午的时间安排中方学生来教唱。你们将会在晚会结束时与中方学生合唱这首歌。

To celebrate the impending New Year and to promote the exchanges between the Chinese and international students, we will host the New Year Party with Chinese students on the evening of (DD/MM). The gala is characterized by dances, songs and games. The university leaders and teachers will be invited to the gala. We hope that you would take your performances seriously to fully show your artistic talents and charm, and that you will enjoy the gala. We will choose the best programs which are popular with the audience and will grant awards to performers after the party. Recently you are supposed to:

1. Get ready for the performances. Each country will prepare for a single performance which mainly consists of body movements like traditional folk dance and mime. You are encouraged to cooperate with other countries. Your families are welcome to participate in the show if they are interested and skilled in stage performance. After the meeting, the duty student will ask every country leader to fill out this playbill in detail. The duty student will deliver the playbill to us on (DD/MM). We will select the most desirable performances from the playbill for the party.

2. Learn the Chinese song *A lovely Family*. You will learn the song from Chinese students in the afternoons. And you will join the chorus with Chinese students at the end of the party.

4.3 征文摄影活动 Essay and Photographing Competitions

4.3.1 活动启事 Call for Essays and Photographs

为庆祝中华人民共和国成立70周年，分享留学生对中国及甲大学的理解和认识，展示你们在校期间丰富多彩的学习生活，9月至10月将举行第×届以"我眼中的中国"为主题的征文及摄影比赛。有关事项如下：

一、参赛作品要求

1. 征文使用英、法两种语言撰写，体裁不限，每人1篇，字数在400~1000字。要求主题突出、语言生动，内容可包括对中国的理解或认识；对甲大学的了解或在此的学习感受；对中国人民特别是大学师生的印象等。征文排版格式可参考《我眼中的中国(20××年文集)》，借阅此书可到1号教学楼7楼课间休息室及图书室。

2. 参赛照片可使用相机、手机、iPad 等设备拍摄，照片格式统一为

JPEG，数目不限。要求与中国或中国人相关，抓住最美好的瞬间，展现中国的发展成果、大学完善优美的办学环境及学校人员（包括留学生）的精神风貌等。除统一组织的采风以外，留学生只允许在《留学生行政管理规定》指定的非禁区内拍摄。

3. 每件作品都要有标题、作者国别及姓名，以电子文件形式提交。

二、作品征集时间

摄影、征文截止时间为 9 月 20 日。同一人的所有作品打包压缩后交给本班班长。9 月 20 日 17:00 前，由各班班长收齐交给留学生办公室。

三、评审人员

评审工作将由英语及法语教授、任课教师、中外学生代表共同完成。

四、奖励安排

征文及摄影比赛各设一等奖 1~2 名、二等奖 2~4 名、三等奖 3~6 名。9 月 30 日将举行征文及摄影比赛颁奖仪式。征文及摄影比赛作品将作为"参观见学"的课程作业，其完成情况按有关比例计入课程成绩。10 月底，所有征文将集结出版。

The College of International Exchange will host the ×th Essay and Photographing Competition on *China in My Eyes* to mark the 70th anniversary of the founding of China, share international students' experiences at our university and display students' rich and colorful lives in China. The details are as follows:

Ⅰ. Submission Requirements

1. The language is either English or French and there are no genre restrictions. Each student is expected to write only one essay with 400~1000 words. In the essay the topic should be highlighted and the language should be vivid and succinct. You can write about your understanding of China, your insight and experiences gained from our University, your interactions with Chinese people, and especially with the teachers and students at our university. Please refer to the collections of *China in My*

Eyes 20×× for the topics and format. They are available in the lounge and library on the 7th floor in the NO. 1 classroom building.

2. The photographs can be taken with a camera, a cell phone, an i-Pad and other devices. The format is JPEG and there is no limit to the number of photos you submit. The most wonderful moments should be related to China or Chinese people, highlighting Chinese achievements, the university's excellent facilities and attractive environment for education, as well as the morale of teachers and (international) students. With the exception of those shot during the visits organized by the College of International Exchange, other photos are supposed to depict the scenario in non-restricted places indicated in *Administrative Regulations for International Students.*

3. The title, nationality, and name of the writer should all be included in the essay or photos. Please submit in soft copy/electronic version.

Ⅱ. Timetable

The closing date/deadline for submissions is September 20th. The works of the same student should be compressed in one package and delivered to respective course leaders. The prefect shall collect all submissions and deliver them to the administration office by 17:00 on September 20th.

Ⅲ. The reviewer team

The works will be reviewed jointly by English and French language academics, instructors, and Chinese and international student representatives.

Ⅳ. Awards

The prizes will be awarded to writers and photographers separately, with 1 ~ 2 first prize winners, 2 ~ 4 second prize winners and 3 ~ 6 third prize winners for each competition. The award ceremony will take place on September 30th. Your essays and photos will be used as assignments for the subject *"Visit and Study Tour"*, and will be graded on a percentage basis. All the essays will have been compiled and published in a book by the end of October.

"外国留学生眼中的中国共产党"征稿启事

今年是中国共产党成立 100 周年。走过百年光辉历程的中国共产党，已发展成为世界上最大的马克思主义政党，并带领全国各族人民奋发图强、艰苦创业，创造了举世瞩目的成就，让中华民族实现了从站起来、富起来到强起来的伟大飞跃。

进入新时代，中国共产党不忘初心，不仅带领中国人民打赢了脱贫攻坚战、全面建成小康社会，还坚定地履行大国担当，携手各方勠力同心，共同推动人类命运共同体建设，为弘扬多边主义、加强全球治理、促进亚洲和世界的繁荣发展提振了信心、增添了动力。即日起，J 日报特开设"外国留学生眼中的中国共产党"专栏，邀请外国留学生投稿，以外国留学生的视角感受中国共产党的百年奋斗征程。

Call for Papers: "The Communist Party of China (CPC) through My Eyes"

This year marks the centennial of the Communist Party of China (CPC). As the world's largest Marxist ruling party, the CPC has united the people of various ethnic groups across the country through concerted efforts, and shared weal and woe with the people throughout its 100-year history. The world has seen the great achievement created by the CPC that guided the nation through the backwardness to a major economy by leaps and bounds.

In the new era, while remaining committed to its original aspiration and mission, and uniting the whole nation, the CPC eradicated absolute poverty and made great strides towards a moderately prosperous society in all respects. China, as a responsible major country, has jointly advanced the efforts in the building of a global community with a shared future. In this way, China boosted confidence and injected impetus for multilateralism, global governance, and prosperity of Asia and the world. The endeavors generated by the CPC has won global acclaim. The *J Daily* offers a new feature called "The CPC Through My Eyes" to encourage contributions from overseas students. Contributors are supposed to elaborate on their perspectives on the CPC's growth over the past 100 years.

4.3.2　颁奖典礼主持词 Host Speech at the Award Ceremony

朋友们：

　　下午好！

　　为庆祝中华人民共和国成立 70 周年，经学校批准，4 月份，我们面向留学生开展系列活动。这些活动得到了我校全体留学生的积极响应和热情参与。你们还拿起手中的笔和照相机，完成并上交了××部征文和摄影作品，用你们独特的视角，刻画了中国、中国人及学校师生的对外形象，展现了中外人员的友好情谊。经过认真评审，我们从中遴选了×部优秀作品。今天，大学领导专程出席中华人民共和国成立 70 周年招待会，并为获奖人员颁奖。出席的领导有：大学校长刘鹏海，副校长白晓林。让我们对他们的到来表示热烈的欢迎和衷心的感谢。

　　接下来，有请大学副校长白晓林宣读获奖人员名单。

　　……

　　接下来，请留学生代表、征文比赛一等奖获得者 S 国查那卡发言。

　　……

　　现在，让我们用热烈掌声欢迎大学校长刘鹏海致辞。

　　……

Dear friends,

Good afternoon!

To celebrate the 70th anniversary of the founding of the People's Republic of China, with the approval of the university authorities, in April, we organized a series of events for all international students. We also witnessed active response and participation of all the international students. At the same time, you used your pen to express emotions and your camera to capture images. Additionally, you handed over ×× peices of work to us. Your work reflects your unique viewpoint on China, the Chinese people, and teachers and students at our university, while also demonstrating the positive relationships between Chinese students and international students. We selected × pieces of exceptional work from all submissions following a thorough evaluation. Today we are honored to invite the university authorities to our National Day reception and we will award winners. The leaders are professor Liu Penghai, president of the university and professor Bai Xiaolin, vice president of the university. Let's welcome them with a round of warm applause.

Let's now welcome professor Bai Xiaolin, vice president of the university to announce the winners.

...

Let's welcome Mr. Chanaka from Country S, the first prize winner to make a speech.

...

Let's now welcome professor Liu Penghai, president of the university to address the reception.

4.3.3 获奖证书样稿 Honor Certificate Samples

1. "我眼中的中国"主题征文比赛。

查那卡：

你获得 20××—20××学年"我眼中的中国"主题征文比赛一等奖，特发此证，以资鼓励。

2. "我眼中的中国"主题摄影比赛。

西农：

你获得 20××—20××学年"我眼中的中国"主题摄影比赛一等奖，特发此证，以资鼓励。

1. Essay competition：" China in My Eyes".

Dear Chanaka，

You won the first prize in the essay competition：" China in My Eyes". The certificate is issued as a token of encouragement.

2. Photographing Competition：" China in My Eyes".

Dear Sinon，

You won the first prize in the photographing competition：" China in My Eyes". The certificate is issued as a token of appreciation.

4.3.4　获奖文章选登 Winners' Essays

爱上武汉不需要理由

T 国留学生　法　莫

也许在地图上，武汉不过是一个小小的点。但我知道武汉高校众多，在校大学生超过了 110 万，是中国在校大学生人数最多的城市。而且武汉汇聚了 140 多个国家 1 万多名像我一样的外国留学生，可以说武汉是一个教育强市，是一座留学之城。我先后两次留学中国，对中国的感情非常深。如果有可能，我希望能够加入中国国籍。中国是世界上经济发展速度最快的国家，其发展成就举世瞩目。能有机会到中国学习，对我们个人发展和国家建设来说，重要性都是不言而喻的。记得第一次留学是在中国南京，回国后我的职业生涯有了重要飞跃。这一次到武汉后，我发现这里的教育环境更优越、师资更强大、生源更集中。我深信在武汉的留学深造一定会帮助我在更高级的职位竞争中脱颖而出，实现新的飞跃。

　　中国的语言叫汉语，中国的文字叫汉字，中国的传统服饰叫汉服，大部分的中国人是汉族人。有意思的是，武汉这座城市的名字里面也有个"汉"字。这里历史悠久，有很多名胜古迹和漂亮的人文自然景观。比如，蜚声中外的黄鹤楼、千年古刹——归元寺、武汉人的后花园——东湖公园，还有城市新名片——楚河汉街。武汉号称"九省通衢"，地处长江黄金水道与京广铁路大动脉的十字交汇处，是全国四大铁路枢纽和六大航空枢纽之一。武汉新机场的建成更是大大提升了其国际化速度。随着多条高铁的开通，武汉至北京、上海、广州、香港、成都等地的交通缩短至 5 小时左右。武汉因其特殊的地理环境和繁荣的经济，素有"江城"之称和"东方芝加哥"的美誉。来武汉后，我参加了学校组织的"中国日"文化体验活动，到武汉江滩、解放公园、中山公园等各类场所参观、采风、拍照，触摸了这座魅力之城的发展脉搏。白云黄鹤的传说，吉庆街的欢唱、再加上过江隧道和地铁的开通……武汉呈现给我们和世界的，不仅是一座气质独特的历史文化名城，更是一座生机勃勃的现代化大都市。我和同学们都觉得武汉发展得越来越好了，武汉的天更蓝了，水更清了，草更绿了，空气更洁净了，市容更优美了……我们希望成为武汉国际化进程中的新主人，一起追寻武汉梦、中国梦！我们相信新武汉人的生活会越来越幸福！

　　在我眼里，武汉人热情好客、直率朴实、善良真诚，和他们在一起，我很开心。我觉得武汉人那股火辣辣的性格代表的是武汉文化最底层、最本土的精神。比如说，尽管在非洲和 T 国，足球氛围也很浓厚，但是还是没有武汉人在一起踢球和看球时那么热闹和疯狂。来武汉不久，我就加入了学校留学生足球队，和中国朋友一起踢球、聚会，就像一个快乐的国际大家庭。我们来自五湖四海，为了共同的学习目标走到一起，不一样的生活环境，不一样的风俗习惯，不一样的语言，给教学安排带来了很多困难，但是武汉的老师们，出点子、想办法，认真备课，课堂讲解深入浅出，带领我们逐步完成了预定的学习目标。他们还悉心照顾我们的饮食起居，帮助我们度过"思乡"关，以最快的速度适应了"第二故乡"——武汉的生活。我真担心毕业回国后，会不习惯呢！学习之余，我们经常会用不太熟练的汉语与武汉市民打招呼、聊天，讲一些我们自己国家好玩的事情。通过参加学校组织的中华传统文化系列讲座，我们结识了不少武汉的朋友。和他们在一起，我们感受到了开放、自信和包容。我想说友情之船，一旦铸成，永不下沉。

武汉吃的东西也不含糊，有武昌鱼、藕夹、珍珠丸子、洪山菜薹、精武鸭脖、泥蒿炒腊肉、排骨藕汤……每天早上芝麻酱的香气飘洒在江城的每一个地方。武汉夏天的美食很多，有凉面、绿豆汤，还有年轻人的最爱——烧烤。

江城武汉是我的新家，各位朋友要是有空，欢迎来这里做客！

Need No Reason to Love Wuhan

Famohamed Conteh, Student from Country T

I looked up the map and searched for the city of Wuhan. It looked like a small spot compared with the big world. But I know Wuhan is home to universities with an enrollment of over 1.1 million students and ranks number one with the largest number of enrolled university students in China. More than 10 thousand international students like me from over 140 countries are now gathering in Wuhan, a city of education and a city for overseas study. I came to study in China twice. I must confess that I would feel grateful to China, if I had way to apply for citizenship in China. China is the fastest growing country in the world in economy and in its developmental orientation, a nation that was griping for development has now become the light of the universe. To be very precise, we come from various countries to seek modern knowledge in different disciplines which will be of greatest importance to us as individuals, and to our countries as a whole. I came to study in Nanjing a few years ago (it was the first time I had come to China), which aids me in the challenging appointments I have had back home and helps me realize the important leap in my career. When I came to study in Wuhan this time, to my surprise, the educational environment is much better, the teaching staff here are more professional, the number of the international students here is amazing. I believe that my career progression, a new leap in senior division will be realized when I go back. The Chinese language is known as Han Yu, the Chinese characters are named as Han Zi, the Chinese traditional costume is called Han Fu and Han Zu accounts for the majority of Chinese people. The funny thing is that there is a "Han" in the name of Wuhan. Wuhan is a time-honored city and has quite a few of scenic spots and historical sites as well as perfect natural attractions and cultural heritage like the world famous attraction Yellow Crane Tower, the thousand-year-old temple—Guiyuan temple, the back garden of Wuhan people—East Lake scenic area and the new urban card—Chu River and Han Street. Wuhan has long been known as the "thoroughfare to nine provinces". Wuhan is located in the blessed land of the intersection between the golden passage of Yangtze River and the main artery of Jingguang Railway (Beijing to Guangzhou) while it is one of the national transportation hubs of the four key railways and the six key airlines. A new airport terminal has been built and the internationalization of Wuhan is on its unstoppable way. The opening of the high speed railways has reduced the travelling time to 5 hours or so from Wuhan to Beijing, Shanghai, Guangzhou, Hongkong, Chengdu, etc. Wuhan is reputed as the "River City" and the "Chicago of China" for its unique location and prosperity. I participated in the "Culture-Oriented Events on China Day" organized by our university shortly after my arrival. We went sightseeing in different places like Yangtze River Beach, Jiefang Park, Zhongshan Park, etc. taking pictures, learning local customs and habits, exploring the city's development. The legend of the white clouds and the yellow crane, the singing of the Jiqing Street, the opening of the underwater tunnel and the subway... All these have made Wuhan not only a city of culture with unique temperament in history, but also a dynamic and modern metropolis. My classmates and I have seen the city is developing better and better with improved environment like the blue sky, clean water and air, green grass, etc. We are looking forward to being identified as new inhabitants in the course of the city's internationalization. We are sure that the new generation of local people will enjoy a happier life.

In my eyes, hospitality, honesty and kindness are the characteristics of wuhan people. I feel delighted when I communicate with them. Their passion and enthusiasm represent the profound local culture. I can elaborate this in an example: in Africa and in Country T, people are keen to play football while in Wuhan people are crazy when they watch the football game and play football. I joined the international student football team of our university. I made a lot of Chinese friends in the football field. We gather together as if we are a happy international family. We are from different parts of the world and get together for the same aim of studying. Although different social background, customs, habits, languages bring about difficulties for the teaching process, the teachers of Wuhan help all of us accomplish the scheduled study task by providing us good ideas and methods, preparing for the lessons carefully and lecturing complicated subjects in simple terms. The teachers take care of our everyday life carefully and have helped us overcome the painful homesickness. Now we recognize Wuhan as our "second hometown". I am afraid that when I go back to my country, I will be a stranger there. In spare time, we like chatting with local people in our shaky Chinese and tell funny stories of our countries. We attended the lecture on "China's Traditional Culture Series" sponsored by our university and made a lot of friends who have the spirit of opening-up, confidence and inclusiveness. I would like to say that true friendship is the best ship that can ever be built, so difficult yet if achieved truly… unsinkable.

In Wuhan you can enjoy delicious food every day. The famous delicacies are: blunt-snout bream, deep fried lotus root sandwich, meat ball with glutinous rice, purple flowing stalk, duck neck, stir-fried cured meat with mud artemisia, and spareribs with lotus root soup as well. Every morning, the smells of the delicious aroma of the sesame paste fill the air. In summer, you are attracted by various delicacies like cold noodles with sesame sauce, sweet mung bean soup and barbecue which is popular with young people at parties.

Wuhan is my new home. Welcome to my home at your convenience.

这里给了我第二次职业生命

S 国留学生　查那卡

去年 9 月，我和近十名同胞来到中国甲大学留学。我仍然清晰地记得通过飞机窗口第一次看到武汉上空的白云和蓝天；还记得第一次感受到武汉的热风、繁忙的车流和热闹的街道。进入大学，平整的道路，高大的松树，郁郁葱葱的校园，设施齐全的教学训练场馆，中国学生自信的脚步，中国教师忙碌的身影，还有每天清晨田径场上练太极拳的老人……这里的一切，对我来说，都充满着迷人的魅力和如此多的新鲜感！

中国和 S 国两国友谊源远流长，可以追溯到公元前 1 世纪。甲大学在 S 国的知名度非常高。20 世纪××年代，贵校首次开展留学生教育时，我们国家就选派了多名人员到此留学。当时的领队贾斯汀今天已提拔为重要的领导人。他为 S 国建设做出了突出贡献，已成为 S 国的骄傲和我们效仿的榜样。去年贵校评选的优秀留学生 S 国贾瑞尔回国后很快就晋升为高级官员。所以，我们 S 国人员都争相来这里留学。到校后，我全身心投入大学安排的各种丰富多彩的专业学习和文体活动。这里的课程学习起点高、专业性强、内容全面，和我之前留学过的 B 国、Y 国等国家相比，我觉得来对地方了。在国际交流学院，来自××个不同国家的留学生，像家人一样互相帮助、互相照顾。国际交流学院组织的中国国庆节、中秋节、春节等庆祝活动，让我们感受到了中国的文化和风俗，体验了很多过去只有通过电影、纪录片和杂志才能了解的中国生活。在参观见习活动中，我们见到了令世界称奇的三峡大坝工程。我永远无法忘记我在三峡听到的有史以来最美妙的音乐，那是一位美丽的中国女子乘坐一只木筏，在三峡溪流里吹奏长笛的声音。

当所有的事情都在美好平静地发展的时候，去年 12 月一个让我终生难忘的日子里，由于我的一个疏忽，我的右脚踝粉碎性骨折了，这差点使一切都发生改变了。我记得医生告诉我，伤势非常严重，若不尽快进行手术，可能会落下残疾，以后可能无法再继续我热爱的事业了。这个消息犹如晴天霹雳，身体的疼痛、高额的医疗费、术后残疾、中断学业被召回国，这些问题、困难和危机，让我备受折磨，我感到十分沮丧和消沉。现在回想起来，幸好我的生活里面有你们，一群热情友善、真诚而富有同情心的中国朋友。我住院后，大学各级领导对我非常关心。你们与我国驻华使馆反复协商，帮助我顺利在中国完成手术。否则，我将在没有行走能力的情况下踏上归途，那种痛苦和危险对我来说，是无法想象的。最让我感动的是，贵校从国家之间的友谊和对我个人前途发展负责的角度出发，同意我继续在中国留学。国际交流学院院长还联系武汉市多家医院进行专家会诊，邀请武汉市××医院外科主任亲自为我主刀，这确保了我手术后一个月就能独立行走，没留下任何行走隐患。他还与医院方面多次协商，最终医院为我安排了 VIP 病房，并提供了周到的护理，而且还为我减免了很多手术费用。如果没有国际交流学院全体人员轮流到医院看望我、鼓励我，我不知道会怎么熬过那些日日夜夜。我明白是你们的不懈努力使我留了下来。为此，我国有关部门领导撰写亲笔信，向中国致以崇高敬意，我国驻华使馆也专门致函，向贵校表示感谢和敬意。

手术虽然过去 4 个月了，但一切都好像还和昨天一样，让人记忆犹新。现在，我已经恢复了所有的正常学习和训练。我更有热情和信心过好在大学的每一天，不断积累专业知识。在这里，我收获了真正的友谊，学到了课堂上没有的知识。尽管去过很多国家，也在很多国家留学过，但是不得不说，我在甲大学和中国不仅学到了专业知识，而且还了解了中国文化和最了不起的中国人民，这是在其他地方不曾有过的经历和感受。我想大声说，这里为我的职业腾飞打下了坚实的基础，给了我第二次职业生命！

My Career Life Salvaged by University A

Chanaka, Student from Country S

Last September with about 10 countrymates, I came to study in University A which is a prestigious Chinese university. I still remember the white clouds and the blue sky passing by my window of the air craft on my way from Beijing to Wuhan. I also remember the hot breeze and the densely populated streets with vehicles and people on both sides. As we entered University A, what jumped into my eyes was the campus scenery: the broad streets, the tall pine trees, the lush surroundings, the various teaching and training venues, the young Chinese students marching in confident strides, the hard-working teacher, and the elderly people practicing Tai-chi every morning. All these are full of charm and freshness for me.

The friendship between Country S and China has a long history which dates back to the 1st century BC. University A is very famous in our country. When the university first carried out the foreigner training program in 1990s, our country sent some students to study here, with Justin as the team leader. He has been doing very well in our country and becomes the pride and example for us. It was not by chance that Mr. Gurui, the excellent student selected by our university last year, was appointed to a prominent position when he was back. No wonder people of our country are eager to study here. I threw myself into studying the subject contents and attending the extra-curricular activities in University A after I came here. Compared with Country B and Y where I studied as overseas student before, I think the education here is more useful with characteristics of higher starting point, more comprehensive and professional. In the College of International Exchange, the international students from ×× countries help and take care of each other like family members. The events organized by the College of International Exchange, such as the visit tours and celebrations on the Mid-Autumn Day, the National Day, the Spring Festival, offer great opportunities for us to appreciate the Chinese culture and custom. The visit to the world miracle—the Three Gorges Dam in Yichang impressed me very much. I will never forget the most beautiful music I heard from a lady who was playing the flute on a wooden boat in the Streams of the Three Gorges.

When everything was moving forward in peace and hope, I had an unfortunate accident last December, which is indelible in my life. Due to my own cursoriness, I suffered a comminuted fracture on my right ankle which almost changed my life totally. I remembered that the doctor told me to have an immediate surgery in order to avoid deformity. I felt very depressed on thinking of all the unfortunateness, such as the pain on the right ankle, the expensive medical fees, the possibility of deformity, the recalling back to my country, and thereafter the difficulties I would face in my country... Fortunately, it was you—warm hearted, most sympathetic and kind hearted Chinese friends who had offered timely and tremendous help at the critical moment and so lucky I was in this university. After I was admitted to the hospital for my surgery, the leaders of this university gave me a lot of care. After the repeating diplomatic discussions going on between China and our Embassy in Beijing, I finally had the chance to accept the surgery in China. If in any case, I would have been recalled back to my country and had to return home with no walking ability. I was deeply touched when the news arrived that I could continue my study here and the hospital waives much of the medical fees for me. And I knew that it was the painful attempts taken by the Dean of the College of International Exchange that made it possible for me to continue my study here after my surgery in China under the safe and secured hands of well experienced doctors in ×× hospital in Wuhan. The Dean went to several hospitals to organize the expert consultation and invited the chief of the surgical department of Wuhan ×× hospital to carry out the surgery for me. Thanks to his miraculous talent in carrying out my surgery, I was able to walk again within a month from the operation. What's more, the hospital had managed to arrange a VIP ward for me and I received an attentive nursing care. Without every slightest help, encouragement and care from all the staff of the College of International Exchange, I don't know how to get over those days. I bear it in mind that your untiring efforts makes it possible for me to stay here. The leader of relevant authority in our country wrote a letter in person to show his respect to China. And the Embassy of our country in China also sent a letter to the university to convey their sincere appreciation and gratitude.

Although 4 months have passed, everything has been fresh in memory as if it had happened just now. I now return to my daily study and training and become more enthusiastic and confident than ever, take my course day after day to learn more knowledge. Here I not only establish great friendship with other international students and staff of the College of International Exchange, but also learn a lot. As a person who has travelled and studied in many countries in the world, I honestly feel that the experiences I gained in University A and in China in terms of the subject knowledge and the exposure to the culture and the wonderful people here are the most impressive. I am pleased to announce that training at University A has laid solid foundation for my career.

4.4 体育竞赛 Sports Competitions

4.4.1 田径运动会 Sports Meeting

田径运动会参赛报名通知

我校计划于 11 月 1 日至 2 日举行年度田径运动会。国际交流学院将组队参加比赛，欢迎各位留学生踊跃报名参加。为留学生设置的比赛项目有：(1)100 米赛跑；(2)400 米赛跑；(3)3000 米赛跑；(4)4×100 米接力；(5)12×60 米迎面接力；(6)跳高；(7)跳远；(8)铅球。大家可以找值班留学生马卡拉和杰西自由填报，每人限报 3 项。报名截止时间为 9 月 30

日。10 月中旬国际交流学院将组织内部预赛，并为参赛队员提供运动服。

表 4.1 田径运动会报名表

项目 姓名	100 米	400 米	3000 米	4×100 米接力	跳高	跳远	铅球

Sports Meeting Sign-up

Our university will host a sports meeting in early November. The College of International Exchange will organize an athlete team to compete in the sports meeting. We are looking forward to your active involvement in the sporting events listed below: (1) 100-meter dash; (2) 400-meter race; (3) 3000-meter race; (4) 4×100-meter relay; (5) 12×60-meter relay; (6) high jump; (7) long jump; (8) shot put.

Each of you is limited to three events. You can sign up with Makara and Jesse, the duty students. September 30 is the deadline for the sign-up. A preliminary match will be held at the College of International Exchange in mid-October. We will provide sportswear for the players who are chosen at the preliminary round.

Table 4. 1　The Sign-up Page for the Sports Meeting

Item Name	100m	400m	3000m	4×100m Relay Race	Hign Jump	Long Jump	Shot Put

4.4.2　乒乓球赛 Table Tennis Match

"校庆杯"乒乓球赛规则

1. 每次比赛由 3 场组成，每场比赛 11 分。赢 2 场比赛者获得 3 分并晋级，赢 1 场比赛者获得 1 分，弃权者得 0 分。

2. 第一轮各组之间进行循环赛，每组由 5 名选手组成，前 3 名选手晋级下一轮。

3. 第二轮开始淘汰赛，决赛前 3 名为冠军、亚军和季军。

4. 接发球顺序由猜硬币决定。由猜对的选手选择发球或接球，对手选择使用乒乓球桌的某一边。

5. 每 2 分后选手交替发球，直到得到 11 分且至少领先对手 2 分，或者直到两名选手都得到 10 分。如果两名选手都达到 10 分，那么之后每得

1 分后发球交替，直到一名选手获得 2 分的优势。

6. 每场比赛后，选手交换场地。在第三场比赛中，无论轮到谁发球，当一个选手得 5 分后交换场地。

7. 选手必须从基线后面击球，使球在桌子半边反弹一次，并在对手的半场至少弹跳一次。如果球击中网，但没有击中对手的半桌，那么对手得 1 分。如果球击中网在另一边反弹，则被称为放网。此时选手须再次发球。放网数量不受限制，不会造成任何处罚。

8. 对于比赛中的以下任何错误，对手得分：

(1)球在自己身边弹跳 2 次。

(2)双击球。请注意，手腕下方的部分被视为球拍的一部分，并允许从手握球拍的手或手指上做出回球，但击中手或手指，然后击中球拍是双重击球。

(3)球在对手半场没有反弹(即没有做出"好"的回球)。

Rules of "University Anniversary Cup" Table Tennis Match

1. Each mach is composed of 3 games, 11 points each game. The winner is the player who wins 2 games and will gain 3 points. The loser will gain 1 point. Those who waive the right to play will gain zero.

2. The trial match undertakes round robin among groups, each group composed of 5 players. The player who takes up the top 3 standings will advance to the next round.

3. The elimination series is adopted from the second round. The winners in the finals are the champion, the runner-up and the second runner-up.

4. The service is decided by a coin toss. The player with a right guess can choose to serve or to receive, but the other can choose which

side of the table to use.

5. The service alternates between opponents every two points until a player reaches 11 points with at least a two-point advantage, or until both players have 10 points. If both players reach 10 points, then the service alternates after each point until one player gains a two-point advantage.

6. After each game, players switch sides of the table and in the third round, players switch sides when one player scores 5 points, regardless of whose turn it is to serve.

7. The player must hit the ball from behind the baseline so that it bounces once on his half of the table, and then bounces at least one time on the opponent's half. If the ball strikes the net but does not strike the opponent's half of the table, then a point is awarded to the opponent. However, if the ball hits the net, but nevertheless goes over and bounces on the other side, it is called a let (or net-in). The play must be stopped and the ball must be served again with no penalty. The number of the let is unlimited.

8. Points are awarded to the opponent for any of the following errors:

(1) Allowing the ball to bounce on one's own side twice.

(2) Double hitting the ball. Note that the hand below the wrist is considered part of the racket and making a good return off one's hand or fingers on the racket-holding hand is allowed, but hitting one's hand or fingers and subsequently hitting the racket is a double strike and an error.

(3) Causing the ball not to bounce on the opponent's half (e.g. , not making a "good" return).

"校庆杯"乒乓球决赛及颁奖安排

时间：×月××日

地点：国际交流学院综合训练场

参加人员：国际交流学院领导及工作人员，全体留学生

主持人：国际交流学院留学生教师吴君鹏

着装：运动服

奖项及奖品：一等奖，运动服；二等奖，跑步鞋；三等奖，足球鞋

议程：

1. 举行乒乓球半决赛、决赛。

2. 国际交流学院领导为获奖学生颁发奖品。

3. 国际交流学院领导与所有参赛学生合影。

4. 国际交流学院院长讲话。

Arrangements for the Award Ceremony of "University Anniversary Cup" Table Tennis Final Match

Time：DD/MM

Location：Multi-purpose training ground of the College of International Exchange

Participants：College leaders and staff, all international students

Host：Mr. Wu Junpeng from the college administration office

Dress code：Sportswear

Prize：Sportswear for the first prize winner, jogging shoes for the second prize winner, and soccer shoes for the third prize winner

Agenda：

1. The semi-finals and finals kick off in a row.

2. College leaders award the winners.

3. All players join the group photo with leaders.

4. Dean of the college makes a speech.

"校庆杯"乒乓球赛颁奖仪式

下面我宣布：

获得"校庆杯"乒乓球赛三等奖的是×××专业××组，获得二等奖的是×××专业××组，获得一等奖的是×××专业××组。

下面请国际交流学院领导为获奖学生颁发证书和奖品。

……

下面请各位领导与全体参赛学生合影。

……

下面请国际交流学院院长讲话。

……

Award Ceremony of "University Anniversary Cup" Table Tennis Match

I am pleased to announce the following results from the "University Anniversary Cup" table tennis match：

The third prize winner is team ×× from the course ×××, the second prize winner is team ×× from the course ××× and the first prize winner is team ×× from the course ×××.

Let's invite leaders of the College of International Exchange to issue certificates and prizes to winners.

…

All players please join leaders to take a group photo.

…

Let's now welcome dean of the college to make a speech.

…

国际交流学院院长在"校庆杯"乒乓球颁奖仪式上的讲话

女士们、先生们、朋友们:

　　下午好! 很高兴和大家一起, 全程参与和观看了这次令人难忘的比赛。在庆祝大学建校 70 周年的日子里, 由国际交流学院组织的第三届"校庆杯"乒乓球比赛, 经过 10 天 5 轮的激烈角逐, 已结束全部赛程, 取得圆满成功。首先向获得冠军、亚军和季军的 3 名选手表示祝贺! 向全体运动员、裁判员、记分员表示敬意!

　　回顾比赛的整个过程, 从抽签、分组, 到训练、比赛, 全体留学生都能积极参与、认真准备, 服从安排。刚开始, 有不少留学生朋友告诉我, 来中国前, 他们碰都没碰过乒乓球。几轮比赛下来, 大家不仅了解了乒乓球的基本打法, 而且也慢慢喜欢上了这一项被称作中国国球的运动。我看到不少朋友即使是在课间, 也会去打上几拍。业精于勤, 像科内、哈桑、阿拉克这几位零起点的非洲朋友, 课余时间自觉训练, 进步都很大, 成为了前八名, 甚至是前四名。虽然我们选手不多, 但这同样是涉及十多个国家的"国际赛事", 取得这样的成绩是值得骄傲和自豪的。

　　中国有句名言, "友谊第一、比赛第二"。我们举办这次乒乓球比赛, 主要是为了锻炼身体、促进交流、增进友谊, 构建一个更加和谐的国际大家庭。在比赛过程中, 我注意到不少值得称赞的事情, 比如, 7 名裁判员、记分员, 相互配合, 及时召集人员, 公正评判, 认真记录, 为比赛的顺利进行牺牲了不少个人时间, 做了很多保障和服务性工作。再比如, 马卡拉手把手地教会了很多非洲留学生打乒乓球。每次比赛, 总有很多观众为选手加油助威, 有的还热心地给选手出谋划策。瑟萨多次带着他 3 个可爱的小孩不惧寒冷前来观战。还有些留学生在赛程、赛制安排上给我们提了很好的建议。这些都拉近了我们彼此的距离。我要特别指出来的是, 比赛结束后, 每场次比赛成绩单, 将作为历史资料长期保存。我相信, 我们的友谊和比赛时的那一幕幕, 也将长期珍藏在各位朋友心中。

　　今后, 我们还会安排羽毛球比赛、趣味运动会等多种不同类型的比赛。我们将一起筹划、一起组织、一起落实。希望大家保持热情，团结协作，积极参与，奋力拼搏，敢为人先，永争第一。最后，衷心祝愿各位朋友身体健康、生活幸福！谢谢！

Speech from the Dean of the College of International Exchange at the "University Anniversary Cup" Table Tennis Match Award Ceremony

Ladies and gentlemen, friends,

Good afternoon! I am very glad to participate in and watch this unforgettable game along with you. To commemorate the 70th anniversary of the university, the College of International Exchange hosted the third "Anniversary Cup" table tennis match. Now, this match has come to a successful conclusion after a 5-round intense competition in 10 days. Let's offer our congratulations to the champion, the runner-up and the second runner-up and pay tribute to all players, referees and scorekeepers!

From the drawing lots and grouping to the training and competition, all friends took the match seriously, prepared carefully, followed the directions, and participated enthusiastically throughout the whole process. At the beginning, some friends told me, before coming to China, they had never handled table tennis balls. However, after rounds of competition, you not only have learned basic skills, but also enjoyed playing table tennis which is renowned as China's national game. I saw that many friends even made use of class breaks to shoot a few rounds. Practice makes perfect. Several beginners from Africa including Kone, Hassan, and Arak spent their spare time training. And they made tremendous progress in such a short period of time, climbing to the top eight and even making it to the top four. Although there are only a few students from several countries take part in this match, it is an international competition. So you have every reason to be proud of your accomplishments.

There is a saying in China that goes, "friendship first, match second". We hosted this match to improve our bodies, promote our exchanges and enhance our friendship to build a more harmonious multinational family. During the match, I witnessed a lot of memorable moments. For example, the 7 referees and scorekeepers cooperated with each other, assembled players on time, judged impartially and recorded carefully. They paid much time supporting and assisting during the match. Makara was able to teach several African friends how to play table tennis. And many friends came to watch and cheer on the players and some gave advice and suggestions to the players. Despite the cold weather, Joseph brought his three lovely kids to watch the games for many times. Some friends gave us good advice on match schedules. What you have done warm our hearts. In particular, I want to point out that the score record papers of each game will be saved as historical materials. I believe that our friendship as well as every moment of the game will be treasured in our memories.

In the future, we will host a range of events, including badminton matches and recreational games. We will all contribute in planning, coordinating, and implementing our ideas, just like we did throughout this match. We hope you will sustain your passion, collaborate with each other, participate actively, and work hard with a pioneering spirit to strive for the best. Finally, I wish you good health and a happy life! Thank you very much.

4.4.3　校园马拉松 Campus Marathon

一、微型国际马拉松比赛议程

时间：4 月 14 日 15:00—16:30

地点：大学教学区(含田径场)

参加人员：全校教职员工

活动安排：

1. 大学领导、嘉宾、参赛选手代表签名留念。

2. 大学领导讲话。

3. 马拉松比赛开始。

二、微型国际马拉松比赛主持词

各位选手，中外朋友们：

大家好！今天我们在此举办大学微型国际马拉松比赛。

首先，我介绍一下出席马拉松比赛的各位领导：大学副校长白晓林，大学基础教育学院何勇教授，我是国际交流学院院长王建东。参加本次马拉松比赛的还有全体留学生，学校教职员工、中方学生、家属代表，以及来自深蓝国际俱乐部的学生，让我们对各位朋友的到来表示热烈的欢迎。

下面有请大学副校长白晓林和各位嘉宾及参赛选手代表签名留念。

……

现在，让我们以热烈的掌声欢迎大学副校长白晓林致辞。

……

开幕式到此结束，请各位参赛选手就位。

三、大学领导在微型国际马拉松比赛上的讲话

各位参赛选手：

大家好，今天是一个值得喝彩的日子！在这生机勃勃、惠风和畅的春光里，大学 200 多名师生齐聚赛道，共同迎来了大学微型国际马拉松大赛。在此，我代表学校领导，向大家表示热烈祝贺！

为传播中国文化，促进中外友好交流，丰富中外学生校园生活，展现大学师生的风采，我们隆重举办系列庆祝活动。此次马拉松比赛是系列活动的首项活动。比赛面向全校教职员工，包括国际留学生，可以说这是一项群众性、国际性的体育赛事。赛程设置合理，既有 3 公里趣味跑、5 公里健康跑，也有挑战自我的 10 公里耐力跑，选手们可视情自由选择。此外，赛道线路均沿大学校园显著建筑物及优美景观设置，参赛者既能享受快乐奔跑的魅力，又能近距离地感受校园的美丽景致。让我们在美丽的校园尽情奔跑吧！

希望所有参赛者都能发扬挑战自我、超越极限、坚忍不拔、永不放弃的马拉松精神，秉承友谊第一、比赛第二的原则，赛出风格，赛出水平，用激情和力量演绎无限精彩，用奔跑和速度彰显我们蓬勃的活力。

最后祝愿本次活动取得圆满成功，祝愿全体参赛人员跑出健康、跑出活力、跑出风采！

Ⅰ. International Campus Marathon Agenda

Time: 15:00-16:30, April 14

Location: Areas for educational activities (including training grounds)

Participants: Teachers and students

Agenda:

1. Leaders, guests and runner representatives give their autograph as a memento.

2. University leader delivers a speech.

3. The campus marathon kicks off.

Ⅱ. Host Address at the International Campus Marathon

Dear participants and friends,

Good afternoon! Today, our university will host the International Campus Marathon. To begin, please allow me to introduce the authorities present today: professor Bai Xiaolin, vice president of the university, and professor He Yong, from the School of Basic Education. My name is Wang Jiandong, dean of the College of International Exchange. Additionally, the marathon is attended by all international students, teacher representatives, Chinese student representatives, families, and members from the Blue Water International Workshop. Let's express our warm welcome to all of them with a round of applause.

Let's now welcome professor Bai xiaolin, vice president of the university, distinguished guests, and runner representatives to sign their names on the board.

…

Let's now welcome professor Bai, vice president to address us.

...

This is the end of the opening ceremony. Runners please take your places.

Ⅲ. Speech by University Leader at the International Campus Marathon

Dear participants and friends,

Good afternoon! Today is a day to celebrate. In the vibrant, breezy spring, over two hundred teachers and students are gathered at the tracks to kick off the international campus marathon. Hereby, on behalf of university authorities, I would love to offer my heartfelt congratulations to all of you.

We will host a series of celebrations with the goal of promoting Chinese culture, fostering friendly exchanges between China and other countries, enriching campus life, and demonstrating the ethos of our faculty and students. The marathon is the first event of the festivities. The competition welcomes participation from all teachers and students, including international students, making it a truly mass and international sporting event.

Today's marathon boasts its sensible distance. You can choose whatever distance to take. We have a delightful 3-kilometre fun run, a 5-kilometre health run, and a 10-kilometre charm run where you can test yourself. Whether you run 3, 5 or 10 kilometers, you'll pass by famous landmarks and breathtaking sceneries. Runners will experience the thrill of athletics and come face to face with nature's splendor. Let's enjoy the marathon!

I hope that all participants will keep the marathon spirit alive by challenging themselves, pushing their limitations, persevering through adversity, and never giving up. I hope you will all follow the philosophy of "friendship first, competition second", play fairly and make the most of your competence. I hope that passion and power will rule the tracks, and that endurance and speed will propel our booming strength to new heights.

Finally, I wish the event a big success. May we all run for our health, strength, and honor.

4.4.4 "战疫五项"趣味活动"Fight Five" Fun Games

"战疫五项"趣味活动颁奖仪式议程

时间：5月3日11:00

地点：国际交流学院综合训练场

参加人员：国际交流学院领导及工作人员，留学生志愿者及获奖人员

主持人：国际交流学院留学生教师吴君鹏

着装：中方人员着白色T恤，留学生着黄色T恤

活动流程：

1. 健身操表演。

2. 国际交流学院教学办公室主任蒋平为活动志愿者颁发证书。

3. 国际交流学院副院长赵长江为"个人全能奖"颁发证书、纪念品，赠送鲜花。

4. 国际交流学院院长王建东为"小组全能奖"颁发证书、纪念品、奖杯，赠送鲜花。

5. 国际交流学院院长王建东总结讲评。

Award Ceremony Agenda for "Fight Five" Fun Games

Time: 11:00 on May 3

Location: Multi-purpose training ground of the College of International Exchange

Participants：Leaders and staff of the College of International Exchange，volunteers and winners

Host：Mr. Wu Junpeng from the administration office of the college

Dress code：White T-shirt for Chinese staff and yellow T-shirt for international students

Agenda：

1. Setting-up exercises.

2. Mr. Jiang Ping，head of the administration office of the college presents volunteers with certificates.

3. Professor Zhao Changjiang，deputy dean of the college presents "individual all-around" winners with certificates, mementos and flowers.

4. Dean of the college presents "team all-around" winners with certificates, mementos, cups and flowers.

5. Professor Wang Jiandong，dean of the college delivers a speech.

"战疫五项"趣味活动颁奖仪式主持词

各位领导、留学生朋友们：

大家上午好！5 月 1 日至 3 日，学院举办了中外"战疫五项"趣味活动，至此，"战疫五项"活动圆满结束，感谢大家的积极参与。鉴于目前依然处于疫情防控阶段，所以要严格控制颁奖现场的人数，只安排获奖人员到现场领奖。当然，我们会通过微信群向大家分享颁奖现场的情况，欢迎大家观看。

下面进行活动第一项，请活动志愿者代表和颁奖领导出场，颁奖领导是国际交流学院教学办公室主任蒋平。

有请国际交流学院教学办公室主任蒋平为志愿者颁发证书。

谢谢蒋平主任。

活动第二项，请获得"个人全能奖"的留学生和颁奖领导出场，颁奖领导是国际交流学院副院长赵长江。

获得三等奖的是来自 R 国的达西。有请赵长江副院长为获奖留学生颁发证书和纪念品，赠送鲜花。

获得二等奖的是来自 S 国的马特。有请赵长江副院长为获奖留学生颁发证书和纪念品，赠送鲜花。

获得一等奖的是来自 T 国的约翰。有请赵长江副院长为获奖留学生颁发证书和纪念品，赠送鲜花。

朋友们，请肃静，奏 T 国国歌。

有请颁奖领导与获奖留学生合影。

感谢颁奖领导。

祝贺获奖留学生。

活动第三项，请获得"团体全能奖"的留学生和颁奖领导出场，颁奖领导是国际交流学院院长王建东。

获得第三名的是来自 M 国的伽玛，泰勒，迪诺。有请王建东院长为获奖留学生颁发证书和纪念品，赠送鲜花。

获得第二名的是来自 T 国的贾曼，雷诺，海蒂。有请王建东院长为获奖留学生颁发证书和纪念品，赠送鲜花。

获得第一名的是来自 C 国的纳斯，孟杜，马杜胡。有请王建东院长为获奖留学生颁发证书、纪念品和奖杯，赠送鲜花。

朋友们，请肃静，奏 C 国国歌。

有请颁奖领导与获奖留学生合影。

感谢颁奖领导。

祝贺获奖留学生。

活动最后一项，请王建东院长致辞。

谢谢王建东院长！

下面，我宣布国际交流学院"战疫五项"趣味活动到此结束。

A Host Speech at the Award Ceremony

Respected leaders, dear friends,

Good morning! We hosted the "Fight Five" fun games from May 1st to May 3rd. So far we have wrapped up all five events. Thank you for your hard work! Given the pandemic prevention and control response, we imposed a limit for the number of people at the ceremony, with all winners present. However, we will share the ceremony via a Wechat group. Everyone is invited to watch through the wechat group.

Let's now welcome volunteer representatives and Jiang Ping, head of the administration office.

Jiang Ping will now award volunteers with certificates.

Thank you very much Mr. Jiang.

Let's welcome the leader, and "individual all-around" winners.

Professor Zhao Changjiang, deputy dean of the College will now honor "individual all-around" award to Darcy from Country R, the third prize winner with the certificate, memento and flowers.

The second prize winner is Matt from Country S. Professor Zhao Changjiang will now award Matt with the certificate, memento and flowers.

The first prize winner is John from Country T. Professor Zhao Changjiang will now award John with the certificate, memento and flowers.

Friends, attention please, now play the national anthem of Country T.

The leader will now take a group photo with prize winners.

Appreciated. Congratulations to awardees.

Let's now welcome "team all-around" winners and the leader,

professor Wang Jiandong, dean of the College.

The third-place team members are Gamma, Taylor, and Dino from Country M. Professor Wang Jiandong, dean of the College will now award winners with the certificate, memento and flowers.

The second-place team members are Jarman, Reno, and Heidi from Country T. Professor Wang Jiandong, dean of the College will now award winners with the certificate, memento and flowers.

The first-place team members are Nas, Mendo and Maduhu from Country C. Professor Wang Jiandong, dean of the College will now award winners with the certificate, memento, cups and flowers.

Friends, attention please, now play the national anthem of Country C.

The leader will now take a group photo with prize winners.

Appreciated. Congratulations to honorees.

Let's welcome professor Wang Jiandong, dean of the college to deliver a speech.

Thank you so much, professor Wang.

The "Fight Five" fun games concluded.

第五章 综合保障篇
Chapter Five Extensive Logistical Support

5.1 教学场所消毒管理措施 Rules for Disinfection at Educational Facilities

留学生楼及留学生教学场所消毒工作由专业消杀公司组织力量实施。消毒方式以喷洒消毒药物进行消杀为主，按照大学相关规定实施，重点对留学生教室、会议室、功能室、食堂、宿舍、厕所、电梯、楼梯、扶手、垃圾桶等重点场所的环境卫生开展全覆盖消毒。

开课前对各留学生教室进行彻底的卫生清扫、全面消杀，保证教室恢复到常规使用状态，为正常开课做好准备。上课后，留学生教学场所每日定时通风换气且不少于两次，对物体表面和室内空气等进行定期消毒。

The disinfection of the international students' building and the educational facilities of international students is carried out by professional disinfection companies. The disinfection method is primarily spraying disinfectants, and in accordance with the relevant regulations of the university, key areas such as classrooms, offices, canteens, dormitories, toilets, elevators, stairs, handrails, trash cans, etc. for international students will all be disinfected.

Before class, a full cleanliness and complete disinfection of the classrooms for international students will be conducted to ensure that classrooms return to normal use and are ready for regular classes. After class, the teaching place should be ventilated at least twice a day, and the surface of objects and the indoor air should be disinfected regularly.

5.2 看病就医 Visiting Doctors

入学阶段，大学为留学生安排一次体检。学制一年以上，每年增加一次常规体检。留学生患病后，由大学医院提供门诊治疗，必要时，转入指定医院诊治。

1. 需要就诊治疗时，请填写看病申请表，并逐级向留学生领队、留学生值班员和中方值班教师报告，中方值班教师会及时给予回复。遇到急重病情可直接向中方值班教师报告。

2. 普通疾病的治疗，如感冒、发烧、腹泻等，国际交流学院将安排人员陪同前往校医院或指定医院，由医生决定医疗措施；进行口腔保健、镶配义齿、矫正生理缺陷、购买营养滋补品等，治疗来华前已患有的各种慢性病、皮肤病以及到非指定医院就诊的，由留学生自行安排，国际交流学院可视情协助。

3. 患重大疾病须做手术的，征得其驻华代表机构同意后方可手术；情况紧急的，须由本人或领队在医院的手术告知书上签名，并由本人或领队及时将病情及治疗过程上报所在国驻华代表机构。

During the enrollment period, the university arranges a medical check-up for international students. In addition, for students whose course duration is one year or more, a medical check-up will be scheduled once a year. If necessary, the sick are to be transferred to the designated hospital from the university hospital which provides outpatient care.

1. In the event of illness, please complete the form of Application for Visiting a Doctor. Then report the illness to the country group leader, the duty student, and the Chinese duty staff. The Chinese duty staff will re-

act as soon as possible. Inform the Chinese duty staff directly if you are seriously sick.

2. For common illnesses such as cold, fever and diarrhea, the college's Chinese staff will accompany the sick student to the university hospital or a designated one, where the doctor will provide medical treatment. In the following cases, the college will provide assistance on a conditional basis: dental care, dental prosthetics, physiological defect treatment, and nutritional supplement purchase. The same conditional policy applies to students who have had chronic illnesses before their arrival in China, and students who seek medical treatment outside of the designated hospital.

3. Those who require surgery for a serious sickness must obtain prior approval from their embassies in China. In the event of an emergency, the sick or the country group leader must sign the surgical confirmation and notify the Embassy in China about the disease and the treatment.

5.3 陪读家属 Accompanying Families

陪读家属管理规定

1. 留学生在华培训期间，本人配偶、父母、子女（以下简称"家属"）可来华陪读或探亲，但须提前15天向国际交流学院提出书面申请，待批准后方可成行。家属来华陪读各种出入境手续自行办理。

2. 家属来华陪读、探亲的期限，不准超过留学生学习期限。留学生对陪读家属负有管理教育的责任和义务。

3. 家属在华陪读、探亲，可以自主选择住宿地点，安全责任自负。如需租住大学提供的家属公寓，应提前提出书面申请，签订租住协议，按时缴纳房屋租金及水电气等费用。

4. 家属来华陪读、探亲，可自主选择就餐方式。如需在国际交流学院餐厅就餐，应按照标准缴纳伙食费。

5. 家属在华陪读，大学不提供交通、医疗等保障。如遇特殊情况，可向大学提出申请，并按照当地标准缴纳相应费用。

6. 陪读家属在华期间，不得就业或者从事其他经营性活动。

Rules for Accompanying Families

1. International students' spouse, parents and children (hereinafter referred to as family) can stay in China during the courses. However, international students should submit a written application to the College of International Exchange 15 days before their families arrive in order to obtain prior clearance from the college to substantiate the request. Families should go through the formalities of entry and exit by themselves.

2. The international students' families are not allowed to overstay the courses. It is the students' responsibility and obligation to manage and instruct their families.

3. Families can choose where to live after receiving permission from the college, but they must also be responsible for their own safety. If the family requests university-provided housing, they must submit an application in advance and sign a leasing agreement. The family must pay the rent and utility bills, such as water, electricity and gas on time.

4. Families can choose where to eat. It is supposed to pay for the food as per the standards if the family dines in the mess of the College of International Exchange.

5. Neither transportation nor free medical treatment is provided by the university for families. In the event of a necessity, families can file an

application and pay for the service according to local standards.

6. Family members are not allowed to work or do business while in China.

公寓租金标准及缴纳方式

1. 留学生陪读家属公寓室内使用面积为 80 平方米，含起居室 2 间，客厅、小餐厅、厨房和卫生间各 1 间。

2. 公寓租金标准参照大学周边地区同类房屋平均租赁价格制定，每平方米每天租金×元。

3. 公寓租金须按月缴纳，租住时间不满一月，按实际天数收费。

4. 留学生及陪读家属入住时应缴纳当月租金，并在每月 25 日前缴纳下月租金。

Rent for Apartment

1. Each family apartment is 80 square meters in size and has two bedrooms, one living room, one dining room, one kitchen, and one bathroom.

2. The rent for the apartment is × yuan per square meter per day, based on the typical rate for similar apartments near our university.

3. The rent will be paid monthly. If the rental duration is less than one month, the fee is calculated on a daily basis.

4. International students and their families should pay the first month's rent when they move into the apartment, and then pay the rent before the 25th of each month.

日常生活费用收费标准及缴纳方式

1. 留学生及陪读家属租住公寓期间的水电费、网费、有线电视费、电话费等日常生活费用由其个人自理。

2. 水电费。每月缴费金额以当地水电部门下发的水电费用缴纳通知单为准。

3. 网费。公寓接入 ADSL 宽带网络，使用费为×××元/月，如不需要网络服务，可向国际交流学院申请关闭。

4. 公寓内电话已开通市内短途和国内长途，按中国电信资费标准收取费用。如需开通国际长途，须另行申请。

5. 国际交流学院负责每月统一向相关部门缴纳以上费用，留学生根据缴费单据向国际交流学院财务部门支付相关费用。

Payment of Bills

1. International students and their families must pay for utilities such as water, electricity, Internet, cable TV, and home phone service in family apartments.

2. Water and electricity bill. The cost is calculated based on the monthly bill issued by the municipal water and power board.

3. The Internet. The apartment has access to the ADSL broadband network. The monthly charge is ×××Yuan. Students may request that the Internet be turned off.

4. The apartment has a local call service as well as a domestic long distance call service. The cost is set in accordance with China telecom tariff standard. Submitting an application is necessary for international call service.

5. On a monthly basis, the College of International Exchange pays the above-mentioned charge to the appropriate authorities. The financial office of the College of International Exchange is where students pay their bills.

公寓内部设施使用须知

1. 家用电器：公寓内统一配备液晶电视、台式电脑、电冰箱、洗衣机、电热水器、油烟机、电话机、电熨斗、微波炉、电烤箱、电磁炉、电子密码保险柜等家用电器。

2. 家具：公寓内统一配备床、沙发、写字台、梳妆台、餐桌、衣柜、椅子、鞋柜等家具。未经同意，留学生及陪读家属不得私自改变床、床头柜以及写字台等屋内物品摆放位置。

3. 留学生及陪读家属应爱护公寓内的家具、门窗及各种设施，不得私自拆卸、改装以及移动屋内的固定设施，以免造成损坏。若不慎人为造成屋内设施损坏，将承担相关维修费用：

（1）房间地板均为木制，如因人为原因造成房间地板损坏，须按照受损面积承担维修费用。

（2）不准在房间内墙面上贴画、钉钉子、粘贴挂钩等，破坏墙面整洁及美观。一经发现，国际交流学院将进行清除，并视墙面损坏情况向相关人员收取维修费用。

（3）不准在浴室毛巾架晾晒衣物，如因此造成毛巾架脱落或下塌，将承担全部维修费用。

（4）不准将烟头、屋内垃圾等废弃物丢入坐便器，如因人为原因造成下水道堵塞，疏导费用由留学生及陪读家属个人承担。

（5）留学生及陪读家属应保持阳台整洁，不准在阳台上堆砌物品或向阳台外丢弃废弃物。

（6）不准在各种木质家具表面刻字、钉钉子、粘挂钩等，一经发现将进行清除，维修费用由留学生及陪读家属个人承担。

4. 租住公寓的留学生及陪读家属入住前须向国际交流学院缴纳房屋设施押金×××元。退房时，经检查屋内各项设施如保持完好，将全额退还押金。

The Usage Instructions of the Interior Facilities

1. Electrical household appliances: the apartment is equipped with the following electrical household appliances: LCD television (Liquid Crystal Display television), desk computer, fridge, washing machine, electric geyser, range hood, telephone, iron, micro-wave oven, electro-magnetic stove and electric cipher safe.

2. Furniture: the apartment is equipped with the following furniture: bed, sofa, dressing table, dining table, wardrobe, chairs and shoe case. Without permission, the layout of the furniture cannot be changed. If the change of the layout is really necessary for special purpose, please apply for permission.

3. Please take good care of the furniture, doors, windows and other facilities. Do not dismantle or transform the facilities. Do not change the layout of the fixed facilities. If any man-made damages are done to the facilities, you will have to pay for the repair.

(1)The floor in the room is wooden, therefore, it could be easily damaged by water or cigarette ends. If any man-made damages are done to the floor, you will have to pay for the repair according to the size of the damaging area.

(2)Do not paste picture or hook onto the wall or drive in a nail to spoil the wall. Once found, we will clean the wall and you will have to pay for the repair of the wall.

(3) Do not hang clothes on towel rail in the bathroom. You will have to pay for the repair if any damages are done.

(4) Do not throw cigarette butts, garbage in the house and other wastes into the toilet. If the sewer is blocked due to man-made reasons, the cost of the dredging will be borne by the international students and their families.

(5) International students should keep the balcony tidy, and are not allowed to pile objects on the balcony and discard waste outside the balcony.

(6) Do not scratch or paste paintings, nail nails, or stick hooks on the surface of the wooden furniture. Once found, they will be removed. The maintenance costs will be borne by the international students and their families.

4. International students and their families should hand over ×××　yuan to the College of International Exchange for a deposit before moving in. Before returning to the home country upon graduation, the deposit will be returned in full if all facilities in the house are in good condition after inspection.

其他注意事项

1. 租住期间，留学生及陪读家属的安全责任由留学生自行负责。

2. 邀请校内外人员(含学生、任课教师)到公寓做客，须事先向国际交流学院报备。

3. 未经国际交流学院批准，不准在公寓内自行添置、使用大功率电器。严禁将易燃、易爆、剧毒等危险物品带入房间内。除配备的厨具外，严禁在公寓内使用电炉、酒精炉、煤油炉等设备进行烹饪、煮食或加热取暖。因违反规定引起火灾等事故造成损失者，将追究其责任，并视情赔偿损失。

4. 公寓只限留学生及陪读家属居住，不准私自转租、改变使用性质或供非法用途。

5. 要注意保管好个人用品，留学生及陪读家属离开公寓时应随手将门窗关好锁好，贵重物品要采取安全措施，以防丢失。任何经济损失均由留学生及陪读家属个人承担。

6. 留学生及陪读家属要自觉保持走廊、宿舍和卫生间的整洁，严禁在走廊堆放私人物品，严禁饲养各种小动物。国际交流学院工作人员有权处理走廊上的杂物。

7. 留学生及陪读家属租住公寓期间，日常卫生由其自行负责打扫。

8. 留学生及陪读家属入住公寓前，须认真阅读本规定，认定无误后，须在指定位置签字。

表 5.1　国际交流学院陪读家属公寓生活设施赔偿价格表

序号	设施名称	赔偿价格	备注
1	客厅空调	5750 元	
2	液晶电视	4900 元	
3	电脑	4500 元	
4	电冰箱	2800 元	
5	卧室空调	2850 元	
6	洗衣机	2500 元	
7	油烟机	2150 元	
8	热水器	1950 元	
9	微波炉	950 元	
10	电子密码保险柜	950 元	
11	电烤箱	550 元	
12	电磁炉	550 元	

续表

序号	设施名称	赔偿价格	备注
13	电熨斗	285 元	
14	电话机	200 元	
留学生入住时，请确认房间内物品完好无损，并在指定位置签字。 租住方签字：_____			

Other Instructions

1. During the rental period, the international students and their family members are responsible for their own safty.

2. International students must notify the college in advance if they want to invite guests (including teachers and students) from outside to their apartments.

3. Without the approval of the College of International Exchange, it is not allowed to purchase or use high-power electrical appliances in the apartment. It is strictly forbidden to bring flammable, explosive, highly toxic and other harmful items into the room. Except for the kitchenware, it is strictly forbidden to use electric stoves, alcohol stoves, kerosene stoves and other equipment for cooking or heating in the apartment. Those responsible for damages caused by fires or other incidents caused by violations of regulations shall be held accountable and appropriate compensation will be required.

4. The apartment is only available to international students and their family members. Subletting, changing the nature of the use of the house, or using it for illicit purposes are all prohibited.

5. International students and their families should take care of their personal belongings, close and lock their doors and windows before leaving the department, and take precautions to avoid valuables from being stolen. Any financial losses will be borne by international students and their families.

6. International students and their families should make an effort to keep the corridors, dormitories and bathrooms clean and tidy. It is strictly forbidden to stack personal belongings in the corridors, as well as keep small animals. The staff of the College of International Exchange has the authority to handle the debris in the corridor.

7. International students and their families are responsible for the daily hygiene during the rental period.

8. International students and their families must carefully study these regulations before inviting family members to live in the department, and sign on the designated place after all the rules are confirmed correct.

Table 5.1   Compensation Price List for Living Facilities in the Apartment

No.	Facilities	Price	Remarks
1	AC in the living room	5750 yuan	
2	Television	4900 yuan	
3	Computer	4500 yuan	
4	Refrigerator	2800 yuan	
5	AC in the bedroom	2850 yuan	
6	Washing machine	2500 yuan	
7	Kitchen ventilator	2150 yuan	
8	Water heater	1950 yuan	

Continued

No.	Facilities	Price	Remarks
9	Microwave oven	950 yuan	
10	Safebox	950 yuan	
11	Electric oven	550 yuan	
12	Induction cooker	550 yuan	
13	Electric iron	285 yuan	
14	Telephone	200 yuan	

Please confirm that all items in the room are in good condition and sign in the designated place when you check in.

Signature：_____

5.4 训练场所 Training Placilities

5.4.1 体育馆 Gymnasium

体育馆内设有游泳馆和球类馆。馆内可以开展游泳、体操、拳击、篮球、排球、羽毛球、乒乓球等多种运动的训练和比赛，能容纳观众 5000 人。

The gymnasium is divided into two sections: one for various balls and the other for swimming. It is a good place for various sports traing and competitions, including swimming, gymnastics, boxing, basketball, volleyball, badminton, and table tennis. It has a capacity of 5,000 audience.

5.4.2 田径场 Athletic Field

大学田径场改造完成于 2012 年 9 月，占地 26240 平方米，建有标准环形塑胶跑道、天然草足球场和 3000 人看台，并配备 LED 大屏、音响系统、照明系统。可进行包括田径运动项目的教学、训练和比赛，承担了学校开学典礼、校庆集会、田径运动会等大型活动。

The renovation of the athletic field was completed in September 2012. It covers an area of 26,240 square meters. There are a typical circular plastic track, a natural grass football field and a 3,000-seat audience stand in it. It's also eguipped with a giant LED screen, a sound system, and a lighting system. It may conduct instruction, training, and competitions in a variety of sports, including track and field, as well as large-scale events such as school opening ceremonies, anniversary celebrations, and sports meetings.

5.4.3 工程训练中心 Engineering Training Center

工程训练中心主要承担"金工实习""机修金工基础与实践""专业焊接实习"等课程的教学，旨在培养学生实践能力、工程素质与创新意识。工程训练中心分为车工实习区、钳工实习区、焊工实习区及现代加工实习区。除实习外，学生也可以在这里开展课外创新实践活动。工程训练中心有 3D 打印实习区。采用 FDM(工艺熔沉积制造)打印方法，学生可以自己建模，也可以利用开源模型来打印机器零件、工艺品等，这有助于培养学生创新思维能力。工程训练中心还配备了普通车床和数控车床。在普通车床的实习中，学生可以了解车床的组成、工作原理、操作方法等，并练习各种基本的车削工艺。学生进行普通车床实习并具备一定的车削加工基础后，可进行数控车削实习。经过工程训练，可以让学生了解机械制造全过程，增强其工程实践能力，培养其大工程意识和创新意识。

The engineering training center primarily offers lessons in Metalworking Practice, Machine Repair and Metalworking Fundamentals, and Welding Practice. The center is dedicated to cultivate the practical ability, engineering abilities and innovative awareness of the students. It is separated into areas dedicated to lathe work, bench work, welding, and modern processing. Apart from practicing, it is open for extracurricular activities centered on creativity. There is a 3D printing area in the center. Students can create new models or modify existing ones to print machine parts and crafts with the FDM (Fused Deposition Modeling) method. It is beneficial for them to put their unique ideas into practice. The center is also equipped with regular lathes and CNC (Computer Numerical Control) lathes. (In regular lathe practice, students can learn about the composition, working theory, and operating mechanism of the turnery, as well as the basic cutting skills.) After completing regular lathe practice, students will go on to the CNC lathe practice. After the engineering training, students will gain an understanding of the entire manufacturing process and build related talents. Their awareness of important engineering projects and innovation will also be improved.

5.4.4　主要实验场所 Major Labs

机械工程实验室

这里是大学机械工程实验室。这个实验室主要用来给本科学生上机械方面的实验课，包括基础性试验、综合性试验、创新性试验和维修训练等。首先可以看到很多奖杯和荣誉证书，它们都是我们的学生在全国各项竞赛中所获得的，比如全国大学生机械创新设计大赛和先进成图大赛。稍后可以看到和这些奖励相关的参赛作品。请往这边走。这个实验室成立于

19××年，截至目前已有近××年的历史。展柜中展示的是各种各样的教学模型，比如齿轮、凸轮、万向联轴器等。其中的一些模型是我们自己设计制作的。这些模型能够帮助学生了解机械运动原理。我们左手边有一些机械模型，学生可以使用这些模型做一些基础性试验，比如齿轮减速器的拆装、齿轮的测量和绘制等。这个试验平台叫作综合创新试验台，学生可以进行综合性、创新性的试验。这个区域主要用来进行维修训练，比如液压系统维修、切割和焊接等。这些是离心泵维修平台，学生可以进行离心泵维修。这些是冷藏设备，学生可以进行制冷管路的制作和加工训练。这个系统用于管路维修，设计有多种类型的故障管路，学生可以进行堵漏训练。设备的底座可以摇摆，模拟船舶航行过程中船体摇摆的环境，高度还原现场情况。这台机电设备用于舵机和锚机的电气控制技能实训。这个区域展示的主要是学生的创新作品。其中的部分作品是大学生机械创新设计大赛获奖作品。这项竞赛每2年举办一次，而且每次比赛都有不同的主体。学生在任课老师的指导下进行创新设计，这些作品不仅让学生收获了奖励，也为我们学校赢得了荣誉。这些是数控设备，简称CNC，是Computer Numerical Control的缩写，包括数控机加工中心、数控铣床、数控车床和线切割机。它们都是由电脑编程控制的，所以精度远高于传统的加工方法。它们也为学生实作训练提供了必要条件。

Mechanical Engineering Laboratory

This is the mechanical engineering laboratory. It is mainly used for undergraduate mechanical experiments, including basic experiment, comprehensive experiment, innovative experiment and maintenance operation. These trophies and certificates are awarded to our students in various national competitions, for example, the College Students' Machinery Innovative Design Competition and Advanced Mechanical Drawing Competition. Up to now, our students have won numerous awards, including the national first and second prize, and provincial prizes. We'll see these prize-winning designs later. This way, please. Founded in 19×× , our lab has a history of nearly ×× years. These are models for teaching, including gear wheel, cam and universal coupling. Some of them were designed and made by our colleagues. They help students understand the principle of mechanical movement. On your left, you'll find a variety of mechanical models. Here, students conduct fundamental experiments such as disassembly and assembly of the gear reducer, as well as measurement and mapping of the gear wheel. This kind of test beds is used for comprehensive and innovative experiments. This section is mainly for maintenance training, such as hydraulic system maintenance, cutting and welding, and so on. These are centrifugal pump test benches used by students to practice maintenance. This is refrigeration equipment for practicing tube expansion and bending. This system is designed for pipeline maintenance. It is composed of many types of defective pipes that students can use to practice plugging. This base can reproduce the pitch and roll of a machine functioning on a navigating ship in a maritime setting.

This electromechanical apparatus is used to practice electrical control of the steering engine and windlass. This area displays the students' creative works. As mentioned before, some of them are prize-winning works. Every two years, the College Students' Machinery Innovative Design Competition is organized with a different topic. In the competition, students create works under the guidance of their teachers. They received awards for themselves as well as for our university. This is a collection of six computer numerical control (CNC) machines, comprising a CNC machining center, two CNC milling machines, two CNC lathes, and a wire cutting machine. Because they are completely computer-programmed, the precision is significantly higher than with traditional processing methods, and it also creates circumstances for hands-on practice.

船舶总体数字实验室

这是大学船舶总体数字实验室。它从传统的以手工设计为主的船舶总体专修室发展成为职能化、多通道立体投影的综合教学科研平台。学生在这里可以进行船舶设计、船舶建造工艺、修理技术等课程的实验与毕业设计。下面请大家观看船舶设备吊装仿真演示。

Ship General Digital Lab

This is the Ship General Digital lab. It develops from a ship design classroom into a functional, multi-passage comprehensive teaching and scientific research platform. In this lab, students can conduct different experiments of classes like ship design, ship building technique and repair technique, as well as complete their graduation preject. Next, please watch the simulation show of the ship equipment hoisting.

机械基础教学实验中心

这里是大学机械基础教学实验中心。本中心开设多项机械基础教学和科研实验。这里可以同时容纳 200 名学生进行基本演示实验、综合实验、创新实验。

Experiment Center for the Foundations of Machinery Engineering

This is the Experiment Center for the Foundations of Machinery Engineering at University A. This center may conduct a variety of educational and scientific research experiments on mechanical foundations. It can accommodate up to 200 students conducting a variety of experiments such as demonstration experiments, comprehensive experiments, and innovative experiments.

电子技术实验中心

这里是大学电子技术实验中心。在这里学生可以进行高、低频电子线路实验、数字与逻辑实验、电子设计自动化实验和电工技能培训。

Electronic Technological Experiment Center

This is the electronic technological experiment center. Students can conduct experiments on high and low frequency electronic circuits, digital and logic circuits, electronic design automation, and participate in electrician skill training at this center.

基础实验中心

这里是大学基础实验中心。在这里可以开展物理、力学、材料学、数学等学科的教学与科研工作。学生能在这里进行工程力学、物理、金属工艺等实验。现在请各位参观位于一楼的工程力学实验室、位于二楼的金属工艺实验室和位于四楼的物理演示实验室。

Basic Experiments Center

This is the Basic Experiments Center at our university. This facility is capable of conducting a variety of educational and scientific research activities in the fields of physics, mechanics, materials science, and mathematics. Students can do experiments in engineering mechanics, physics, and smithcrafts here. Please visit the engineering mechanics lab on the first floor, the smithcrafts lab on the second floor, and the physics demonstration lab on the fourth floor.

第六章　国际交往篇

Chapter Six　International Exchanges

6.1　团组来访 Welcoming Foreign Delegations

6.1.1　接待方案 Reception Plans

表 6.1　外方院校代表团来访行程单

时　间	活 动 内 容
10 月 31 日（星期四）	
08：00	乘高铁由北京前往武汉
12：17	抵武汉站
12：30	出发前往饭店
13：10	抵达，入住，午餐
14：00	乘车赴船舶综合试验训练中心
15：30	参观第七届世界军人运动会比赛场馆和相关训练设施。依次参观浮动码头、游泳馆、障碍场、航海技术平台
16：30	乘车返回酒店
18：00	酒店晚餐（自助餐）
19：30	视情推荐代表团游览江滩，观赏夜景
11 月 1 日（星期五）	
07：30	酒店早餐

续表

时　间	活　动　内　容
08：40	出发前往学校
09：00	参观学校教学训练设施(工程训练中心、机械基础教学实验中心、船舶设备仿真工程实验室、损管模拟训练系统和内燃动力实验室)
10：35	抵达学校大接待室，刘鹏海校长在大接待室门前迎接，门前合影
10：40	茶歇
10：50	双方就人才培养进行座谈交流 观看大学介绍片 刘鹏海校长介绍大学专业设置和人才培养情况 外方团长介绍人才培养情况 双方进行交流
11：55	双方交换校徽，外方团长在留言簿留言
12：00	刘鹏海校长宴请代表团成员
13：00	返回酒店
14：00	退房
14：15	出发前往武汉站
16：01	乘高铁返京

Table 6.1　The Itinerary for the Visiting Delegation

Time	Activities
	31 Oct. （Thursday）
08：00	Take the high-speed rail from Beijing to Wuhan
12：17	Arrive at Wuhan Railway Station
12：30	Proceed to the hotel
13：10	Check in and have lunch
14：00	Depart for the Ship Testing and Training Base by vehicle
15：30	Tour venues and training facilities for the 7th Military World Games, from the pontoon, natatorium, obstacle course to seamanship course

Cintinued

Time	Activities
16:30	Return to the hotel by vehicle
18:00	Buffet dinner at the hotel
19:30	If possible, take a tour to the Riverside Park for a night view
1 Nov. (Friday)	
07:30	Breakfast at the hotel
08:40	Depart for University A
09:00	Visit educational and training facilities. Campus tour: Engineering Training Center—Mechanical Lab—Ship Equipment Simulation Engineering Lab—Ship Damage Control Simulation System—Internal Combustion Engine Power Lab
10:35	Arrive at the Grand Reception Hall. The university's president Liu Penghai greets the delegation in front of the hall and then joins them for a group photo
10:40	Coffee break
10:50	Presentation and discussion on talent development A documentary about our university Presentation on the university's education programs and talent development by professor Liu Penghai, president of the university Presentation on talent development by head of the delegation Discussions
11:55	Exchange emblems and leave a message in the guestbook
12:00	Lunch reception hosted by professor Liu Haipeng, president of the university
13:00	Return to the hotel
14:00	Check out
14:15	Proceed to Wuhan Railway Station
16:01	Return to Beijing by high speed rail

6.1.2 会见辞 Speech at the Meeting

尊敬的柯尔院长，各位 R 国朋友：

上午好！我是中国甲大学校长刘鹏海。

首先，我代表大学领导和全校教职员工，对各位同行的到来表示热烈欢迎！

下面，我向院长介绍参加会见的校方人员。这位是办公室主任曹荣先生，负责国际合作；这位是教务处处长蔡亚波先生，负责教学训练的筹划组织和实施。

中 R 两国有着深厚的传统友谊，是最早同新中国建交的国家之一。

今年是中 R 建交 70 周年，两国必将在新的历史起点上，在中国—中东欧国家合作框架下推动双边关系迈上新台阶。

之前，院长先生参观了第七届世界军人运动会场馆和学校的教学训练场所。接下来，我还将向你进一步介绍学校人才培养情况，希望院长先生能够对我校的办学理念、人才培养水平和师资力量等有进一步了解，也希望院长先生能为我校与贵国院校的合作提供更多支持。

Respected dean Khol, friends from Country R,

Good morning! I'm Liu Penghai, president of University A. To begin, on behalf of university faculty and students, I'd like to extend my warm welcome to colleagues from Country R. Now I'd like to introduce my colleagues to you. Mr. Cao Rong, head of the Admin Office, is in charge of international cooperation. Mr. Cai Yabo, head of Office of Studies, is responsible for educational planning and implementation.

China and Country R boast a profound tradition of friendship. Counrty R was among the first countries that established diplomatic ties with the People's Republic of China.

This year marks the 70th anniversary of China-Country R diplomatic relations. At this new historical juncture, the two countries will undoubtedly elevate the bilateral ties to new heights within the framework of co-operation between China and Countries of Cetral and Eeastern Europe.

Mr. Khole has taken a tour of the venues for military games and our university's facilities. And I'll proceed with our talent development program. I believe that through my briefing, you are able to gain a clear picture of our educational philosophy, talent cultivation mode and teaching team. It is highly appreciateol if you are able to provide more support to the cooperation between our university and institutions in your country.

6.1.3　中外院校合作协议 Cooperation Agreement Between Chinese and Foreign Universities

中国甲大学与 D 国 K 大学缔结友好学校意向书

中国甲大学是中国重要的国家级综合大学之一，承担各类型学历教育。D 国 K 大学是 D 国最大的一所学校，承担着 D 国所有技术人员的任职培训。经友好协商，中国甲大学与 D 国 K 大学认为：两校间建立长期友好合作交流机制将会使双方院校进一步增进彼此间的了解与信任，以在更广范围内进行实质性的交流与合作。为此，双方于 20××年×月就两校结为友好学校达成如下意向：

第一条　缔结友好学校的原则

学术交流，友好合作

第二条　缔结友好学校的内容与方式

1. 两校管理者定期互访，交流办学和人才培养情况。

2. 两校专家教授定期互邀到对方学校进行学术交流活动。

3. 两校每年互派 1~5 名年轻教师到对方学校进修学习。

4. 两校每年选送 5~10 名优秀学生到对方学校进行短期学习与交流活动。

5. 进行相关专业、课程的专业教材、图书等可共享教学信息资料的互换。

6. 积极推进其他双方感兴趣领域的实质性合作项目。

第三条　联络机构、人员和职责

1. 中国甲大学和 D 国 K 大学分别设立专门的联络工作小组，并指派一名具体负责人进行联络工作。

2. 联络小组的主要职责：就下一步两校如何正式签署友好学校协议及落实意向书所确定的项目进行协调与沟通。

Agreement of Intent on the Establishment of Sister School Relationships Between University A, PRC and University K, Country D

University A of PRC, one of the leading national universities, assumes a variety of higher educational missions. University K, being the largest institution in Country D, is responsible for the on-the-job training of technicians. Following a cordial consultation, University A of China and University K of D reach the consensus: the establishment of the sister school cooperative exchange mechanism will boost mutual understanding and trust, laying a groundwork for pragmatic exchanges and cooperation in more areas. Whereby an agreement for sister schools is made in MM, $20 \times \times / 20 \times \times$ between the two parties and proclaimed as follows:

Article 1: Principles for Establishing Sister Schools

The principles include academic exchanges and friendly cooperation.

Article 2: Contents and Procedures for Establishing Sister Schools

1. At regular intervals, administrators from both schools exchange visits and discuss school administration and talent cultivation.

2. Every year, experts and professors from each school participate in academic exchange events at the invitation of the other school.

3. Every year, one to five young instructors from each school participate in an exchange program to further their education at the other school.

4. Every year, one to ten excellent students from each school participate in an exchange program at the other school.

5. Share educational literature, such as textbooks and publications on pertinent professional domains.

6. Expand pragmatic cooperation into more areas of mutual interest.

Article 3:Liaison Office, Personnel and Responsibilities

1. Both University A of China and University K of D establish liaison offices and appoint a liaison officer from each institution.

2. Responsibilities of liaison offices:

Communicate and negotiate with the other party regarding the official signing of the sister school agreement and the implementation of the agreement of intent's provisions.

6.1.4 宴请 Banquet

宴会请柬

亲爱的柯尔院长:

　　谨于 12 月 22 日中午 12:00 在××自助餐厅举行宴会。

敬请光临!
甲大学国际交流学院院长王建东

Banquet Invitation

Dear Mr. Kohle,

The honor of your presence is requested for the banquet on the twenty second of December, at twelve o'clock in the morning, at ×× Cafeteria.

Wang Jiandong

Dean of the College of International Exchange of University A

6.1.5 祝酒辞 Toast

尊敬的柯尔院长，各位 R 国朋友：

大家好！非常高兴与各位共进午餐。在此，我再次对你们的到来表示热烈欢迎！

今天上午，我与院长先生进行了愉快和高效的交流，就人才培养交换了意见，我认为我们的很多理念和想法都不谋而合，可以在该领域寻求更大的合作空间和更高的合作层次。

如果把我们的合作比作一艘巨轮，那契合的培养理念就是引领之舵，深入的务实合作就是驱动之帆，牢固的双边关系就是稳定之锚。

幸运的是，这三点我们都具备，我相信在不久的将来，这艘巨轮一定会乘风破浪，扬帆远航。

今天下午，院长先生和各位朋友就要离汉返京。分别不是结束，R 国有句谚语，叫作"流水逝去，石头永驻"。请允许我以水代酒，并提议：

为中 R 两国的友谊，为此次访问的圆满成功，为我们大家的身体健康，干杯！

Respected Mr. Khole, friends from Country R,

Good afternoon!

It's my great pleasure to have lunch with you. Once again, I would like to extend a warm welcome to all of you.

In the morning, we had a pleasant and productive discussion on talent development. I think we happen to hold the same view on a number of matters. So I believe we may seek broader space and higher level of cooperation in this field.

If we were to compare our cooperation to a large ship, the common philosophy of education would be the steering rudder; the in-depth pragmatic collaboration would be the driving sail; and the strong bilateral tie would be the stationing anchor.

We are lucky to have all three components. As a result, I am confident that this large ship will have fair winds and a following sea in the future.

Mr. Khole and your delegation are scheduled to depart Wuhan this afternoon. However, parting does not equal ending, as a saying goes in your country, river-stones remains while the water rushes away. Please allow me to propose a water toast:

To the friendship between the two countries, to the success of the current visit, to the health of everyone, cheers!

6.2 团组出访 Visiting Foreign Countries

6.2.1 致 R 国 G 学院院长的信函 A Letter to the Dean of College G in Country R

尊敬的柯尔院长：

您好！在结束了成果丰硕、紧凑愉快的访问行程后，我和代表团成员已经顺利回到了学校。在此，我谨代表全校师生并以我个人名义，对您为此次访问所做的精心安排表示感谢，对贵校所展现出的专业素质和强国底蕴表示钦佩。

此次两院校校长论坛成功举办，且高效而务实，成果丰硕。我们就学生的培养，尤其是领导力的培养进行了深入而详尽的交流，这使我和代表团成员深受启发，受益匪浅。正如我所说的，两校东西文化的交融，将为我们的合作打开新思路，为我们加深了解、增进友谊提供新契机。同时，您务实的工作作风、独特的个人魅力给我留下了深刻印象。我们二人都是新上任的校长，通过此次访问，我想我们之间也建立起了珍贵的个人友谊。此次访问是过往合作的一个很好的总结，更是未来合作的一个良好开端，这将进一步为我们开展深层次交流打下坚实的基础。

我欣喜地告诉您，我们已将此次访问成果和在会谈中提出的合作倡议向相关部门进行了报告，并且正在积极争取将有关意向列入两校年度交往计划，我也希望能早日从院长先生处得知贵校的反馈意见，这将有助于我们尽早着手进行准备，我们也会将有关倡议照会贵国驻华使馆。

借此机会，我谨邀请您于20××年率代表团来我校进行访问，并出席新一届两院校校长论坛，届时双方可就人才培养、教学训练等继续深入交换意见，并在论坛期间共同绘制两校合作的宏伟蓝图。同时，我也可以尽地主之谊，请院长先生品尝中国美食，领略中国文化。

请再次接受我的问候和致意！期待与您在武汉重逢！

中国甲大学校长刘鹏海
20××年×月×日

Respected Mr. Khole,

After a fruitful, compact, and pleasant visit to your country, our delegation successfully returned to our university. Hereby, on behalf of our university's faculty and students, and in my own name, I would like to express my gratitude to you for the meticulous arrangements for this visit, as well as my admiration for your university's professionalism and your country's rich legacy.

The first Education Forum concluded with pragmatic, efficient, and rewarding outcomes. We conducted in-depth and extensive exchanges on the cultivation of students, particularly the development of student leadership, which inspired me and our delegation members tremendously. As I said, the integration of eastern and western cultures at the two universities will bring fresh ideas for our collaboration as well as new possibilities to expand our understanding and strengthen our friendship. At the same time, your pragmatic work style and special personal charm left a deep impression on me. We are both recently appointed deans. I believe we have also established a valuable personal friendship as a result of this visit. This visit serves as a wonderful review of previous collaboration and a good start for future collaboration, laying a solid foundation for our in-depth exchanges. It is worth noting that we have submitted the findings of this visit and the cooperation initiatives proposed during the talks to the Foreign Affairs Ministry of China, and that we are working hard to incorporate the relevant objectives in the two countries' yearly exchange plan. We wish to receive your feedback as soon as possible so that we may be prepared as early as possible. We will also forward the cooperation proposals to your country's Embassy in China.

I would like to take this opportunity to invite you to head a delegation to our school in 20×× to attend the Second Education Forum. At that moment, we may continue exchanging our views on talent development, education, and other topics, and lay out the grand blueprint of cooperation between the two schools; I will also take advantage of the opportunity to invite you to enjoy Chinese cuisine and culture. Please accept my greetings and compliments again! And I am looking forward to seeing you in Wuhan!

Liu Penghai, President of University A

DD/MM/20××

6.2.2 在外方欢迎宴会上的祝酒辞 A Toast at the Welcome Reception Hosted by a Foreign Counterpart

尊敬的柯尔院长，女士们、先生们、朋友们：

我和我的代表团非常高兴能够来贵国访问，对我本人来说，我也非常高兴第一次踏上贵国这片神奇而美丽的土地。

贵国为我们的访问做了精心的安排，使我有机会与贵校的领导人会见并参观贵校，这些会见和参观访问进一步加深了我们对贵国，特别是贵校的了解。我相信这次访问一定会取得圆满成功。两校的友好交流与合作，尤其是专业领域的合作必将取得丰硕的成果。

借此机会，我诚挚地邀请院长先生率团来我校参观访问!

现在，我提议:

为两国人民的友谊，为院长先生的健康，为在座的各位朋友的身体健康，干杯!

Respected Mr. Khole, ladies and gentlemen, dear friends,

My delegation and I are very excited to visit your country. This is my first visit to this beautiful and marvelous land.

You have arranged for us a very nice visiting program, which enables us to visit your campus and meet with college authorities. I believe these meetings and visits will help us learn more about your country and, in particular, your college. I am confident that this visit will be a success, and that the cooperation and exchanges between the two academies, particular in professional domains, will be extremely beneficial.

I'd like to take this opportunity to extend an invitation to Mr. Khole and your delegation to our campus.

May I now propose a toast:

To the friendship between the two countries, to your health, Cheers!

6.2.3　访问 R 国 G 院校谈话提纲 Main Points to Discuss with the College G in Country R

一、开场白

应贵国的邀请，我和我的同事来到 R 国访问，我因此感到非常高兴。院长先生专门会见并全程陪同我率领的考察团，我们感到非常荣幸。这是我第一次访问贵国，我们此次来访主要是为了增进对彼此了解，加深友谊，促进合作，向你们学习有益的建设经验。

二、介绍代表团成员

现在请允许我向大家介绍我的同事。他们是……

三、关于两国关系

中国和 R 国都是历史文化悠久的国家，虽然分处欧亚大陆，相隔万里之遥，但两国人民友谊源远流长，双方在政治、经济、文化、科技、教育等各个领域的合作富有成果。中 R 两国作为联合国安理会常任理事国，和睦相处，互利合作，共同发展，符合两国和两国人民的共同利益。今年是中 R 两国建交××周年，两国睦邻友好与互利合作的关系进入了全面发展的新阶段。

四、关于此次访问

G 院校是一所在国际上享誉盛名的高等院校，贵国为我们安排了一个很好的访问日程。我们甲大学创建于 1949 年，是全国重点、综合性大学，是中国相关领域重要的教学科研基地。我校一直致力于对外合作与交流，吸纳外国办学经验。此次我率考察团来访，与贵校同行就共同关心的问题进行交流，借此契机建立起校际对口交流与合作机制，开展人才培养、联合科研等合作，推动两校在各层次各领域的交流。我们相信，在主人周到的安排下，我们这次访问一定会取得圆满成功，中 R 两国的友好合作关系必将得到进一步的发展。

I. Opening

I feel very delighted to visit Country R with my colleagues at the invitation of your government. It is my great honor that Mr. Dean, could make time in your busy and demanding schedule to meet with my delegation. This is the first time I've been to your country, the goal of this visit is to enhance mutual understanding, deepen friendship and promote exchanges and cooperation between our two universities, and what's more, to learn from you the advanced experience.

II. Introduction to the delegation members

Please allow me to present my colleagues to you. They are ...

III. The bilateral relations

Both China and Country R have a rich history and splendid civilization. The friendship between the two countries dates back to ancient times despite the fact that we are thousands of kilometers apart and located in Europe and Asia, respectively. The cooperation in fields of politics, economics, culture, science and technology, education has yielded fruitful outcomes. As permanent members of the Security Council in UN, China and Country R have developed a harmonious relation, and win-win cooperation which benefits both nations and their peoples. This year marks the ×× th anniversary of the establishment of diplomatic relation between China and Country R, and I believe bilateral good-neighborly friendship and mutually beneficial cooperation have reached a new stage of all-round development.

IV. About this visit

College G enjoys great prestige both at home and abroad. Our colleagues of Country R have arranged a nice program for our visit. Our university, founded in 1949, is the leading and comprehensive university in China, serving as an important base for education and scientific and technological research. Our university always endeavors to strengthen the cooperation and exchanges with overseas academies in order to benefit from their advanced educational expertise. This time I am coming for an in-depth discussion and exchanges on topics of mutual interest. I'd like to take this opportunity to establish the exchange and cooperation mechanism between our two universities in areas of talent development and scientific and technological research, so as to foster interactions across multiple tiers and fields. We appreciate your thoughtful arrangement, which ensures that our visit will be a success, and that the friendly and cooperative ties between the two countries will see further development in the future!

6.3 学术交流 Academic Exchanges

6.3.1 "构建海洋命运共同体"国际研讨交流会议程 The Agenda of the International Forum of "Building a Maritime Community with a Shared Future"

时间：20××年×月×日(周四)15：00—16：30

地点：国际交流学院国际学术交流中心

参加人员：大学领导，教务处、船舶学院、国际交流学院领导，教师代表，研究生代表，全体留学生，在校学习的×××专业学生

主持人：国际交流学院院长王建东

活动流程：

1. 大学副校长白晓林致辞。

2. 郭彩霞教授专题发言。

3. B国留学生瑟琳娜、谢云副教授、M国留学生托赫顿发言。

4. 茶歇。

5. S国留学生马迪纳、中国学生赵珂、D国留学生格莱斯发言。

6. 现场观众提问。

7. 大学领导与发言代表合影留念。

Time：15：00—16：30，DD/MM/20××(Thursday)

Location：Academic Exchange Center of the College of International Exchange

Participants：University leaders, leaders from the Office of Studies, the College of Ship Architecture and the College of International Exchange, teacher representatives, student representatives of the Graduate School, all international students, students from course ×××

Host: Professor Wang Jiandong, dean of the College of International Exchange

Agenda:

1. Professor Bai Xiaolin, vice president of the university delivers a speech.

2. Professor Guo Caixia delivers a speech on a specific topic.

3. Miss Serena from Country B, associate professor Xie Yun and Mr. Joe Hutton from Country M make presentations in a row.

4. Café break.

5. Mr. Martino from Country S, Mr. Zhao Ke, a Chinese student and Mr. Gleis from Country D make presentations in a row.

6. Audience make questions.

7. University leaders take a group photo with presenters.

6.3.2 "构建海洋命运共同体"国际研讨交流会主持词 Host Speech at International Forum of "Building a Maritime Community with a Shared Future"

各位领导、中外朋友们：

为纪念中国改革开放 40 周年，促进中外船舶技术交流，经大学领导批准，船舶学院和国际交流学院联合举办此次构建海洋命运共同体国际研讨交流会。

首先，我向大家介绍出席今天论坛的领导和嘉宾：大学副校长白晓林、教务处处长蔡亚波、船舶学院院长程志涛，我是国际交流学院院长王建东。参加此次研讨的还有相关领域的中外专家、学者和青年学生代表，让我们以热烈的掌声对大家的到来表示热烈的欢迎。

今年是改革开放 40 周年，我们在回顾中国从"赶上时代"到"引领时代"40 年跨越的同时，也看到了中国船舶行业的发展变化。为此，我们秉持着更加开放的视野和态度，组织"构建海洋命运共同体"国际研讨交流会。今天参加交流发言的有来自不同国家的船舶工程师，也有我校的教师代表，还有我校船舶与海洋专业学生代表，可以说是精彩纷呈，值得期待。

下面研讨会正式开始。首先请大学副校长白晓林致辞，大家掌声欢迎！

……

谢谢白晓林副校长。下面请郭彩霞教授进行主题发言。郭教授是研究国际政治与外交的知名专家。今天她发言的题目是……大家掌声欢迎！

接下来，有请 B 国瑟琳娜发言，她的发言题目是……大家掌声欢迎！

接下来，有请谢云副教授发言，她的发言题目是……大家掌声欢迎！

接下来，M 国托赫顿将给我们分享……大家掌声欢迎！

接下来休会 10 分钟，我们在现场准备了热饮和小点心，大家可以边休息，边自由交流。

我们继续开会。接下来，有请 S 国马迪纳介绍……

接下来，请船舶与海洋专业的中国学生赵珂发言，他的题目是……

谢谢赵珂的发言，接下来，有请 D 国格莱斯发言，他的发言题目是……大家掌声欢迎！

所有 8 名代表发言结束了，接下来，进入现场观众提问环节，欢迎大家向发言代表踊跃提问。如果需要向留学生提问，我们可以提供翻译，当然如果大家可以直接用英语提问，那就更好了。

朋友们，刚才各位嘉宾的发言，让我们了解了各国的船舶建设特色，感受了改革开放 40 年中国船舶专业的巨变，这些开阔了我们的研究思路，拓宽了我们的学术眼界。这些发言中有很多是真知灼见，值得我们认真思考和借鉴，也必将成为宝贵的资料。我们将把各位的发言及相关资料汇编成册，以供更多的人参考研读。再次感谢各位的精彩发言。

现在，请大学副校长白晓林向发言代表颁发蓝色讲坛证书并合影留念。

……

我宣布，"构建海洋命运共同体"国际研讨交流会到此结束！

Honorable leaders, dear friends,

Good afternoon! To commemorate the 40th anniversary of Chinese reform and opening-up and to promote technical exchanges between China and other countries, with the approval of the university authorities, in collaboration with the College of Ship Architecture, the College of International Exchange hosts the "Building a Maritime Community with a Shared Future" International Forum.

To begin, let me introduce leaders and guests presented here: professor Bai Xiaolin, vice president of the university, professor Cai Yabo, head of the Office of Studies, professor Cheng Zhitao, dean of the College of Ship Architecture. I am Wang Jiandong, dean of the College of International Exchange. Besides, here with us are professors and experts from both home and abroad as well as all student representatives. Let's extend our warm welcome to them with a big hand.

This year marks the 40th anniversary of China's reform and opening-up. When we review China's role from a follower to a leader over the past 40 years, we also witness the development and changes in the Chinese ship industry. Therefore, with a much broader vision and attitude, we hold the "Building a Maritime Community with a Shared Future" International Forum. Today's presenters include engineers from different countries, instructor representatives from our university and student representatives from majors of ship architecture and marine engineering. We are all looking forward to sharing ideas and benefiting from this fantastic forum.

Let's now welcome professor Bai Xiaolin, vice president of the university to deliver a speech.

...

Thank you professor Bai. Let's now welcome professor Guo Caixia. Professor Guo is a leading expert on international politics and diplomacy.

The title of her presentation is... welcome!

Let's now invite Miss Serena from Country B to make her presentation on... welcome!

Let's now invite associate professor Xie Yun to make her presentation on... welcome!

Let's now invite Mr. Joe Hutton from Country M to share with us his view on...

Let's take a ten-minute break. Hot drinks and snacks are over there. Please enjoy yourselves and feel free to communicate.

The presentation session is resumed. Let's now invite Mr. Martino from Country S to make an introduction on...

Let's now welcome Mr. Zhao Ke, a Chinese student majoring in Ship Architecture and Marine Engineering to make his presentation on ...

Let's now welcome Mr. Gleis from Country D to make his presentation on...

Following the presentations by the eight representatives, let's go to questions. If you have any questions, please do not hesitate to ask them. If you have any questions for international students, we have interpreters available, although it is preferable if you ask them in English.

Dear friends, the preceding presentations describe the characteristics of the ship industry in various nations and the dramatic changes that have occurred in China's ship industry over the last 40 years as a result of the reform and opening-up. These views boost the resources available for our research and widen our horizons in the academic domain. Numerous discoveries are worth analyzing and learning from, and they will accumulate to become a source of wealth for us. We will collect your lectures and assemble them into a book in order to reach a larger audience. Once again, I want to express my gratitude for your amazing presentations.

Now, let's invite professor Bai Xiaolin, the university's vice president, to present Blue Water Forum certificates and take photographs with all presenters.

…

I now declare today's forum closed.

6.3.3 大学领导在"构建海洋命运共同体"国际研讨交流会上的发言 Speech by University Leader at the International Forum of "Building a Maritime Community with a Shared Future"

校长发言

女士们、先生们、留学生朋友们：

下午好！

在全国上下纪念改革开放 40 周年的喜庆日子里，我们迎来了"构建海洋命运共同体"国际研讨交流会的开幕式！借此机会，我谨代表大学领导和全校教职员工，对论坛的成功举办表示热烈祝贺！对参加会议的各国留学生、教师及船舶与海洋专业中国学生代表表示热烈欢迎！

2019 年 4 月，中国国家主席习近平在集体会见出席海军成立 70 周年多国海军活动外方代表团团长时指出，海洋对于人类社会生存和发展具有重要意义。海洋孕育了生命、联通了世界、促进了发展。我们人类居住的这个蓝色星球，不是被海洋分割成了各个孤岛，而是被海洋连结成了命运共同体，各国人民安危与共。海洋的和平与安宁关乎世界各国的安危和利益，需要共同维护，倍加珍惜。习主席希望大家集思广益、增进共识，努力为推动构建海洋命运共同体贡献智慧。这一重要讲话顺应人类社会的共同意愿和基本追求，提出了构建海洋命运共同体的重要倡议。这是对人类命运共同体思想的丰富和发展，是共护海洋和平、共筑海洋秩序、共促海洋繁荣的中国方案，顺应时代潮流，契合各国利益。我们应立足自身，放眼世界，运用有效手段，联合一切积极力量，推动构建海洋命运共同体。

中外同行们，海洋关乎人类安危，必须高度重视。中国人民热爱和平，渴望和平，坚决维护和平，坚定不移地走和平发展道路。中国倡导树立共同、综合、合作、可持续的新安全观，反对海上霸权主义。各国应相互尊重、平等相待、增进互信，加强海上对话交流，深化务实合作，走互利共赢的海上安全之路，合力维护海洋的和平与安宁。我们举办这次国际论坛，就是为了搭建一个中外船舶工程师同堂研讨的平台，创造一个碰撞思想、增进友谊的机会。希望大家聚焦构建海洋命运共同体这个主题，积极交流各国的做法与经验，总结实践成果，思考发展对策，以和平、发展、合作、共赢的方式扎实推进海洋命运共同体的建设。

最后，预祝本届研讨交流会取得圆满成功。

谢谢大家！

Speech by President of the University

Ladies and gentlemen, dear friends,

Good afternoon!

On this auspicious occasion when Chinese people throughout the country are commemorating the 40th anniversary of China's reform and opening-up, we are here to hold the forum of "Building a Maritime Community with a Shared Future". On behalf of university authorities, faculty and students, I would like to take this opportunity to offer my sincere congratulations to the successful opening of this forum and to extend my warm welcome to students from various countries, instructor representatives and Chinese student representatives from majors of Ship Architecture and Marine Engineering.

In April, 2019, at the commemorative event for the 70th anniversary of PLA Navy, the Chinese President Xi Jinping noted that the ocean is of vital importance for the survival and development of human society, since it is where the life begins, the world is connected, and the social progress is achieved. The blue planet we live on is not divided into islands by the ocean, but connected into a community with a shared future. People of all countries share weal and woe. Maritime peace and tranquility bears on the security and interests of all countries and needs to be jointly upheld and cherished. President Xi called on all parties to pool their wisdom, build consensus and contribute their expertise to the building of a maritime community with a shared future. This important speech conforms to the common aspiration and basic pursuit of mankind and puts forward an important initiative of building a maritime community with a shared future. This is the enrichment and development of the idea of building a community with a shared future for mankind. It is China's plan to jointly safeguard maritime peace, build maritime order and promote maritime prosperity. It conforms to the trend of the times and serves the interests of all countries. We must concentrate on our own efforts while maintaining a global perspective, employ effective methods, and join forces to build a maritime community with a shared future.

Dear colleagues, the oceans are vital to the security of mankind, and we must attach great importance to them. The Chinese people are peace lovers, steadfast in their defense of peace, and unwavering in their pursuit of peaceful development. China promotes a new paradigm of shared, comprehensive, cooperative, and sustainable security. To counter maritime hegemony, countries must respect one another, consider one another as equals, strengthen mutual trust, increase marine discussion and exchanges, expand practical collaboration, pursue win-win maritime security, and collaborate to maintain maritime peace and tranquility. The goal of hosting this international forum is to provide a platform for discussion between Chinese and foreign marine engineers and to facilitate the exchange of ideas and friendship. I hope you will keep the theme of building a maritime community with a shared future in mind, actively exchange practices and experiences, reflect on practical accomplishments, and consider development strategies in order to make significant progress toward building a maritime community with a shared future through peace, development, and win-win cooperation.

Finally, I wish a great success of today's forum.

Thank you!

在"一带一路"合作交流中促进
海洋人才国际素养的培养

2013 年 9 月以来，国家主席习近平先后提出了"一带一路""构建人类命运共同体"和"构建海洋命运共同体"倡议。2017 年联合国安理会一致通过第 2344 号决议，首次将"构建人类命运共同体"的重要理念载入其中，这也反映了国际社会的共识。近年来，这些倡议不仅为沿路各国经济腾飞带来了机遇，也铺就了丝路各国增进理解与信任、加强全方位交流的和平友谊之路。作为海洋大国，中国倡导建设和谐海洋，深度参与推行共同的海上安全机制和维护共同的海上安全利益，是携手打造利益共同体、安全共同体、责任共同体的重要力量，也必然要在构建人类命运共同体的不尽探求中、在共筑"一带一路"宽广大道中发挥更大的国际作用、承担更重的国际责任。青年海洋人才是海洋的未来领导者和建设者，也是海上和平的维护者，他们的国际素养将决定未来海洋事业的风姿与色彩。涉海院校的主要责任就是培养海洋人才以迎接日益广泛的国际交流合作。

一、海洋人才国际素养涉及的三个层面

各国对海洋人才国际素养的理解不尽相同，但基于联合国教科文组织提出的定义，通常认为良好的国际素养包括思维、知识和能力三个层面。

（一）开阔的国际视野和国际化思维。21世纪是充满机遇和挑战的海洋世纪。3000多年前中国著名的《周易·乾卦》提出："首出庶物，万国咸宁。"今天的中国正秉承大国担当，携手各国同行在国际海洋安全方面不断深化交流与合作。海上丝绸之路不仅涉及最繁忙的海上贸易生命线，沿线国家也多身处政治、文化、历史和意识形态相对复杂的地区，建设和维护海上安全和共同发展利益，对海洋人才的全球意识和战略思维提出了更高的挑战。

（二）国际化的知识结构。丝路沿岸国家文化起源不同、宗教信仰相别、生活习俗迥异，这就客观要求我们突破种族、文化的限制，熟悉与海洋相关的国际法规，掌握海上通用的职业知识和技能，助力打造文化包容的和谐海洋。

（三）国际交流沟通能力。没有沟通何来相互理解，唯有交流方能促进友谊。通晓国际规则和外交礼仪，能够流利地使用一门或多门外语与外国同行进行无障碍交流，是海洋人才国际素质的基石，是撑起"命运共同体"千尺之台的强大助力。其中，国际海洋规则的灵活运用更是完成不断增多且日益复杂的海上交流活动的保证。

这三个能力相辅相成，共同构筑起海洋人才参与国际海上交流与合作的能力框架。

二、"一带一路"合作交流对培养海洋人才国际素养的需求

"一带一路"倡议是促进沿线各国经济繁荣与区域经济合作，加强不同文明交流互鉴，促进世界和平发展，造福世界各国人民的伟大事业。为了实现习主席这一伟大战略构想，必须有国际化人才作支撑。以"一带一路"合作交流的现实需求为牵引提高海洋人才的国际素养，是当前和今后一个时期涉海院校应该重点予以关注、着力研究解决的重大战略性课题。

（一）适应国家利益拓展、建设海洋事业的现实需求。"一带一路"倡议的推广实施，体现在国家战略利益的不断拓展，体现在海洋事业逐步由单一向多样演变、由国内向海外、由近海到远海的逐步延伸。海洋事业的国际背景更加复杂，内外影响更加广泛，牵动国家政治外交大局，影响各国

对华关系走向。作为维护和捍卫"一带一路"倡议最前沿的力量组成，海洋人才只有深刻认识国家战略利益拓展的时代要求，才能准确理解海洋事业的战略意义和政治分量，有效履行职责使命。只有具备宽阔的国际视野，才能自觉从国家政治外交大局出发观察处理问题。只有熟悉组织海上交流活动必需的国际知识，才能更好地应对复杂局面和突发事件。大力提高海洋人才的国际素养，既是配合国家"一带一路"倡议进行多样化海上交流活动的现实需要，也是有效延伸我国海洋方向建设纵深、维护国家海洋权益的长远需要。

（二）开展对外交流合作、树立大国形象的客观需要。"一带一路"倡议的推广实施，体现在世界各国政治、经济等领域相互依存度的不断提升上，体现在以更重要的身份、在更广的领域、以更多的方式参与的国际交流与合作上。海洋人才将身处海上对外交流活动第一线，不熟悉我国的对外方针政策，就不可能正确掌握对外交往的分寸和策略；不了解对方国家的社会风土人情，就不可能进行主动交往；不掌握国际社会、国际组织的规则和惯例，就不能有效利用其维护国家利益。因此，世界海洋外交领域的一举一动，特别是海洋人才所表现出的国际知识、视野眼界、沟通能力、礼仪修养等，不仅影响着对外交流合作的质量和成效，而且攸关国家利益声誉、反映海洋事业国际形象。为了适应新时代国际海上交流与合作使命任务的需要，必须从树立海洋强国良好形象的高度，大力提高海洋人才的国际素养。

（三）把握海洋地缘格局，赢得外交主动的必然要求。"一带一路"倡议的推广实施，体现在把握地缘战略的有利格局上，体现在赢得国家政治外交的充分主动上。伴随着海洋战略地位的不断上升、经济的全球化发展和海洋大国的群体性崛起，因海洋而起的海洋地缘政治也在悄然兴起，且正在深刻改变世界政治现状，日益影响世界政治未来。未来海上交流合作将为"一带一路"倡议保驾护航，其政治性强、涉及面广，极易引起国际社会的严重关切和政治、外交、经济方面的连锁反应，处置不慎就可能给战略全局带来严重后果。这就要求未来的海洋人才：（1）善于分析和研判国际和周边形势，善于从维护国家安全和利益出发，积极做好各项准备；（2）熟悉掌握国际法规，正确处置各种突发事件，有效防止事态扩大，避免连锁反应；（3）熟悉战略环境，综合利用各种有利因素，高质量完成任务。从某种意义上讲，国际素养已经和信息化素质、领导能力一样，成为能力核心要素。

三、海洋人才国际素养的培养途径

文化的不同造就了世界的缤纷多彩，文化也是青年价值观的源泉。海纳百川，有容乃大。国际素养培养，就是要构筑"和而不同"的跨文化认知和开放办学的理念先导。作为"一带一路"倡议沿线各国海洋外交和文化交流的使者，海洋人才将天然地承担起重要的角色。海洋人才需要在开放、国际性氛围中接受全球观念的熏陶，形成国际视野与意识。尽管各国国情、社情不同，涉海院校的办学模式也有差异，但教育国际化是学生国际素养培养的根本途径，这已成为各国共识。教育国际化主要包括国际化的课程体系、教师队伍和交流平台三个方面。

（一）国际化的课程体系是国际素养培养的基础。跨文化课程、国际法规课程、外交礼仪课程以及海洋事业共有的专业知识、通用职业技能课程的建设是国际素养培养的基础与前提。为了拓展国际视野、训练国际化思维，宜聚焦各类课程教学内容的国际性主题，加强MOOC课程等网络教学资源共建共享，加强对海洋特色、国际特征课程体系的科学设计。

（二）国际化的教师队伍是国际素养培养的关键。院校教学育人的核心环节是"教"。近年来，中国涉海院校在教师海外留学、随船出访、出国学术交流、科研合作等"走出去"方面步伐不断加快，在与外方磋商建立教师互派机制、聘请外籍客座教授、邀请外国专家讲学、学科创新引智计划等"请进来"方面，也与多个国家形成了建设性共识，许多院校与外国涉海院校建立了相应合作机制。伴随课程和教师的国际化，中外涉海院校学分互认、中外同班施训等管理制度也相应地建立起来。海洋人才国际素质培养的探索与研究正逐步向纵深发展。

（三）国际化的交流实践平台是国际素养培养的沃土。"一带一路"倡议

明确提出"扩大相互间留学生规模，开展合作办学"，这对于促进涉海院校
的交流合作、提升海洋人才国际素养具有积极地指导意义。积极搭建国际
海上交流平台、参与国际交流实践、丰富学生的国际经历体验，是各国涉
海院校开放办学的通用做法。在这一点上，我们宜固化中国涉海院校与多
个国家，特别是"一带一路"沿线国家业已形成的互派驻训、互派留学生、
互派学生远海训练、举办国际学生周等合作机制，不断深化学生国际素养
培育成果。比如定期邀请各国青年海洋人才开展模拟联合国大会、外国讲
堂、国际论坛、深蓝国际文化节等国际化主题活动；安排学生担任国际涉
海院校校长论坛、各专业领域学术论坛、来访外国代表团、国际比赛的联
络员、翻译官和志愿者。还可选派学生参加中外联合训练、国际航海技能
竞赛以及远海训练船环球航行等国际海上交流活动，不断丰富合作交流内
涵、创新形式、挖掘潜力，打造中外涉海院校合作精品项目。实践证明，
不同国家青年海洋人才间的这些交流实践活动，不但提升了他们的职业素
质和国际素养，也为他们建立起了良好的友谊。

Developing Marine Students' Global Competence through Cooperation and Exchange under the "Belt and Road" Initiative

Since September 2013, Chinese President Xi Jinping has promoted the "Belt and Road" Initiative, calling for the creation of a "community with a shared future for mankind" as well as a "maritime community with a shared future". In 2017, the UN Security Council included the concept of "creating a community of shared future for mankind" for the first time in Resolution 2344, which reflects international consensus. In recent years, these initiatives have not only provided opportunities for economic growth in related countries, but have also served as a bridge to peace and friendship by increasing mutual understanding and trust and enhancing exchanges in all areas. As a major maritime country, China has proposed and is determined to build a harmonious ocean. In response to the "Belt and Road" Initiative, China has participated in and carried out joint maritime security mechanisms for common interests, being regarded as an indispensable force in establishing a community of shared interests, security, and responsibility. Without a doubt, China will take on more international responsibilities as it progresses toward the community of a shared future and the "Belt and Road" cooperation. The young marine students are the next generation of maritime leaders, builders and peacekeepers. Their global competence will be critical in defining the maritime endeavor in the future. It is the responsibility of maritime institutions to prepare students for the ever-increasing international cooperation and exchange.

I. Three Dimensions of Marine Students' Global Competence

According to UNESCO, the three aspects of global competence are universally recognized as thinking, knowledge, and skills.

1. Global vision and thinking pattern. The twenty-first century has been dubbed the "Ocean Century", with both opportunities and challenges coexisting. More than 3000 years ago, the Chinese book *I Ching* taught us in *Hexagram Qian* that Heaven creates everything so that everyone can live in peace and harmony. Today, China, along with colleagues from other countries, is carrying out a major country's commitment to deepen cooperation and exchange in the field of maritime security. The maritime Silk Road encompasses the busiest sea lanes of trade. And the majority of the countries bordering the Silk Road have complicated domestic situations in terms of politics, culture, history, and ideology. In this situation, marine students' global awareness and strategic thinking are challenged to develop and safeguard maritime security and common interests.

2. International knowledge structure. We should not impose ethnic icons and cultural definitions on countries along the Silk Road because their cultures, religions, customs, and habits are diverse. Instead, we should research international maritime conventions and have a solid understanding of the expertise and skills that serve maritime activities to create a harmonious ocean that is culturally inclusive.

3. Proficiency in international communication. Effective communication is required to achieve mutual understanding. Interaction is required to develop friendship. Marine students are expected to be masters of international rules and diplomatic protocol, as well as fluent speakers of at least one foreign language, which are regarded as the cornerstone of their global competence and a tremendous boost in building a community of a shared future. Furthermore, the ability to use international rules in a flexible manner is a much-needed skill in the ever-increasing complicated maritime interactions. The combination of the aforementioned competencies is intended to serve as the foundation for the capability framework for marine students participating in multilateral collaboration.

II. The Need for Marine Students to Develop Global Competence through "Belt and Road" Cooperation and Exchange

The "Belt and Road" Initiative is regarded as an extraordinary achievement with the original intention of promoting economic prosperity and regional cooperation, strengthening cultural interaction, improving peaceful development, and benefiting people all over the world. The professionals with global competence are laying groundwork for the implementation of President Xi's grand strategic vision. Developing marine students' global competence, guided by "Belt and Road" cooperation and exchange, is the major strategic task to which Chinese maritime institutions should give priority both now and in the future.

1. It is the requirement for the advancement of national interests and the maritime missions. The widespread acceptance and implementation of the "Belt and Road" Initiative has resulted in the continuous development of national strategic interests and the gradual evolution of maritime endeavor from a single task-based to a multi-task-based scenario and from a domestic to an international context, from offshore to high-seas operations. The maritime industry is carrying out tasks against a more complicated international backdrop, where its influence has spread beyond its borders. Furthermore, maritime missions have a significant impact on the political and diplomatic situation, as well as the relationship between China and other countries. The marine students, as members of the forces at the forefront of safeguarding the "Belt and Road" initiative, can clearly understand the strategic importance and political implications of national interests and carry out their duties and missions effectively only when they gain a deep understanding of the reality that the development of national strategic interests must keep up with the times. Only with a broad international perspective can they observe and deal with problems while keeping national political and diplomatic situations in mind; only with a good command of the maritime practical knowledge can they address complicated situations and emergencies much better. On the one hand, improving marine students' global competence is critical in order to carry out diverse tasks in accordance with "Belt and Road" project at sea. On the other hand, it is a response to the future's call to deepen and broaden our maritime endeavor and protect maritime rights and interests.

2. It is a call for international cooperation and defining China as a major country. The implementation of the "Belt and Road" Initiative has been presented in the interdependent relations in the fields of politics, and economy around the world. The maritime endeavor, on the other hand, will engage in multilateral collaboration and exchange in more domains through various channels. Marine students on the diplomatic frontlines, will be unable to apply foreign policy strategies if they are unfamiliar with ours. They are more likely to be pushed into a passive role in maritime interactions if they are unaware of the traditions or habits of their counterparts' countries. It is difficult for them to protect national interests if they are not knowledgeable about the rules and practices of international organizations or the international community. As a result, their knowledge, vision, communicative competence, and etiquette, affect not only the quality and effectiveness of internation cooperation and exchange, but also the national interests and reputation of maritime endeavors in the international community. In response to the mission's call in the new era, every effort must be made to raise marine students' global competence to a new level.

3. It is necessary to be proactive in the diplomatic arena with an eye toward the future geopolitical picture. The "Belt and Road" Initiative has taken advantage of a favorable geopolitical situation and has actively participated in political and diplomatic affairs. With the rising strategic position of the ocean, the development of the economic globalization and the collective rise of maritime powers, marine geopolitical issues emerge, drastically changing the status quo of the world politics and progressively influencing the future of the world. Our future maritime endeavor will safeguard the "Belt and Road" initiative against a politically sensitive and complicated backdrop which is likely to arouse grave concern from the international community and set off a chain reaction in terms of politics, diplomacy, and economics, resulting in disaster for the strategic situation if any missteps in interactions occur. As a result, marine students must be skilled in the analysis and judgment of global and regional situations, as well as be prepared to safeguard national security and development in the future. Furthermore, they are expected to be experts in international laws and rules in order to deal with emergencies properly, prevent the situation from worsening, and avoid a chain reaction. Understanding the strategic settings and taking advantage of favorable factors are also essential to the accomplishment of the mission. To some extent, global competence has been identified as a critical component among all, along with the competences of information technology and leadership.

III. Recommendations for the Development of Marine Students' International Competence

The world is colorful because of its cultural diversity. The young generation's values are also influenced by culture. All rivers, as the Chinese say, flow into the sea. Fostering global competence entails modeling intercultural cognition with "harmony in diversity" in the pursuit of an open-ended environment in education. Marine students, as maritime diplomats and cultural ambassadors, play an important role. That is why, in order to develop global perspective and awareness, they must be immersed in an open and inclusive environment. Despite differences in national conditions, as well as differences in educational settings, we all agree on developing students' global competence through education in an international context, emphasizing the importance of the resources of the curriculum system, instructors, and communication platform.

1. The globalized curriculum is the foundation of global competence development. We value the development of courses in cross-cultural communication, international laws, diplomatic protocol, and maritime knowledge and professional skills. In order to highlight the expansion of international vision, and international thinking training, we also emphasize global challenges in various courses, create online teaching resources such as MOOC, and incorporate more maritime and global elements into curriculum design.

2. Globalized instructors are critical to the development of global competence. As we all know, the primary task of higher education is "instructing". The Chinese maritime institutions have accelerated the process of "going global" in recent years by sending instructors abroad for overseas training, ship port visits, seminars, and research programs. Furthermore, we have reached agreement with our international counterparts on cooperative programs and mechanisms such as instructor exchange, the invitation of professors and experts from other countries to give lectures, and the introduction of overseas talents for disciplinary innovation projects. The management system for mutual recognition of course credit points and for international classes has been developed with the globlization of international courses and the teaching team. The ongoing study of marine students' global competence is now expanding in depth and breadth.

3. The international communication practice platform serves as a hub for the development of global competence. The "Belt and Road" Initiative has made it clear in the educational field that increasing the number of overseas students in a reciprocal manner and implementing cooperative programs, which is guiding global cooperation between maritime institutions as well as the development of marine students' global competence. Following the philosophy of open-ended education, maritime institutions worldwide have encouraged students to participate in a variety of exchanges via the international interaction platform. To this point, we plan to consolidate the cooperative mechanism involving student exchange, overseas training, onboard exchange training, and International Student Week with other nations, particularly those participating in the "Belt and Road"

Initiative. The students' global competence is supposed to be improved in this manner. On a regular basis, we may host global themed events such as Model United Nations Conferences, Foreign Nations' Lecture Rooms, International Forum, and Blue Water Culture Festival, or assign students as volunteers, liaison officers, and interpreters during the education symposiums for deans of maritime institutions, academic seminars, international games and foreign delegation visits. We may send students for nautical activities including joint training, international maritime skill competitions, and training cruises alongside overseas peers. The collaboration is evolving and providing new benefits as a result of the commitment to the inter-college cooperation quality initiative. It turns out that communication practice among marine students worldwide strengthens their global competence and expertise while also fostering friendships that will last throughout their careers.

6.3.4 国际研讨会常用表达 Useful Expressions at International Symposium

一、仪式用语

Ⅰ. Ceremonial Expressions

1. 在这金风送爽的美好时节……

In this golden season of autumn...

2. 在这多彩的深秋时节……

In this lovely season tinted with deep autumn hues...

3. 很高兴同大家相聚在……

It gives me great pleasure to get together with you in/by/at...

4. 我很高兴和荣幸地宣布……开幕。

I am very pleased and honored to declare the opening/commencement of the...

5. 我深感荣幸在北京举办的第××次 ABC 国际大会上致开幕词。

I am greatly honored to give the opening address/speech at this... International Conference of ABC here in Beijing.

6. 我很高兴代表 ABC 学会欢迎你们所有的人来参加第××届 XYZ 国际学术会议。

On behalf of the ABC society, I am delighted to welcome all of you to the... International Symposium of XYZ.

7. 你们远道而来参加会议，我相信各位都能乘兴而来、满意而归！

You have traveled all the way here, and I believe that you will all find your participation in the event worthwhile and rewarding!

8. 谢谢你们的邀请和盛情款待。

Thank you for your kind invitation and gracious hospitality.

9. 此次会议的历史可追溯到 1982 年 9 月，当时 ABC 领域的发展已变得如此重要，组织一次会议显然是必要的。

The history of this gathering/conference goes back to September 1982, when it first became apparent that development in ABC had become so important that a conference seemed mandatory.

10. 这个会议的目标有三点。第一，它必须为参会者在这个属于交叉学科的会议上提供信息交流。第二，它必须为参会者之间提供一个重温旧情并结交新友的机会。第三，它必须激发来自世界各地的参会者尽力进行合作的兴趣。

The goals of this conference are threefold. Firstly, it should be a hub of information between participants in this interdisciplinary meeting. Secondly, it should provide an opportunity to establish and renew personal relationships between participants, and thirdly, it should stimulate the interest and ambition of participants from all over the world to cooperate in their efforts.

11. 这个会议的目标主要是将在几年期间对这个课题已作出贡献的各

位聚在一起。我们的目的是说明有关 ABC 在五个不同领域中的认识现状。

It is the aim of this conference to bring together mainly those who have contributed over a period of years to this subject. Our purpose here is to define the present status of knowledge concerning ABC in five different fields.

12. 这个会议将主要讨论有关 ABC 的各个方面。

This conference will focus on the discussion of the various aspects of ABC.

13. 我希望这次第××届国际 ABC 大会将增进我们对 DEF 的了解。我还希望大会将为个人进行科学结果的交流提供机会，这有利于交流新知识和加强世界各地的科学家(参会者)之间的个人友谊。

I hope that this ×× th International Conference of ABC will improve our understanding of DEF. I also hope that the conference will provide the opportunity for personal exchange of scientific results, facilitate the making of new acquaintances, and strengthen friendships among scientists (participants) from different parts of the world.

二、主持报告会用语

Ⅱ. Chairing Expressions at Presentation

1. 早上好，女士们，先生们，我很高兴欢迎诸位参加 ABC 会议。

Good morning, ladies and gentlemen. It is a great pleasure for me/It is a privilege for me to welcome you to the session on ABC.

2. 我是中国 ABC 大学的高博士。我是今天下午会议的主席。

I am Dr. Gao from ABC University, China, and I am going to chair this afternoon's session.

3. 我先说下基本要求，每个报告限时 15 分钟，在每个报告后有 5 分钟的讨论时间，在会议快结束时，我们将自由讨论任何一篇已报告过的论文。

There are some basic rules. First, please limit your presentation in

15 minutes. After each presentation, there will be 5 minutes for discussion. At the end of the session, we will have an open discussion on any of the papers presented.

4. 遗憾的是，我们要撤去 2 篇论文，即第 10 篇和第 11 篇。

Unfortunately, we have to cancel paper No. 10 and No. 11.

5. 时刻表有改变，第 5 篇和第 6 篇对调。

We have to reverse the order of paper No. 5 and No. 6.

6. 列在节目单上的报告人已有些变动，原定由张博士报告的第二篇论文，因不能出席这个会议，而由谢博士来报告。

There has been some change in the presenter listed on the program. Dr. Zhang who was expected to present the second paper could not attend this meeting, and Dr. Xie will present the paper for him.

7. 今天上午第一篇论文将由 A 大学高分子科学教授刘博士宣读。他的题目是……，有请刘博士。

The first paper this morning will be presented by Dr. Liu, professor of polymer science at A University, and his topic is…, Dr. Liu, you have the floor.

8. 本会场下一个报告是……我想请高博士谈谈这一十分重要的课题。

The next presentation in this session is on… I would like to call on/ ask Dr. Gao to talk about this very important subject.

9. 对不起，议程十分/有点紧，我们没有时间讨论了，所以我们必须继续下一篇报告。

Sorry, the schedule is very/ rather tight. We haven't time for discussion, so we must go on to next paper.

10. 张博士，很抱歉，我们必须往下赶；时间快要到了。

Dr. Zhang, I'm sorry, but we do have to move on; we are running short of time.

11. 感谢您的精彩论文/演讲/报告，张博士。

Thank you, Dr. Zhang, for your excellent paper/ contribution/ presentation/ message/ speech/ lecture / talk/address.

12. 现在是讨论时间, 大家有问题吗?

Time for discussion, do you have any question?

13. 您还有问题或评论要问刘博士吗?

Any more questions or comments for Dr. Niu?

14. 让我们进行下一个问题/专题 XYZ。

Let's turn /move on to the next problem/ the subject of XYZ.

15. 我想这将是结束这次会议/进入到下一个演讲人之前的最后一个问题。

I think that'll be the last /final question before we close this meeting / go on to next speaker.

16. 请各位注意!

May I have your attention, please!

17. 让我们休息五分钟。

Let's take five minutes off.

18. 到结束这次会议的时候了。

It's time for us to close this meeting.

19. 谢谢你们的参与。

Thank you for your attention.

三、学术演讲的通用句型

Ⅲ. Expressions Used in Academic Speeches

1. 谢谢沈博士, 首先感谢您对我热情的介绍。

Thank you, Dr. Shen. Let me first thank you for your kind introduction.

2. 前一位演讲人的论文给了我很多启发。

The previous presentation is very inspiring.

3. 我很荣幸能在……会议上发表此次有关……的演讲。

I am very honored to give this speech on... at... conference.

4. 对有幸介绍我的论文表示感谢。

Thank you for the privilege of presenting this paper.

5. 今天我想向你们报告在 ABC 领域中我们的某些工作。

Today I want to talk about some of our work in the field of ABC.

6. 今天我打算发表用 DEF 方法得到的 ABC 研究的结果，这个工作是 XYZ 大学张、刘、余博士和我完成的。

Today I would like to present the results of ABC studies performed with DEF technique at XYZ University by Drs. Zhang, Liu, Yu and me.

7. 今天下午我报告的目的是总结 ABC 领域某些最近的进展。

I am going to summarize some recent advances in the field of ABC this afternoon.

8. 我打算作的报告分为三部分。第一部分涉及 ABC，第二部分有关 DEF，最后部分是关于 GHI。

I will give this talk in three parts. The first part deals with ABC, the second part DEF, and the last part GHI.

9. 今天我将先讨论 ABC，然后涉及 DEF，最后叙述 GHI。

Today, I will first discuss ABC, then DEF, and finally GHI.

10. 今天下午我打算将我的报告分成三部分，第一……第二……和第三……

I would like to divide my talk this afternoon into three parts. First..., second..., and third...

11. 现在我们将转到 ABC 的下一个问题。

We'll now move on to the next problem of ABC.

12. 我想再用几个幻灯片更详细地说明这一情况。

I would like to elaborate on this matter with some more slides.

13. 我们在后面将更详细地讨论这件事。

We will discuss this matter in a little more detail as we go on.

14. 我恐怕没有时间涉及 ABC 的所有方面。

I am afraid I won't have time to cover everything of ABC.

15. 时间有限，我将非常简略地探讨下面的三点。

Time is limited, I will go through the next three points very briefly.

16. 后面我会再提到这一点。

I will return to this point later.

17. 我将重点讲一下 ABC 的研究和开发。

I will focus on the research and development of ABC.

18. 图一，不好意思，是曲线 1 显示……

The first figure, excuse me, the first curve shows...

19. 现在，我想总结这一研究的结果。

Now, I would like to sum up the results of this research.

20. 小结一下，我们已讨论了 ABC、DEF 和 HIJ.

In summary, we have discussed ABC, DEF and HIJ.

四、学术讨论用语

Ⅳ. Expressions Used in Academic Discussion

1. 我想是这样。

I think so.

2. 那是正确的。

It's true.

3. 我希望不是。

I hope not.

4. 我认为不是这样。

I don't think so.

5. 我同意您关于/ 那个……

I agree with you about /that...

6. 我不同意乔博士的那个观点。

I don't agree with Dr. Qiao on that idea.

7. 我支持这个观点。

I am in favor of that point.

8. 实事求是地讲，我必须说正好相反。

Well, as a matter of fact, I would say just the opposite.

9. 我能看一下……吗？

Can I have a look at... please?

10. 为什么您不继续您的实验？

Why don't you go on with your experiment?

11. 我想就这个题目提出我的意见。

I'd like to offer my opinion on this subject.

12. 重点是此化合物的影响可随浓度而变化。

The point is that the effect of the compound may vary with concentration.

13. 我强调这个理论的局限性。

Let me emphasize the limitations of this theory.

14. 恐怕……是不恰当的。

I'm afraid it may be inadequate to say that...

15. 恐怕我无法给您一个答复。

I'm afraid I can't give you an answer.

五、问答交流用语

V. Expressions Used in Q&A Session

1. 我想问张先生一个问题。

I'd like to ask Mr. Zhang a question.

2. 喻先生，您是否能对这一点解释/评论一下？

Mr. Yu, can you explain / comment on this point?

3. 有关 ABC，我想再了解一些。

I'd like to know a little more about ABC.

4. 这个问题的一个原因已被说明，还有其他原因吗？

One cause of this problem has been stated. Are there other causes？

5. 您能告诉我们为什么您反对用 ABC 吗？

Could you tell us why you object to using ABC？

6. ABC 和 DEF 之间的差别是什么？

What is the difference between ABC and DEF？

7. 陈博士，您是否看到 ABC 和 DEF 之间的一些关系？

Dr. Chen, do you see any relation between ABC and DEF？

8. 在这体系中用这两种化学药品有什么优点或缺点？

Is there any advantage or disadvantage of using these two chemicals in the system？

9. 程博士，您对这个方法有什么经验吗？

Dr. Cheng, do you have / have you had any experience with this method？

10. 维生素 C 能预防感冒，您的证据是什么？

What is your proof that vitamin C will prevent colds？

11. 我能要求您给出您在 ABC 方面的观点吗？

May I ask you to give us your opinion on ABC？

12. 能请您再详细讲讲 ABC 吗？

Could you please give a little more detail about ABC？

13. 对不起，请再说一遍。

I beg your pardon？

14. 这是一个好的问题。

That's a good question.

15. 谢谢您的这个问题。

Thank you for that question.

16. 我对这个问题的回答是……

My answer to that question is that...

17. 遗憾的是，现在我无法回答这个问题。

Unfortunately, I cannot answer that question at the moment.

18. 回答这个问题是很难的。

It is difficult/hard to answer that question.

19. 我们现在正在研究这个问题，如果您同意，我将在几周后回答您的问题。

We are now working on this problem and, if you agree, I will answer your question in a few weeks.

20. 要回答这个问题必须作进一步研究。

The answer to this question need further study.

21. 据我所知，在那方面还没有做过足够的研究。

As far as I know, no enough study has been made on that area.

22. 我的同事程博士在这儿。关于这个问题他知道得比我多。可能他对此有更好的想法和解释。

My colleague, Dr Cheng is here, he may know more about that. Perhaps he has some better ideas and comments on this matter.

23. 我希望这回答了您的问题。

I hope this answers your questions.

六、会场上的技术性用语

Ⅵ. Technical expressions in the conference

1. 你们能听到我的话吗？

Can you hear me?

2. 可以开/关掉灯吗？

May I turn on/off the lights?

3. 现在你可以开灯了。

Now, you can turn the lights on.

4. 能接着放下一张幻灯片吗？

May I proceed to the next slide, please？

5. 如果你看到下一张幻灯片，你们将看到 ABC。

If you look at the next slide..., you will see here ABC that....

6. 我们来看下一张幻灯片。

Let's see the next slide.

7. 能聚焦得好一点吗？

Could you focus it a little bit, please？

8. 时间有限，我只能省略下面一些幻灯片，直接讲最后一张。

Time is limited, I have to pass the following slides and move to the last one.

9. 一直往下放，下一张，下一张，再往下。

Just move on. Next... Next... Go ahead.

10. 我们可以让这张幻灯片停留一会儿。

Perhaps we can just leave that on for a moment.

6.4 国际竞赛 International Competition

青年学生航海综合技能比赛项目规则
Regulations on International Nautical
Competition for Undergraduates

第一章 总 则

一、比赛目的

旨在搭建平台，锻炼和提升各国高等院校青年学生的航海综合技能，加强交流，增进友谊。

二、比赛标志

比赛徽标为竞赛的官方标记。

三、官方语言

汉语、英语。

四、参赛国家及人员

参赛国根据协商确定。

每个国家 1 支代表队，包括 1 个参赛班 8 人，替补队员 3 人。领队、教练、翻译等保障人员不超过 5 人，总人数不超过 16 人。

五、比赛地点

中国××省××市。

六、比赛时间

20××年×月×日至×月×日。

七、比赛内容

（一）障碍赛：参赛队员依次通过跳栏、平衡木、圆桶、高板、立柱、水密门、绳网、起跳板、隧道、平行缆、斜索 11 个障碍，总距离约为 310 米。旨在考验学生的速度、力量、灵敏和协调性等身体素质。

（二）航海技术赛：参赛队员完成桅杆作业(爬桅杆、插木销)、收缆撒缆、绕标划船、锚泊作业 4 个内容。旨在考验学生攀爬桅杆、收缆撒缆等航海技能水平。

（三）水上综合技能赛：参赛班队员完成 60 米水上障碍、440 米着装泅渡、1500 米船只机动 3 个内容，总距离 2000 米。旨在考验学生水中越障、泅渡、划艇等综合技能水平。

八、保障

根据国际比赛组织章程要求，比赛期间中方提供部分英文翻译，为各代表队提供人员及物资运输车辆。VIP 安排在酒店住宿，其余人员在综合楼食宿。综合楼内配备健身、娱乐等设施。

Chapter One　General Regulations

Ⅰ. Purpose

The competition aims at setting up a platform to build up and strengthen the undergraduates' nautical skills, enhance the exchanges and boost the friendship among them.

Ⅱ. Logo

The image of the competition is the official logo.

Ⅲ. Official Languages

Chinese, English.

Ⅳ. Participating Countries and Personnel

Participating countries would be decided through discussion.

Each country forms one team, including one squad of eight competitors and three substitutes (male undergraduate only). The support personnel includes team captain, coach and interpreter and must be no more than five people. The total number of the participants must be no more than sixteen.

Ⅴ. Location

×× City, ×× Province, China.

Ⅵ. Time

From DD/MM to DD/MM, 20××.

Ⅶ. Competition Events

1. Obstacle Race: Competitors shall clear 11 obstacles in turn: hurdle, balance beam, barrel, Irish table, circling poles, watertight door, climbing net, long jump, tunnel, parallel wire, and sloping wire. The distance of the Obstacle Race is about 310 meters. This event aims to test undergraduates' physical fitness such as speed, strength, agility and

coordination.

2. Seamanship Race: Competitors shall perform 4 features, e. g. work on the mast (climbing up the mast & putting the pegs into the holes), cable hauling and line heaving, slalom rowing around buoys, hauling of chain and mooring. The purpose is to test the undergraduates' seamanship skills such as climbing masts, hauling cables, heaving lines and so on.

3. Water Race: Each competitor shall perform 3 features, i. e. 60-meter obstacle swimming, 440-meter swimming in battle gear (swimming in clothes) and 1500-meter boat rowing. The total distance of the Water Race is 2000 meters. The purpose is to test the participants' integrated skills such as water obstacle clearing, swimming across, boat rowing and so on.

Ⅷ. Support

According to the practice of international competitions, the Chinese organizer shall provide some English language translation services and arrange transportation for each participating team during the competition. As for accommodation, hotel stays shall be arranged for VIPs while Accommodation Center for other participants. The building is equipped with facilities for fitness and entertainment.

第二章　参赛队的义务和权利

一、参赛资格

1. 各参赛队在规定期限内递交参赛申请。

2. 各国参赛队员必须是在校注册学生，并通过中方组织的健康检查。

二、参赛须知

1. 熟悉并严格遵守本规则。

2. 参赛班 8 人一旦确定，在比赛期间不得随意更换，如遇伤病原因等需要更换替补队员，须出具医疗证明并提前向裁判委员提出书面申请，经允许后方可参赛。

3. 在规定时间内携带规定的设备、器材参赛。

4. 按照比赛规则要求着装，佩戴统一制作、便于识别的袖标（印有参赛国国旗及名称、队员编号等，由中方提供）。

5. 在指定区域待命，遵守比赛秩序和日程安排。

6. 无条件执行裁判指令。

7. 参赛队员不得同时兼任比赛裁判。

8. 各参赛国领队、教练等管理人员不得干涉裁判的裁决，未经同意不得擅自命令本国队员退出比赛。

9. 比赛期间，各参赛国领队、教练等管理人员和保障人员不得向本国参赛队员提供规定以外的帮助。

三、参赛队员权利

1. 在现场裁判组指定时间内，到指定场地进行热身和训练。

2. 在适应性训练时，可就紧急问题向裁判直接提问，其他问题只能通过领队以口头或书面形式向裁判组反映。

3. 因比赛现场出现突发情况危及自身生命安全或因个人身体原因，参赛队员有权停止或退出比赛。

四、领队职责

1. 在规定时间内提交比赛规则要求的所有文件。

2. 教育队员遵守比赛规则和作息时间，并做好安全防护措施。

3. 在比赛地点待命，如离开须征得总裁判长同意。

4. 向参赛队员通报各项决定、比赛时间及赛事调整情况。

5. 掌握参赛队比赛成绩，对当日情况进行小结，布置后续比赛日任务。

6. 参与比赛抽签。

7. 冷静地解决争议问题。

五、领队权利

1. 在产生异议时，向裁判委员会提出口头或书面声明。

2. 检查督促本国参赛队员按要求做好比赛准备。

Chapter II Obligations and Rights of Participating Teams

I. Eligibility

1. Each participating team shall submit an application for participation before the prescribed deadline.

2. Competitors from all participating countries must be undergraduates currently registered in college, and should pass the health check-up conducted by the Chinese organizer.

II. Information for Participants

1. The rules should be read carefully and followed strictly.

2. No change shall be made arbitrarily during the competition once the 8 competitors in a squad are decided. A medical certificate and a written application must be submitted to the Jury of Appeal in advance when there is a need of substitution due to injuries. The back-up competitor can compete only with permission.

3. Specified and approved equipment may be brought to the venue within the stipulated time before the competition.

4. Dress code should be followed in accordance with competition regulations and recognizable armband (provided by the Chinese organizer, carrying the national flag and the name of the participating country, carrying the reference number of the team member, etc.) should be worn.

5. Competitors shall take standby position in designated area, and

observe the competition schedule.

6. Instructions from the referee shall be followed without any condition.

7. Competitors are not allowed to serve as referees concurrently.

8. Participants other than competitors such as team captains and coaches are not allowed to interfere with the referee's judgement or order their competitors to withdraw from the competition without consent.

9. Competitors are not allowed to be assisted beyond the regulations by other participants in the team.

Ⅲ. Rights of Competitors

1. Competitors may warm-up and train in the designated venue within the time limit specified by the on-site referee panel.

2. During the pre-competition training, competitors can directly ask the referee about urgent issues while other issues should be reported by the team captain to the referee panel in oral or written form.

3. Competitors can stop or withdraw from the competition in case of life-threatening emergencies or personal physical discomfort.

Ⅳ. Obligations of Team Captains

1. Team captains shall submit all documents required by competition regulations within the specified time.

2. Team captains shall instruct team members to abide by the competition rules, safety precautions and daily schedule.

3. Team captains shall stay at the competition venue on standby. They should not leave their position without permission from the chief referee.

4. Team captains shall inform the competitors of all decisions and adjustments regarding competition time and events.

5. Team captains should acquire information on the competition results of their teams, make daily summary and assign tasks for subse-

quent events.

6. Team captains shall draw the lots.

7. Team captains should adopt a calm and unbiased attitude when disputes occur.

Ⅴ. Rights of Team Captains

1. If any protest arises, team captains should submit it to the Technical Jury orally or in written form.

2. Team captains should inspect and urge their competitors to make preparation for the competition as required.

第三章　比赛裁判工作

设置裁判委员会、项目裁判委员会，按相应权限分别行使职责。

一、裁判委员会

由中国甲大学 1 名高级领导担任总裁判长，各参赛国代表队最高领导担任委员，主要负责比赛的申诉受理、争议仲裁工作，行使项目最终裁决权。当赞同票和反对票数相同时，以总裁判长意见为准。

二、项目裁判委员会

项目裁判委员会，由中国甲大学 1 名领导担任裁判长，各参赛国 1 名高级别专业人员担任委员，下设裁判组、监督组。主要负责比赛的组织实施、成绩评定和裁决评判工作。

(一)裁判长职责

1. 领导项目裁判组工作，并依照本规则对各项比赛组织与实施情况进行指导。

2. 任命裁判，监督比赛，检查裁判工作。

3. 复审比赛期间执行比赛规则过程中发生的纠纷，保证比赛规则正确执行。

4. 对于发生严重错判、误判、作弊、篡改比赛成绩的裁判，取消其裁判资格。

5. 对严重违反比赛规则的队员实施禁赛。

6. 对出现异议，经裁判委员会集体表决，仍难以达成共识的争议问题有现场裁决权。

(二)各参赛国裁判委员职责

1. 监督比赛裁决工作，无裁决权。

2. 参加裁判工作会议，有发言及表决权。

(三)项目裁判组组成及职责

项目裁判组组长及助理裁判均由中方派出，负责对单项目比赛进行裁评。

1. 裁判组组长职责

(1)负责单项目比赛检查、监督及裁评工作。

(2)指导监督助理裁判开展工作。

(3)比赛前，检查本规则设置标准，发现问题，采取必要措施解决。

(4)宣布比赛成绩、填写比赛纪要，并上报裁判委员会。

(5)如发现助理裁判违反本规则或不履职尽责，有权终止其裁判资格。

(6)出现影响比赛正常进行、威胁比赛安全和参赛队员健康，以及医疗救护等各项保障不到位的情况，有权推迟或者终止比赛。

(7)禁止违反本规则的队员参加比赛。

(8)对不符合比赛实施标准、继续参赛可能对比赛造成不良影响、威胁到自身或他人安全的队员实施停赛处理。

2. 项目助理裁判职责

(1)比赛开始前，检查参赛队员着装及携带设备、装具、器材等是否符合规定，如不符合，有权禁止其参加比赛，并及时上报比赛主裁。

(2)按照比赛规定时间向参赛队员(班)发出进场信号。

(3)根据比赛规定，负责监督、记录各参赛队员(班)比赛情况。

(4)准确判定并记录每名参赛队员(班)的比赛成绩，并在赛后检查参赛队员着装是否符合规定。

（四）项目监督组组成及职责

监督组人员由各参赛国代表队派出，每队 1 人，主要负责对比赛条件设置、比赛裁评、各国参赛队比赛情况进行监督，出现争议时，上报项目裁判委员会裁决。

Chapter Ⅲ   Competition Referees

Jury of Appeal（JOA）and Technical Jury（TJ）shall be established and perform their duties according to its stipulated authority.

Ⅰ. Jury of Appeal

In the Jury of Appeal, one senior leader of University A shall act as the Chief of JOA and the top leader from each participating team act as jury members. It is mainly responsible for the acceptance of appeal, dispute arbitration and exercise of the final judgment. When the number of votes for and against is the same, the opinion of the Chief shall prevail.

Ⅱ. Technical Jury

In the Technical Jury, one senior leader of the host university shall act as the head referee and one senior professional from each participating team act as jury members. With its two divisions（Refereeing Group and Supervision Group）, it is mainly responsible for the organization and implementation of the competition, the results evaluation and the judging.

（Ⅰ）Duties of the Head Referee

1. Lead the Refereeing Group and guide the organization and implementation of each competition event in accordance with regulations.

2. Appoint referees, supervise the competition, and check referees' work.

3. Review disputes on the implementation of rules during the compe-

tition so as to ensure the correct implementation of competition rules.

4. Disqualify referees with serious misjudgments, mistakes, cheating, or tampering with the results of the competition.

5. Suspend competitors who severely violate the competition rules.

6. Make a ruling on site if a dispute arises and no consensus is reached even after a collective vote by the Technical Jury.

(Ⅱ) Duties of TJ Members

1. Supervise the ruling work of the competition, without the right to make rulings.

2. Participate in refereeing work meetings, with the right to speak and vote.

(Ⅲ) Composition and Duties of the Refereeing Group

The Refereeing Group consisting of a Chief and several assistant referees are assigned by the Chinese organizer, responsible for ruling the single event.

1. Duties of the Chief of Refereeing Group

(1) Responsible for the inspection, supervision and ruling of the race.

(2) Instruct and supervise the assistant referees to carry out their work.

(3) Review the standards set by the regulation and take measures to solve the problems if there are before the race.

(4) Announce the race results, fill in the minutes and report to the Technical Jury.

(5) Disqualify assistant referees in case of violation of the regulation or breach of duty.

(6) Postpone or terminate the race under circumstances where the normal continuing of the race is not allowed, the competition security or

the health of the competitors is threatened, and when vital logistic supports such as medical care are not in place.

(7) Prohibit the competitors violating the regulation from the competition.

(8) Suspend the competitors who do not comply with the competition implementation standards, whose continued participation may have an adverse effect on the competition, and threaten their own safety or the safety of others.

2. Duties of Assistant Referees

(1) Before the start of the competition, check whether the competitor' dress, carry-on gear and equipment are in compliance with the regulations. If not, the assistant referee has the right to prohibit the competitor from participating in the game and should report it to the chief of the group in time.

(2) Send an entering signal to the participating competitor (squad) according to the stipulated time.

(3) Supervise and record the performance of each participating competitor (squad) according to the rules of the competition.

(4) Accurately check and record the score of each participating competitor (squad), and check after the competition whether the dress of the competitor meets the requirements.

(Ⅳ) Composition and Duties of the Supervision Group

The members of the supervision group shall be appointed by each participating team, with one person from each team. The supervision group is mainly responsible for supervising the setting of competition conditions, competition judgements and evaluation, and performance of all participating teams. When a dispute arises, they should report it to the Technical Jury of the event for ruling.

第四章 比赛规则

一、障碍赛

(一)比赛条件

1. 人员及着装

人员：各参赛队 8 人参加。

着装：着运动服、运动鞋、运动帽。

2. 场地设置

赛道内设置起点、终点及跳栏、平衡木、圆桶、高板、立柱、水密门、绳网、跳板、隧道、平行缆、斜索 11 个障碍物。

(二)实施方法

以个人为单位组织实施，抽签确定个人组别和赛道，每组 2 人。

参赛队员位于起点就位，裁判员逐一检查参赛队员着装，若不符合比赛要求，则须调整至符合比赛要求。

裁判员发出出发信号并开始计时，参赛队员通过所有障碍到达终点后计时停止，比赛用时为队员完成时间与罚时之和。

障碍通过方法：

跳栏：从上方自由通过，允许用手或脚辅助。

平衡木：利用软梯攀上并通过平衡木，并于 1 米线(白色标识)外着地。

圆桶：从圆桶上方自由通过，允许用手或脚辅助。

高板：任意姿势通过高板，允许无意触碰支柱，但不得有意借用支柱爬上高板。

立柱：环绕立柱的姿势不限，顺时针或逆时针皆可，但须保持方向一致。经每个柱子时，参赛者须绕柱子一圈，同时沿身体纵轴旋转 360°。环绕时，允许抓柱子。

水密门：打开水密门，穿过后须将其完全锁住。

绳网：攀爬上网。抵达第一根横杆后，沿水平钢丝移动，姿势不限，直至手碰触第二根横杆。利用索绳自由下滑，摆动着陆在白色标识线后方，即距第二根横杆3米处。

起跳板：跳过所示区域（起跳板前沿至白色标识线）。脚趾可超过起跳板前缘但不得触及沙面。参赛者身体的任一部位，比如手、脚等，不得碰到起跳板至白色标识线中间4米区域。

隧道：以任意姿势进入并通过隧道，从圆柱体顶部爬出。

平行缆：参赛者须在较低的一根平行索上行走，跨越沙坑（如有必要，可抓上面一根绳索辅助），不得碰触起跳板和白色标识线之间的沙坑区域以及侧边拓展区域。向右环绕障碍架跑，允许手触支柱。任意姿势爬上斜木（一根、两根均可），利用脚缆向前方移动，直至碰到木板对面的横杆，跳下，可以借助侧边柱。

斜索：任意姿势攀爬斜索，不得触碰沙坑，可以借助支柱。通过平台时，须整个脚掌站立在方板上（允许单脚通过），跳下后继续向终点前进。

（三）罚则

1. 若参赛队员未能正确通过障碍，须重新通过直至正确通过，否则每个错误罚时20秒。

2. 参赛队员须在各自跑道内完成比赛，故意越道罚时20秒。

（四）成绩评定

根据各参赛队员的比赛用时判定名次，用时少者名次列前，第1名积N+1分，第二名积N-1分，第三名积N-2分，以此类推（N为参赛队员总人数）。

二、航海技术赛

（一）比赛条件

1. 人员及着装

人员：各参赛队8人参加。

着装：着运动服、运动鞋，戴运动帽。

2. 场地设置

赛场设置起点、终点、桅杆作业区、撇揽区、水上赛道。其中桅杆高6米；撇揽绳长约28米，一端系有300克的重物，撇揽距离不少于22.5米；粗缆绳长10米，一端圈成绳环；水上赛道上设置5个浮标，3号浮标上用小"U"形扣系一条铁链，铁链长约5米，重约5千克，5号浮标上系一个大"U"形扣，重约3千克。使用单人双桨手划艇。

(二)实施方法

以个人为单位组织实施，抽签确定个人组别和赛道，每组3人，在比赛开始前参赛队员领取桅杆作业使用的木销。

参赛队员位于起点就位，裁判员逐一检查参赛队员着装，若不符合比赛要求，则须调整至符合比赛要求。

裁判员发出出发信号并开始计时，参赛队员从起点出发，按要求完成桅杆作业、收缆撇揽、绕标划船、水上作业，到达终点后计时停止，比赛用时为队员完成时间与罚时之和。

桅杆作业：坐在吊板上拉绳升至桅杆顶部，将木销插入对应颜色的孔中然后滑下。

收揽撇缆：从水中拉起10米长粗缆绳，撇细缆绳超过22.5米，每个参赛队员均有三次机会，若第一次失败必须进行第二次，第二次失败必须进行第三次，然后将细缆绳用单套结和粗缆绳绳环部分连接。

绕标划船：参赛队员从码头跳上小艇划两个来回，第一圈须"S"形绕标，第二圈不需要绕标。

水上作业：划艇第二圈经过3号浮标时解下链条固定至4号浮标，若铁链掉落仍须用手触摸4号浮标，经过5号浮标时卸下"U"形环带至终点。

(三)罚则

1. 未将木销插入对应颜色的孔中，每错1个罚时20秒。

2. 三次撇缆未超过规定距离，罚时20秒。

3. 单套结错误或打在绳环外，罚时20秒。

4. 绕错浮标，每个错误罚时20秒。

5. 未将铁链固定在4号浮标，罚时40秒。

6. 未用手触摸 4 号浮标，罚时 20 秒。

7. 大"U"形环和螺丝未带回终点，缺少 1 个罚时 20 秒。

(四)成绩评定

根据各参赛队员的比赛用时判定名次，用时少者名次列前，第 1 名积 N+1 分，第二名积 N−1 分，第三名积 N−2 分，以此类推(N 为参赛队员总人数)。

三、水上综合技能赛

(一)比赛条件

1. 人员及着装

人员：各参赛队 8 人参加。

着装：着运动服、运动鞋，戴运动帽，穿相关携行具。

2. 场地设置

赛场设置起点、终点、水上障碍区、泅渡区、划艇区。水上障碍区设置高台滑梯、圆管、圆木、油污池、浮台等 5 个障碍物；泅渡区域为自然水域；划艇使用班用橡皮艇。比赛全程中方提供完善的安全防护措施。

(二)实施方法

以班为单位组织实施，抽签确定出发顺序。

参赛班位于起点就位，裁判员逐一检查参赛班每名队员装具及着装，若不符合比赛要求，则须调整至符合比赛要求。

裁判员发出出发信号并开始计时，参赛班每名队员均须按要求通过全部障碍，沿规定线路泅渡至对岸后推艇下水，然后划艇到达终点，到达终点后，班长清点人员装具，到齐后报告"项目完成"，计时停止，比赛用时为全班完成时间与全班所有队员罚时之和。

队员之间全程可互帮互助，但个人装具不得离身和交给他人，最前方一名队员和最后方一名队员之间的距离不能超过 50 米。

障碍通过方法：

高台滑梯：攀上平台，沿滑梯滑下。

圆管：钻过圆管。

圆木：从圆木上方攀过。

油污池：从油污池下潜过。

浮台：攀上浮台。

(三)罚则

1. 未按要求通过障碍，须返回该障碍物重新通过，未重新通过者，每个障碍每人次罚时 30 秒。

2. 划艇过程中人员落水，每人次罚时 60 秒。

3. 各参赛队有 1 人未完成比赛，该队本项目总时间加罚 10 分钟，2 人(含)以上未完成比赛，该队本项目计 0 分。

(四)成绩评定

根据各参赛班的比赛用时判定名次，用时少者名次列前，第 1 名积 N+1 分，第二名积 N-1 分，第三名积 N-2 分，以此类推(N 为参赛班的数量)。

Chapter Ⅳ　Competition Rules

1. Obstacle Race

(Ⅰ) Conditions

1. Personnel and Dress Code

Personnel：8 competitors from each participating team.

Dress code：sports clothes, sports shoes, and sports caps.

2. Characteristics

Besides the start and finish, there are 11 obstacles in the track, including the hurdle, balance beam, barrel, Irish table, circling poles, watertight door, climbing net, takeoff plank, tunnel, parallel wire and sloping wire.

(Ⅱ) Methods

This race is organized on an individual basis. Heat and track number of the individual competitor are determined by drawing lots, with two people in each heat.

The competitors take position at the starting point while the referees will check the dress of the competitors one by one. If the dress does not meet the requirements, it must be adjusted for compliance.

The referee sends a start signal and starts timing. The time counting stops when the competitor reaches the finish after clearing all obstacles. The game time is the sum of the competitor's completion time and penalty time.

Method of clearing:

Hurdle: Pass over the hurdle in free-style. Support with hands and/or feet are allowed.

Balance beam: Climb the ladder. Move forward and descend further than the one-meter line (white marker) on the ground.

Barrel: Pass over the barrel in free style. Support with hands and/or feet are allowed.

Irish table: Pass over the irish table in free style. A competitor may unintentionally touch a post, but may not use it intentionally as a support to get up onto the table.

Circling poles: Circle around the poles in free style either clockwise or counter-clockwise but always in the same direction. At each pole the competitor's body itself must turn 360°, and must also turn 360° around each pole. Grasping or holding the pole is permitted.

Watertight door: Open and pass through the watertight door free style, close and lock it completely.

Climbing net: Climb up the net. After reaching the first crossbar, coordinate hands and feet to pass through the wire rope free-style until the hand touches the second crossbar. Descend free-style using the fiber rope, swing and land at least 3 meters from the second crossbar after the white marker-line.

Takeoff plank: Jump over the area (measured from the front edge of the takeoff plank to the white marker line). Toes may cross the edge of the plank but may not touch the ground in front of the takeoff plank. Successful completing of this obstacle means that at no time may the competitor's body, foot, hands, etc. touch the sand between the takeoff plank and the 4-meter mark.

Tunnel: Enter in and pass through the tunnel free-style. Exit through the top of the cylinder.

Parallel wire: Cross the sandpit by running on the lower wire (and, if necessary, holding onto the upper wire) without touching the sandpit inside the area between the takeoff plank and the white marker line or their lateral extensions. Run around the stand to the right. Hand support on the posts is allowed. Ascend the plank or planks in freestyle. Move sideways along the yard using the footrope and touch the crossbar opposite the planks. Descend in freestyle. Using the side-post is allowed.

Sloping wire: Climb in freestyle up the sloping wire without touching the sandpit. Use of the posts is allowed. Pass over the platform standing flatfooted on the platform (one foot is allowed). Jump down and continue to the finish.

(Ⅲ) Penalties

1. If a competitor fails to pass the obstacle correctly, he must repass until he overcomes the obstacle correctly. Otherwise, there will be a 20-second penalty for each fault.

2. Competitors must complete the game on their respective tracks. If a competitor deliberately crosses the track, there will be a 20-second penalty.

(Ⅳ) Result Evaluation

Time spent by each competitor is used to decide the ranking. The competitor with the least time ranks first and receives N+1 points in scoring, then N - 1 points for the second place, N - 2 points for the third place, and so on (N is the total number of competitors).

Ⅱ. Seamanship Race

(Ⅰ) Conditions

1. Personnel and Dress Code

Personnel: 8 competitors from each participating team.

Dress code: sports clothes, sports shoes, and sports caps.

2. Characteristics

The course consists of a start, a finish, a mast operation area, a cable hauling and a line heaving area, and water tracks. Among them, the mast is 6 meters high; the heaving line is about 28 meters long with a 300g object tied at one end; the distance of the line heaving is no less than 22. 5 meters and the cable is 10 meters long, with one end having a loop; 5 buoys are set along the water tracks; a chain is fastened to buoy No. 3 with a U-shape shackle and the chain is 5 meters long and weighs approximately 5kg; a larger U-shape shackle weighing 3kg is fastened to buoy No. 5 and a single boat with two oars is applied in this race.

(Ⅱ) Methods

This race is organized on an individual basis. Heat and track number of the individual competitor are determined by drawing lots, with three people in each heat. Competitors are given the wooden pegs for work on mast before his heat.

The competitors take position at the starting point while the referees will check the dress of the competitors one by one. If the dress does not meet the requirements, it must be adjusted for compliance.

The referee sends a start signal and starts timing. The competitor starts from the start, and finishes the mast operation, the hauling of the cable and the heaving lines, the slalom rowing around buoys, and the hauling of the mooring chain according to the requirements. The time counting stops when the competitor reaches the finish. The game time is the sum of the competitor's completion time and penalty time.

Work on the mast: The competitor sits on a boatswain's chair and hoists himself up to the top, puts the pegs into the holes of corresponding colors and then descends.

Hauling the cable and heaving lines: The competitor hauls the 10-meter long cable from the water and throws the heaving line further than 22.5 meters. Each competitor can make up to three attempts. After a successful heaving, the competitor must tie the end of the heaving line to the bight of the cable with a bowline knot.

Slalom rowing around buoys: The competitor jumps on the boat and must pass each of the five buoys four times during the two laps in the race. In the first lap, the competitor must row slalom; while in the second lap, slalom is optional.

Hauling the mooring chain: Loosen the shackle from buoy No. 3, haul the chain and move it to buoy No. 4 and fasten it there with the same shackle. If the competitor does not fasten the chain to buoy No. 4, he has still to touch buoy No. 4 with one hand. Row to the buoy No. 4 and loosen the shackle. Take the shackle and the pin in to the boat and bring them to the finish line.

(Ⅲ) Penalties

1. If a competitor fails to put the pegs into the holes of corresponding colors, there will be a 20-second penalty for each fault.

2. If a competitor fails to throw the heaving line over the stipulated distance within three attempts, there will be a 20-second penalty.

3. If the knot is found not to be a bowline or is fasten outside the loop, there will be a 20-second penalty.

4. If a competitor fails to round a buoy correctly, there will be a 20-second penalty for each fault.

5. If a competitor fails to fasten the chain to buoy No. 4, there will be a 40-second penalty. Moreover, if a competitor fails to touch buoy No. 4 with one hand, there will be another 20-second penalty.

6. If a competitor fails to bring the shackle and the pin to the finish line, there will be a 20-second penalty for each missed item.

(Ⅳ) Result Evaluation

Time spent by each competitor is used to decide the ranking. The competitor with the least time ranks first and receives N+1 points in scoring, then N-1 points for the second place, N-2 points for the third place, and so on (N is the total number of competitors).

Ⅲ. Water Race

(Ⅰ) Conditions

1. Personnel, Equipment and Dress Code

Personnel: 8 competitors from each participating team.

Dress code: sports clothes, sports shoes, belts and carry-on gear.

2. Characteristics

The course consists of a start, a finish, a water barrier area, a swimming area and a rowing area. Five obstacles are set in the water obstacle area, including high slide, tube, log, oil pool and floating platform. The swimming area is a natural water body. Rubber boats for squad are used in rowing. The Chinese organizer will provide thorough safety protection throughout the race.

(Ⅱ) Methods

This race is organized on squad basis. The starting order of the squads is determined by drawing lots.

The squads take position at the start while the referees will check the dress of the competitors one by one. If the dress does not meet the requirements, it must be adjusted for compliance.

The referee sends the start signal and starts timing. Each competitor of the squad must clear all the obstacles as required, swim along the specified route to the opposite bank, push the boat into the water, and then row the boat to the finish. Time counting stops as the squad leader counts the competitors and gears, and then reports "task completed". The game time is the sum of the completion time and penalty time of all the competitors in the squad.

Squad members can assist each other throughout whole process, but the carry-on gear shall not be put aside or handed over to others. The distance between the first member and the last member shall not exceed 50 meters.

Method of clearing:

High slide: Climb up the platform and descend along the slide.

Tube: Enter in and crawl through the torpedo tube.

Log: Climb over the log.

Oil pool: Dive and cross below the oil.

Floating platform: Climb over the floating platform.

(Ⅲ) Penalties

1. If the competitor fails to complete the obstacle correctly, he must return to the obstacle and pass again. If the competitor fails to complete the obstacle again, there will be a 30-second penalty for each fault.

2. In the process of rowing, if the competitor falls into the water, there will be a 60-second penalty for each person/time.

3. If the carry-on gear is dropped and left behind, there will be a 5-minute penalty.

4. If one member fails to complete the race, a 10-minute penalty will be added to the total time of the squad in this race. If two members or above fail to complete, the squad will score 0 point for this race.

(Ⅳ) Result Evaluation

Ranking of the squad is decided by its game time, those who use less time rank higher. The points obtained by the squad correspond to the squad ranking (for example: if there are 5 squads, the first place scores 5 points, and the fifth place scores 1 point).

第五章 申 诉

一、申诉须在初始成绩公布后 30 分钟内提交至裁判委员会, 裁判委员会对当天的申诉进行裁决。申诉裁决后不得再申诉。

二、各国参赛队认为受到不公正裁决时, 可向裁判委员会提起申诉。

三、提出申诉时应确保证据充分, 须注明队员或裁判违反了本规则中的章节和条款, 附上需要审议和裁决的争议点照片或录像, 指出争议问题并记录时间和地点, 必要时可申请回放现场视频录像。

四、对参赛队提出的申诉, 裁判委员会在接收相关材料后 6 小时内, 或正式宣布比赛成绩前, 形成正式决议并书面通告各参赛国领队。

Chapter Ⅴ Protests

Ⅰ. A protest can be submitted to the Jury of Appeal not later than thirty (30) minutes after the announcement that the preliminary results are posted visible in the race area. The JOA shall give their verdict on that day. No further protest is allowed after a verdict is reached.

Ⅱ. All participating teams may submit a protest to the JOA if they believe that they have been unfairly judged.

Ⅲ. When a protest is submitted, it shall be ensured that the evidence is sufficient. The protest shall refer to the articles of this regulation that the competitor or the referee has violated, attach the photos or videos of the disputed points, point out the disputed issues and record the time and place. If necessary, the playback of the video recording can be applied.

Ⅳ. For the protest submitted by the participating teams, the Technical Jury shall reach a formal verdict and notify the team captains of the participating countries in written form within 6 hours after receiving the relevant materials or before officially announcing the results of the competition.

第六章　奖项设置及奖励办法

设立单项奖、个人奖、团体奖。

一、单项奖

给每个单项前三名的个人(班)颁发奖牌和证书。

二、个人奖

给三个项目总积分前三名的个人颁发奖牌和证书。

三、团体奖

给三个项目总积分前三名的参赛队颁发奖杯、奖牌及证书。如果总积分相同，则在水上综合技能项目中积分高者名次列前。

Chapter Ⅵ　Awards

There are single event awards, individual awards and group awards.

Ⅰ. Single Event Awards

Medals and certificates will be awarded to the top three individuals (squads) in each event.

Ⅱ. Individual Awards

Based on the results of all 3 events, certificates and awards will be given to the top three individuals for their excellent performances.

Ⅲ. Group Awards

Trophies, medals and certificates will be awarded to the top three teams in terms of total points of the three races. If the total scores are the same, the team with the higher score in the Water Race will precede.

附　　录
Appendix

附录一　高校机构和岗位名称
Appendix 1　Names of University Sections and Posts

中文名称 Chinese	英文名称 English
职能部门 Functional Offices	
校长办公室	President's Office
党委办公室	Office of the CPC ＊＊ University Committee
党委组织部	Organization Office of the CPC ＊＊ University Committee
党委宣传部	Publicity Office of the CPC ＊＊ University Committee
纪委办公室	Discipline Inspection Office of the CPC ＊＊ University Committee
监察处	Supervision Office
教务处	Office of Studies
科研处	Office of Scientific Research and Development
研究生院	Graduate School
人事处	Office of Human Resources
财务处	Office of Finance
发展规划处	Office of Development and Planning

中文名称 Chinese	英文名称 English
学生工作部	Student Affairs Office
团委	＊＊University Communist Youth League Committee
武装部	Office of National Defense Education
保卫处	Security Office
国际交流与合作处	Office of International Exchange and Cooperation
港澳台办公室	Office of Hong Kong, Macao and Taiwan Affairs
实验室及设备管理处	Office of Laboratory & Equipment Management
基建处	Infrastructure Management Office
后勤管理处	Logistic Affairs Office
审计处	Auditing Office
离退休工作处	Office of Retirement Affairs
工会办公室	Trade Union Office
院系 Schools and Departments	
海洋学院	School of Marine Science
机械工程学院	School of Mechanical Engineering
电子工程学院	School of Electronical Engineering
新能源研究院	Institute of New Energy Technology
法学院	School of Law
管理学院	School of Management
交通工程学院	School of Transportation Engineering
信息科学技术学院	School of Information Science and Technology
化学工程学院	School of Chemical Engineering
数理学院	School of Mathematics and Physics
马克思主义学院	School of Marxism
人文学院	School of Humanities
社会科学学院	School of Social Sciences
外国语学院	School of Foreign Languages

续表/Continued

中文名称 Chinese	英文名称 English
医学院	School of Medicine
新闻传播学院	School of Journalism and Communication
国际教育学院	School of International Education
继续教育学院	School of Continuing Education
附属机构 Affiliated Units	
图书馆	Library
信息网络中心	Information and Network Center
信息资源中心	Information Resource Center
档案馆	Archives
校史馆	University Museum
校医院	University Hospital
后勤服务总公司	Logistic Affairs Company
开发总公司	Development Company
学生公寓管理公司	Student Dormitory Management Company
院校岗位名称 Faculty Post	
校长	President
副校长	Vice-President
党委书记	Party Secretary
办公室主任	Chief of the Office, Office Director
院长、系主任	Dean
副院长、系副主任	Deputy Dean
教授	Professor
副教授	Associate Professor
讲师	Lecturer
客座教授	Visiting Professor
辅导员	Student Advisor

附录二　本科专业(课程)目录

Appendix 2　Undergraduate Major(Course) Directory

学科门类及名称 Disciplines	一级学科名称 First-level Disciplines	专业名称 Majors
哲学 Philosophy	哲学 Philosophy	逻辑学 Logics
		伦理学 Ethics
		宗教学 Science of Religion
经济学 Economics	经济学 Economics Sciences	经济学 Economics
		经济统计学 Economic Statistics
	财政学 Public Finance	财政学 Public Finance
		税收学 Taxation
	金融学 Finance	金融学 Finance
		金融工程 Financial Engineering
		保险学 Insurance
		投资学 Investment
	经济与贸易 Economics and Trade	国际经济与贸易 International Economics and Trade
		贸易经济 Trade Economics
法学 Law	法学 Science of Law	法学 Law
	政治学 Political Science	政治学与行政学 Politics and Public Administration
		国际政治 International Politics
		外交学 Diplomacy

学科门类及名称 Disciplines	一级学科名称 First-level Disciplines	专业名称 Majors
	社会学 Sociology	社会学 Sociology
		社会工作 Social Work
		人类学 Anthropology
	民族学 Ethnology	民族学 Ethnology
	马克思主义理论 Theory of Marxism	科学社会主义 Scientific Socialism
		中国共产党历史 History of Communist Party of China
		思想政治教育 Ideological and Political Education
		马克思主义理论 Theory of Marxism
	公安学类 Public Security Science	治安学 public order policing science
		侦查学 Public Order Policing Science
		边防管理 Border Control
教育学 Education	教育学 Education Science	教育学 Pedagogy
		科学教育 Science Education
		人文教育 Humane Education
		教育技术学 Educational Technology
		艺术教育 Art Education
		学前教育 Preschool Education
		小学教育 Primary Education
		特殊教育 Special Education

续表/Continued

学科门类及名称 Disciplines	一级学科名称 First-level Disciplines	专业名称 Majors
教育学 Education	体育学 Sports Science	体育教育 Physical Education
		运动训练 Sports Training
		社会体育指导与管理 Instruction and Management of Social Sport
		武术与民族传统体育 Wushu and Traditional Chinese Sports
文学 Literature	中国语言文学 Chinese Language and Literature	汉语言文学 Chinese Language & Literature
		汉语言 Chinese
		汉语国际教育 Teaching Chinese to Speakers of Other Language
		古典文献学 Studies of Chinese Classical Text
		中国少数民族语言文学 Chinese Ethnic Language and Literature
	外国语言文学 Foreign Languages and Literatures	英语 English Language and Literature
		俄语 Russian Language and Literature
		法语 French Language and Literature
		德语 German Language and Literature
		日语 Japanese Language and Literature
		西班牙语 Spanish Language and Literature
		阿拉伯语 Arabic Language and Literature
	新闻传播学 Journalism and Communication	新闻学 Journalism
		广播电视学 Broadcasting and TV
		广告学 Advertising
		传播学 Communication
		编辑出版学 Editing and Publishing
	新闻传播学(交叉专业) Journalism and Communication (interdisciplinary subject)	会展 Convention-exhibition

学科门类及名称 Disciplines	一级学科名称 First-level Disciplines	专业名称 Majors
历史学 History	历史学 History	历史学 History
		世界史 The World History
		考古学 Archaeology
		文物与博物馆 Antiquity & Museology
理学 Natural Science	数学 Mathematics	数学与应用数学 Mathematics and Applied Mathematics
		信息与计算科学 Information and Computing Science
	物理学 Physics	物理学 Physics
		应用物理学 Applied Physics
		核物理 Nuclear Physics
	化学 Chemistry	化学 Chemistry
		应用化学 Applied Chemistry
	天文学 Astronomy	天文学 Astronomy
	地理科学 Geography	地理科学 Geography
		自然地理与资源环境 Physical Geography and Resource & Environment
		人文地理与城乡规划 Human Geography and Urban-Rural Planning
		地理信息科学 Geographical Information Science
	大气科学 Atmospheric Sciences	大气科学 Atmospheric Science
		应用气象学 Applied Meteorology
	海洋科学 Oceanographic Sciences	海洋科学 Marine Science
		海洋技术 Marine Technology
		海洋资源与环境 Marine Resource & Environment

续表/Continued

学科门类及名称 Disciplines	一级学科名称 First-level Disciplines	专业名称 Majors
理学 Natural Science	地球物理学 Geophysics	地球物理学 Geophysics
		空间科学与技术 Space Science and Technology
		防灾减灾科学与工程 Disaster Prevention and Mitigation Science and Engineering
	地质学 Geology	地质学 Geology
		地球化学 Geochemistry
	生物科学 Biological Sciences	生物科学 Biological Science
		生物技术 Biotechnology
		生物信息学 Bio-informatics
		生态学 Ecology
	心理学 Psychological Sciences	心理学 Psychology
		应用心理学 Applied Psychology
	统计学 Statistical Sciences	应用统计学 Applied Statistics
		统计学 Statistics
工学 Engineering	力学 Mechanics	工程力学 Engineering Mechanics
		理论与应用力学 Theoretical and Applied Mechanics
	机械 Machinery	机械工程 Mechanical Engineering
		机械设计制造及其自动化 Mechanical Design & Manufacturing and Their Automation
		材料成型及控制工程 Materials Processing and Controlling Engineering
		机械电子工程 Mechatronics Engineering
	仪器 Instrument	测控技术与仪器 Measurement Control Technology and Instruments

续表/Continued

学科门类及名称 Disciplines	一级学科名称 First-level Disciplines	专业名称 Majors
工学 Engineering	材料 Materials	材料科学与工程 Materials Science and Engineering
		金属材料工程 Materials Physics
		材料科学 Materials Chemistry
		冶金工程 Metallurgical Engineering
	能源动力 Energy and Power	能源与动力工程 Energy and Power Engineering
	电气 Electrical Engineering	电气工程及自动化 Electrical Engineering and Automation
	电子信息 Electronic Information	通信工程 Telecommunication Engineering
		微电子科学与工程 Microelectronic Science and Engineering
		光电信息科学与工程 Opto-electronics Information Science and Engineering
		信息工程 Information Engineering
	自动化 Automation	自动化 Automation
	计算机 Computer	计算机科学与技术 Computer Science and Technology
		软件工程 Software Engineering
		网络工程 Network Engineering
		信息安全 Information Security
	土木 Civil	土木工程 Civil Engineering
		建筑环境与能源应用工程 Building Environment and Energy Engineering

学科门类 及名称 Disciplines	一级学科名称 First-level Disciplines	专业名称 Majors
工学 Engineering	水利 Water Conservancy and Hydraulic Engineering	水利水电工程 Water and Hydropower Engineering
		水文与水资源工程 Hydrology and Water Resources Engineering
		港口航道与海岸工程 Harbour, Waterway and Coastal Engineering
	测绘 Geodesy and Geomatics	测绘工程 Geodesy and Geomatics Engineering
		遥感科学与技术 Remote Sensing Science and Technology
	化学与制药 Science of Chemical & Pharmaceutical Engineering	化学工程与工艺 Chemical Engineering and Technology
		制药工程 Pharmaceutical Engineering
	地质类 Earth Resource and Geological Engineering	地质工程 Geological Engineering
		勘查技术与工程 Exploration Technology and Engineering
		资源勘查工程 Resource Prospecting Engineering
	矿业 Mining Category	采矿工程 Mining Engineering
		石油工程 Petroleum Engineering
		矿物加工工程 Mineral Processing
		油气储运工程 Oil & Gas Storage and Transportation Engineering
	纺织 Textile Science	纺织工程 Textile Engineering
		服装设计与工程 Apparel Design and Engineering
	轻工 Light Industry	轻化工程 Light Chemical Engineering
		包装工程 Packaging Engineering
		印刷工程 Printing Engineering

续表/Continued

学科门类及名称 Disciplines	一级学科名称 First-level Disciplines	专业名称 Majors
工学 Engineering	交通运输 Science of Traffic & Transportation	交通运输 Transportation
		交通工程 Traffic Engineering
		航海技术 Navigation Technology
	海洋工程 Science of Ocean Engineering	船舶与海洋工程 Naval Architecture and Ocean Engineering
	航空航天 Aeronautics	航空航天工程 Aeronautical and Astronautical Engineering
		飞行器动力工程 Flight Vehicle Design and Engineering
		飞行器设计与工程 Flight Vehicle Manufacturing Engineering
		飞行器制造工程 Flight Vehicle Power Engineering
	核工程 Nuclear Engineering	核工程与核技术 Nuclear Engineering and Technology
		辐射防护与核安全 Radiation Protection and Nuclear Safety
		工程物理 Engineering Physics
		核化工与核燃料工程 Nuclear Chemical and Fuel Engineering
	农业工程 Agricultural Engineering	农业工程 Agricultural Engineering
		农业机械化及其自动化 Agricultural Mechanization and Automation
		农业电气化 Agricultural Electrization
		农业建筑环境与能源工程 Agricultural Structure, Environment and Energy Engineering

学科门类及名称 Disciplines	一级学科名称 First-level Disciplines	专业名称 Majors
工学 Engineering	林业工程 Forestry Engineering	森林工程 Forest Logging Engineering
		木材科学与工程 Wood Science and Engineering
		林产化工 Chemical Processing of Forest Products
	环境科学与工程 Environmental Science and Engineering	环境科学与工程 Environmental Science and Engineering
		环境工程 Environmental Engineering
		环境科学 Environmental Science
		环境生态工程 Ecological Engineering of Environment
	生物医学工程 Biomedical Engineering	生物医学工程 Biomedical Engineering
	食品科学与工程 Food Science and Engineering	食品科学与工程 Food Science and Engineering
		食品质量与安全 Food Quality and Safety
		粮食工程 Grain Engineering
		乳品工程 Dairy Engineering
	建筑 Architecture	建筑学 Architecture
		城乡规划 Urban and Rural Planning
		风景园林 Landscape Architecture
	安全科学与工程 Safety Science and Engineering	安全工程 Safety Engineering
	生物工程 Biology Engineering	生物工程 Bioengineering
	公安技术 Public Security & Technology	刑事科学技术 Criminal Science and Technology
		消防工程 Fire Protection Engineering

学科门类及名称 Disciplines	一级学科名称 First-level Disciplines	专业名称 Majors
农学 Agricultural Sciences	植物生产 Plant Production Sciences	农学 Agronomy
		园艺 Horticulture
		植物保护 Plant Protection
		植物科学与技术 Plant Science and Technology
	自然保护与环境生态 Nature Conservation and Environmental Ecology	农业资源与环境 Agricultural Resources and Environment
		野生动物与自然保护区管理 Wildlife and Natural Reserve Management
		水土保持与荒漠化防治 Soil and Water Conservation and Combating Desertification
		生物质科学与工程 Biomass Science and Engineering
	动物生产 Animal Production Sciences	动物科学 Animal Science
	动物医学 Science of Veterinary Medicine	动物医学 Veterinary Medicine
		动物药学 Veterinary Pharmacy
	林学 Forestry	林学 Forestry
		园林 Landscape Gardening
	水产 Fishery Science	水产养殖学 Aquaculture
		海洋渔业科学与技术 Marine Fishery Science and Technology
	草学 Pratacultural	草业科学 Prataculture Science
		草坪科学与工程 Turf Science and Engineering

续表/Continued

学科门类 及名称 Disciplines	一级学科名称 First-level Disciplines	专业名称 Majors
医学 Medicine	基础医学 Preclinical Medicine	基础医学 Basic Medical Sciences
	临床医学 Clinical Medicine Sciences	临床医学 Clinical Medicine
	口腔医学 Stomatology	口腔医学 Oral Medicine
	公共卫生与预防医学 Journal of Public Health and Preventive Medicine	预防医学 Preventive Medicine
		食品卫生与营养学 Food Hygiene and Nutrition
		妇幼保健医学 Maternal and Child Health Medicine
	中医学 Traditional Chinese Medicine	中医学 Chinese Medicine
		针灸推拿学 Acupuncture & Moxibustion and Tuina
		藏医学 Traditional Tibetan Medicine
		蒙医学 Mongolian Medicine
	中西医结合 Chinese-Western Medicine Integration	中西医临床医学 Clinical Science of Integrated Chinese Medicine and Western Medicine
	药学 Pharmacy	药学 Pharmacy
		药物制剂 Pharmaceutics
	中药学 Traditional Chinese Material Medica	中药学 Traditional Chinese Material Medica
	法医 Forensic Medicine	法医学 Medical Jurisprudence

学科门类及名称 Disciplines	一级学科名称 First-level Disciplines	专业名称 Majors
医学 Medicine	医学技术 Medical Technology	医学检验技术 Medical Inspection Technology
		医学实验技术 Medical Laboratory Technology
		医学影像技术 Medical Imaging Technology
		眼视光学 Optometry and Ophthalmology
		康复治疗学 Rehabiliation Therapy
	护理学 Nursing Science	护理学 Nursing
管理学 Management Science	管理科学与工程 Management Science and Engineering	管理科学 Management Science
		信息管理与信息系统 Information Management and Information Systems
		工程管理 Construction Management
		房地产开发与管理 Real Estate Development and Management
	工商管理 Science of Business Administration	工商管理 Business Administration
		市场营销 Marketing
		会计学 Accounting
		财务管理 Financial Management
	农业经济管理 Agricultural Economics and Rural Development	农林经济管理 Economics and Management of Agriculture and Forestry
		农村区域发展 Rural and Regional Development
	公共管理 Science of Public Management	公共事业管理 Public Affairs Management
		行政管理 Public Administration
		劳动与社会保障 Labor and Social Security
		城市管理 Urban Management
		土地资源管理 Land Resources Management

续表/Continued

学科门类 及名称 Disciplines	一级学科名称 First-level Disciplines	专业名称 Majors
管理学 Management Science	图书馆、情报与 档案管理 LIS & Archives Management	图书馆学 Library Science
		档案学 Archival Science
		信息资源管理 Information Resource Management
	物流管理与工程 Logistics Management and Engineering	物流管理 Logistics Management
		物流工程 Logistics Engineering
	工业工程 Industrial Engineering Discipline	工业工程 Industrial Engineering
	电子商务 E-Commerce Professional Category	电子商务 Electronic Business
	旅游管理 Tourism Management	旅游管理 Tourism Management
		酒店管理 Hospitality Management
艺术学 Arts	艺术学理论 Arts Theory	艺术史论 Theory and History of Arts
	音乐与舞蹈 Music and Dance Studies	音乐表演 Music Performance
		音乐学 Musicology
	戏剧与影视 Theatre Film and TV Studies	表演 Performing Art
		戏剧学 Theatre Studies
	美术学 Fine Studies	美术学 Fine Arts
		绘画 Painting
	设计学 Design	艺术设计学 Designtology
		视觉传达设计 Visual Communication Design

附录三 校园常用标识语
Appendix 3 Public Signs on Campus

一、文化宣传语 Inspiring Signs

1. 让我们的校园更文明，让我们的心灵更高尚。

Let's make our campus environment even more harmonious and our soul even more exalted.

2. 英语常说才流利，汉语常说才练达。

English becomes more fluent with much practice; Chinese becomes more brilliant with much use.

3. 静心才能虚心，虚心方可进步。

Stillness in one's heart can make one modest and modesty can make one progressive.

4. 学习的兴趣源于学习的过程。

Enthusiasm for learning is stimulated in the course of learning.

5. 乐于学习，善于沟通，敢于承担，勇于创新。

Be keen on learning, good at communicating, courageous in undertaking, and brave in innovating.

6. 忌满地挖坑，要钻井出水。

Never give up easily; dig the tunnel through.

7. 只有永远的努力，没有永远的成功。

There is no constant success without constant effort.

8. 不怕困难，就怕畏难。

Fear not difficulties, but be fueled by them.

9. 把失败当作起点，把成功也当作起点。

Regard both defeat and success as starting blocks.

10. 学中外语言，通亚洲文化。

Learn different languages to master the world culture.

11. 知之者不如行之者。

To do is better than to say.

12. 成功者永远在做事，失败者永远在许愿。

The winner is always striving and the loser is always promising.

13. 学生的笑脸就是校园的阳光，家长的满意就是学校的生命。

Students' faces bring life to the campus; Parents' contentment bring hope for the school.

14. 让家长省心放心，让孩子成人成才。

Save the parents from anxiety and prepare the children for brilliant future.

15. 教师的敬业就是学校的希望，社会的认可就是学校的成功。

The teacher's devotion is the hope of the school and the society's acceptance is the success of the school.

16. 尊重学生的人格，尊重学生的发展，尊重学生的选择。

Respect the student's personalities, development and choices.

17. 严在防患于未然，爱须真诚到细微。

Discipline is about nipping things in the bud while love is always subtle and sincere.

18. 成绩不说跑不了，问题不说不得了。

Achievements remain even when unnoticed; problems, however, becomes worse when not pointed out.

19. 成功永远属于用心做事的人。

Success always belongs to those who work hard.

20. 我们不会被对手打败，只会被自己打败。

We are not defeated by our opponents, but by ourselves.

21. 所谓的成功就是把每一件具体的事都做好。

Success means to do every job well, no matter how small it is.

22. 让学生从你的目光中找到自信，让孩子从你的微笑中体会温馨。

Let the students find confidence in your eyes and let children feel warm from your smile.

23. 要尽量多地要求学生，也要尽量多地去尊重学生。

Ask students as much as possible, and respect students as much as possible.

24. 爱是教育的翅膀。

Love is the propeller of education.

25. 孩子不犯错误才是错误。

It is an erroneous belief that children make no mistakes.

26. 坦坦荡荡做人，扎扎实实做事。

Be frank and honest with people; be persistent and practical with work.

27. 只有你想到，你才能做到。

You can hardly do what you have not even expected.

28. 以平常心，做非凡事。

Be common in mind, do uncommon wok.

29. 天下兴亡，我的责任。

Everybody is responsible for the rise and fall of the nation.

30. 用心做事，方能成就大事。

No pains, no gains.

二、文明标识语 Regulatory Signs

1. 靠右走 Right side!

2. 保持安静 Silence !

3. 禁止吸烟 No smoking!

4. 不要随地扔东西 Don't litter!

5. 播种生活，收获习惯；播种习惯，收获性格；播种性格，收获命运。Habits are framed in daily life, then form personality and finally determine destiny.

6. 上下楼梯，注意安全。Be cautious when taking the stairs!

7. 小心! Be careful!

8. 请节约用水! Save water, please!

9. 不要把手伸向向你微笑的花朵。Do not pick flowers smiling at you.

10. 请及时归还! Return in time!

11. 好书如挚友。A good book is a good friend.

12. 良好的秩序是一切的基础。Good order is the foundation of all.

13. 行动胜于空谈。Deeds, not words.

14. 有个好习惯，事事皆不难。Custom makes all things easy.

15. 正在开会，请保持安静。Meeting in progress, quiet please.

三、方向标识语 Guide Signs

1. 入口 Entrance

2. 出口 Exit

3. 推 Push

4. 拉 Pull

四、校园设施 Identification Signs

1. 校长办公室 President's Office

2. 副校长办公室 Vice-President's Office

3. 院长办公室 Dean's Office

4. 校长助理室 Assistant President's Office

5. 教学楼 Classroom Building

6. 后勤服务中心 Service Center

7. 会议室 Meeting Room

8. 学生中心 Student Center

9. 留学生中心 International Student Center

10. 洗手间 Toilet

11. 文具室 Stationery Office

12. 急救室 Emergency Room

13. 药房 Pharmacy

14. 阶梯教室 Lecture Theater

15. 文印室 Copier Room

16. 语音室 Language Lab

17. 图书馆 Library

18. 自修室 Study Room

19. 电子阅览室 Electronic Reading Room

20. 多功能演示室 Multi-functional Demonstration Room

21. 体育馆 Gymnasium

22. 步行街 Pedestrain-only Street

23. 美食街 Food Street

24. 书屋 Book Store

25. 电影院 Movie Theatre

26. 快递取件点 Courier Station

27. 超市 Supermarket

28. 银行 Bank

29. 邮局 Post Office

30. 布告栏 Bulletin Board

31. 传达室 Reception Room

32. 学生宿舍楼 Dormitory Building

33. 茶水间 Pantry

34. 宿管处 Dormitory Management Office

35. 洗衣房 Laundry Room

36. 熨衣房 Ironing Room

37. 盥洗室 Lavatory

附录四　常用符号及数学词汇简表
Appendix 4　Mathematical Symbols and Terms

符号 Symbols	中文名称 Chinese	英文名称 English	符号 Symbols	中文名称 Chinese	英文名称 English
+	加号，正号	plus	$\sqrt{\ }$	平方根	（square）root
—	减号，负号	minus	∵	因为	since; because
±	正负号	plus or minus	∴	所以	hence
×	乘号	is multiplied by	::	等于，成比例	equals, as（proportion）
÷	除号	is divided by	∠	角	angle
=	等于号	is equal to	⌒	半圆	semicircle
≠	不等于号	is not equal to	⊙	圆	circle
≡	全等于号	is equivalent to	○	圆周	circumference
≅	等于或约等于号	is equal to or approximately equal to	△	三角形	triangle
≈	约等于号	is approximately equal to	⊥	垂直于	perpendicular to
<	小于号	less than sign	∪	并，合集	union of
>	大于号	more than or greater than sign	∩	交，通集	intersection of
≮	不小于号	is not less than	∫	……的积分	the integral of
≯	不大于号	is not more than	Σ	总和	（sigma）summation of
≤	小于或等于号	is less than or equal to	°	度	degree

符号 Symbols	中文名称 Chinese	英文名称 English	符号 Symbols	中文名称 Chinese	英文名称 English
≥	大于或等于号	is more than or equal to	′	分	minute
%	百分之……	per cent	″	秒	second
‰	千分之……	per mill	#	……号	number
∞	无限大号	infinity	℃	摄氏度	Celsius system
∝	与……成比例	varies as	@	在	at

附录五　常用计量单位简表

Appendix 5　Units of Measurements

类别 Classification	中文名称 Chinese	英文名称 English	缩写 Abbreviation
重量 Weight	毫克	milligram	mg
	克	gram	g
	千克(公斤)	kilogram	kg
	吨	ton	tn/t
	磅	pound	lb
	盎司	ounce	oz
长度 Length	公里	kilometer	km
	米	meter	m
	厘米	centimeter	cm
	毫米	millimeter	mm
	英里	mile	mi
	英寻	fathom	fm
	码	yard	yd
	英尺	foot	ft
	英寸	inch	in
	海里	nautical mile	nm
	链	cable	cab
面积 Area	平方米	square meter	sq m
	平方公里	square kilometers	sq km
	公顷	hectare	ha
	平方英里	square mile	sq mi
	英亩	acre	a

续表/Continued

类别 Classification	中文名称 Chinese	英文名称 English	缩写 Abbreviation
	平方码	square yard	sq yd
	平方英尺	square foot	sq ft
	平方英寸	square inch	sq in
容积 Capacity	升	liter	l
	毫升	milliliter	ml
	蒲式耳	bushel	bu
	加仑	gallon	gal
	品脱	pint	pt
体积 Volume	立方米	cubic meter	cu m
	立方码	cubic yard	cu in
	立方英尺	cubic foot	cu ft
	立方英寸	cubic inch	cu in

参 考 文 献
Bibliography

[1]喻子敬，邓波. 涉外交流学概论[M]. 武汉：武汉大学出版社，2015.

[2]赵冰华. 应用型本科院校优秀教学团队建设与管理[M]. 南京：东南大学出版社，2019.

[3]张秋平. 推进我国高校双语教学建设研究[J]. 对外经贸，2017(11).

[4]张奕. 双语教学模式下的国际化人才培养策略研究[M]. 天津：天津科学技术出版社，2017.

[5]马永红. 课堂英语[M]. 合肥：中国科技大学出版社，2001.

[6]萧宗六. 学校管理学[M]. 北京：人民教育出版社，2018.

[7]鄢文海，任雪玲. 高校基层教学组织建设与管理[M]. 北京：高等教育出版社，2020.

[8]熊建辉. 我国教育国际化最新进展与宏观形势——新时代职业教育国际化发展战略与创新路径思考[J]. 中国职业技术教育，2019(12).

[9]李明岩. 高校留学生管理工作理念及管理机制的创新思考[J]. 才智，2015(23).

[10]班秀萍，叶云龙. 全面质量管理与高校人才培养[M]. 长春：东北师范大学出版社，2017.

[11]曹洁，闫妍，李薇. 文化管理视角下的非洲来华留学生管理问题研究[J]. 农村经济与科技，2017(4).

[12]冯大鸣，乔伊·麦希施密特. 学校管理双语手册[M]. 上海：上海教育出版社，2005.

[13] 周淳. 英语课堂用语手册[M]. 北京：科学出版社，2009.

[14] 高兰英，孙清祥. 英语课内外用语手册[M]. 北京：中国海洋出版社，2004.

[15]《实用双语教育手册》编委会. 实用双语教育手册[M]. 苏州：苏州大学出版社，2004.

[16] 张鸣宇. 高校留学生跨文化管理与服务策略分析[J]. 中国校外教育，2014(9).

[17] 申伟华. 大学体育英汉双语教程[M]. 北京：人民邮电出版社，2013.

[18] 刘笑冰，李宇佳，王靓楠，等. 审核评估背景下高校双语教学的问题与对策研究[J]. 教育教学论坛，2019(37).

[19] 刘晓澜. 对高校教育管理体质改革的分析与思考[J]. 亚太教育，2016(18).

[20] 张燕. 课堂英语的特点及应用[J]. 桂林师范高等专科学校学报，2002(4).

[21] 熊建辉. 从跟跑到领跑　40 年中国教育对外开放之路[J]. 神州学人，2018(6).

[22] 张小锋. 新冠肺炎疫情防控对中国高等教育的多重影响[J]. 北京教育：高教版，2020(4).

[23] 教育部语言文字信息管理司. 公共服务领域英文译写指南[M]. 北京：外语教学与研究出版社，2016.

[24] 邓波. Develop Naval Cadets' Global Competence through "Belt and Road" Initiative Cooperation and Exchanges[J]. 海外英语，2021(3).

[25] 文君，蒋先玲. 用系统思维创新高校"一带一路"国际化人才培养路径[J]. 国际商务，2015(5).

[26] 沈鹏熠. "一带一路"倡议下我国高校国际化人才培养研究[J]. 职业技术教育，2017(31).

[27] 武汉市人民政府. 武汉概况[DB/OL]. http://www.wuhan.gov.cn/.

[28] 邓波，尹敬湘. 海上联演常识 100 问[M]. 北京：海洋出版社，2020.

后　　记
Afterword

　　"以心相交者，成其久远。"习近平总书记常说，国与国友好的基础是否扎实，关键在于人民情谊是否深厚。与其他交流活动相比，高校交流合作具有研学时间长、身心距离近、交流互动深等特点和优势，是增进人民之间情谊的重要手段。如果说对外交流是一片蓊蓊郁郁的森林，那么高校教学工作就是其中最有朝气和活力的一棵树苗，需要我们精心浇灌，悉心培养，才能种树成林，成为国际交往与合作中一道亮丽的风景线。

　　《高校教学工作双语手册》由海军工程大学邓波负责书稿纲目的拟定和全书统稿；邓波、程飞霞编写了各章节中文内容，徐茜、程飞霞、龚梅翻译了各章节英文内容；卢甜、金倩、吴振亚参与了许多重要内容的修订和附件收集。本书取材广泛，得到了很多专家及同行的支持与帮助，参考了大量国内外文献和互联网资料，借鉴了国际交流合作教育的一线实践成果，也吸收了外国留学生和涉外选修课学生的优质文函和积极建议。王伟任、李成兵、汪静静、何飞等兄弟院校、单位的专家教授审阅了书稿，并提出了很多宝贵而中肯的意见。武汉大学出版社对本书出版给予了大力支持。在此，谨对所有给予本书帮助和支持的单位和个人表示衷心感谢。

编者

2021 年 9 月